EMPOWERED BELIEVERS

Empowered Believers

The Holy Spirit in the Book of Acts

Gonzalo Haya-Prats

Edited by Paul Elbert
Translated by Scott A. Ellington

CASCADE *Books* • Eugene, Oregon

EMPOWERED BELIEVERS
The Holy Spirit in the Book of Acts

Copyright © 2011 The Foundation for Pentecostal Scholarship, Inc. All rights reserved. Except for brief quotations in critical publications or reviews, no part of this book may be reproduced in any manner without prior written permission from the publisher. Write: Permissions, Wipf and Stock Publishers, 199 W. 8th Ave., Suite 3, Eugene, OR 97401.

Scripture quotations, unless otherwise designated, are from the New Revised Standard Version Bible: Anglicized Edition, copyright © 1989, 1995, Division of Christian Education of the National Council of the Churches of Christ in the United States of America. Used by permission. All rights reserved.

Cascade Books
An Imprint of Wipf and Stock Publishers
199 W. 8th Ave., Suite 3
Eugene, OR 97401

www.wipfandstock.com

ISBN 13: 978-1-60899-778-7

Cataloguing-in-Publication data:

Haya-Prats, Gonzalo.

    Empowered believers : the Holy Spirit in the Book of Acts / Gonzalo Haya-Prats, edited by Paul Elbert, translated by Scott A. Ellington.

    xxvi + 290 p. ; 23 cm. Includes bibliographical references and indices.

    ISBN 13: 978-1-60899-778-7

    1. Bible. N.T. Acts—Criticism, interpretation, etc. 2. Holy Spirit—Biblical teaching. I. Elbert, Paul. II. Ellington, Scott A. III. Title.

BS2625.2 H25 2011

Manufactured in the U.S.A.

Cover art image: An 11th century fresco of the evangelist and doctor Luke symbolised as a bull holding his gospel in the UNESCO listed frescos of the ancient basilica of Aquileia in Italy.

Contents

List of Illustrations and Tables | vi
Author's Prologue to the English Edition | vii
Foreword by Paul Elbert | ix
Acknowledgments | xiii
Preface | xv
List of Abbreviations | xxi

PART ONE: The Lukan Understanding of the Spirit

1 "The Holy Spirit": Establishing the Greek Term with the Double Article (τὸ) πνεῦμα (τὸ) ἅγιον | 3
2 The Inbreaking of the Divine | 30
3 The Holy Spirit—Gift and Promise of God | 48
4 The Holy Spirit's Mode of Action | 72

PART TWO: The Effects of the Holy Spirit

5 Testimony and Evangelization | 97
6 The Beginning of the Christian Life | 130
7 The Development of the Christian Life | 155
8 The Prophetic Direction of the People of God | 193
9 Conclusions | 234

Appendix | 249
Bibliography | 251
Index of Names | 273
Index of Ancient Literature | 277

Illustrations and Tables

1. Use of the Adjectival Article in Reference to the Holy Spirit in the Synoptics | 22
2. Use of the Adjectival Article in Reference to the Holy Spirit in Acts | 24
3. Luke's Choice of Verb Tenses in the Spirit Passages of Acts | 55
4. "Testimony" in Acts | 101
5. Elements of the Process of Conversion in Acts | 136
6. The Pentecost of Cornelius: An Analysis of the Parallels | 250

Author's Prologue to the English Edition

FORTY-THREE YEARS AGO I prepared this dissertation for my doctorate in theology. At that time I knew a fair bit about biblical exegesis, but now, wrapped inevitably in other pursuits, I have forgotten a fair bit of what I once knew, but I have acquired slightly more from experience. Now I understand that the Spirit of God, who hovered over the face of the waters, came into that figure of clay infusing it with life: thought, feelings, autonomy, the image and likeness of the creator, and the impulse to commune with Him.

I believe that God's Spirit is manifested in us through various qualities—charismas. In some the Spirit manifests as thought, in others as poetry, in others art, in others affection, in others action—*in all for love*. These are the habitual, daily declarations of the Spirit.

The Spirit manifests to the degree in which our earthen limitations allow. Our words are forged by the culture that surrounds us, and they cannot express beyond what they have reached in our greatest experiences. Our hearts are burdened by our instinct of self-preservation, causing any declaration of the Spirit to be ambiguous, colored by our limitations. Nevertheless, there are extraordinary moments in which the Spirit erupts from some more gentle heart to overcome the cultural structures that normally stifle the voice—this is the time of the prophets, at any time and in any culture.

I hope this book helps us perceive the indwelling Spirit that cries Abba, Father, and share that Spirit with our neighbors by means of festive word and action that leads to solidarity.

I am grateful for the professionally rendered services of the translator and the editor, respectively, in the translating and in the updating of notes and bibliography. I am particularly pleased that it is The Foundation for Pentecostal Scholarship which disseminates this thesis originally completed at the Gregorian University of Rome. It demonstrates that the same Spirit breathes in and animates both.

—Gonzalo Haya-Prats

Madrid
June 1, 2010

Foreword

WHILE THE IMPORTANT THESIS in Spanish at the Pontifical Gregorian University, Rome, by Gonzalo Haya-Prats, S.J., was given a French translation by Romero and Faes some thirty-five years ago,[1] the present translation allows Haya-Prats' many theological, pneumatological, and exegetical insights to be more widely available. When this thesis was advanced in the late sixties there already was an increasing awareness among many in the major sectors of Christendom and within biblical scholarship in particular that the activities of the Holy Spirit as described in the New Testament were underexplored areas of investigation. Today, this appraisal has not abated[2] and Haya-Prats' contribution to our understanding of the work of the Spirit in the book of Acts is as timely as ever.

Regarding the nature of Spirit activities and functions described in Luke-Acts, new discoveries have continued to emerge in the interpretive methodology of Haya-Prats that are taking on fresh relevance,[3] hence

---

1. Haya-Prats, *L'Esprit Force*.

2. R. B. Hays, in a paper given at the Center for Catholic and Evangelical Theology at Duke Divinity School on "Preaching, Teaching, and Living the Bible" suggested several components of valid interpretative practice which are capable of producing such fresh and authorial attentive readings. An essential faculty for this work is a "Spirit-led imagination, an imagination converted by the word" (Hays, "Reading the Bible with Eyes of Faith," 15).

In our view, this sober quality of interpretation is amply demonstrated both by Haya-Prats' thesis and by the work of his thesis supervisor, I. de la Potterie (see, for example, the latter's *La vérité dans Saint Jean* and "Le sens spiritual de l'Écriture," 627–45). Professor de la Potterie is remembered for his loyalty to the Church and profound apostolic endeavor, as well as for being a devoted and strict director of more than thirty dissertations (Lambrecht, "In Memoriam: R. P. Ignace de la Potterie, S. J.," 592–93) of which Haya-Prats' thesis is one.

3. Beginning decidedly in 1974, shortly after Haya-Prats undertook the methodological challenge of an interpretive strategy unfettered by the imposition of arbitrary

the appropriateness of revisiting an exploration of their thematic origins as originally advanced by Haya-Prats. In addition to the initial insights of I. de la Potterie,[4] to which Haya-Prats is obviously indebted, we would particularly like to draw attention in these introductory remarks to several complementary studies that both support and illustrate the contemporary relevance of Haya-Prats' exegetical work. Perhaps the following observations might whet appetites anew for the heuristic content of this English version.

For example, H. Mühlen reflects that Spirit-reception demonstrates that "The Holy Spirit is One Person in many persons."[5] Y. Congar concludes that "The Renewal can open the way to a different kind of Christian practice which is especially valuable in communicating faith in the Lord Jesus Christ."[6] F. Martin finds that John the Baptist's prophecy

---

and artificial temporal intervals upon the text of Luke-Acts as previously employed in a thesis from the Reformed tradition at the University of Greifswald by an Estonian Lutheran pastor, H. von Baer's *Geist Der Heilige Geist in den Lukasschriften*, new exegetical works of fresh relevance and interpretive energy have continued to emerge. These biblical efforts engage in various ways with the topical analyses and attempted narrative sensitivity similarly advanced by Haya-Prats and perhaps might be briefly illustrated by the following studies: Giblet, "Baptism in the Spirit in the Acts of the Apostles," 162–71; Sullivan, "'Baptism in the Holy Spirit,'" 54–61; Sullivan, Wörner, and Baumert, *Die charismatische Erneuerung*; Mainville, *L'Esprit dans l'oeuvre de Luc*; Menzies, *The Development of Early Christian Pneumatology with Special Reference to Luke-Acts*; Stronstad, *The Prophethood of All Believers*; Shelton, *Mighty in Word and Deed*; Kim, *Die Geisttaufe des Messias*; Montague, *The Holy Spirit*; Baumert, *Charisma, Taufe, Geisttaufe, I: Entflechtung einersemantischen Verwirrung; II, Normativität und persönliche Berufung*; Hur, *A Dynamic Reading of the Holy Spirit in Luke-Acts*; and Kim, "A Narrative Preaching of the Holy Spirit in Luke-Acts."

4. A portion of this important pioneering work is available to English readers in de la Potterie and Lyonnet, *The Christian Lives by the Spirit*, a portion of which appeared previously in de la Potterie's "L'onction du chrétien par la foi," 12–69, and in his *La vie selon l'Esprit*.

5. Vondey, *Heribert Mühlen*, 307. See too, Mühlen, "Der Beginn einer neuen Epoche der Geschichte des Glaubens," 28–45; idem, "The Renewal of the Church," in his *A Charismatic Theology*, 347–60, and also Mühlen, "The Person of the Holy Spirit," in *The Holy Spirit and Power*, 11–33 (McDonnell's ET of "Die epochale Notwendigkeit eines penumatologischen Ansatzes der Gotteslehre," 275–87).

6. Congar, "The Positive Contribution of the 'Charismatic Renewal' to the Church," in his *I Believe in the Holy Spirit*, 2:155. Just five years after Haya-Prats' thesis at Pontifical Gregorian University, Congar published the following two ground-breaking theological observations: "Actualité renouvelée du Saint-Esprit," 543–60 and "La pneumatology et théologie catholique," 250–58. This background underpinned the famous work by Suenens, *A New Pentecost?*

as recorded by the Evangelists (Matt 3:11; Mark 1:7–8; Luke 3:16; John 1:27, 33) is in continuity with New Testament tradition and that "the substantive form of the expression accentuates the aspect of a personal moment of grace,"[7] and R. Stronstad finds that this personal moment of grace "is that prophetical, vocational, charismatic experience which the disciples, themselves, received on the day of Pentecost."[8] There is a growing realization that Luke's narrative-rhetorical interest in the Holy Spirit and the resurrected Jesus' charge to disciple-believer-witnesses at Acts 1:8 should be further explored. The contextual injunction that "You will receive power when the Holy Spirit has come upon you; and you will be my witnesses in Jerusalem, in all Judea and Samaria, and to the ends of the earth" is testimony that should not be marginalized, but rather be incorporated into the experience of the historic Christian faith. As W. Kurz reminds us, "Jesus' promise and call of his disciples to be filled with the Holy Spirit and to be his witnesses to the ends of the earth (Acts 1:8) retains its significance for contemporary Christians."[9] R. Cantalamessa also argues that "The Holy Spirit is the soul of the tradition. If it is removed or forgotten, what remains of the tradition is only the dead 'letter.'"[10] Cantalamessa stresses that we must not demand that "he adapt to our truth, instead of we to his."[11]

All would agree, we believe, that in order to be submissive our reason must be purified by the critical agency of the Holy Spirit.[12] Accordingly, it would certainly not be amiss to suspect that a balanced consideration of Haya-Prats' historically significant but often neglected thesis should assist such adaptation to truth mediated by the Spirit of Jesus.

It is a privilege then to serve as the editor of this heuristic thesis which is worthy of fresh attention. Like all human endeavor, scholarship is a creature of its time. It reaches back into the work of others in the past which we may have overlooked and need to revisit, stimulates the

---

7. Martin, *Baptism in the Spirit*, 54–55. This is a revised version of his "Le baptême dans l'Esprit," 23–58.

8. Stronstad, "On Being Baptized in the Holy Spirit," in *Trajectories in the Book of Acts*, 186.

9. Kurz, "From the Servant Isaiah to Jesus and the Apostles in Luke-Acts to Christians Today," in *Between Experience and Interpretation*, 193.

10. Cantalamessa, *The Mystery of Pentecost*, 43.

11. Cantalamessa, *Mystery*, 43.

12. So, Johns, "Of Like Passion," in *The Pontificate of Benedict XVI*, 111.

discoveries of the present, and looks forward eagerly to the relevancy of future investigations. Gonzalo Haya-Prats, under the supervision of Professor Ignace de la Potterie, offers us herewith this opportunity to so explore. Without intruding into the text, some additional relevant documentation via some additional footnotes will occasionally be introduced along the way. This editorial material, along with citations in this Foreword, will hopefully serve to assist readers as to investigative contexts and pertinent points of scholarship that are especially germane to arguments and analysis as advanced by Haya-Prats himself. These will all be added to the bibliography.

—Paul Elbert

Pentecostal Theological Seminary
Cleveland, Tennessee

Acknowledgments

THE 2006 CONFERENCE OF the Society for Pentecostal Studies had ended, and I was enjoying Sunday breakfast at the Hilton Pasadena with scholars Paul Elbert and David Reed when I turned the conversation to an unusual name that I had come across a number of times in the past few years—*Gonzalo Haya-Prats*. Whether in books or articles related to the role of the Holy Spirit in Acts, it seemed that Haya-Prats' name kept surfacing. Robert Menzies interacted with him extensively in *Empowered for Witness* (1994), agreeing with him much of the time. Matthias Wenk, in the introduction to his *Community-Forming Power* (2000), summarized the theses of eleven scholars, allotting more space to Haya-Prats than to any other, including Gunkel, von Baer, Büchsel, Schweizer, Menzies, and Turner.

My perusal of the literature related to the Holy Spirit in Acts brought the name of Haya-Prats into sharp relief. His work, however, was written in Castilian Spanish (as a doctoral dissertation at the Gregorian University of Rome in 1967) and translated only into French, *L'Esprit, force de l'église* (1975; now out of print). As such, it was inaccessible to the person who reads only English, and I was convinced that it was too important a work to languish unreadable to such a large sector of Christendom.

So as I enjoyed the breakfast that Sunday morning with Paul and David, I turned the conversation to Haya-Prats. I was eager to hear their opinion about the idea of having the Foundation sponsor the translation of his dissertation into English. Paul, a Lukan scholar who had read Haya-Prats in Cerf's French edition and had cited it on occasion, thought the idea had merit. We would discuss it at greater length on our flight back to Atlanta. David, more the historical theologian, agreed that such a project was worthwhile on the grounds that there was great interest in the Holy Spirit in the church and that the work filled a gap in scholarly writing on the Holy Spirit. Thus was birthed the book now resting in your hands.

In July of 2006, the Foundation gratefully received Haya-Prats' permission to translate his dissertation into English; the same year, we contracted with Scott Ellington to perform the translation (he also translated most of the German quotations). In 2007, Scott delivered the literal translation I had requested, which I then copyedited and delivered to Paul for his pertinent scholarly notes that update the work to the current year.

It should be noted that this monograph is a translation of the complete, original Spanish dissertation, not a translation of Cerf's French edition, which omitted Chapter 1 and parts of others. And to make the work more accessible to the non-scholar, all contemporary foreign language quotations in the text have been translated into English, but for the scholar, the original language follows in the footnotes (excepting *TWNT*); where page citations of an English translation occur, the page citations of the original edition usually follow.

Along this journey, a few individuals contributed unselfishly toward the completion of this project, not the least of whom was Paul, who accepted no remuneration for the contribution of his Foreword and notes and for his many hours of editorial work, and this on top of his work as the founding editor of the *Journal of Biblical and Pneumatological Research*; the Foundation echoes his gratitude to the administration and colleagues at the Pentecostal Theological Seminary (Cleveland, Tenn.) for the supportive and cordial atmosphere which they provided as friends of scholarship. Stéphanie Bélanger, kindly translated passages from the French scholars. Steve Gossett, who serves on the Foundation's Board of Directors along with C. Scott Johnson, kindly provided the graphic of the final illustration. I am grateful to all of these individuals for their support of this project.

—Robert W. Graves, President

The Foundation for Pentecostal Scholarship
Pentecost Sunday 2010

Preface

THIS STUDY IS INTENDED to contribute to the development of biblical moral theology, which, it has been accurately observed, is a new label that as yet lacks a definite meaning. It is clear, though, that it should be understood as that part of biblical theology that pertains particularly to the moral aspect of the message. Currently, there is a growing desire and hope that biblical theology will contribute a primary elaboration of the biblical facts to the renewal of moral theology, as it is already doing with dogmatic theology. Pius XII, in the "Divino afflante Spiritu," reminded exegetes of the need to expound on the moral sense of the various sacred books. The Second Vatican Council asserted in the "Dei Verbum" that a study of the Holy Scripture "is . . . the soul of sacred theology" (num. 24) and, in the decree concerning priestly formation ("Optatam Totius"), recommended that "Special care must be given to the perfecting of moral theology. Its scientific exposition, nourished more on the teaching of the Bible, should shed light on the loftiness of the calling of the faithful in Christ and the obligation that is theirs of bearing fruit in charity for the life of the world" (num. 16).[1]

The present work is limited to the concept of the Holy Spirit and its influence in the Christian life of the primitive community according to the book of Acts. This certainly touches, in part, on an aspect of moral theology, although perhaps it is tempting to consider it secondary or even entirely outside the scope of moral theology. If moral theology wishes to distinguish itself from philosophical ethics, though, it must receive from revelation not only its specific objective but also the light of

---

1. [This English translation of the decree "Optatam Totius" is taken from the Vatican website: www.vatican.va/archive/hist_councils/ii_vatican_council/documents/vat-ii_decree_19651028_optatam-totius_en.html], accessed August 1, 2006. Trans.]

its principles. The action of the Holy Spirit may pass by a psychologist or a philosopher unnoticed, but it cannot be ignored by moral theology.

The fearlessness of Peter before the Sanhedrin can be a manifestation of his integrity or heroism, according to his ethic, but a moral theology cannot ignore the fact that this event describes a human action that takes place *within the fullness of the Holy Spirit*. The object of moral theology is not human action in an exclusively anthropologic sense, but rather it is seen in the light of revelation, and by revelation we know that no Christian action exists that does not involve the participation of God. Christian action is not merely conformity to human nature or right reasoning but to the dynamism of the kingdom of God, as an expression of divine charity and filial devotion. The fearlessness of Peter, the wisdom of Stephen, and the joy of the disciples: these are human behaviors, but they are also the result of an intervention by the Holy Spirit. The moral theology that forgets this intervention of the Spirit would cease to be either theological or Christian.

Looking ahead, ethics will be able to demand integrity of a person, but only moral theology will be able to promise the presence of the Holy Spirit. Furthermore, moral theology demands integrity—the first duty of a Christian is to allow the presence of God to invade his or her own activities.

The intervention of God is discovered through the light of revelation, and to forget this would be to reduce moral theology to a judicial code or a philosophical ethic. Even in the Holy Scripture, observation confirms that the Spirit (*Ruach*) rarely appears in the legal texts. The study of the Holy Spirit in Acts renders an important service to moral theology, even if it only modifies the pagan hero archetype by adding the notion of the "man full of the Holy Spirit," which Acts inherited from biblical tradition.

The second limitation of this study is its narrow focus on the book of Acts. It was necessary to confine the study to a single biblical author in order to present a homogeneous consideration of the topic in all its richness, without corrupting it with modern interpretations or diluting it by drawing on other biblical authors. The selection of Acts presents both advantages and disadvantages for a study of the action of the Spirit with a particular concern for its application to moral theology. The first advantage is to deal with the book that could be called, even though the expression is not an entirely satisfactory one, The Gospel of the

Holy Spirit. Another motive for giving preference to Acts is the limited development that the theology of this book has achieved since the commencement of the study of each individual sacred writer. Grässer and Guthrie, in their annotated bibliographies, have noted this lack of study of the theology of Acts. With respect to the understanding of the Holy Spirit that we find in Acts, it is common to see it interpreted from the perspective of other New Testament authors, thus diluting this book's unique message. One may, for example, see the interpretation of Pentecost in the few allusions found in the *Dogmatic Constitution on the Church: Lumen Gentium, Solemnly Promulgated by His Holiness, Pope Paul VI on November 21, 1964* (num. 4.19.24) and the more comprehensive mention made in *Decree on the Missionary Activity of the Church* ("Ad Gentes,"), n. 4. One could also call attention to the scant use of Acts in developing the themes of the charismatic gifts and of the church as the people of God.

A third advantage of studying Acts is its contribution to a theology both ancient, with respect to its origins, and modern, through comparisons with the Synoptics and with a large part of the Epistles. The difficulty that this presents from the very beginning is that Acts did not develop an understanding of the Holy Spirit as sanctifier such as we find in the writings of Paul and John. Many authors maintain that Acts simply carries on the notion of the prophetic gift found in the Old Testament, while others attribute to the Pentecostal gift the life of the community described in the Lukan summaries in Acts. The disharmony among these authors spurred me to undertake this work. An initial reflection over the diverse references to the Spirit in Acts will expose a type of Spirit-influence on moral order, even though it concentrates on marginal facts with no exact reference to a sanctifying effect. In chs. 6, 7, and 8, I will describe and analyze this problem, which could be called the nucleus around which this work has developed.

The need to think about Acts within its own context, and not in light of our own current issues, obligates us to study first of all how Luke perceived the Spirit. We may then examine the Spirit's effects according to the importance they have in Acts and not according to the issues with which we ourselves are preoccupied.

The results of this study confirm the Holy Spirit's influence in the extraordinary empowering of the Christian life, even though one could not call this a sanctifying action, nor does sanctifying action occupy an important place in the Lukan concept of the Spirit. A more important contribution to moral theology could be reevaluating the concept of the Holy Spirit as a promoter of the history of salvation—more important, at least, for a moral theology that wishes to renew itself "by means of a more vivid contact with . . . the history of salvation" (Vatican II). This study reveals that Acts, always through its narrative style, teaches us of the existence of the Spirit's action, of the need to immerse ourselves in the Spirit, and of the means by which we recognize the Spirit.

The bibliography that deals specifically with the Holy Spirit in Acts is very scant and in fact could be reduced to the following works: the monograph by von Baer, *Der Heilige Geist in den Lukasschriften* (The Holy Spirit in the writings of Luke), published in 1926;[2] the section that Schweizer dedicates to the study of Luke and Acts in the *TDNT* article, "πνεῦμα, κτλ,"[3] and a rather general article by Lampe on the Holy Spirit in Luke's writings.[4]

From Mattill's bibliography I have learned of various theses written on the same theme and defended in various universities in the United States, but I have encountered no other description or mention of such works. I give the full citation of these materials in the bibliography, where I also gather the excursions that several commentaries devote to an all-embracing vision of the Holy Spirit in Acts. Also, a number of encyclopedias and biblical theologies published in recent years dedicate a section to the Holy Spirit in Acts. Previously, it was customary to deal with Acts together with the Synoptics or combined with other themes from the Epistles, such as the concept of the primitive community. Much more important have been both comprehensive and partial observations concerning the Holy Spirit in Acts that we find in studies of either the overall structure of Luke's work or of certain specific passages. However, commentaries and articles frequently examine various technical questions in such passages while failing to interpret the activities of the Spirit. Pentecost is naturally the primary topic to be examined, but attention is frequently diverted to descriptive details.

---

2. Von Baer, *Der Heilige Geist in den Lukasschriften*.

3. Schweizer, "πνεῦμα," *TDNT* 6:389–455.

4. Lampe, "The Holy Spirit in the Writings of St. Luke," in *Studies in the Gospels*, 159–200.

I should give special recognition for the direction that has been given, with respect to its content or methodology, to the works of Dupont, de la Potterie, Trocmé, Menoud, Dibelius, Haenchen, and Lohse.

The *method of interpretation* should never overshadow what Luke wanted to communicate to his readers. To that end, I have always had before me all the passages in Luke-Acts that mention the Holy Spirit (or the particular theme dealt with in each section). To the extent possible in a book like Acts, I have tried to look for an interpretation that is valid for all the passages in Luke-Acts, or at least an interpretation that can provide a coherent meaning for the majority of passages, accompanied by an explanation for any aberrant passages. Along side of this all-embracing vision, I have analyzed each passage to determine its sense, starting with the particular meaning of its vocabulary, then the construction of each phrase or sentence, the structure of the paragraph, and the way that it is integrated in the unity of the larger narrative and of the overall work. Vocabulary is always the starting point and the guiding thread of my study. In the investigative scheme, a Lukan term always acts as an epigraph or key term for each section, even though I may shift later to a more harmonized development and presentation.

It has been through all the analysis of the structures and the comparison of the parallels that I have been able to penetrate more deeply into the intentions of Luke. I employed this method especially to study the episode of Cornelius and, more particularly, the triple narration of the coming of the Holy Spirit, using it as a filter to examine the Cornelius episode until it was reduced to its essential meaning in the Jerusalem Council.

I acknowledge in particular P. Ignace de la Potterie for guiding me in the methodology of this work and for other valuable observations.[5]

---

5. [With regard to this acknowledgement of methodological guidance from his distinguished dissertation director, Prof. Dr. I. de la Potterie, S. J., perhaps it may be helpful at the outset of reading Haya-Prats' thesis to underscore two significant points that he makes in his Preface about message dilution due to imported and imposed perspectives, which he particularly seeks to avoid throughout. First, while Haya-Prats mentions his occasional justifiable indebtedness to von Baer's thesis, *Heilige Geist*, done a half-century earlier, he does not at all follow or employ the interpretive method of that thesis. This is consistent with Haya-Prats' stated desire that a method of interpretation should never overshadow or obliterate the original communicative intention. On the other hand, von Baer, an Estonian Lutheran pastor, invokes and imposes artificial periodizations or epochs on the text of Luke-Acts as an arbitrary interpretive technique. Neither Luther nor Calvin employed this pseudo-epochal tactic.

Von Baer is apparently the originator of this narratively destructive interpretive imposition within the Reformed tradition. His artificially divisive temporal epochs are rightly perceived as an ineffective and misleading interpretive tool that obliterates the original rhetorical intention. They lead dogmatically to claims about Lukan characters and events that fit the Protestant theology of some. Haya-Prats does not imitate this approach. He avoids it.

For example, following von Baer's epochal imagination, it is claimed, ignoring substantial narrative evidence, that no characters in Jesus' earthly ministry experienced lasting faith, forgiveness, repentance, or salvation since the terms of salvation were supposedly not met until another salvific epoch arrived at the first Jerusalem Pentecost. The deleterious effects of continuing to employ and embellish this artificial methodology, which Haya-Prats does not do, are especially to be avoided. To Haya-Prats' credit and contextual objectivity, he does not adopt or import von Baer's simplistic and narratively distortive methodology of epochal imposition, probably under the wise and guiding influence of his director. In de la Potterie's many preeminent studies on the Fourth Gospel one never encounters such narratively disruptive epochal impositions employed as an interpretive technique. Such pseudo-narratival impositions could be used there in order to make extraordinary claims, similar to how they have been employed to overshadow the communicative intent of Luke-Acts, namely that none of the characters in the Fourth Gospel who believe in Jesus experienced salvation during the earthy ministry of Jesus and that John 20:22 was salvific for all these characters, or that even if faith and salvation did occur in Jesus' ministry it was destined to fade away without the special Spirit-reception event for selected characters. Neither de la Potterie nor Haya-Prats employs this interpretive method.

Second, the other significant point Haya-Prats makes in his Preface about message dilution is equally astute. He rightly observes that when Luke-Acts is interpreted through a filtered perspective deduced from another NT writer, proper interpretive methodology is not achieved. Interpretations attuned to this or that understanding of Paul have often been used to impose a false perspective onto Luke-Acts without adequate narrative reflection, supposedly then making Luke distinctive or diverse from Paul. The idea that the activities of the Holy Spirit in Luke-Acts are "distinct" from Pauline pneumatology and theology appears to be a long-standing a priori notion. Pressing beyond common expressions for Christian experience, an extreme notion of "distinctness" is then dovetailed in some Protestant scholarship with an uncritical imitation and embellishment of von Baer's anti-narrational periodizations.

In many respects then the thesis of Haya-Prats is a quite refreshing, heuristic, and independent counter-balance both to quick and dogmatic impositions of snippets from other NT writers upon Luke-Acts and to overshadowing claims and embellishments controlled by an artificial and narratively divisive epochal scheme that are long overdue for retirement. Of great worthiness, Haya-Prats' thesis is relatively unencumbered by these particular imported perspectives. Accordingly, Haya-Prats allows us to much more freely and critically become engaged in a journey of progress toward what W. C. van Unnik called a *"living* contact with Luke's world" where we may "walk with him along his roads, to see and hear with his eyes and those of his contemporaries" ("Luke's Second Book and the Rules of Hellenistic Historiography," in *Les Actes des Apôtres*, 60). —Ed.]

Abbreviations

AB	Anchor Bible
ABR	*Australian Biblical Review*
AmClergé	*Ami du clergé*
Ang	*Angelicum*
ASNU	Acta seminarii neotestamentici upsaliensis
AsSeign	*Assemblées du Seigneur*
ATANT	Abhandlungen zur Theologie des Alten und Neuen Testaments
AThR	*Anglican Theolgical Review*
AtSettBibl	*Atti della Settimana Biblica Italiana*
BAC	*Biblioteca de autores cristianos*
BAGD	Bauer, W., W. F. Arndt, F. W. Gingrich, and F. W. Danker. *Greek English Lexicon of the New Testament and Other Early Christian Literature*, 1979
BDF	*A Greek Grammar of the New Testament and Other Early Christian Literature*. Ed. F. Blass, A. Debrunner, and R. W. Funk. Chicago: University of Chicago Press, 1961
Beginnings	*The Beginnings of Christianity: The Acts of the Apostles*. 5 vols. Ed. F. J. Foakes Jackson and Kirsopp Lake. Vol. 5 ed. K. Lake and Henry J. Cadbury. London: Macmillan, 1920–1933
BETL	Bibliotheca Ephemeridum Theologicarum Lovaniensium
BEvT	Beiträge zur evangelischen Theologie
BFCT	Beiträge zur Förderung christlicher Theologie
BHT	Beiträge zur historischen Theologie
Bib	*Biblica*
BibOr	Biblica et orientalia
BK	*Bibel und Kirche*

BR	*Biblical Research*
BSac	*Bibliotheca Sacra*
BVC	*Bible et vie chrétienne*
BZ	*Biblische Zeitschrift*
BZNW	Beihefte zur Zeitschrift für die neutestamentliche Wissenschaft und die Kunde der älteren Kirche
CBQ	*Catholic Biblical Quarterly*
Coll	*Collationes*
CTM	*Concordia Theological Monthly*
DBSup	*Dictionnaire de la Bible: Supplément.* Ed. Louis Pirot and A. Robert. Paris: Létouzey et Ané, 1928–
Ebib	Etudes bibliques
EcuR	*Ecumenical Review*
EgT	*Eglise et Théologie*
EKK	Evangelisch-Katholischer Kommentar zum Neuen Testament
ErJb	*Eranos-Jahrbuch*
EstBib	*Estudios bíblicos*
EstEcl	*Estudios eclesiásticos*
ET	English Translation
ETL	*Ephemerides theologicae lovanienses*
EvT	*Evangelische Theologie*
Exp	*The Expositor*
ExpTim	*Expository Times*
FRLANT	Forschungen zur Religion und Literatur des Alten und Neuen Testaments
FS	Festschrift
Greg	*Gregorianum*
HKNT	Handkommentar zum Neuen Testament
HNT	Handbuch zum Neuen Testament
HP	Héritage et Projet
HPR	*Homiletic and Pastoral Review*
HSNT	Die Heilige Schrift des Neuen Testaments
HTKNT	Herders theologischer Kommentar zum Neuen Testament
HTR	*Harvard Theological Review*
HTS	*Harvard Theological Studies*
IBQ	*Irish Biblical Quarterly*
IBS	*Irish Biblical Studies*

ICC	International Critical Commentary
Int	*Interpretation*
JBL	*Journal of Biblical Literature*
JBPR	*Journal of Biblical and Pneumatological Research*
JPTSup	Journal of Pentecostal Theology Supplement Series
JSNTSup	Journal for the Study of the New Testament Supplement Series
JTI	*Journal of Theological Interpretation*
JTS	*Journal of Theological Studies*
KEK	Kritisch-exegetische Kommentar über das Neue Testament
LD	Lectio divina
LNTS	Library of New Testament Studies
LumVie	*Lumière et vie*
LumVit	*Lumen Vitae*
MCom	*Miscelánea Comillas*
MTZ	*Münchener theologische Zeitschrift*
NIV	New International Version
NovT	*Novum Testamentum*
NovTSup	Supplements to *Novum Testamentum*
NRSV	New Revised Standard Version, 1995
NRTh	*La nouvelle revue théologique*
NS	new series
NT	New Testament
NTAbh	Neutestamentliche Abhandlungen
NTD	Das Neue Testament Deutsch
NTF	Neutestamentliche Forschungen
NTM	New Testament Monographs
NTOA	Novum Testamentum et Orbis Antiquus
NTS	New Testament Studies
NZM	*Neue Zeitschrift für Missionswissenschaft*
OC	One in Christ
OT	Old Testament
Protest	*Protestantesimo*
RB	*Revue biblique*
RCB	*Revista de cultura bíblica*
RechBib	Recherches Bibliques
RevDiocTour	*Revue diocésaine de Tournai*

RevExp	Review and Expositor
RevistB	Revista bíblica
RevSR	Revue des sciences religieuses
RGG	Religion in Geschichte und Gegenwart. Ed. K. Galling. 7 vols. 3rd ed. Tübingen: Mohr/Siebeck, 1957–1965
RHPR	Revue d'histoire et de philosophie religieuses
RHR	Revue de l'histoire des religions
RNT	Regensburger Neues Testament
RSPT	Revue des sciences philosophiques et théologiques
RSR	Recherches de science religieuse
RThom	Revue thomiste
SB	Sources bibliques
SBLDS	Society of Biblical Literature Dissertation Series
SBS	Stuttgarter Bibelstudien
ScEccl	Sciences ecclésiastiques
SchuolC	Schuola Cattolica
Scr	Scripture
SE	Studia Evangelica
SklPhil	Studien zur klassischen Philologie
SP	Sacra pagina
ST	Studia theologica
St	Studium
StPatr	Studia patristica
Str-B	Herman L. Strack and Paul Billerbeck. *Kommentar zum Neuen Testament aus Talmud und Midrasch*. 6 vols. Munich: Beck, 1922–1961
SUNT	Studien zur Umwelt des Neuen Testaments
SymBU	Symbolae biblicae upsalienses
TDNT	*Theological Dictionary of the New Testament*. 10 vols. Ed. Gerhard Kittel and Gerhard Friedrich. Trans. Geoffrey W. Bromiley. Grand Rapids: Mich.: Eerdmans, 1964–1976
TF	Theologische Forschung
TGl	Theologie und Glaube
THKNT	Theologischer Handkommentar zun Neuen Testament
TLZ	Theologische Literaturzeitung
TRu	Theologische Rundschau
TS	Theological Studies
TSK	Theologische Studien und Kritiken

TWNT	*Theologisches Wörterbuch zum Neuen Testament*. 10 vols. Ed. Gerhard Kittel and Gerhard Friedrich. Stuttgart: Kohlhammer, 1933–1978
TZ	*Theologische Zeitschrift*
VD	*Verbum domini*
VE	*Vox evangelica*
VS	*Verbum Salutis*
VSpir	*Vie spirituelle*
VTSup	*Supplements to Vetus Testamentum*
WMANT	*Wissenschaftliche Monographien zum Alten und Neuen Testament*
WUNT	*Wissenschaftliche Untersuchungen zum Neuen Testament*
ZAW	*Zeitschrift für die alttestamentliche Wissenschaft*
ZKG	*Zeitschrift für Kirchengeschichte*
ZKT	*Zeitschrift für katholische Theologie*
ZNW	*Zeitschrift für die neutestamentliche Wissenschaft und die Kunde der älteren Kirche*
ZST	*Zeitschrift für systematische Theologie*
ZTK	*Zeitschrift für Theologie und Kirche*

PART ONE

The Lukan Understanding of the Spirit

I

"The Holy Spirit"

Establishing the Greek Term with the Double Article
(τὸ) πνεῦμα (τὸ) ἅγιον

1.1 Forerunners of the Lukan Expression

THE STUDY OF THE term τὸ πνεῦμα τὸ ἅγιον, which Luke employs with notable consistency, provides an introduction to his concept of the Spirit. Only, though, as an introduction, because two words, even when adopted as the proper name for a reality, cannot express all of the richness of being and of action that the author perceives. The knowledge of a suitable name can prepare us for a direct encounter, but can by no means replace it. First, we observe that the term is not original with Luke, but it was he who fixed it in the New Testament tradition as the proper name for the Spirit of God. The process is complex and subtle. It does not deal only with fixing a name for a concrete and precise reality, but deals rather with trying to define this intangible reality by means of a name and a corresponding density of content.[1]

---

1. The evolution of thought concerning the Holy Spirit has been handled frequently as an introduction by NT scholars, see Shoemaker, "Use of *Ruah*"; Lake, "Holy Spirit"; Gächter, "Zum Pneumabegriff des hl. Paulus"; Kleinknecht et al., "πνεῦμα κτλ."; Schwiezer, "Gegenwart des Geistes"; Guillet, "Révélation progressive du Saint-Esprit"; Cadbury, *Book of Acts in History*. See also the introductions of Goguel, *Notion johannique*; and Arnal, *Notion de l'Esprit*. [A number of recent studies about the Spirit in

From the first page of Genesis, the Spirit of God is spoken of, but the content of this term remains imprecise throughout the entire Old Testament. The Spirit is a power originating in God that invades a man, enabling him to complete God's plans. It is frequently designated as πνεῦμα Θεοῦ, πνεῦμα Κυρίου, but also according to the effect produced, e.g., πνεῦμα αἰσθήσεως (Exod 28:3), ζηλώσεως (Num 5:14), συνέσεως (Deut 34:9; Sir 39:6), σοφίας (Wis 7:7), πνεῦμα Θεῖον σοφίας (Exod 31:3; 35:31), καινόν (Ezek 11:19; 36:26), ἅγιον πνεῦμα παιδείας (Wis 1:5), τὸ πνεῦμά σου τὸ ἀγαθόν (Neh 9:20; Ps 142:10), τὸ ἄφθαρτόν σου πνεῦμα (Wis 12:1), and the seven gifts of Isa 11:12. The mention of an evil spirit, πνεῦμα Θεοῦ πονερόν (1 Sam 18:10), raises the question of the consequence of those spirits originating in God.

The occurrence of the term τὸ πνεῦμα τὸ ἅγιον in Ps 51:11, "Do not cast me away from your presence, and do not take your holy spirit from me," and in Isa 63:10-11, "But they rebelled and grieved his holy spirit. . . . Where is the one who put within them his holy spirit?"[2] appears to insinuate a strong identification of the Spirit with God. The adjective קדוש indicates something more than the going forth of God; it indicates that the entity of the Spirit itself pertains to the sphere of God; it is in intimate contact with him. It can also be applied to the covenant, the promised land, and Jerusalem.[3] In Psalm 51 and in Isaiah the term *Holy Spirit* appears to reach a greater profundity. However, it reappears only in the Wisdom of Solomon (Wis 1:5; 9:17).[4] We can say, however, that Luke has not taken the term *Holy Spirit* from these passages. It is precisely these four passages that situate the action of the Spirit in an ethical atmosphere that has scarcely left its footprints in Acts (see my chs. 6 and 7). Only Isaiah 63:10-11 could have been echoed by Luke via the resistance to the Spirit. Nevertheless, Luke presents himself as the heir of the Old Testament concept of the Spirit of God, especially in the Spirit's dimension of prophetic gifting. In the Gospel, he gives special place to the citation of Isa 61:1 as the consecration of Jesus for his mes-

---

biblical and Qumran texts, in addition to those above and in notes 5 and 9 below, are cited in Elbert, "Contextual Analysis," 8–11. —Ed.]

2. [Unless otherwise designated, all biblical citations in English are from the NRSV. —Trans.]

3. See Procksch, "ἅγιος."

4. The variants of certain texts may also be added: Ps 142:12; Wis 48:12; Dan 5:12; 6:4.

sianic work (Luke 4:18), and in Acts he proposes the quote from Joel 2:28–32 as an explanation of Pentecost.

The typical themes concerning the Spirit in the Old Testament have had a more muted influence on the background of Acts: physical-psychic intervention upon elect men to save the people of God on specific occasions (Samson, Othniel, Gideon, Jephthah, Saul) or in a permanent form (Moses, the seventy elders, Joshua, Saul, David), and in a very specific way upon the prophets. The fullness of this power of the Spirit would rest upon the Messiah. According to certain texts, in the messianic times the spirit of prophecy and a spirit of moral renewal would spread among the people. These themes have been assimilated by Luke, but we cannot say that they have directly determined his concept of the Spirit. Also apparent are small traces left by expressions from the Septuagint in the Lukan redaction.[5]

The majority of the verbal terms that Luke has employed are in the Septuagint. He applies them to the Spirit of God, but the correspondence is merely general and not detailed. In some cases of parallel ideas, the formula previously employed by the Septuagint is lacking. The inheritance of the themes has carried its vocabulary with it, but the fact that this vocabulary reappears only in its archaic form indicates that the essential background of a concept, more than its precise ideas, has been inherited.

Ἔρχομαι can be found in Ezek 2:2; 3:24; Wis 7:7; and Num 5:14. In comparing Isa 32:15 with Luke 24:49 and Acts 1:8, we are surprised by the similarity of content and the disparity of formulation. The verbs δίδωμι, ἐπιπίπτω, and πίμπλημι have sufficient precedents in the Septuagint, but only in different contexts and expressions.[6] The inbreak-

---

5. The theme of the Holy Spirit in the OT can be found summarized in any biblical theology or biblical dictionary. Special interest is merited by the articles of Imschoot: "L'Action de l'Esprit"; "L'Esprit de Jahvé source"; "L'Esprit de Jahvé et l'Alliance"; "L'Esprit de Jahvé, Principe." See also Koch, *Geist und Messias*; Enciso, "Manifestaciones naturales"; Goitia, "La noción dinámica."

6. Δίδωμι (Acts 5:32; 8:18; 11:17; 15:8) is an obvious verb in the treatment of gifting and has abundant antecedent references to the Spirit: Isa 42:1 (ἔδωκα), Ezek 11:19 (new spirit); 36:27; 37:6, 14; Num 11:29; 2 Kgs 19:7 (disturbing spirit). Ἐπιπίπτω (Acts 10:44; 11:15; 8:16) has appeared already in its simple form in Ezek 11:5 (and in 1 Kgs 18:10a, referring to an evil spirit). Πίμπλημι appears in the theological passive (Acts 2:4; 4:31; and 9:17) and in the passive participle (Acts 4:8 and 13:9). It has appeared in the OT in the theological passive applied to the Spirit in Prov 15:4; Sir 39:6; Luke 1:15, 41, 67, and in the composite ἐνπλέω in an active form in Exod 28:3; 31:3;

ing of the Spirit as speaking, guiding, seizing, and sending also have their antecedents, although they are less fixed. The terms that consciously repeat an Old Testament theme are ἐκχέω, καταβαίνω, and χρίω. Ἐκχέω (Acts 2:17–18), taken from Joel 2:28, appears at first glance to exert a direct influence by the prophetic text on the author of Acts; however, this citation, noticeably, has two perspectives in the discourse of Peter. On one hand, it is introduced in order to explain the phenomenon of glossolalia; on the other hand, he warns that its principal end is to demonstrate that Jesus has been exalted as Messiah. The quotation was lengthened in order to arrive at the consequence, "Then everyone who calls on the name of the Lord shall be saved." It appears, therefore, that the text pertains to a christological discourse that has been utilized to explain Pentecost.[7] Καταβαίνω has also been taken into the tradition, and it is that term that the four Gospels employ for the coming of the Spirit in the baptism of Christ. The tradition may have been taken from Isa 63:14. Χρίω is the only one of the three terms with antecedents in the LXX whose application to the Spirit has no footprints in the tradition.[8] Its application to Christ (Luke 4:18; Acts 4:27; 10:38) could indicate, though, its earlier usage in flowering primitive Christologies. Furthermore, it deals with a theme that occupies only a limited space in the Lukan concept of the Spirit.

In this brief journey through the root themes and expressions from the Old Testament, it can be deduced that Luke has inherited from it his themes and many of his formulas. This unsystematic inheritance has served as a fertile field for the growth of a more precise concept that

---

35:31, and in a passive form in Deut 34:9 and Sir 48:12. I will deal more fully with this radical in the study of the adjective πλήρης in sec. 7.1.

7. See Dupont, "L'Utilisation apologetique," especially the conclusions. See also the interesting article by Ghidelli, "Citazioni dell' Antico Testamento." Haenchen notes that the Septuagint translation "name of the Lord" in the place of "name of Yahweh" permitted the christological use of this text in Hellenistic preaching (Haenchen, *Acts of the Apostles*, 179; idem, *Apostelgeschichte*, 142). Concerning the construction of the discourse by Luke himself, the thesis of Dibelius (*Reden der Apostelgeschichte*, 120–62) has prevailed. A synthesis of the diverse tendencies can be seen in Dupont, *Études*, 41–56. [Dupont continued his interest in Pentecost narrative material in Acts with the following two studies: "Nouvelle Pentecôte" and "Dieu l'a oint d'Esprit Saint." —Ed.]

8. 2 Cor 1:21 relates this anointing to the Christian but with only a distant relationship to the Spirit. In Heb 1:9, this term refers to Christ, even though it cites Ps 44:8 and has no relationship to the Spirit. On the theme of the anointing in Paul, John, and in the tradition, see La Potterie, "L'onction du chrétien."

required new characteristic terms and that, most important, established a single proper term.

Pre-Christian Judaism had used the term *holy spirit* with greater frequency than the canonical books, even with a certain normalcy. At times, it referred to the spirit of a man who had been favored by God. Allusions can be found in the Qumran sect to the sanctifying spirit. The most common conception of the Spirit of God in pre-Christian Judaism, though, refers to the inspiration of sacred Scripture and to the spirit of prophecy.[9] The first occupies in Acts a minimal place, while the second develops a new richness as the sign of a more radical gift. During this period the term *holy spirit* has become more fixed but has progressed little in its content. The influence that it may have had on Luke appears to be merely ambient, only preparing the linguistic mold.[10] The term is already set, but it has not been systematically adopted, nor does it reflect the richness of content that it possesses in Christianity.

The true birth of the term *Holy Spirit*, corresponding substantially to its actual content, can be located in the primitive Christian tradition. Even though in this period no true teaching concerning the Spirit existed, we find already the firmly established transmission of three sayings referring to the Spirit concerning blasphemy, assistance before tribunals, and the baptism in the Spirit. The theme of blasphemy against the Holy Spirit, with slight variations of form, we see repeated in the three Synoptic Gospels, even though the context in which Luke places the account changes the sense of Mark's interpretation. We will return to this theme in sec. 7.3, but for now it is of interest to affirm the formal aspect. Mark 3:29 employs the expression εἰς τὸ πνεῦμα τὸ ἅγιον, while Matt 12:32 employs the preposition with a genitive and the double

---

9. Baumgärtel, Bieder, and Sjöberg, "Spirit in Judaism." For *Spirit* in Judaism see Str-B 2:126–38; Asensio, "Espíritu de Dios"; Förster, "Heilige Geist im Spätjudentum"; Nötscher, "Geist und Geister"; Coppens, "Don de l'Esprit d'après"; Benoit, "Qumran et NT"; Fitzmyer, "Jewish Christianity in Acts." [Re: the concept of charismatic prophecy in pre-Christian Judaism, see also Menzies, *Development*, chs. 2–5; Forbes, *Prophecy and Inspired Speech*, passim. —Ed.]

10. For example, Asensio ("Espíritu de Dios," 33) observes that "The apocryphal literature alone, more than giving new light, if we exempt the single apparent use of 'Holy Spirit,' reinforces its diffuse use throughout the pages of the Old Testament"; equally Gächter, "Pneumabegriff"; and Gunkel, *Wirkungen des heiligen Geistes*, 10. [See also the English translation of Gunkel's monograph in the bibliography (here, 19–20). —Ed.] Braun, "Qumran und das Neue Testament," is representative of the unanimous sense among critics concerning the merely superficial influence of Qumran on Acts.

article: κατα τοῦ πνεύματος τοῦ ἁγίου. Luke 12:10 does not employ the double article, but inserts an adjective in the construction: εἰς τὸ ἅγιον πνεῦμα. It is not clear why Luke avoided in this passage the expression with the double article, but it appears probable that he avoids the double article with the preposition. We will examine the question in more detail in sec. 1.2, which deals with the use of the article. This theme has left few traces in Acts, being only remotely referred to in passages such as Acts 5:3, 9; 6:10; and 7:51.[11]

The saying about the Spirit's assistance before tribunals appears to be a more vital theme in the primitive tradition. Its formal instability is perhaps indebted to a true assimilation which repeats it in new expressions. Mark 13:11 uses the expression τὸ πνεῦμα τὸ ἅγιον; Matt 10:20 "the Spirit of our Father;" Luke 12:12 uses the inserted adjective "the Holy Spirit"; and Luke 21:15 attributes this assistance to Christ himself. The theme is important for the author of Acts, at least as one of the aspects of the apostles' testimony.[12] In his Gospel, Luke omits in these passages mentioning the Sanhedrin found in Mark 13:9 and Matt 10:17. It is probable that he reserved this aspect for the book of Acts, especially in the cases of Peter (Acts 4:8) and Stephen (6:10). The similarity of expression between Acts 6:10, "But they could not withstand the wisdom and the Spirit with which he spoke," and Luke 21:15, "For I will give you words and a wisdom that none of your opponents will be able to withstand or contradict," is especially noticeable.[13]

The saying concerning the baptism in the Holy Spirit is the most firmly established in the primitive Christian tradition, and it maintains a rigid invariability in Acts and John. Nevertheless, the term does not appear to have found a concrete interpretation in the tradition. On the other hand, Luke had seen the realization of the baptism in the Spirit in the gifting of the Pentecostal Spirit both to the apostles (Acts 1:5) and likewise to the house of Cornelius (11:16) (as detailed in sec. 6.4). With respect to the formal expression, all authors (except Mark) use the term

---

11. See sec. 7.3.

12. The diverse aspects of testimony will be examined in ch. 5 and testimony offered before tribunals, specifically, in sec. 5.3.

13. Even though Luke will use up to triplicate repetition for important scenes, there is no lack of examples of these omissions in the Gospel that reappear in Acts, such as the accusation of blasphemy against the temple in the proceedings against Jesus (Matt 26:61; Mark 14:58, cf. Luke 22:54–71) that Luke applies to Stephen in Acts 6:13–14.

ἐν πνεύματι ἁγίῳ (Matt 3:11; Luke 3:16; John 1:33; Acts 1:5; 11:16). The mentioning of fire in Matt 3:11 and Luke 3:16 appears to correspond to the eschatological character of the Baptist's preaching.

The term (τὸ) πνεῦμα (τὸ) ἅγιον, therefore, is found in the first tradition with a rather imprecise content (blasphemy against the Spirit, baptism in the Spirit) but in a solemn context that specifically exceeds the assistance of the Spirit of Yahweh given to judges and prophets in the Old Testament. Procksch believes that the title *Holy Spirit* came from Christ himself when he referred to the Pentecostal Spirit in the sayings concerning the Spirit's help before tribunals and blasphemy against the Spirit. Other more general expressions would have been employed when not referring to the Pentecostal Spirit.[14] It appears probable that Jesus used the term *Holy Spirit*, already in current use in Judaism, for his initial teachings on the Spirit, but it is arbitrary to distinguish in Jesus a Pentecostal teaching as opposed to a more general one about the Spirit.[15] In reality we do not have sufficient indications that Jesus used other titles for the Spirit. The consistency of the term *Holy Spirit* in Mark, albeit in a very limited number of passages, is a better indicator of the stability of the expression of Jesus transmitted by the tradition (Mark 1:8; 3:9; 12:36; 13:11; an anaphoric article may occur in 1:10). Matthew, on the other hand, does not maintain the consistency of the term *Holy Spirit* (Matt 10:20; 12:28). In the baptism of Jesus, he employs the form πνεῦμα Θεοῦ without the article (Matt 3:16); Mark 1:10 employs τὸ πνεῦμα; Luke 3:22 employs his more solemn and characteristic formula τὸ πνεῦμα τὸ ἅγιον. This passage was formed in the more primitive tradition. The non-Lukan occurrences attempted to emphasize the help of the Spirit for the messianic work, but perhaps did not attach particular importance to the term that designates the Spirit. Luke, on the other hand, wished to emphasize the identity of the Spirit that was upon Jesus and that Jesus placed upon his disciples for the extending of his work unto the ends of the earth; for this reason Luke introduced here the double article that is his preferred expression in Acts.

---

14. Procksch, "ἅγιος," 105–7.

15. This question is examined in greater detail in the next section. Procksch himself recognizes many exceptions to the norm that he proposes. Note also the use of the double article in 7:51, referring to the resistance to the Holy Spirit in ancient times (see sec. 7.3).

Comparing the texts of Luke with its corresponding parallels in the Synoptics, it is apparent that Luke used the complete expression *Holy Spirit* (without encountering it in Matthew or Mark) in Jesus' journey into the desert (Luke 4:1a; cf. Matt 4:1 and Mark 1:12), in the so-called Jubilee hymn (Luke 10:21; cf. Matt 11:25), and in the fruits of prayer (Luke 11:13; cf. Matt 7:11, ἀγαθά). On the other hand, Luke did not mention the Spirit in a citation of David (Luke 20:42; cf. Matt 22:43, "in spirit"; and Mark 12:36, "in the Holy Spirit"). Nevertheless, he attributed to the Spirit in Acts the inspiration of David and of Isaiah (1:16; 4:25; 28:25). More important is the substitution of "by the finger of God" in Luke 11:20 for "by the Spirit of God" in Matt 12:28.[16]

The relation between the author of Acts and Paul presents numerous problems.[17] With respect to the Spirit, they held clearly divergent

---

16. We have already noted that Luke changes the expression of Mark, "the Holy Spirit," with the double article, by the use of the inserted adjective between the article and the noun. But this observation has little effect on the use of the term *Holy Spirit* as much as do the nuances of the use of the article. The complete list of parallel texts in the Synoptics that refer to the Spirit is as follows: incarnation (Matt 1:18, 20; Luke 1:35), baptism in the Spirit (Matt 3:11; Mark 1:7–8; Luke 3:16; cf. John 1:33; Acts 1:5; 11:16), the baptism of Christ (Matt 3:16; Mark 1:10; and Luke 3:22), the desert (Matt 4:1; Mark 1:12; Luke 4:1), the Jubilee hymn (Luke 10:21; Matt 11:25, which does not mention the Spirit), the fruit of prayer (Luke 11:13; Matt 7:11, ἀγαθά), blasphemy against the Spirit (Matt 12:32; Mark 3:29; Luke 12:10), and help before tribunals (Matt 10:20; Mark 13:11; Luke 12:12; Luke 21:15, which does not mention the Spirit). With respect to exorcisms in Matt 12:28, the parallel in Luke 11:20 avoids the reference to the Spirit. Finally, there is the inspiration of David (Matt 22:43 and Mark 12:36, without Luke 20:42 mentioning the Spirit).

17. See Haenchen, *Acts*, 112–16 = *Apostelgeschichte*, 99–103, 657–59; Dibelius, "Paulus in der Apostelgeschichte," in his *Aufsätze zur Apostelgeschichte*, 175–80. [See the English translation of *Aufsätze* in the bibliography. —Ed.] The differences that appear between Paul as he appears in his letters and the image that Luke presents to us have been noted (Vielhauer, "Zum 'Paulinismus' der Apostelgeschichte"). In particular, the disparity between the two in the chronology of their accounts of the visits to Jerusalem has been studied (see the critical review of divergent hypotheses by Dupont, *Études*, 56–72, and also the various articles by Dupont on Pauline problems in the second part of *Études*). Wikenhauser, in his *Apostelgeschichte*, 177–81, and his *Apostelgeschichte und ihr Geschichtswert*, 169–286, demonstrates a reconciliation of disparities. [On the reconciliation of perceived disparities, see also the occasional arguments of Hemer, *Book of Acts*, passim. —Ed.] I agree with Trocmé (*Livre des Actes et l'Histoire*, 143) that Luke is nothing more than a periodic companion of Paul. Kilpatrick, in a brief note ("Spirit, God and Jesus in Acts"), rejects the similarity that Lake ("Paul's Conversion," 219) establishes between the Pauline doctrine of the Spirit and that of Acts. This is also discussed by Knox, "Acts and the Pauline Letter." [For an intertextual analysis yielding evidence for the similarity of Lukan and Pauline Pneumatology, cf. Elbert, "Possible Literary Links." —Ed.]

concepts. Paul distrusted the charismatic gifts (1 Cor 14) and preferred the theme of moral renovation by means of the Spirit as announced in Ezek 36:24–28 and Jer 31:31–34. Luke, on the other hand, starts from the charismatic reality of Pentecost and interprets it in light of Joel 2:28–32, understanding the gift of the Spirit always in a charismatic sense, either as a testimony of God or as an extraordinary animation *(reactivación extraordinaria)* of faith.[18] With respect to the terms used by both, we note that Paul uses the form *Holy Spirit* some 12 times, but this designation is proportionally very meager in comparison with the approximately 123 times that Paul mentions the Spirit of God. Paul follows the practice of using the separate titles for the Spirit, calling it the *Spirit of God*,[19] *of the Lord*,[20] *of Christ*,[21] or according to the effects that it produces.[22] There exist some consonance, such as the expression "in the Holy Spirit" (that proceeds from the baptism in the Spirit) and the verb λαμβάνω, which were not used by the LXX in relation to the Spirit. We also find a degree of consonance in certain themes referring to the Spirit, such as faith, wisdom, promise, and joy, even though they are treated in different ways. However, totally lacking in Luke are the themes of indwelling,[23] the Spirit of divine brotherhood, and the opposition between the flesh and the spirit, which pertain more directly to the order of salvation reserved by Luke exclusively for Christ.[24] On the other hand, Paul lacks the term ἐπλήσθη, characteristic of Pentecost.

As a complementary observation, we note that John employs the term *Holy Spirit* only three times in his Gospel: John 1:33 is the obliga-

---

18. Gächter, "Pneumabegriff," reviews in three principle points the different conception of Paul and of Acts: (a) Acts refers to the intervention of the Spirit in the external growth of the church, while Paul considers it to be directed to the internal growth of each individual member; (b) in Acts, the action of the Spirit is an observable, charismatic, normal experience of every Christian, while for Paul the action of the Spirit is an object of faith at least as much as an experience, and he knows that the great majority of Christians do not have this experience; (c) according to Acts, Christ sent the Spirit to the disciples so that they could complete his work, while according to Paul the Spirit brings about in Christians their being in Christ.

19. Rom 8:9, 14; 1 Cor 2: 14; 3:16; 6:11; 7:40; 12:3; and the singular form, the Holy Spirit of God, in Eph 4:30.

20. 2 Cor 3:17.

21. Rom 8:9.

22. Rom 1:4; 8:15; 11:8; and Eph 1:17.

23. [To the contrary, see Shelton, "'Filled with the Holy Spirit.'" —Ed.]

24. See the observations in sec. 2.3 with regard to healings.

tory citation that mentions the baptism in the Holy Spirit; John 14:26, "But the Advocate, the Holy Spirit, whom the Father will send in my name" (with the double article); and John 20:22 on the gifting after the resurrection (the Johannine Pentecost, without the article). Peter employs it two times (1 Pet 1:12 and 2 Pet 1:21) and Jude one time (20). It is notable that the Epistle to the Hebrews adopts the term *Holy Spirit* in five of the twelve passages that mention the Spirit.

Before concluding this review of the antecedents of the Lukan concept of the Holy Spirit, it is necessary to make a reference to Hellenism. The idea of the divine spirit is expressed regularly in the Greek world with the terms πνεῦμα Θεῖον and πνεῦμα ἱερόν. In their development, we encounter certain details that coincide with the New Testament, but their essential characteristics are completely distinct.[25] The defender of the antecedent nature of the Hellenistic concept of the Spirit has been Leisegang.[26] Von Baer completely rejects this interpretation, refuting it in various chapters of his work on the Holy Spirit in the writings of Luke, arguing that "Leisegang's opinion requires at the very least a restriction. When the Holy Spirit appears as the bearer of the historical revelation of God, it is thought of in completely non-Greek terms. Yet the Spirit-statements in Luke's gospel are completely embedded in this non-Greek frame."[27]

1.2 The Use of the Article

The term *Holy Spirit* is presented on some occasions without an article, on others with an article, and on still others with a double article. The complexity of the reasons that could be put forward to explain this diversity necessitates examination. A detailed comparison of the texts

---

25. H. Kleinknecht, "πνεῦμα in the Greek World," esp. 336, and the whole paragraph dedicated to "the Greek concept of the spirit and the New Testament."

26. Leisegang, *Pneuma Hagion*.

27. ". . . dass die Ansicht Leisegangs zum mindestens einer Einschränkung bedarf. Wenn der Hl. Geist als Träger der geschichtlichen Offenbarung gottes erscheint, so ist das vollkommen ungriechisch gedacht. In diesen ungriechischen Rahmen sind aber die Geistesaussagen in Lukasevangelium eingebettet" (Baer, *Heilige Geist*, 112–13). In his introduction (4), von Baer observes that the differences between the religious concepts of the Hellenistic world and the concept of the Spirit in the NT are so fundamental that, in comparison with these differences, the diverse nuances of the NT disappear and give the impression of a tight unity.

reveals no unique principle that explains either the lack of the article or its use. It appears, rather, that grammatical, stylistic, and perhaps even ideological determinants influenced its use. Procksch proposes that the article, especially the double article, refers to the Pentecostal Spirit, while expressions without the article refer to a more general and Old Testament sense of the Spirit. However, he recognizes the tenuous nature of his affirmation: "In general it may be said that the definite form . . . only became the possession of the Christian community in the event of Pentecost (Acts 4:31) in which He now works with sovereign creativity. On the other hand, the indefinite πνεῦμα ἅγιον works less as conscious will than as unconscious power of a creative (Luke 1:35 and 4:1) or prophetic nature (1:15, 41, 67, etc.), although this cannot be pressed too hard."[28]

This observation by Procksch appears to be correct with regard to references to the pentecostal Spirit in Luke's understanding and redaction. Perhaps, some of the variants in the use of the article in reference to Pentecost that Procksch examines can be understood as remnants of the older story that is utilized by Luke in his final composition.

In the Gospel of Luke, we encounter three consecutive texts (Luke 2:25, 26, 27), the first without an article, the second with a double article, and the third with only a single article. This case can only be explained as a later reworking. Luke 4:1a, 1b, 14 refer to the Spirit first without an article, then the next two with the single article, not for conceptual but for grammatical reasons (through lack of an adjective or perhaps as an anaphoric article). The arrival of Pentecost is described with the formula ἐπλήσθησαν . . . πνεύματος ἁγίου (Acts 2:4a) without an article. This deals with a typically prophetic formula, and, therefore, it does not appear that an opposition between prophetic and Pentecostal forms can be established. Acts 2:4b uses the article for grammatical reasons (lack of an adjective, it is a subject, perhaps an anaphoric article). The double article and article are found in 2:33 and 2:38, respectively, but both cases are in the determinative genitive. In 4:31, the formula ἐπλήσθησαν . . . τοῦ ἁγίου πνεύματος (with an article and an inserted adjective) appears to

28. "*Im allgemeinen* lässt sich sagen, dass der determinierte Begriff . . . erst im Pfingstereignis zum Gemeinbesitz der Christenheit wird, (Ag 4,31) in der er fortan schöpferisch und regierend wirkt, wahrend das underterminierte πνεῦμα ἅγιον weniger als unbewusste Kraft schöpferischer (Lc 1,35; 4,1) oder prophetischer Art (1,15.41.67 etc) wirksam ist, *obwohl die Rechnung nicht vollstandig aufgeht*" (Procksch, "ἅγιος," 104; emphasis added); BDF, n. 257 (2).

be an exception because previously in 4:8 and subsequently in 9:17 and in 13:9 (very similar cases include 6:3, 5 and 7:55) it is repeated without an article. It would appear that the distinction between prophetic and Pentecostal movings in these cases is an arbitrary one.

A grammatical and not conceptual difference exists between the three consecutive formulas: 13:2 (a double article for a subject and for the predominance of the double article in the second part of Acts); 13:4 (an article with an inserted adjective in order not to use the double article in the genitive agent with ὑπό); and 13:9 (without an article as a circumstantial object of πλησθείς according to the Pentecostal formula). More surprising is the double article in 5:3, "lying to the Holy Spirit," with the same meaning as the Old Testament expression used in 5:9, "to the Spirit of the Lord," possibly an adaptation of the primitive story that was joined to the book of Acts.[29]

The prophetic Spirit, in the restricted sense of prophetic oracles, appears in the second part with the double article (20:23; 21:11; and perhaps 20:28). Equally, the inspiration of the Old Testament prophecies is attributed three times to the Holy Spirit, designated with the double article (1:16 and 28:25) and without an article in 4:25 (without doubt to be governed by the preposition).

It appears, therefore, that *a conceptual value from the use or absence of the article cannot be deduced.* Usage is affected by a combination of diverse grammatical norms and stylistic preferences of the author or of the various redactors, even though such preferences lead us to suspect a particular conception. For now I offer the observation—merely as a approximation, among other reasons, for later reworkings—that the Pentecostal story and Luke 1–2 prefer the Old Testament formula ἐπλήσθησαν πνεύματος ἁγίου without the article. At other times, however, Luke prefers (even to the point of adapting his sources) the double article that appears in the sayings of Christ according to the primitive tradition. In effect, in the Pentecostal story we only encounter the double article in one important text (2:33) and in an occasional citation concerning the inspiration of David. However, the double article is typical of the narrative of Cornelius with its objective in the Jerusalem Council (10:44, 47; 11:15; and 15:8, 28) and of the narrative concerning Paul (13:2; 19:6; 20:23, 28; and 21:11).

---

29. See sec. 7.3.

I will collect here the more or less constant norms concerning the article that can be verified in the comparison to all of the texts in Acts that refer to the Holy Spirit. To improve the clarity of the explanations, consult the table at the end of this section, which presents all the diverse particulars concerning the use of the article in reference to the Holy Spirit, both in the Synoptics and in Acts (see the various notes in sec. 1.2).

Those passages that *lack the article* are more significant since they deal with a concrete substantive. These passages may be grouped in the following manner:

(a) *Prepositional expressions* frequently lack an article, which has no special significance since in the same classic tongue, and especially in Hellenism, the tendency of the article to disappear is accentuated in such expressions.[30] In Acts, this deals with a rather weak tendency that gives way easily to other conventions. The article is lacking with the preposition διά and ἐν (1:2, 5; 4:25; 11:16), but we also encounter the article with these same prepositions (11:28; 19:21; 21:4), probably because of the lack of an adjective. The preposition ἀπό takes the article in the quote from Joel 2:27–28.[31] The subject agent in the genitive with ὑπό is constructed with an article and the adjective is inserted.

(b) *The circumstantial object of material* with πίμπλημι or its derivatives and with χρίω *always* appears without an article, both in the Synoptics and in the Septuagint. The only exception is Acts 4:31 that narrates a coming of the Holy Spirit upon the disciples (as mentioned previously). This consistency in the lack of the article could perhaps originally be due to the partitive sense, in a certain manner, of the verb, but above all we note that it is one of the characteristic expressions with regard to the Holy Spirit in the Septuagint. It is very probable that the first author of this Pentecostal story had thought with pre-existing Old Testament categories. The same Pentecostal universalism appears to be a Jewish type of universalism—proselytes from all the world—while true universalism begins with the entry of Cornelius.[32] It is possible to speak, therefore, of a less personalized conception of the Spirit in the Pentecostal

---

30. Zerwick, *Biblical Greek*, n. 183: "There are thus three cases in which the absence of the article with a concrete and determinate substantive cannot be insisted upon: proper names, prepositional phrases, and nouns with a following genitive (i.e., where influence of the Semitic construct state is possible)."

31. The preposition ἀπό followed by the article is also found in Num 11:17, 25.

32. See sec. 8.4.

story. Nevertheless, for this narrative to be inserted as the basis for the whole work, the conception of the Holy Spirit is in certain ways adapted to the conception that the author manifests in the whole work.

(c) There is a prevalent lack of the article in the Samaritan pericope (8:14–25) and in the Ephesian pericope (19:1–7) that is not easily explained in terms of grammatical motives nor, perhaps, by conceptual ones.[33] The reception of the Spirit by the Samaritans lacks the article in 8:15, 17, and 19. On the other hand, the intermediate verse 8:18 uses the article, probably because the Spirit takes on the role of the subject (in the preceding verses it had the role of the direct object of λαμβάνω) or because of its lack of an adjective (in the other verses it is accompanied by an adjective). Also, one could speak of an anaphoric article, but it appears arbitrary to see an anaphoric article in the midst of the other three texts that repeat tirelessly the same expression without an article. It is clear that in the redaction of this pericope the lack of the article has prevailed, and only for a grammatical or stylistic motive was the article introduced on a single occasion. The Spirit that the Samaritans received is, evidently, according to the structure of the entire work, the same Spirit that Peter had promised in 2:38 (with an article and an inserted adjective in the genitive) and to whose testimony 5:32 refers (double article). It deals, therefore, with the same Pentecostal Spirit already promised by Jesus. There is no other explanation for the lack of the article in this pericope than the assigning of it to a pre-Lukan origin, which Luke did not feel the need to reshape.

The case of the Ephesian disciples appears similar, even though it is not as clear. 19:2a and 19:2b lack the article, while 19:6 uses the double article. In the first mention, the Spirit functions as the direct object of λαμβάνω (as in the Samaritan pericope). In 19:2b, the anaphoric article is expected, but what occurs is οὐδ' εἰ πνεῦμα ἅγιον ἔστιν without an article, even though it is a subject. Conceptually, as well, what is expected is the use of the double article, or at least the single article, alluding to the Pentecostal Spirit, since it does not have the sense that the disciples of the Baptist had not already heard about the Spirit sent by Jesus (that one supposes would be expressed with an article) but rather that they did not know that the Holy Spirit exists (without the article), a doctrine known from the Old Testament and from pre-Christian Judaism. The

---

33. These passages are examined in the treatment of the relationship between baptism and the Holy Spirit in sec. 6.4.

best solution to this contradiction is that the author does not examine in detail the meaning of the use or of the absence of the article. The lack of an article in the first two mentions could arise from the primitive story (λαμβάνω as in the Samaritan pericope). However, the third mention of the Holy Spirit with the double article (19:6) could have been introduced, or retouched, by the author in order to highlight the moment of the coming of the Holy Spirit with a formula that is almost identical to that in the story of Cornelius (10:44 and 11:15).

The use of the article is constant in diverse circumstances that may be called a stylistic norm or device of Acts, even though in many cases it would not be easy to say which of these circumstances has been the decisive one for the use of the article. Many of the texts that use the article can be explained simply with the known device of the anaphoric article.[34] As such, the suspicion of an anaphoric article would serve to remove importance from the use of the article in specific passages—as in 2:4b and in 8:18—given that the article would not represent any conceptual meaning, but merely a stylistic one. The problem in many passages is in determining if an article is merely anaphoric or, if in addition to pertaining to the meaning of the noun, it takes advantage of this resource of the anaphoric article.[35]

The same difficulty for interpretation resident in the use of the anaphoric article is also presented by the two following norms concerning the article that compensates for the lack of the adjective and the article that accompanies the subject. Technically, in a specific case, it is difficult to say to which of these three stylistic devices the use of the article is due. It appears that the most firmly established device is the compensation of the adjective (with only a single exception). On the other hand, it is not as certain that the author desires to use the anaphoric article, since it is

---

34. BDF, n. 252.

35. In Acts 2:4b it would remain to be resolved if (a) the mention of 2:4a without an article is made necessary by being a circumstantial object and the author avails himself of the first occasion (2:4b) to use the article, or if on the other hand (b) the author has not considered the article (2:4a) and is only obliged to use it as an anaphoric article or by giving it the role of the subject (2:4b). I am inclined to accept this second answer, since in the first case he would have employed the complete term, *the Holy Spirit*, better in 2:4b, which is repeated three times in a row in 8:15–19 and two times in 13:2, 4. In 8:18, the preference is clearly for the lack of the article, and 8:18 fills the requirement for an article by the use of the anaphoric article (or of the article as the subject or by the lack of the adjective).

missing from texts such as 8:17, 19 and 19:2b (even though their absence could arise from another source).

Another three texts in Acts could be explained as an anaphoric article, at least in a sense: 8:29; 10:19 = 11:12. No mention of the Holy Spirit precedes these texts, but they are preceded by a celestial intervention that in both anecdotes is equivalent in style to a spirit, and it appears that these texts refer to one of these spirits and not to the Holy Spirit.[36] As noted above, an article that compensates for the lack of an adjective is a constant norm, or device, and is founded logically on the article assuming the determinative value of the adjective. We observe this device in the following texts: 2:4b; 6:10; 8:18, 29; 10:19; 11:12, 28; 19:21; 20:22; 21:4. The only exception is 6:3, "full of the Spirit and of wisdom," in which both substantives are mutually determined and which corresponds to the spirit of wisdom in the Old Testament; nevertheless, the similar formula in 6:10 uses the article.

It is more difficult to explain why the adjective has been substituted for the article. In certain cases it can be attributed to stylistic brevity. In cases such as 8:29, 10:19, and 11:12 ("the Spirit said"), it could suggest a difference of the Pentecostal Holy Spirit, as noted above. This same explanation would be possible, even though it does not seem probable, in Paul's decisions in 19:21 and 20:22. We find no explanation for the lack of the adjective in 11:28 or 21:4 because the oracles of such prophets are clearly attributed to the Holy Spirit, as in 20:23 and in 21:11 (with the double article). The article is almost always used when the Holy Spirit serves as the subject of the verb. The exceptions that we find are in the clearly Old Testament-style text, 8:39 ("the Spirit of the Lord snatched Philip away"; cf. Luke 1:35 and 2:25), and the text already mentioned, 19:2b.

The use of the article with the subject agent in the genitive with ὑπό is notable. In these cases, the inserted adjective is employed (13:4 and 16:6), except in Luke 2:26, which employs the double article. The term *Holy Spirit* when used as a *determinative genitive* (subjective or as an added explanation) occurs *without exception* with an article and almost always with an inserted adjective (see 1:8; 2:38; 9:31; 10:45; and with a double article in 2:33). Regarding the use of the inserted adjective, of the thirty-nine passages in Acts where the complete term *Holy Spirit* occurs, only seven passages insert the adjective between the article and the noun.

---

36. See sec. 2.2 and 8.3.

Four of these passages are in the determinative genitive (1:8; 2:38; 9:31; and 10:45), another two are in the agent genitive with ὑπό (13:4 and 16:6), and the other is in a circumstantial object without preposition (4:31), which is, as previously noted, an irregular use of an article with ἐπλήσθησαν.

The use of the inserted adjective in the expression *the Holy Spirit* is not found in the Septuagint, or Mark, or Matthew except for the late baptismal formula in Matt 28:19.[37] It deals, therefore, with a characteristic formula of Luke's Gospel and Acts. Comparing the use of the inserted adjective with the use of the double article reveals that the inserted adjective is never found in a nominative or in a direct or indirect object, but only in a determinative or agent genitive and only once in a circumstantial object. The double article, by contrast, is found ten times in the nominative, three in a direct object, and two in an indirect object, only one time in a genitive determinative and never in a circumstantial object. This comparison suggests that the inserted adjective is a stylistic device in Luke to avoid using the double article in these oblique cases. Thus, it could explain the use in Luke 12:10 of an inserted adjective in order to avoid using the double article with a preposition as Mark 3:29 does. However, this does not explain why Luke 12:12 has changed the double article with a subject in Mark 13:11 for the inserted adjective.

The identicalness of content between the emphatic form of the double article and the construction of the inserted adjective can be seen in the comparison of the following texts. It does not appear that any difference of content exists between Acts 2:33, where Christ has received from the Father "the Promise of the Holy Spirit" (double article exceptional in the determinative genitive) in order to impart it to his disciples, and Acts 2:38, where Peter, in the same Pentecostal discourse, promises to those who are baptized "the gift of the holy Spirit" (inserted adjective).

Acts 10:44–47 is extremely significant with the mixture of the construction of the double article (as subject and direct object) with the construction of the inserted adjective: "the Holy Spirit [double article] fell upon all who heard the word . . . the gift of the Holy Spirit [inserted adjective] had been poured out even on the Gentiles . . . these people who have received the Holy Spirit [double article with direct object] just as we have?" Also 13:2–4 supposes the identical content in both expressions: "the Holy Spirit [double article accompanying the subject]

---

37. Similar formulas could be Wis 9:17; Rom 8:11; 1 Cor 6:19.

said, 'Set apart for me Barnabas and Saul.' . . . So, being sent out by the Holy Spirit they went down to Seleucia" (inserted adjective with a genitive agent with ὑπό). A grammatical equivalence in understanding is also recommended because, as in the expression τὸ πνεῦμα τὸ ἅγιον, so too in τοῦ ἁγίου πνεύματος, the adjective enjoys the attributive construction.

The use of the double article is something characteristic, although not exclusive, to Acts. This expression is encountered in Ps 51:11 and in Isa 63:10–11 and in similar formulas in Num 11:17; Neh 9:20; Ps 142:10; and Isa 59:21. In the Synoptics it occurs once in Matt 12:32, on blasphemy against the Holy Spirit, and in three of the six references to the Holy Spirit in Mark. Luke employs the expression three times in his Gospel, but not in the texts corresponding to Mark's. Luke uses this expression of the double article with deliberateness. It is the normal manner of presenting *the Holy Spirit* as a subject in Acts, especially in the central structure and in the second part. *The Spirit* as subject with only one article supposes that the lack of an adjective has a special motive, that is, it does not function as an inserted adjective with the nominative. The double article is used two times with an indirect object (7:51 and 15:28, in this latter text, it is equivalent to a subject), three times as a direct object (about which I have been unable to establish any norm with respect to the article), and exceptionally one time in the determinative genitive (2:33). In the Gospel of Luke it is used as a subject in the genitive agent with ὑπό (Luke 2:26); a very singular case, as much for the construction (which would have been more normal with the inserted adjective) as for introducing this formula in the story of Simeon. Luke 10:21 uses it in the Jubilee hymn as a causal dative.

Does the use of the double article in Luke suppose a particular intention? It is very significant that Luke 3:22 has introduced the double article to the narrative of the baptism of Christ in contrast to its parallels in Matt 3:16 (without an article) and Mark 1:10 (with a single article that is perhaps anaphoric), whereas Luke has only returned to using it in his Gospel referring to Christ in 10:21 (if we discount the exceptional case of 2:26) and has changed it for an inserted adjective in the sayings about blasphemy and persecutions.

As previously observed, the identification of the expression of the double article with the Pentecostal Spirit seems to be correct, although some exceptions can be found in which the double article is not used, perhaps owing to the use by Luke of older narratives in his final redaction. It seems probable that the use of the double article is a Lukan characteristic. The formula would come from the sayings concerning blasphemy and persecutions. Luke identifies this help before tribunals as the power for testimony—even in a positive and optimistic sense—experienced in the communities. He makes use of the Pentecostal story as a description of the initial and solemn moment of its fulfillment and respects the expressions of the original author without seeing any opposition with the expression of the double article that he prefers to use.

Luke speaks in Acts always of the same Spirit promised by Jesus, even though, perhaps, the concept of the Spirit in the incorporated narratives does not coincide exactly with the nucleus of the work (i.e., Cornelius and the Jerusalem Council). The double article would not indicate, therefore, a different conception of the Holy Spirit but the distinct imprint of Lukan expressions. In general, the expressions represent the Lukan conception, but the lack of the double article does not indicate a concept that claims distinction in the collection of the work. Still more, the expression with the double article could have been copied in the second part and may not correspond to the entire Lukan concept. The use or lack of the article can be a sign worth bearing in mind, but it cannot be taken as a discriminative norm for interpreting the extent of each expression. In examining the texts, it is fitting to retain the verifications that have been shown to be more consistent. The article can be explained as compensation for the adjective (ten cases and one exception), as an anaphoric article, or as a companion to the subject (twenty cases, two exceptions) and in the determinative genitive (five cases and no exceptions). The lack of the article is constant in the circumstantial object without the preposition (ten cases, two exceptions).

Luke's rationale for selecting these combinations of terms is, ultimately, elusive. It is possible that Luke's preference for the article, and even the double article, was motivated by a progressive tendency to personalize the Holy Spirit. However, in this tendency lurks a danger of attributing to the Holy Spirit such an overpowering personality that it would absorb the human action. Such an excess of personality would lead paradoxically to a depersonalization of both God and believer.

The following two tables may assist in acquiring a grammatical overview of Luke's efforts with respect to usage by Mark and Matthew.

Use of the Adjectival Article in Reference to the Holy Spirit in the Synoptics

Gospel	Context	No Article	One Article	Two Articles	Type of Adjective	Grammatical Construction/ Preposition
Matthew	Incarnation	1:18			Predicate	ἐκ
	Incarnation	1:20			Predicate	ἐκ
	Bapt. in H. S.	3:11			Predicate	ἐν
	Bapt. of Jesus	3:16			-	Direct Object
	Desert		4:1		-	ὑπό (subject)
	Person		10:20		-	Subject
	Messiah		12:18		-	Direct Object
	Exorcism	12:28			-	ἐν
	Blasphemy		12:31		-	Object Genitive
	Blasphemy			12:32	Attributive	κατά
	Inspiration	22:43			-	ἐν
	Baptism		28:19	*	Inserted	Determinative Genitive
Mark	Bapt. in H. S.	1:8			Predicate	Circumstantial Complement
	Bapt. of Jesus		1:10		-	Subject
	Desert		1:12		-	Subject
	Blasphemy			3:29	Attributive	εἰς
	Inspiration			12:36	Attributive	ἐν
	Person			13:11	Attributive	Subject

* = constructive equivalent

The Holy Spirit   23

Gospel	Context	No Article	One Article	Two Articles	Type of Adjective	Grammatical Construction/ Preposition
Luke	John the Baptist	1:15			Predicate	Material Genitive
	Incarnation	1:35			Predicate	Subject
	Elizabeth	1:41			Predicate	Material Genitive
	Zechariah	1:67			Predicate	Material Genitive
	Simeon	2:25			Predicate	Subject
	Simeon			2:26	Attributive	ὑπό (subject)
	Simeon		2:27		-	εου
	Bapt. in H. S.	3:16			Predicate	εου
	Bapt. of Jesus			3:22	Attributive	Subject
	Desert	4:1a			Predicate	Material Genitive
	Desert		4:1b		-	εου
	Desert		4:14		-	Determinative Genitive
	Messiah	4:18			-	Subject
	Exultation			10:21	Attributive	Circumstantial Complement
	Petition	11:13			Predicate	Direct Object
	Blasphemy		12:10	*	Inserted	ειος
	Person		12:12	*	Inserted	Subject

USE OF THE ADJECTIVAL ARTICLE IN REFERENCE TO THE HOLY SPIRIT IN ACTS

Context	No Article	One Article	Two Articles	Type of Adjective	Grammatical Construction/ Preposition
Instructions through the H. S.	1:2			Predicate	διά
Baptized in the H. S.	1:5			Predicate	ἐν
H. S. coming upon		1:8	*	Inserted	Determinative Genitive
The H. S. spoke			1:16	Attributive	Subject
Filled with H. S.	2:4a			Predicate	Material Genitive
Spirit gave utterance		2:4b		-	Subject
Pour out Spirit		2:17		-	ἀπό
Pour out Spirit		2:18		-	ἀπό
J. rec'd promised H. S.			2:33	Attributive	Determinative Genitive
Receive gift of H. S.		2:38	*	Inserted	Determinative Genitive
Peter filled with H. S.	4:8			Predicate	Material Genitive
Spoke by the H. S.	4:25			Predicate	διά
Filled with H. S.		4:31	*	Inserted	Material Genitive
Lie to the H. S.			5:3	Attributive	Direct Object
Test the Spirit	5:9			-	Direct Object
H. S. witnesses to			5:32	Attributive	Subject
Full of the H. S.	6:3			-	Material Genitive
Full of the H. S.	6:5			Predicate	Material Genitive
Stephen spoke by the S.		6:10		-	Indirect Object
Resist the H. S.			7:51	Attributive	Indirect Object
Filled with H. S.	7:55			Predicate	Material Genitive
Receive the H. S.			8:15	Predicate	Direct Object

* = constructive equivalent

Context	No Article	One Article	Two Articles	Type of Adjective	Grammatical Construction/ Preposition
Received the H. S.	8:17			Predicate	Direct Object
Spirit was given		8:18		-	Subject
Receive the H. S.	8:19			Predicate	Direct Object
The Spirit told Philip		8:29		-	Subject
The Spirit took Philip	8:39			-	Subject
Filled with H. S.	9:17			Predicate	Material Genitive
Encouraged by the H. S.		9:31	*	Inserted	Determinative Genitive
The Spirit said to him		10:19		-	Subject
J. anointed with H. S.	10:38			Predicate	Material Genitive
H. S. fell on			10:44	Attributive	Subject
Gift of H. S. poured out		10:45	*	Inserted	Determinative Genitive
Received the H. S.			10:47	Attributive	Direct Object
Spirit told Peter		11:12		-	Subject
H. S. fell on			11:15	Attributive	Subject
Baptized in the H. S.	11:16			Predicate	ἐν
Full of the H. S.	11:24			Predicate	Material Genitive
Agabus predicted by the S.		11:28		-	διά
The H. S. said			13:2	Attributive	Subject
Sent out by the H. S.		13:4	*	Inserted	ὑπό (subject)
Paul, filled with H. S.	13:9			Predicate	Material Genitive
Filled with joy and the H. S.	13:52			Predicate	Material Genitive

Context	No Article	One Article	Two Articles	Type of Adjective	Grammatical Construction/ Preposition
Giving the H. S. to them			15:8	Attributive	Direct Object
Seemed good to the H. S.			15:28	Attributive	Indirect Object
Kept by H. S. from preaching		16:6	*	Inserted	ὑπό (subject)
S. of Jesus would not allow		16:7		-	Subject
Fervent in the Spirit		18:25		-	Circumstantial Complement
Receive the H. S.	19:2a			Predicate	Direct Object
Not heard there is a H. S.	19:2b			Predicate	Subject (εἰμί)
The H. S. came on them			19:6	Attributive	Subject
Paul resolved in the Spirit		19:21		-	ἐν
Paul, bound by the Spirit		20:22		-	Circumstantial Complement
The H. S. witnesses to Paul			20:23	Attributive	Subject
H. S. appointed overseers			20:28	Attributive	Subject
Disciples urge Paul through S.		21:4		-	διά
The H. S. says			21:11	Attributive	Subject
The H. S. spoke			28:25	Attributive	Subject

1.3 Conclusions

I have dedicated this first chapter to a study of the term τὸ πνεῦμα τὸ ἅγιον in its formal aspect. The results are neither abundant, nor significant. Style is a reflection of thought, but a very conditioned reflection, as much by grammar as by expressions common to the tradition, or by context. The formal investigation is especially uncertain in a book like

Acts, which contains numerous antecedent stories. These modest results, however, may introduce us to the Lukan concept of the Spirit.[38]

As we have seen, the Old Testament uses various expressions to designate the Spirit of God, and in four passages it uses the term *holy spirit*. Pre-Christian Judaism had frequently used the term *holy spirit*, but without advancing beyond the Old Testament understanding. It was the primitive Christian tradition that affixed the term *Holy Spirit* to three gospel sayings with a new perspective, even though probably without having assimilated the sense of blasphemy against the Spirit or of baptism in the Holy Spirit. Mark has remained faithful to the tradition in his use of this term. On the other hand, Matthew has returned to Old Testament expressions such as *the Spirit of God*. Nor has Paul felt bound to the term *Holy Spirit*. Even less so with John, who uses it only three times. But the relatively frequent use of the term in the Epistle to the Hebrews is notable.

I believe that the fixing of the term *Holy Spirit* as a proper name for designating the Spirit of God can be ascribed to Luke and, more specifically, to Acts. This does not have to do merely with a more constant repetition of the term, but with combining the Old Testament inheritance with the developing perspective principles of the gospel message. The Pentecostal story has permitted Acts to interpret the sense of the baptism in the Holy Spirit[39] and to develop, with abundant nuances, the Spirit's help to the disciples. This fixing of a proper name to a substantially finished content is perhaps the major contribution of Luke to the Christian understanding of the Holy Spirit. The Spirit texts of Acts are

---

38. Conzelmann, *Mitte der Zeit*, n. 1, at Acts 1:11, appeals also to those inevitable disagreements of style: "Naturally it must be reckoned with, that it does not fit every individual place. There can be found remnants from the sources used that are not completely melted down. Especially one notices much inattentiveness. It does not go too far, what (good) ancient historians are used to [Natürlich ist damit zu rechnen, dass sich ihm nicht jede einzelne Stelle einfügt. Es finden sich Restbestände aus den benutzten Quellen, kie nicht vollständig eingeschmolzen sind. Uberhaupt bemerkt man viele Unachtsamkeiten. Sie überschreiten aber nicht das Mass dessen, was man bei (guten) aintiken Historikern gewohnt ist]." Zerwick (*Biblical Greek*, n. 118) prevents the deception of expecting from the grammar an intimate sense of an expression: "We must beware of the notion that words and grammatical usage have of themselves a certain definite and invariable content of meaning. They are in reality conventional signs whose sense is usually fairly general, the exact meaning being in each case determined by usage and above all by the subject matter."

39. See sec. 6.4.

cited fairly infrequently and, when they are, very frequently they are interpreted in the Pauline sense. Nevertheless, the term *Holy Spirit* has remained definitely fixed as a true proper name.

The preceding section has discussed whether or not the use, or the absence, of the article in the term *Holy Spirit* reflects a conceptual divergence. The relation that Procksch establishes between the article—especially the double article—and the Pentecostal Spirit appears to be correct. We find, however, some exceptions that may be attributed to the use Luke made of some older story. The lack of the article would generally indicate a more Old Testament understanding. I recognize that there is a progressive tendency toward the article, but its application is subject to other grammatical norms and to influences of diverse sources in such a way that a concrete norm could scarcely be established that interprets such a tendency. This irregularity is shown by the various examples in which the use or lack of the article in the same context demonstrates that we are dealing with a grammatical and not a conceptual difference. The coming of the Holy Spirit upon Cornelius is described at times with a double article (10:44, 47; 11:15; and 15:8) and at other times with the adjective inserted between the article and the subject (10:45), but it is most valuable interpreted as the baptism in the Holy Spirit (without an article; 11:16), just as in the Pentecostal coming (2:4a) with which it is identified. In the same way, I have compared the diverse expressions of 13:2, 4, and 9.

Even along the conceptual lines, I do not believe that a progressive advance exists in the book of Acts. The foundation is the Pentecostal story, which is loaded with an Old Testament sense (its expression without an article resemble Luke 1–2). The principle point is the story of Cornelius and the Jerusalem Council, which conditions the entire structure of Acts. The Pauline narrative (which conserves the double article from the story of Cornelius) returns to an Old Testament sense of the action of the Spirit but in a more superficial sense than that of the Pentecostal narrative.

These observations suggest a hypothesis that leaves us open to an ulterior consideration. It is probable that the expression τὸ πνεῦμα τὸ ἅγιον is the characteristic of the principal author of Acts, who has organized the structure, supporting it with the Cornelius-Jerusalem Council complex. The author has respected the style of the older Pentecostal narrative (ἐπλήσθησαν), which has served as a base of departure, and of other narrations, such as that of Stephen and that of the Samaritans. More archaic expressions are encountered in the anecdote of Ananias and Sapphira ("Spirit of the Lord," 5:9), of Philip (ἥρπασεν, 8:39), and of the vision of unclean animals (10:19). The Pauline story, in the last part, can be attributed to the same author or can be an imitation of the style of the first part of the work.[40]

As an orientation with respect to Luke's use of the article, I have grouped the texts in a way that presents a uniform explanation. *The lack of the article*: (a) generally the prepositional phrases; (b) the circumstantial object of the subject; (c) the episode of the Samaritans and of the Ephesians frequently lack the article without our being able to discover a grammatical reason to justify it. *The employment of the article*: (a) in those texts that can explain it as an anaphoric article; (b) as compensation for the lack of an adjective; (c) when the Spirit is the subject of the action; (d) when it is used as a determinative genitive. My examination of the double article and the use of the inserted adjective leads me to believe that this latter construction substitutes equally for the double article in the expressions with a determinative genitive or agent.

The vagaries and uncertainties in which the evolution of the term *Holy Spirit* develops appear to reflect the perception of the Spirit as an impersonal force, a literary personification, and, finally, a person.[41]

---

40. I do not claim to go into the complicated questions concerning the sources and composition of Acts. I have no other choice, however, than to affirm the divergent nuances in the conception of the Spirit and in its expressions in the diverse parts of the work. The diversity of the author between the first and second parts of Acts has been amply studied without a satisfactory explanation having been achieved. With respect to the theme of the Holy Spirit, the difference between both parts is absolute as we will have occasion to note throughout this work. The impression is of an imitation of the first part, without attaining its profundity of inspiration. The Jerusalem Council belongs to the first part, as does perhaps the end of the work itself. On the other hand, certain inserted reworkings could pertain to the second part, before the Jerusalem Council. For the purpose at hand, it is enough to verify the differences, leaving to the investigators of the sources of Acts the search for the causes of such diversities.

41. See sec. 4.4.

2

The Inbreaking of the Divine

2.1 The Spirit and the Power (δύναμις)

The actions attributed to the Holy Spirit are one form of intervention by God, but they are by no means the only form, as illustrated by Luke in the book of Acts. These illustrations better define the Lukan concept of the Holy Spirit. The term δύναμις denotes an intervention of God and appears at times to designate the same content as the term πνεῦμα. Various passages call attention to the affinity between these two concepts. Pentecost is interpreted by Jesus both as an abiding concept in order that disciples may be "clothed with power from on high"[1] (Luke 24:49) and as the reception of the power of the Holy Spirit (Acts 1:8). In the story of the Annunciation (Luke 1:35), we encounter this description: "The Holy Spirit will come upon you and the power of the Most High will overshadow you." Peter tells us, alluding to the descent of the Holy Spirit at the Jordan, that Jesus was anointed with the Holy Spirit and with power (Acts 10:38).

There exist certain parallels between the Holy Spirit and supernatural power; nevertheless, they are not equivalent terms.[2] Both terms arrive

---

1. It is difficult in translating δύναμις to retain all of the nuances and suggested meanings of the Greek word. The various translations employ different terms in the diverse passages of Luke and Acts.

2. The only case of true equivalence is Luke 24:49, in which the expression "until you have been clothed with power from on high" quite evidently refers to the Spirit of Pentecost and not simply a prodigious energy. For this reticence to use the term *Holy Spirit* at the end of Luke, two explanations can be suggested: (a) Luke may wish to leave for his second work the introduction of the Pentecostal theme and is content

at their point of contact carrying their own particular nuances. Neither are the terms in the same category. The term δύναμις is invariably personified. With ingenuity that does not lack irony, Simon the magician intentionally represented himself to the people as "the power of God that is called Great"[3] (Acts 8:10). The power appears to put him in the service of the Spirit as the property or extension of the Spirit, operating in the name of the power of the Holy Spirit (Luke 4:14; Acts 1:8).[4]

Δύναμις signifies, in the Gospel of Luke, a superhuman power (Luke 21:27) that, like πνεῦμα, can also be applied to demonic powers (Luke 10:19) but which is almost always understood as divine power. The effects of this supernatural power can be of a creative-fructifying type (Luke 1:35) or can bring victory against impure spirits (Luke 4:36; 9:1) and against the sickness that results from their tyranny (Luke 5:17; 6:19; 8:46; Acts 3:12; 4:7). Particularly from this last aspect comes the meaning of miracles that acquire the plural form δυνάμεις (Luke 10:13; 19:37; Acts 2:22; 8:13; 19:11).[5] It should be noted that the affinity in the terms δύναμις and πνεῦμα (Luke 1:35; 4:14; 24:49; Acts 1:8; 10:38) is encountered in those passages in which the divine power is manifested with a more complex character that embraces diverse aspects. Nevertheless, to differentiate them, this divine power is designated either as the *Holy Spirit* or as *power*.

Luke attributes exclusively to the Holy Spirit prophetic utterances, speaking in tongues, the compulsion to speak the good news, and embolding the believer's confession under persecution. He attributes exorcisms and healings to δύναμις. Exorcism of unclean spirits is accomplished by the power (Luke 4:36; 9:1; Acts 10:38). Furthermore, he appears to avoid expressly

---

with a vague allusion in Luke 24:49; (b) if we accept that Luke's writings were originally a single work and that in the pursuant separation into two works a few light finishing touches were added, a redactor might have chosen two such similar terms.

3. Luke also concedes the article in other passages, but we discover in them a grammatical reason: Luke 4:14 and 22:69 use the article with a genitive determinative. Luke 10:19 uses the article, together with the adjective πᾶς in the predicate form, in order to rule out every exception (Zerwick, *Biblical Greek*, n. 188).

4. Grundmann, "δύναμις," expounds the two concepts of this theme: (a) an impersonal energetic substance, common to manistic and magical religions; (b) personal interventions by God in nature and history. Naturally, the personal intervention by God is a fundamental concept of the Bible; nevertheless, some texts echo a manistic concept, the most significant examples of this being Luke 6:19 and 8:46.

5. Luke 22:69 appears to be a theological periphrasis of the name *Yahweh*. See also Schweizer, "πνεῦμα," 404–6.

attributing to the Spirit the efficacy of exorcisms in a pair of highly significant texts: (a) when Matthew 12:28 cites the argument of Christ, "If it is by the Spirit of God that I cast out demons," and (b) when Luke 11:20 uses the expression that appears only here in the New Testament, "If it is by the finger of God that I cast out the demon." It is uncertain that Luke knew of an attribution to the Spirit in his sources, making the avoidance of it a conscious decision, but this appears most probable.

Von Baer believed that the expression used by Luke (an allusion to Exod 8:15) would be the original one for Christ and that it would emphasize the immediacy of the moving of God in him, in contrast to the indirect method of invoking the name of God used by the Jewish exorcists.[6] It appears, however, that von Baer carries his conclusions too far, guided by his general principle: "He (Christ) is the bearer of the new Messianic spirit. Everything that was done by him is, at the same time, also being valued by Luke as a work of power by the Holy Spirit, because the Messianic spirit worked through Jesus."[7] Even though this principle is fundamentally valid, I believe it preferable to respect the terminology of Luke, who in no passage attributes to the Spirit this faculty of exorcism, neither prior to Pentecost (Luke 9:1; 10:19) nor following it (Acts 16:18), but rather attributes it to the δύναμις or to the ἐξουσία.[8]

George has recently summarized the question about this text and deduced that Luke exchanged the mention of the Holy Spirit for the expression "the finger of God" for two reasons: (a) to emphasize the figure of Christ as the new Moses by means of the allusion to Exod 8:15, and

---

6. "The nature of the expressions πνεῦμα Θεοῦ [spirit of God] and δάκτυλος Θεοῦ [finger of God] appear to be of equal value in this case. Also Luke had seen in this statement of Jesus a confirmation of this, that upon Jesus the abiding, unique Messianic spirit had brought about this wonder [Dem Wesen nach sind die Ausdrücke πνεῦμα Θεοῦ und δάκτυλος Θεοῦ in diesem Falle als gleichwertig anzusehen. Auch Lukas wird in diesem Ausspruch Jesu eine Bekräftigung dafür gesehen haben, dass der auf Jesu ruhende einzigartige Messiasgeist diese Wunder bewirkte]" (Baer, *Heilige Geist*, 136).

7. "Er (Christus) ist der Träger des neuen Messiasgeistes. Alles, was von ihm gewirkt wird, ist gleichzeitig auch als Kraftwirkung des Heiligen Geistes von Lukas bewerten worden, den durch Jesus wirkte der Messiasgeist" (Baer, *Heilige Geist*, 69). The intention of Luke is to highlight the imprint that the prophetic consecration at the Jordan, by means of the Holy Spirit, produced in Christ. This idea presides over the construction of chs. 3 and 4, which are very personal to Luke, and sets the agenda for the rest of the gospel (4:31—24:43), just as Pentecost does for Acts.

8. Von Baer, on the other hand, expressly attributes exorcisms to the action of the Spirit (*Heilige Geist*, 196–98).

(b) to avoid attributing exorcisms to the Holy Spirit. I subscribe completely to his words: "But Luke attaches more importance than Mark and Matthew to defining the precise role of the Spirit in the activity of Jesus. With respect to their differences, he does not attribute the exorcisms and healings of Jesus to the Spirit, but to his power. . . . For Luke, the Spirit is the source of the message, the divine power that consecrates Jesus to proclaim the Gospel. . . . Without doubt it is that Lucan concept of the role of the Spirit which explains the placement of the unique passage on blasphemy against the Spirit in the third Gospel."[9]

Works equally characteristic of the power are *healings*. Luke 5:17 states expressly of Jesus, "And the power of the Lord was with him to heal." With slight variations, we encounter the same thought in Luke 6:19; 8:46; 9:1. Acts also attributes healings to the power or the name of Jesus, as seen in the healing of the lame man at the temple (Acts 3:12; 4:7).[10] The citation of Isaiah 61:1 that Luke uses in the discourse at the synagogue in Nazareth could be significant in interpreting the prophetic work of Jesus as the anointing of the Spirit promised to the Messiah (Luke 4:18–19.) Luke eliminates the intermediate phrase "to bind up the broken-hearted" and continues with the proclamation of the message to the captives and the blind, so as to avoid confusion with regard to a remarkable healing.[11]

My analysis confirms the observation of Schweizer: "Though the miracles are important for Luke, they are never ascribed to the Spirit. . . . Though Luke can use δύναμις and πνεῦμα almost as synonyms,

---

9. "Mais Luc s'attache plus que Marc et Matthieu à définer le rôle précis de l'Esprit, dans l'activite de Jésus. A leur différence, il n'attribue pas les exorcismes et les guerisons de Jésus à l'Esprit, mais à sa Puissance . . . Pour Luc, l'Esprit est la source du message, la puissance divine qui consacre Jésus pour proclamer l'Evangile . . . C'est sans doute cette conception lucanienne du rôle de l'Esprit qui explique la place du logion sur le blasphè me contre l'Esprit dans le troisiè me évangile . . ." (George, "Note sur quelques"). Also, Yates, "Luke's Pneumatology," maintains a conscious retouching on Luke's part. See also Rodd, "Spirit or Finger." [For further study, cf. Woods, *"Finger of God" and Pneumatology*. —Ed.]

10. Concerning the name of Jesus, see sec. 2.3, where it is made evident why Luke does not attribute exorcism and healings to the Spirit.

11. This omission is much more significant than that of the term ἰάομαι (used here by Isa 61:1 in a figurative sense) that always has in Luke the sense of a physical healing. Luke would avoid, at least consciously, the possible misunderstanding from an attribution of healings to the Spirit.

the distinction between them is clear at this point."[12] It is no accident that in neither the Gospel nor Acts does Luke attribute healing to the Holy Spirit. The Spirit inspires the prophetic word; the power produces the clearly extraordinary phenomena, be it healing, exorcism, or any other demonstration of superhuman intensity that can be perceived by the senses. Intentionally exaggerating the distinction between the two in order better to understand it, it could be said that the Spirit represents the intervention of God in the area of the *intellect*, and the power in the area of the *senses*.

This distinction is confirmed in the relationship observed between the Spirit and the power *with respect to testimony*. The Spirit teaches the believer what to say before tribunals (Luke 12:12); Peter rises up full of the Holy Spirit while making his first defense of Jesus before the Sanhedrin (Acts 4:8) in the same way that, under the influence of the coming of Pentecost, he had given testimony with his discourse and "with many other arguments" (Acts 2:40). The summaries distinguish well between intrepid evangelization which they attribute to the Spirit (4:31) and testimony given with great power (4:33) and with wonders and signs (5:12).[13] However, the testimony is not given with words alone but also with wondrous manifestations. Jesus was endorsed (ἀποδεδειγμένον) by God with miracles (δυνάμεσι), wonders and signs (τέρασι καὶ σημείοις) (Acts 2:22), and "with great power the apostles gave their testimony," (δυνάμει μεγάλῃ ἀπεδίδουν τὸ μαρτύριον, Acts 4:33).

The signs and wonders (σημεῖα καὶ τέρατα) are characteristics of testimony. At times they appear in the context of an intervention of the Spirit (Acts 2:19; 4:30; 6:8; 15:12), and it is easy to consider them an effect of the Spirit. Nevertheless, it should be noted that not only does Acts never attribute them expressly to the Spirit, but they are clearly attributed directly to God. Certainly, we see a type of parallelism in those passages that present the same person on some occasions as endowed

---

12. Schweizer, "πνεῦμα," 407. "Obwohl Lukas die Wundertaten sehr wichtig sind, warden sie nicht ein einziges Mal auf den Geist zurückgeführt. . . . Obwohl Lukas δύναμις und πνεῦμα fast synonym verwenden kann, ist in dieser Frage die Unterscheidung klar." [In this edition of Haya-Prats' thesis, Bromiley's *TDNT* translation of the *TWNT* is quoted in the text, unless otherwise noted. —Ed.] Note that the blindness of Elymas is attributed directly to the hand of God (13:11), permitting a mere prophetic sense to the action of the Spirit over Paul (13:9). The deaths of Ananias and Sapphira are even less related to the action of the Spirit (see sec. 7.3).

13. See sec. 7.2.

by the Spirit and on others as having the power to work wonders. Of Stephen, "a man full of faith and the Holy Spirit" (6:5), it is said that "full of grace and power, he did great wonders and signs" (6:8). Jesus, attested to by the wonders and signs "that *God did* through him among you" (2:22, emphasis added), is also presented as "anointed with the Holy Spirit and with power" (10:38).

This correlation of the gift of the Spirit and the gift of wonders in the same person does not permit us to derive the second from the first; on the contrary, it is probable that Acts 6:5 substitutes mention of the Spirit for that of power precisely because it deals with the working of wonders and signs. The parallelism with Acts 10:38 appears to be merely generic: Christ had been anointed with the Spirit for the prophetic proclamation of the message, and with power for the execution of wonders which attested to his ministry.[14] Spirit and power are associated with two distinct effects of interventions by God. This contrast helps shape the Lukan concept of the Spirit. Other interventions of God help identify more precisely the content of the Lukan conception of the Spirit.[15]

Χείρ Κυρίου designates "the finger of God" (as previously seen in regard to exorcism) and is a direct intervention of God. Gentiles and Jews united together "to do whatever your hand and your plan had predestined to take place" (4:28). Stephen cited Isa 66:2: "Did not my hand

---

14. More difficult to interpret is the parallelism in Luke 1:35. I believe that we are not dealing with two identical terms but with the prophetic aspect and with the wondrous aspect of the intervention of God. See sec. 8.2.

15. Von Baer (*Heilige Geist*, 38–43) proposes various terms as correlative terms for the Spirit. However, from the beginning, the danger of taking as equivalent these parallel terms, which frequently surpass a mere rhythmic doubling and add new aspects, is apparent. Even more dangerous is to take as synonyms the diverse terms that each evangelist employs to describe the same scene, because the new term has frequently been introduced consciously in order to propose a different interpretation of the event. We tend to disregard the term ἐξουσία, which appears two times in the gospel together with δύναμις, in Luke 4:36 and 9:1. Its proper sense, though, is almost of a judicial character, and we could translate it by "dominion," "power," "ability," or "right." Only in Luke 10:19 does this ability seem to involve of necessity something physical. Acts applies this term to God (1:7), to the dominion of Satan (26:18), and, in the words of Simon the Magician, to the ability that the apostles had to impart the Spirit (8:19). The remaining passages have the sense of profane power. In the Gospel, it appears more frequently with its religious sense. I believe that this term, with its more qualitative-judicial than substantive value, does not offer a comparison with the term *Spirit*, which designates the same reality that executes action. I would add that the Spirit appears to act with its own freedom, without the need to complete it (as with the power that the disciples received) with the addition of ἐξουσία.

make all these things?" (Acts 7:50). The hand of God works healings and wonders (4:30; 11:21; 13:11) by means of Moses (7:25) and of the apostles (5:12; 11:30; 14:3; 19:11; probably also 2:33). In the cases cited, the hand of God produces effects similar to those of the power, but it alludes to a more direct intervention by God, while the power refers to an energy that is transferred to the ones who are sent. For the exaltation of Christ, a formula is used demonstrating intense respect for the hand of God: Jesus was exalted at the *right hand of God* (2:33; 5:31).

Indirect references to the intervention of God are encountered through the adjective δυνατός or the verb δύναμαι. These have, naturally, their ordinary meaning, which we could call profane or neutral, with respect to the religious intervention of God. Nevertheless, in certain passages an allusion to a need or impediment that surpasses human forces is apparent. The profane sense of δυνατός is evident in Luke 14:31 and Acts 20:16; 25:5, while an intermediate and more ambiguous sense can be seen in Acts 18:24. The religious sense appears in Luke 1:49, where God is called ὁ δυνατός; in Luke 18:27, which asserts, "What is impossible for mortals is possible for God"; and in Luke 24:19, which describes Christ as "mighty in deed and word before God," an expression that in Acts 7:22 is applied almost word for word to Moses. We also encounter the religious sense of divine intervention in Acts 2:24 and 11:17, which express the *impossibility* of restraining Christ under the dominion of death or of resisting the inbreaking of God in favor of the Gentiles. These supernatural interventions are attributed directly to God, not to the Spirit. Even in Acts 11:17 the resistance spoken of would properly be against the intervention of God and not specifically against the Spirit that is his sign.

The verb δύναμαι, more frequently used than the adjective, has not remained as fixed in its religious sense. In Acts we encounter religious tones only in certain passages in the first part of the book.[16] In 4:20, when Peter responds to the Sanhedrin, "For we cannot keep from speaking about what we have seen and heard," the author refers without doubt to the promise of the Spirit that had been asserted in 1:8, completed in

---

16. Of the thirteen passages in the second part, only 20:32 has a religious sense: "a message that is able to build you up and to give you the inheritance." This does not necessarily depend on a different use of the vocabulary but, more likely, on a profane licentiousness that dilutes the religious density of these statements.

Pentecost, and repeated in 4:31. The impulse of the Spirit impels them almost irresistibly to the proclamation of the message.[17]

Reviewing the analysis of the diverse expressions that indicate an intervention by God (leaving aside until later sections interventions by means of angels and by means of Christ), three groups emerge: (a) the *hand* or the *finger* or the *right hand* of God indicate such interventions by God; (b) the power resembles a superhuman energy, but with an almost material character, which proceeds from God but is transmitted to humans; and (c) between these two groups would be situated interventions by means of the Holy Spirit. Other allusions are too general, imprecise, or clearly different from the subject theme.

Keeping in mind the points of similarity and the distinctions between the *Spirit* and the *power*, the following may be concluded: both signify the intervention of the power of God in history, determining events of salvific importance. The difference between the two terms appears to be rooted in Luke's tendency to see in the Spirit a more personalized reality that assumes in itself the right to act, even though it acts as one sent by God, and whose intervention is of a non-material nature, on a plane appropriately called intellectual acting. In the power, Luke sees a communicated energy of a more material type, yet without becoming manistic, that does not allow us to understand the mode of its use (ἐξουσία) and is destined to carry out more material interventions.[18] Consequently, the Spirit assumes the principal place in the interventions of God, while the power is substituted in actions that would have results that are too material for the Spirit, or that for another motive Luke does not want to attribute to it. In a certain sense, some effects of the power would be attributable to the Spirit, since Luke appears to speak of the power being subordinated to the Spirit in Luke 4:14 and in Acts 1:8, but

---

17. A somewhat similar case of the irresistible action of the Holy Spirit could be 6:10 and perhaps 19:20. Other texts such as 5:29; 8:31; and 13:38 refer to the impotence of human beings before the things of God, although it remains unclear whether this impotence would have to be made up for by the Spirit or whether it would be attributed to another class of intervention by God.

18. This does not mean at all that the power is to be interpreted as the presence of a special substance, as the interpretation of Grundmann ("δύναμις," 299–305) might suggest, being too inclined to encounter in Luke allusions of a manistic concept. I believe that mention of the power would only be an allusion to the personal intervention of God with physical repercussions, an effect that Luke avoids attributing to the Spirit.

it would be violating Luke's thinking to dispense with the distinction he has maintained so consistently in various passages.

Yet another more conceptual and theological interpretation could be given, independent of the preceding one, but which could more or less consciously have been its foundation. Perhaps Luke had witnessed in the power the submission brought by Christ that began to blot out the marks of sin, such as demonic possession and sickness. But these miracles were accomplished with power and in the name of Jesus, even after the gift of the Spirit. On the other hand, Luke had seen in the Spirit the anticipation of the gift of the last days, which consisted of exultant participation in the knowledge of God, translated in prophetic songs and the gift of tongues. The testimony of God would consist as much in the supernatural imprint of healings—an aspect that is preferred in our times but which was secondary in Luke—which is attributed to the power, as in the spreading of the prophetic gift according to the promise of Joel, which Luke attributes to the Spirit.[19] This latter aspect is the one preferred by Luke, who had without doubt experienced it in his communities, while miracles would be a much less frequent phenomenon.[20]

2.2 The Holy Spirit and Angels

Some passages appear to introduce the action of an angel as comparable or equivalent to the action of the Spirit. This section examines these to determine to what extent they influence Luke's concept of the Holy Spirit. The story of the eunuch in Acts 8:29 introduces the Spirit with an article and without an adjective, in a construction that appears to be an anaphoric article. There is no mention of the Spirit in the immediate context, as the use of the anaphoric article would suppose, but rather the words of an angel. It appears that the text identifies the angel with the Spirit, but it is very doubtful that the spirit mentioned would be the Holy Spirit. The entire story presents characters that are very foreign to the

---

19. Prophecy in its sense of superhuman exaltation as a spokesperson of the Spirit is the sense found in the story of Zechariah, Elizabeth, and in the gift of tongues. See sec. 8.1.

20. The prophetic gifts in the Pauline communities were solidly attested to in his letters. With regard to miracles, there remain a number of narratives in Acts with a suspicious parallelism between the miracles of Paul and those of Peter narrated in the first part. It is perfectly evident that Luke had a preference for prophetic experience, which he considered to be normal in all the communities.

Pentecostal concept of the Holy Spirit, particularly in the direct mode of intervention communicating a precise message,[21] or the snatching of Philip, or the violent action of the Spirit in Mark 1:12 that Luke 4:1b corrects. Even the formal expressions are ambiguous and not the accustomed ones, such as εἶπεν δὲ τὸ πνεῦμα without the characteristic adjective, as in the πνεῦμα Κυρίου in 8:39 with its Old Testament flavor.[22]

In the stories of Cornelius, we note certain conventions in the attribution of the visions to the Spirit, to an angel, or to a voice from heaven. A certain planned logic, very detailed and solemnly prepared, is apparent in which there is an angel that speaks to Cornelius in order not to anticipate an intervention of the Holy Spirit prior to his coming upon him. To Peter, on the other hand, a voice from heaven speaks first and afterwards the Spirit speaks, also introduced with an anaphoric article, which was not used when he spoke to him in the preceding context, i.e., with an article that can refer to the supernatural subject that has just finished acting.[23] According to the words of the Spirit, it had been he himself who had sent the emissaries of Cornelius (10:20). This assumes, although in an implicit and unnoticed form of the narrative itself, that the Spirit had acted through the will of Cornelius, whether directly or by means of the angel. On the other hand, the emissaries explicitly attribute the announcement to God (χρηματίζω) by means of a holy angel (10:22). I believe that, as with the angel, so too the spirit is only presented as a messenger of God and that the spirit mentioned here is clearly different from the Holy Spirit that Luke will use again without difficulty in the principal scene of the coming upon Cornelius. In the episode of Cornelius, we notice more than in any other passage in the first part that the author has interpreted a supernatural event, staging the details according to his own conceptions.

---

21. The second part of Acts alludes to messages from the Holy Spirit, but they are presented in diverse forms, through a prophet (21:11), that do not deal, as is the case here, with an anthropomorphic dialogue with the Spirit. See sec. 4.1.

22. The expression "Spirit of the Lord" had occurred already in 5:9, another Judaic anecdote with an OT flavor, put there in parallel with the expression of the double article. Because of the strange sense of the episode, I am inclined to see in 5:3 a retouching of an OT form of the original story. See sec. 7.3.

23. These occur as much in the direct narrative (10:13, 19) as in the repetition (11:7, 12), excluding, therefore, the attribution to diverse sources. See a more detailed study of this passage in sec. 8.3.

Reviewing briefly the interventions of angels in Acts, we see that groups of such interventions are encountered in the trial and discourse of Stephen before the Sanhedrin (five times)[24] and on the two occasions when Peter was freed (seven times).[25] We also encounter them in the punishment of Herod (12:23) and in the trial of Paul before the Sanhedrin (23:8–9), as well as the aforementioned passages that concern the eunuch and Cornelius. Note that all of these passages develop in a Jewish environment, except for 27:23, which pertains to Paul's final journey. All of these concern incidental narrative additions incorporated by the author according to a general plan, but they maintain original characteristics that are very foreign to the organic conception of the work. In none of these do we encounter a directly Pentecostal consciousness. They deal with stories from the Old Testament (the discourse of Stephen) or with Jewish anecdotes which are almost superstitious (12:15–16). In the dispute that Paul provoked among the members of the Sanhedrin, there appears to be an inclination among the Pharisees to accept the intervention of angels or spirits (as virtually equivalent terms): "What if a spirit or an angel has spoken to him?" (23:9).

The only passage in which this popular Jewish style appears to be inadequate would be the story of Cornelius, which occupies a key position in the structure of Acts. Nevertheless, these Judaic elements could pertain to the original anecdote of the story. Luke (or his Hellenistic-Palestinian source) would have reworked it, placing the accent on the Pentecostal part, and would have left the mention of the angels and spirits in the prologue in order to avoid an intervention by the Holy Spirit upon Cornelius prior to his formal coming.[26] When Luke edited the central episodes to fit with his Pentecostal conception of the Holy Spirit, he totally dispensed with the angelic interventions. In the Jewish mentality, angels are frequent messengers of God in certain types of circumstances.[27] Luke, on the other hand, is fascinated by the manifestation of the power of God in the imparting of his own Holy Spirit, which is much more valuable and permanent than the interventions of angels.

24. Acts (6:15); 7:30, 35, 38, 53 refer to the history of Israel.

25. Acts 5:19; 12:7–11, 15.

26. See sec. 8.3.

27. Bonsirven, "Angélologie," in his *Le judaïsme palestinien au temps de Jésus-Christ*, passim; Grundmann et al., "ἄγγελος, κτλ." Angels, celestial messengers, were also known in the Greek culture. But in our narratives all of the characters have a Judaic style.

The ontic reality (i.e., noumenal or real) of the communication of the message of God can in many cases be the same as the normal experience of reality. Nevertheless, the writers of Scripture were able to gauge its importance by interpreting it—or experiencing it—as an action of the Holy Spirit or as words of an angel. This is not to say that God has always communicated to human beings in the same manner but only affirms that the description of such manifestations pertains at times to the individual style of the writer. These attributions to different causes on the part of the writers of Scripture may be theological interpretations, albeit under the influence of inspiration.

I conclude from my exposition that the intervention of the angels in Acts, rather than being parallel or subordinate to the Holy Spirit, is more like spontaneous growth rooted in the Spirit.[28]

2.3 The Holy Spirit and the Interventions of Christ

The intervention of God in the life of the community is at times described by Acts as appearances or messages from Christ. Von Baer asks if such interventions are considered by Luke as actions of the Holy Spirit or if they develop on an independent level.[29] Answering this question helps determine the role that Luke has attributed to the Spirit in the life of the community. Note, however, that this section does not attempt to study the action of the Spirit on the Messiah,[30] but rather the extent to which one or the other acts in the Pentecostal communities. Conzelmann supposes that the Spirit provides a substitute for the action of Jesus in the post-resurrection life of the community.[31] This study concludes that Acts refers to some interventions by Jesus (through the use of his name or through faith in him) and to others as *interventions*

---

28. Baer, *Heilige Geist*, proposes the question of the relation between the Spirit and angels as he deals with concepts related to the Spirit (43), and he dedicates a brief section to this theme in the second part of the book (199–201). His observation that angels do not act in the interior of individuals as does the Spirit appears accurate to me (e.g., to be full of the Holy Spirit). On the other hand, the angel carries out exterior actions that only in the unusual case of the eunuch are attributed to the Spirit. Luke did not resort to angelic interventions on his own, but, more likely, he simply respected those accounts that he encountered in his sources.

29. Baer, *Heilige Geist*, 39–42.

30. See sec. 8.2.

31. Conzelmann, "Lukasanalyse," 31.

of the Spirit. Von Baer divides the interventions of Christ approximately into the following groups: (a) the experience on the road to Damascus (9:1–9; 22:6–11; 26:13–18), (b) visions of or hearing Christ (7:55; 9:10; 18:9–10; 22:17–18; 23:11), and (c) the Spirit of Jesus (16:7). I will add some observations about (d) the name of Jesus.

(a) *The Damascus experience* (9:1–18; 22:5–16; 26:9–18) is an exceptional case. Paul includes it among the resurrection appearances (1 Cor 15:8). Luke had closed the cycle of such appearances with the ascension; however, he gives the reader to understand sufficiently that in this case we are dealing with an authentic personal appearance of Christ and not with a spiritual vision. Von Baer's first argument is the absence of the characteristic terms for visions such as ἐν ἐκστάσει, ἐν ὁράματι, ἐν πνεύματι, even though the term ὀπτασίᾳ does appear one time (26:19). The most important argument contributed though is the authority that this vision confers on Paul, designating him as a witness to the fact that visions of the temple and messages received in dreams had not ceased.[32] Von Baer concludes correctly that this case deals with a direct intervention by Christ, not attributable to the Spirit, that will be granted to Paul by means of Ananias.[33]

---

32. If the term *witness* retains in these two passages the sense that Luke had given it in the first part and very decidedly in 1:25 and 10:41, its value as a proof in this case would be strengthened. In order for Paul to be established as a witness to the fact of the resurrection of Jesus, it is necessary that the Damascus experience be of the same order as the appearances to the apostles. Still, even though the term does not retain here more than a mixed meaning, it is evident that Luke justified with this appearance of Jesus the role, immediately alongside the Twelve, that he assigns to Paul. See also sec. 5.1, n. 5.

33. Conzelmann (*Apostelgeschichte*, 59) comments in this way about the sense of this passage: "Luke had not compared the event with the Easter appearance. He fundamentally distinguished, unlike Paul, this vision from the other appearance. Paul was not an apostle by means of it. Behind it stands no anti-Pauline tendency. Luke simply follows the restraints of his 'salvation history' schemas. Paul is the link that connects the apostolic period and the present. As such he should become integrated into the present church (the church that is represented through Ananias) [Lk hat den Vorgang nicht den Ostererscheinungen angeglichen. Er unterscheidet ja– anders als Paulus – diese Vision grundsätzlich von jenen. Paulus wird durch sie nicht Apostel. Dahinter steht keine antipaulinische Tendenz. Lk folgt einfach dem Zwang seines heilsgeschichtlichen Schemas. Paulus ist das Bindeglied zwischen Apostelzeit und Gegenwart. Als solches wird er in die vorhandene Kirche (die durch Ananias repräsentiert wird) eingegliedert.]." On the historicity of this act, see the commentary on this passage in Haenchen, *Acts*, 315–29 = *Apostelgeschichte*, 265–77. The triple story is precisely the proof of the importance that is attributed to this event, without having to look for an explanation in diverse sources. See also Lake, "Conversion of Paul"; Lohfink, "Eine altestestamentlische Darstellungsform."

(b) Von Baer considers *the visions* as the realization of the programmatic citation of Joel 2:28–32 (Acts 2:17–21) and attributes them, therefore, to the action of the Holy Spirit. This is clear in 7:55, where the fullness of the Spirit is mentioned as the cause of the vision that filled Stephen with joy. I do not believe, however, that this case can be generalized. Luke did not repeat the terms ὅρασις and ἐνύπνιον that appear in Joel's quote. He applies the equivalent term ὅραμα to the vision of Moses (7:31). In the vision that summoned Paul to Macedonia (16:9–10), he attributes the calling directly to God, in spite of the fact that he had just attributed it to the Holy Spirit (16:6), and he attributes to the Spirit of Jesus (16:7) the direction of their itinerary. In 18:9; 22:17–18; and 23:11 it is Christ who speaks to Paul in the vision, and likewise in 9:10 to Ananias. This lack of the footprints of Joel's quotation in the different visions leads one to think that Luke had not tried to apply the description of the prophet in all its details.[34]

These visions multiply in the Pauline stories, alternating between decisions made in the Holy Spirit and warnings related by the prophets endowed by the Holy Spirit. This type of parallelism implies that the redactor of the second part saw little difference between the communication of God by means of a vision and by means of the Holy Spirit, emphasizing only the most superficial aspect of the Pentecostal Spirit. There appears to be no motive for resolving this parallelism of visions and Spirit, as both are considered to be effects of the Spirit. The author did not relate the visions to the Spirit (except in 7:55), and not until later is the reader given any sufficient basis for affirming it. The fact that such visions were multiplied in the second part with a notably distinct tone extricates us from the possible connection to the quotation of Joel that the author, in the first part, had just related to visions.[35]

(c) *The Spirit of Jesus* in 16:7 is mentioned in close proximity to the Holy Spirit (16:6 with the adjective equivalently interspersed, as noted, in the emphatic form). The escalation of the two verses clearly indicates their redactional character.[36] The author wishes to show us that it was

---

34. This is even more evident if Luke is not the original redactor of Pentecost but had only integrated it into his work.

35. As previously noted, the visions of Peter and Cornelius do not present signs of an authentic actuation of the Holy Spirit; see secs. 2.5 and 8.3. Concerning the visions in the NT, see Michaelis, "ὁράω, κτλ," 350–55.

36. [The redactional signal is attuned to the fact that here the Holy Spirit and the Spirit of Jesus are practically placed in *parallelismus membrorum*. See Pervo, *Acts*, 390. —Ed.]

God himself who had directed Paul's steps toward Europe. It is not easy to know whether the author employed three distinct formulas—Holy Spirit, Spirit of Jesus, and a vision—as mere stylistic variation of a single, equivalent reality, or if he intended to have three subjects intervene, each with distinct attributes. The situation is not presented in a grand fashion, as though we were to see an invocation of three great divine forces that would guide the development of the church—God, Jesus, and Spirit—but they may have been grouped by way of summary.

The decisions concerning the Pauline itinerations are generally attributed to the Spirit, be it in the more ambiguous form "in the spirit" (19:21; 20:22)[37] or with a clearer reference to the Holy Spirit that acts through prophets (20:23; 21:4; 21:11). However, we have seen that in three passages it is Christ himself, in visions, who determines Paul's plans (18:9; 22:17; 23:11), and on at least one occasion (27:23), in a less important case, it is assured by an angel. Von Baer attributes, in general, such indications to the Spirit, and he sees throughout the book of Acts, in a coherent and almost continuous line, the work of the Spirit directing the avenues of evangelization.[38] It appears there is no lack of points to fill in this line; however, there are many other points that do not correspond to such a line. The persecutions, for example, had played an important role in the first part, and perhaps the impediment mentioned in 16:6–7 is a supernatural intervention—attributed to the Holy Spirit—of some hostility. The acceptance of the Gentiles as a result of testimony in support of Cornelius is clearly due to the Holy Spirit, but then this, more than an itineration, is the exact thesis of the book of Acts. I have already mentioned the ambiguous beginning to the story of Cornelius and of the episode of the eunuch. In the second part attribution to the Spirit predominates, but it does not absorb the other interventions.

This variation of attributions, even in the second part, obscures the interpretation of the phrase *the Spirit of Jesus*.[39] It is, perhaps, more

---

37. A similar formula applies to Apollos in 18:25. See discussion of these expressions in 3.2.

38. Baer, *Heilige Geist*, 104–8, 112–13.

39. The commentaries are in the habit of expounding on the change in itinerary without giving much attention to the precise sense of the expression *Spirit of Jesus*. Steinmann refers to the explanation of Acts 1:2 from which we may only deduce that the Holy Spirit is the same Spirit that Jesus possessed (*Apostelgeschichte*, 133). Leal (*Sagrada Escritura*, 111) identified it expressly with the Holy Spirit. It may be said that in general the allusion is understood to refer to the Holy Spirit. See too the brief note by Kilpatrick, "Spirit, God and Jesus," 63.

probable that the author is thinking of an intervention by Christ—the sum of the three supernatural forces—through the Spirit that has possessed him since the Jordan baptism and that was transmitted to the disciples in his exaltation to the heavens. This is to say, we are encountering a borderline case in which the thought goes beyond its direct boundary, which is the Spirit, retaining still the attention in the original boundary of action, which is Christ. The Spirit of Jesus would be, therefore, the Holy Spirit, somewhat objectively as in the thought of the author. Nevertheless, in this expression, Christ is still explicitly recognized as the ultimate subject of attribution.

The expression *the Spirit of Jesus* would be differentiated from the term *Holy Spirit* because in the first the thought still notes *explicitly* the active presence of Jesus, while the second only *implicitly* supposes the presence, without making it clear. Such an implicit supposition must be clear to the exegete from other passages.[40] The fact that Luke had preferred the term *Holy Spirit* to other expressions that expressly recall its origin—*Spirit of Jesus, Spirit of the Lord, Spirit of Yahweh*—may indicate an important link in the process of personification in the concept of the Spirit.[41]

(d) *The name of Jesus* is a frequent expression in Acts, and it clothes itself in diverse nuances: invoking the name of Jesus, baptizing in the name of Jesus, suffering for the name of Jesus, evangelizing the name of Jesus and in the name of Jesus. At times, the name of Jesus is the term for the action of the apostles. At other times, it is invoked in order to carry out, as an active subject, forgiveness, salvation, or healing. For the moment, only this active force of the name of Jesus is of import.[42] The

---

40. We encountered one of these limiting expressions before in which the mind is isolating a concept, personifying it, by the same means that it lets the base concept that originated it fall into the implicit supposition, in essence, forgetting it. It is difficult to say when to attribute to such a concept a separate nature from the original concept, or, if it deals with active, conscious subjects, when to attribute a separate personality to it. Customarily, it is the philosophers who, reflecting on language and other spontaneous manifestations, come to oppose both concepts—or both conscious subjects—demonstrating by this its different identity.

41. [As to narrative personification in Luke's "Spirit of Jesus" (16:7), see also Stählin, "Τὸ πνεῦμα Ἰησοῦ"; George, "L'Esprit Saint," passim. —Ed.]

42. Bietenhard, "ὄνομα, κτλ," 269–79. Referring to Acts 4:7, he writes that "Power (δύναμις) and Name (ὄνομα) are parallel concepts" (277). Generic parallelism, I would add, in that they are interventions of God; however, the subject of attribution in both cases is different.

primary effect of the name of Jesus is salvation. The quotation from Joel 2:32, "everyone who calls on the name of the LORD [Κυρίου]," is evidently applied to Christ (2:21–36). Salvation exclusively in the name of Jesus is expressly affirmed in 4:12. Christians are "those who invoke the name of Jesus," those who have been baptized in his name. There is no doubt that salvation is always directly attributed in Acts to Jesus, which continues operating through faith and baptism.

Other effects attributed to the name of Jesus in Acts are healings and the casting out of demons. As previously discussed, these works dealt with the concept of δύναμις, and we concluded that Luke avoided attributing them to the Spirit. Here, Luke does attribute them to the name of Jesus or, in a more general manner, to God himself. When faced with the threats of the Sanhedrin, the community burst forth in prayer (4:29–31): "grant your servants to speak your word with all boldness [παρρησία], while you stretch out your hand to heal, and signs and wonders are performed through the name of your holy servant Jesus." The effect of the prayer is a new outpouring of the Holy Spirit, a spontaneous source of new boldness and of miracles. However, the author only attributed to it the first effect—"and spoke the word of God with boldness"—a limitation already insinuated in the redaction itself of the supplication which attributes healings and wonders to the hand of God and to the name of Jesus. We cannot, therefore, extend the effects of this new outpouring of the Holy Spirit to miracles, guided solely by the proximity of the words or the concepts, when the author has left clear indications to the contrary, both in this text and in the constant attribution of healings and exorcisms to the name of Jesus.

In 9:34, Peter employs an expression that is still more direct in the healing of Aeneas: "Jesus Christ heals you; get up and make your bed!" Exorcisms take place in the name of Jesus beginning with the mission of the seventy-two disciples (Luke 10:17) and equally in Acts (16:18), even though the frequency is decreasing. Certain Jewish exorcists attempted, unfortunately, to seize upon the power of the name of Jesus (19:13), something that others who are not identified (Luke 9:49) had done with greater success and, it appears, with better intention and faith. We can discover the key to this attribution of healings and exorcisms to Jesus in the healing of the paralytic in the temple, narrated evidently as an example of the miraculous works of the apostles. Both in the narration (Acts 3:6) and in the interpretation by Peter (3:16; 4:7, 10), Luke insists on attributing it to the name of Jesus (or more precisely to faith in his name). Peter concludes, as a lesson from the miracle, "There is salvation [σωτηρία] in no one else, for there is no other name under heaven given among mortals by which we must be saved" (4:12). In this symbolic proximity of healing with salvation—of exorcism with the forgiveness of sins—resides the theological key to the constant attribution to Jesus of healings.

In conclusion, Acts sees the salvific action of Christ continually actualized in communities. The communication of the Spirit to the disciples is not, therefore, a total substitute for Christ, but rather the transfer of his prophetic mission—in the full sense of the word—as a spokesman of the message of God. The magnitude of this prophetic mission becomes clear in the study of the effects of the Holy Spirit. In combining the separate elements, it could be said that Christ transmits to his apostles the presence of the Spirit that he received at the Jordan and, in a joyous order, the anticipation of the eschatological gift that he received in his exaltation.

3

The Holy Spirit—Gift and Promise of God

3.1 The Gift of the Holy Spirit

THE HOLY SPIRIT REPRESENTS an intervention of God that is superior to messages conveyed by angels or the power to effect exorcisms and miraculous healings. Such an intervention was announced in the Old Testament, and Luke does not hesitate to call it "the Promise of the Father" (1:4) and "the gift of God" (8:20). The manifestation of the Spirit on the day of Pentecost is interpreted in light of Joel 2:28–32 as a sign that Jesus, "having received from the Father the promise of the Holy Spirit, . . . has poured out this that you both see and hear" (2:33). As a consequence of the discourse, Peter exhorts the Jewish audience to be baptized "and you will receive the gift of the Holy Spirit. For the promise is for you . . ." (2:38–39).

This chapter examines what Acts says about the gift of the Holy Spirit, first through an analysis of the four expressions that Luke uses to talk about this gift (δωρεά), then through an examination of the verbs of gifting and especially their possible temporal value. Finally, we will observe this gift as it integrates into the joint elements of the Promise and the eschatological kingdom.

In Acts, we encounter the term δωρεά four times in reference to the Holy Spirit—two times in the explicit manner of "the gift of the Holy Spirit" (ἡ δωρεὰ τοῦ ἁγίου πνεύματος, 2:38; 10:45) and two times as references: "the gift of God" (8:20) and "the same gift" as on the day of

Pentecost (11:17). Δωρεά is considered expressly by Philo as an intensive term that signifies a great gift and emphasizes, more than δῶρον, the aspect of most free gratitude.[1] We encounter it with a religious sense in two passages of the Wisdom books and in five Pauline passages.[2] But in only two other passages is it used in reference to the Spirit: John 4:10, "if you knew the gift of God," and Heb 6:4, "For it is impossible to restore again to repentance those who have once been enlightened, and have tasted the heavenly gift, and have shared in the Holy Spirit, . . . and then have fallen away" (6:6a; doubtlessly echoing the theme of blasphemy against the Holy Spirit). The proximity of this theme in Acts with two of the more typically Jewish passages is suggestive and calls for greater scrutiny.

In the Samaritan "Pentecost," the form *the gift of God* (8:20) evidently expresses, in the genitive, the donor subject. With respect to the content of the gift, it remains somewhat ambiguous. Does it signify the ability of transmitting the Spirit, the Spirit himself, or his charismatic manifestations? In pure logic, we say that it deals with the ability to transmit the Spirit, which Simon wanted to buy (ἐξουσία).[3] However, it does not appear that Peter took into account these nuances of the proposal, and the narration emphasizes only the sin of trying to make commercial that which is a gift of God.[4] From this passage alone, we cannot deduce if it deals with prophetic charisma or with a more radical gift. But this is not strange, as it deals only with a marginal reference.

The texts 10:45 and 11:17 pertain to the story of Cornelius, a decisive passage for the admission of the Gentiles.[5] The force of the argument lies precisely on the equality of the gift received by Cornelius with the gift received by the disciples at Pentecost. For this reason, the three

1. Büchsel, "δίδωμι, κτλ," 166–68.

2. Wis 7:14; 16:25; Rom 5:15, 17; 2 Cor 9:15; Eph 3:7; 4:7.

3. As Weiss (*Schriften des Neuen Testaments*, 563) interprets it; see Holtzmann, *Apostelgeschichte*, 64.

4. I examine the passage according to the intentions of Luke, whose thought I am studying, dispensing here with historic precision with regard to details and the meaning that they could have in their original sources. We can see this in Haenchen, *Acts*, 305–8 = *Apostelgeschichte*, 256–59, who reviews the diverse interpretations concerning the historicity of this event. [See also Schneider, "Philippus und die Samaria-Mission." —Ed.]

5. The episode of Cornelius is narrated three times: a direct account of the story (10:44–48), Peter's justification before the community at Jerusalem (11:15–18), and a reference as a decisive argument in the called council at Jerusalem (15:7–14). These accounts are studied more closely later.

narrations of this event each insist on noting this equality (10:45, 47; 11:15, 17; 15:8).[6] It is in these contexts that the two occurrences of *the gift of the Holy Spirit* warranting analyses are found. In the first narrative, the story is related from the viewpoint of Peter's companions: they "were astounded that the gift of the Holy Spirit had been poured out even on the Gentiles, for they heard them speaking in tongues and extolling God" (10:45–46). The mention of glossolalia might cause one to think that Peter's companions perceive in the gift of the Holy Spirit nothing more than the exterior charisma. However, it is the author who describes the scene, and he wishes to emphasize that the glossolalia is the cause (ἤκουον γὰρ) that induced them to think about the equality of the gift. His use of ὅτι καὶ alludes to a first term of comparison, that is, to the Spirit received by the disciples and by all the Jews that have been baptized (2:38; 5:32). Ἐκκέχυται alludes to the prophecy of Joel 2:28–32, which served to explain the Pentecostal manifestation of the Spirit.

If it is possible for some doubt to remain concerning that which the companions of Peter might have thought in the first moment, there remains no doubt concerning what Peter himself thought and even less concerning what the author of the story thought. The gift of the Holy Spirit is the same gift that the disciples received at Pentecost. The forthcoming analysis of the passage in its entirety demonstrates what the content contributes to the meaning of this Pentecostal gift.

The other passage, pertaining to the second narration of the event and placed in the mouth of Peter to justify the baptism of Cornelius to the community in Jerusalem, is yet more significant: "If then God gave them *the same gift* that he gave us when we believed in the Lord Jesus

---

6. Is this gift exactly the same as the Pentecostal gift? Luke certainly presents it as such. The small descriptive differences, such as the violent wind and the tongues of fire, certainly do not affect the equality of the gift received. A more serious objection would be the interpretation of Pentecost in 1:8 as a force for testimony, since Luke reserves for the apostles the mission of being witnesses. However, this interpretation of 1:8 is nothing more than a particular application to the apostles (yet we note a broader application when all the characters in Luke 24 are considered). The true interpretation is in 1:5 as baptism in the Spirit (on the other hand, in 1:8, testimony is understood in an expanded sense as evangelization). It is probable that at Pentecost the 120 disciples, who are not presented here as witnesses (but see the inclusive use of witnesses, Luke 24:48), also received the Spirit. Although the correspondence of all the details is lacking, there is coherence in a harmonic conception, albeit one that is flexible. Moreover, the identity refers to eschatology, which is its essence. [At the first Jerusalem "Pentecost," the narrator goes beyond the perception of an exterior charisma, adding the interior description of being "filled with the Spirit"; see Shelton, "'Filled with the Holy Spirit.'" —Ed.]

Christ, who was I that I could hinder God?" (11:17; emphasis added). The force of Peter's justification is in the equality of the gift received by Cornelius and the gift received by the disciples. Peter (i.e., the author through Peter) understands this gift as the actual reception of the Holy Spirit, that is to say, the gift that *is* the Holy Spirit. In the first narrative, Peter proposed the same argument for allowing Cornelius to be baptized, but with an equivalent expression: "Can anyone withhold the water for baptizing these people who have received the Holy Spirit just as we have?" (10:47). Still, in the third narration of the event before the Jerusalem Council, Peter repeated a similar expression: "And God who knows the human heart, testified to them by giving them the Holy Spirit, just as he did to us" (15:8). The stylistic parallelism between this passage and the text at hand is notable:

15:8: Θεὸς ἐμαρτύρησεν αὐτοῖς δοὺς τὸ πνεῦμα τὸ ἅγιον καθὼς καὶ ἡμῖν

11:17: τὴν ἴσην δωρεὰν ἔδωκεν αὐτοῖς ὁ Θεὸς ὡς καὶ ἡμῖν

Peter places full value on the comparison of the gift received by Cornelius with the Pentecostal gift (τὴν ἴσην δωρεὰν), coming to understand it as baptism in the Holy Spirit: "And I remembered the word of the Lord, how he had said, 'John baptized with water, but you will be baptized with the Holy Spirit'" (11:16). He specifically finds support for this interpretation by adducing the equality of the gift: "*If then* God gave them the same gift that he gave us" (11:17; emphasis added). This resemblance to the baptism in the Spirit promised by Jesus is even more consciously elaborated in as much as Peter dispensed with the temporal determination that would appear to limit it in 1:5: "but you will be baptized with the Holy Spirit *not many days from now*" (emphasis added).

It is apparent, then, that in these passages the gift of the Holy Spirit signifies the same gift that the disciples received at Pentecost, understood in its fullest sense as baptism in the Spirit. It does not deal, as such, with a charismatic gift such as glossolalia, whose author is the Holy Spirit (a genitive that would express the giving subject), but rather with a gift that is the same Holy Spirit (epexegetic or added-clarifying genitive).[7]

---

7. Zerwick (*Biblical Greek*, n. 45), in dealing with the epexegetic genitive or genitive of apposition, also proposes Acts 2:38 as one of his grammatical examples: "'you will receive the gift of the Holy Spirit' (Acts 2:38) is not to be understood of a gift to be given by the Holy Spirit, but of the Holy Spirit Himself to be received as a gift."

Lastly, Acts 2:38 has provoked major controversy and is at the center of the Pentecostal message. Peter exhorts his listeners in his Pentecostal discourse, "Repent, and be baptized every one of you in the name of Jesus Christ so that your sins may be forgiven; and you will receive the gift of the Holy Spirit. For the promise is for you . . ." This text has frequently been interpreted as a promise of the gift of the Holy Spirit by means of water baptism and, by spontaneous extension, as a reception of the Spirit that sanctifies. A later detailed examination considers the possible relation between baptism and the Holy Spirit and performs a detailed analysis of this text. Here, I will put forward the conclusion that Acts does not present the gifting of the Spirit as occurring through baptism, but rather (in ordinary cases) by means of the laying on of hands, although the two rituals may commonly be supposed to occur in close proximity. Even less credible is the opinion that Peter promises in this text the imparting of the sanctifying Spirit that will appear ultimately as a fruit of baptism in an anticipated theology.

The significance of Peter's expression "and you will receive the gift of the Holy Spirit" needs to be understood in light of the entire discourse. On one hand, Peter takes as a point of departure the manifestation of glossolalia, which had attracted the attention of his listeners, and interprets it in the light of Joel 2:28–32 as the pouring out of the Spirit announced for the end times. On the other hand, the resurrection of Jesus, of which they were witnesses, proves according to the citation of Psalm 16:10 that he is the Messiah. Peter continues: "Being therefore exalted at the right hand of God, and having received from the father the promise of the Holy Spirit [τήν τε ἐπαγγελίαν τοῦ πνεύματος τοῦ ἁγίου is evidently an epexegetic genitive], he has poured out this that you both see and hear" (2:33). The gift of the Holy Spirit is for Peter a visible sign that the Messiah has completed his work and has received from the Father the inauguration of the end times.

In the discourse, there is a certain interchangeability between the Holy Spirit and its charismatic manifestation: "this that we both see and hear." This might lead one to believe that the gift of the Holy Spirit can be reduced to the charisma of glossolalia or of prophecy. Such a minimalist interpretation would, at the very least, contradict the importance that the author attributes to the Pentecostal episode. In the text of Joel 2:28, it is doubtful that it promises much more than a dissemination of prophetic charisma. Nevertheless, already in the Old Testament, we encounter signs that the prophetic charisma was indicative of a more radical and permanent possession by the Spirit of God. In Numbers, a significant episode occurs where Yahweh sends Moses to select seventy elders to help him with the governing of the people (11:16). He then takes the Spirit that was on Moses and places it on the seventy elders: "And when the spirit rested upon them, they prophesied. But they did not do so again" (11:25). The two elders that had remained in the camp also prophesied. Evidently, the narrator wished to convey that the prophetic charisma was a perceivable sign for the people that the Spirit rested upon the seventy elders in order to help them and to lend authority to their decisions. The prophecy was certainly coming from the Spirit that had rested upon the elders, but it was no more than an initial sign of its future activity that would be less visible. Moses expresses this same idea with a universalism that corresponds exactly to the conclusion of Joel's citation: "Would that all the LORD's people were prophets, and that the LORD would put his spirit on them!" (Num 11:29).[8]

In Luke's interpretation, it is even more evident that the gift of Pentecost cannot be reduced to a mere prophetic charisma. He prepares the way for the Pentecost narrative with the warnings of Jesus to the disciples that they await "the promise of the Father" (1:4), and he describes it solemnly "you will be baptized with the Holy Spirit" (1:5), which for the disciples would mean receiving "power when the Holy Spirit has come upon you; ... [to] be my witnesses ... to the ends of the earth" (1:8). The same coming of the Spirit is described by Luke with the characteristics of a true theophany: tongues of fire and violent wind that come from heaven and invade the place. The consequences of this abiding fullness of the Spirit surpass the *strictly* prophetic manifestations; at times they will be manifested as power, other times as wisdom, as joy, as comfort, and as testimony. We are able to include all of these manifestations in the fuller sense of prophecy, understanding that this variety supposes the presence of an activity of the Spirit that is manifested in diverse forms according to the circumstances. It was necessary to show the content of the gift of the Holy Spirit because the interpretation falls easily into one of two extremes: at times it is interpreted as the giving of the sanctifying

---

8. I do not presume that this passage has been taken into account in the redaction of the prophecy of Joel or in its application to Acts, but merely propose it as a demonstration of the biblical mentality with regard to the Spirit, even among the earliest writings.

Spirit, of which Paul speaks to us, while at other times it is reduced to a prophetic charisma, in the most restricted sense of the phrase.[9]

Thus, the context of Pentecost gives us no occasion to interpret the promise of Peter as the sanctifying Spirit, but I reserve this question for the section that refers to baptism (6.4). With regard to the second minor interpretation, it is a shortsighted consideration which limits itself to that which the biblical authors had presented as an exterior sign of the presence of the Spirit. This presence is verifiable only through such manifestations, but the Spirit is the force that produces them, in itself an unverifiable and great gift of God in the messianic times.

The content of this gift is refined in Part 2, "The Effects of the Holy Spirit." For now, effort must be made to extricate ourselves from a difficulty concerning the temporal value of this gift, which appears to be suggested by the use of the aorist form of the verbs used to express the giving of the gift.

3.2 Verbs of Gifting—The Predominant Aorist Tense and Others

Certain aspects of the Pentecostal gift of the Spirit are implied in the verbs that describe the diverse comings of the Holy Spirit.[10] The Spirit is given by God (δίδωμι in the active form with the subject expressed, or in the theological passive; 5:32; 8:18; 11:17; 15:8) and received by the disciples (λαμβάνω, 1:8; 2:33, 38; 8:15, 17, 19; 10:47; 19:2), who remain full of the Holy Spirit (πίμπλημι, 2:4; 4:8, 31; 9:17; 13:9; Luke 1:15, 41, 67; πληρόω, Acts 13:52). The Spirit falls from above upon them (ἐπιπίπτω, 8:16; 10:44; 11:15; ἐπέρχομαι, 1:8; 19:6; Luke 1:35; 24:49), and is sent by Jesus (ἐξαποστέλλω, Luke 24:49), is spread by God (ἐκχέω, 2:17, 18; ἐκχύνω, 10:45) or by Jesus, who had already been anointed with it during his earthly life (χρίω, 10:38; Luke 4:18) and who received it in his exaltation in order to spread it (2:33). A sense of gifting emerges from the convergence of these terms.

A maximum of eight repetitions of the same term is used (λαμβάνω), a term that is unique in that it has no precedents in the

---

9. Adler (*Erste christliche Pfingstfest*, 66–69) noted that the commentaries remain dazzled by the gift of glossolalia and forget that the central point of Pentecost is in the fullness of the Spirit, whose effects are going to be manifested by degrees throughout Acts.

10. Previously examined, briefly, in sec. 1.1.

Septuagint. λαμβάνω expresses a fundamentally passive behavior like "taking" or "receiving something that is given." Acts 20:35 records the saying of Christ, "It is more blessed to give than to receive [λαμβάνειν]," and 26:10 refers to the "authority received from the chief priests." However, a greater emphasis on the active sense is also frequent (highlighted by its grammatical form), signifying in certain cases an initiating and widespread action.[11] In the texts that refer to the Spirit, the passive sense of receiving a gift stands out, even though this act of gifting is always made to those who are prepared to receive it by means of faith, prayer, repentance, or alms.[12]

More interesting than the nuances of meaning of these verbs is the temporal form that Luke uses almost constantly. The following table highlights the temporal form of Luke's choice (the four categories in the left column should not be taken too strictly):[13]

LUKE'S CHOICE OF VERB TENSES IN THE SPIRIT PASSAGES OF ACTS

	Acts	Present	Imperfect	Future	Aorist	Perfect
Jerusalem	1:8				ἐπελθόντος	
	2:4		ἐδίδου		ἐπλήσθησαν	
	2:17			ἐκχεῶ		
	2:33				λαβών ... ἐξέχεεν	
	2:38			λήμψεσθε		
	4:8				πληθείς	
	4:31				ἐπλήσθησαν	
	5:32				ἔδωκεν	

---

11. See Zorell, *Lexicon Graecum Novi Testamenti*, λαμβάνω: "1) fere passive [mildly passive], *alqa. re donor*, . . . *erhalten* [get, receive], *bekommen* [obtain, receive] . . . 2) magis active: [more active], *sumo* [to take], . . . *arripio* [take hold of], *accepto* [receive] . . . *hinnehmen* [take, accept] . . . *manu accipio* [take the hand], . . . *alqm. prehendo* [to lay hold of someone]." [See also the various examples of the usage of λαμβάνω in Danker, *Concise Greek-English Lexicon*, 212. —Ed.]

12. See sec. 6.2.

13. Omitted are the anthropomorphic type of manifestations of the Spirit that are also in the aorist: 8:29, 39; 10:19; 11:12; 13:2; (15:28); 16:7; 20:28. Likewise omitted are references to the inspiration of Scripture: 1:16; 4:25; 28:25.

56 PART ONE: THE LUKAN UNDERSTANDING OF THE SPIRIT

	Acts	Present	Imperfect	Future	Aorist	Perfect
Samaria	7:55	ὑπάρχων ...πλήρης				
Samaria	8:15				λάβωσιν	
Samaria	8:16					ἦν ἐπιπεπτωκός
Samaria	8:17		ἐλάμβανον			
Samaria	8:18	δίδοται				
Samaria	8:19	λαμβάνῃ				
Caesarea (Gentiles)	9:31		ἐπληθύνετο			
Caesarea (Gentiles)	10:38				ἔχρισεν	
Caesarea (Gentiles)	10:44				ἐπέπεσεν	
Caesarea (Gentiles)	10:45					ἐκκέχυται
Caesarea (Gentiles)	10:47				ἔλαβον	
Caesarea (Gentiles)	11:15				ἐπέπεσεν	
Caesarea (Gentiles)	15:8				ἐμαρτύ—ρησεν ... δούς	
Pauline	11:24		ἦν ... πλήρης			
Pauline	13:4				ἐκπεμφθέ—ντες	
Pauline	13:9				πλησθείς	
Pauline	13:52		ἐπληροῦντο			
Pauline	16:6				κωλυθέντες	
Pauline	19:2				ἦλθε	
Pauline	20:22					δεδεμένος
Pauline	20:23	διαμαρτύ—ρεται				

In this table it appears evident that almost all of the verbs have been used in the aorist form. Only in the Samaritan episode can a certain diversity be observed, probably due to the adaptation of an earlier story. This use of the aorist raises the question of whether the writer of Acts had understood these comings or giftings of the Spirit in a transitory form, since this is the proper sense of the aorist form. The answer to this question could be very important for illuminating, from the grammatical angle, the characteristics of the gift of the Spirit. Note, in the first place, that the grammatical norm is not strict. It could concern an ingressive aorist, typical of those verbs that signify a state, or of a complex aorist that omits the duration of the action that can at times extend for more than a year, as in Acts 18:11 and 11:26.[14]

The reason for the diverse verbal forms that appear in the table will become apparent shortly. The use of the *future* tense is logical in a promise, like that made in 2:38. The *present* tense in 2:17–18 is a prophetic present that lends liveliness and certitude to the future fulfillment of the promise.[15] In 8:19, a subjunctive is dealt with that has no implication of absolute time; stronger yet is the present in 8:18, even though it appears to be a theoretical and atemporal enunciation.[16] In 20:23, the present refers to a series of actions, probably by a variety of persons. The only present tense form with its whole character of a concrete duration is in 7:55, ὑπάρχων δὲ πλήρης, to which can be added 6:3, 5, and 10, even though they lack the verbal copula. The meaning of these texts will be addressed in the treatment of the adjective πλήρης.[17]

The *imperfect* verbs in 2:4b and 8:17 refer to a group and have a distributive sense and a certain repetitive mode. The global action is imperfect or partial, considered in each individual. In 9:31 and 13:52, they denote more clearly a repetitive and progressive action. The imperfect in 11:24 is the only one that denotes a permanent state (which the author

---

14. Zerwick (*Biblical Greek*, n. 288) arrives at the following conclusion: "It is to be noted that the choice between aorist and perfect is not determined by the objective facts, but by the writer's wish to connote the special nuance of the perfect; if this be not required, the aorist will be used. The use of the perfect in the NT thus shows that the author has in mind the notion of a state of affairs resultant upon the action." See BDF nn. 318–56.

15. BDF n. 323.

16. Jacquier (*Actes des Apôtres*, 260) believes that Θεασάμενος is a more exact reading than ἰδών because Simon would observe those charismatic manifestations. Nevertheless, the theoretical-atemporal character of δίδοται, as explained, agrees better with the current reading ἰδών and implies that the author is categorizing the case more than describing it. Haenchen (*Acts*, 307–8 = *Apostelgeschichte*, 258) believes that Luke took advantage of the narrative of Simon the Magician (as in 13:6–12 and 19:13–20) to demonstrate the superiority of the powers that the church had received from God over the wondrous magic of the contemporary religions.

17. See sec. 7.1(a). We find another present tense in 21:11, which I believe has merely a narrative value on the lips of Agabus.

would express with a present participle, as in 7:55, if the action was current), but it returns to deal with the adjective.

The *perfect* is the form that we would expect to encounter in Acts. Christ had promised the disciples help with the testimony that they would deliver during their entire lives. It would thus be logical that Luke would have narrated the giving of the Spirit, making its permanent effects stand out through the use of the perfect tense. However, we only encounter three perfects applied to the Spirit, two of them in 8:16 (in negative expression) and 10:45 as an obligatory construction substituting for a pluperfect to express relative time with respect to the principal verb.[18] Only in 20:22 does the perfect have its true sense of permanent effect.[19]

From this analysis, it appears that the *aorist* is not just the most frequent form but is also the normal form Luke uses to express the coming of the Spirit. The other forms are used when they are grammatically obligatory or claim to express a circumstance exterior to this same coming of the Spirit.

As for Luke's use of the aorist tense, there are three possible causes, though it is not clear to what extent each of these has influenced Luke; indeed, it is possible that at an earlier time they influenced one another. The first reason could be *grammatical*. Actually, we observe that the perfect tense (passive or active, passive participle) of the verbs that Luke used is in the majority of cases unusual and very rare in the Greek Bible. The passive perfect of πίμπλημι is rare, as is the active perfect of χρίω. The passive perfect of λαμβάνω is very rare. This does not explain, though, why he did not use ἐλήλυθα[20] or πέπτωκα,[21] even though these verbs would prolong the same coming of the Spirit more than its effects. Above all he could have used δέδωκα.[22] A brief look through a concordance reveals that these verbs have an almost absorbent tendency toward the aorist.

The second reason could be *traditional*. In the Old Testament, there are only two perfect tense verbs that refer to the action of the Spirit of

---

18. BDF n. 345 expressly cites 10:45. Jacquier (*Actes*, 259–60, 335) explains this same text as depending on an affective verb.

19. Without referring to the Spirit, but contained in the Pentecostal narrative, we encounter a very graphic perfect verb in 2:13.

20. See Luke 5:17, 32; 7:33–34; (8:46); Acts 8:27; 9:21; 18:2; 21:22.

21. See Rev 2:5; 9:1; 8:3.

22. See Luke 10:9; 19:15; Acts 4:12.

God: Haggai 2:5 with the verb ἐφίστημι, which taken in the perfect signifies permanence, and the Wisdom of Solomon 1:7 (πεπλήρωκεν in the active form). However, the Old Testament would be perfectly familiar with the permanent imparting of the Spirit, albeit partially (Num 11:17; 27:18; 1 Sam 16:14). In Deut 34:9, "Joshua . . . was full [ἐνέπλησθη] of the spirit of wisdom. . . ," which would apparently accompany him during his entire administration. Paul had also used the aorist to refer to the giving or the receiving of the Spirit: λαμβάνω (Rom 8:15; 1 Cor 2:12; Gal 3:2, 14), ἔδωκε (Rom 11:8; 2 Tim 1:7), δούς (2 Cor 5:5; Eph 1:7; and he uses διδόντα once in 1 Thes 4:8), and ἐξαπέστειλεν (Gal 4:6), all with the clear sense of permanent effects for those expressly referred to by the texts. Perhaps the most significant case is Eph 1:13, ". . . were marked [ἐσφραγίσθητε] with the seal of the promised Holy Spirit."

The third reason for the election of the aorist could have been the *conception* itself of these comings of the Spirit. Luke, and in general the biblical authors, in recording the gifts of God would have invoked, directly, the solemn *moment* of its impartation, to function as verifiable testimony granted intentionally by God with that aim in view. This is the implication encountered in Num 11:25 on the imparting of the Spirit to the seventy elders.[23] This same explanation can be applied to the Pauline texts, but more than anywhere else it applies perfectly to the texts in Acts. Luke focused more than any other author on the value of prophetic exultation as testimony.[24] Therefore, it is natural that in referring us to the giving of the Spirit, he may have lingered to describe the first perceptible moment that testifies to the obtaining of the gift.

Luke had inherited from the Old Testament the idea of a permanent endowment of the Spirit. This is evidently assumed in the promise of Acts 1:8 as assistance for the disciples in their testifying unto the ends of the earth. It deals, therefore, with a permanent gift, or, more precisely, with a *permanent offering* of the assistance of the Spirit that would be realized in those moments when it was needed. The expression *permanent offering* avoids the idea of an inhabiting which is totally alien to Acts and expresses well the new comings of the Spirit to those who had already received it (see 4:8; 4:31; 9:31; 13:52).

---

23. See sec. 3.1.

24. I have alluded frequently to those passages that form the nerve center of the book: 2:17, 33; 5:32; the episode of Cornelius, and the key text, 15:8. See ch. 5, particularly secs. 5.4–5.

I conclude, therefore, that Luke did not use the aorist with the sense of a transitory impartation, at least not in the exclusive sense which this expression suggests. The aorist does not constrain us to reduce the effects of the gift to the immediate charismatic manifestations, given the nature of the ingressive aorist. The grammar, therefore, leaves the door open for exegesis to determine the subsequent effects that Luke associates with the gift of the Holy Spirit. Luke has focused on the first perceivable moment that testifies to the imparting of the gift of the Spirit, the permanence of which would not consist in a latent presence but in a readiness to help the disciples.

3.3 Eschatological Gift—The Promise and the Kingdom

The Holy Spirit is clearly mentioned in Acts 1:4 as "the Promise of the Father." However, the content of the Promise is rather imprecise, in both the Old and the New Testaments. In the Septuagint, the term ἐπαγγελία hardly appears. This lack catches our attention because we are accustomed to seeing the Old Testament with Paul's eyes, i.e., as a promise. Certainly, the theme of promise exists, but designated by diverse expressions such as "God said," "the oath of Yahweh," and most often, "the covenant." The term ἐπαγγελία was already coined by Judaism and associated with the law.[25] The successive amalgamation of the promise of God and its frequent expression through symbols makes exact precision in describing its content more difficult.

In the New Testament, we find vacillations in the way the content of the Promise is interpreted. It speaks of the partial promises made to the patriarchs as a symbol of the full Promise[26] or of the promise in a general sense, even at times using plural references to the collection of blessings that the Promise contains.[27] Only a very few texts relate it to the Spirit: Gal 3:14 and Eph 1:13. The more precise idea of the Promise appears to have been rather late in forming and applies to eternal life (2 Tim 1:1; Heb 4:1; 9:15; 10:36). First John 2:25 attributes to Christ himself this aspect of the Promise: "And this is what he has promised us, eternal life."

---

25. Schniewind and Friedrich, "ἐπαγγέλλω, κτλ"; Scharbert, "Verheissung."

26. Rom 9:9; Heb 6:15; 11:9, 33.

27. Rom 4:13–20; 9:8; 2 Cor 1:20; Gal 3:16–29; 4:23, 28; Eph 2:12; 3:6; 6:2; Heb 6:17; 11:39; 2 Pet 3:4, 9. In the plural form: Rom 9:4; 15:8; 2 Cor 7:1; Heb 6:12; 11:13, 17.

Apparently, the Promise covers the range of messianic blessings that can be expressed through some of its more typical characteristics.

Also in Luke-Acts, we find certain vacillations as the writer tries to identify a single object for the Promise. Four texts present the Holy Spirit as the fulfillment of the Promise, while another text speaks in general of the times of the promise (Acts 7:17), and three other texts speak of the coming of Jesus according to the promise (13:23, 32 and 26:6).

Luke 24:49, "I am sending upon you what my Father promised," evidently refers to Pentecost. Acts 1:4, ". . . to wait for the promise of the Father," is explained as baptism in the Holy Spirit (1:5) and as "power when the Holy Spirit has come upon you" (1:8), referring as well to Pentecost. Acts 2:33 expressly states that Jesus, ". . . having received from the Father the promise of the Holy Spirit, . . . has poured out this that you both see and hear." This same imparting of the Spirit is that which Peter promised to those who are baptized, mentioning it indistinguishably as Promise and as gift: ". . . and you will receive the gift of the Holy Spirit. For the promise is for you . . ." (2:38). The three texts in Acts that relate the Promise with the coming of Jesus, and the diverse nuances of interpretation of the Promise in the New Testament, indicate that the Holy Spirit cannot be identified as the exclusive content of the Promise.

The author has sensed that a new impulse takes possession of the disciples once the gift of the Spirit at Pentecost is given. The gift of the Spirit and its manifestations are for him a sign that the last days announced in the Promise had commenced. The Spirit is already a gift of the Promise, even more significant in as much as it is not the fundamental gift but something that pertains to the exuberant fullness (*plenitude exuberante*) of the Promise. The fulfillment of the Promise could evoke in the disciples nothing less, as an equivalent reality, than the *establishment of the Kingdom*: "Lord, is this the time when you will restore the kingdom to Israel?" (1:6).[28]

In the Synoptics, the kingdom of God has a dense and complex meaning, comparable to the coming together of the Promise. At times it applies to eternal life, at other times to the church, and perhaps to Christ himself. There remains a certain vacillation between the terrestrial and

---

28. Similar questions had been asked by the Pharisees (Luke 17:20) and the disciples (Luke 21:7), to which Jesus also responded with immediate applications while avoiding the question of time.

the celestial character of the kingdom.[29] Acts has no special preference for the phrase *the kingdom of God*; it is employed to allude to the content of Jesus' teaching (1:3), to which it adds at times, almost in parallel, a more specific teaching about Jesus himself (8:12; 28:23, 31). In a general manner, it warns that "it is through many persecutions that we must enter the Kingdom of God."[30] This appears to deal with a term that the author received but which is losing its great Judaic resonance.

We cannot say that Luke explicitly established a relationship between the Holy Spirit and the kingdom.[31] If the kingdom equates to the fulfillment of the Promise, the Holy Spirit is a gift of the kingdom. It would be useless to linger over this theme if the question had not been expressly raised. With it we enter into *the eschatological aspect of the gift of the Spirit*. Conzelmann has seen in the evasive response of Jesus to the question about the kingdom a relationship between the Holy Spirit and the kingdom. The adversative particle, ". . . but [ἀλλά] you will receive power when the Holy Spirit has come upon you . . ." (1:8), may indicate that Jesus promises them the Spirit as a substitution for the kingdom, and he concludes that "The Spirit is no longer the eschatological gift itself, but rather the temporary substitute for the possession of the final salvation; it enabled the existence of believers in the midst of the on-going world, in the persecution; it offered power for mission and for endurance."[32] This conclusion does not result naturally from an

---

29. Schmidt, "βασιλεία (τοῦ θεοῦ)." Conzelmann (*Mitte der Zeit*, 109) reproaches Schmidt for having combined the texts of the three Synoptics and thereby obtaining an abstract result. See also Michaelis, *Täufer, Jesus, Urgemeinde*; Semain, "L'Esprit et le royaume"; Bonsirven, *Règne de Dieu*; Dodd, *Parables of the Kingdom*; idem, *Apostolic Preaching*; Ladd, *Jesus and the Kingdom*.

30. Noack, *Gottesreich bei Lukas*; Wilckens, *Missionsreden der Apostelgeschichte*; and Schnackenburg, *Gottes Herrschaft und Reich*, especially his discussion in pt. 3, sec. 1 on the kingdom and the post-Easter community.

31. On the variants of the second petition of the Lord's prayer to "send Your Holy Spirit upon us and cleanse us" in place of "Your kingdom come" (Luke 11:2) see sec. 6.2. [On the possible relation between the kingdom and the Spirit, Klein's observation in "Vor dem Einbruch der Gottesherrschaft" (in *Lukasevangelium*, 566–76) deserves consideration in its surrounding narrative context. The matter is explored in some detail by Cho (*Spirit and Kingdom*, 110–95). —Ed.]

32. "Der Geist ist nicht mehr selber die eschatologische Gabe, sondern der vorläufige Ersatz für den Besitz des endgültigen Heils; er ermöglicht die Existenz der Gläubigen in der fortdauernden Welt, in der Verfolgung; er schenkt die Kraft zur Mission und zum Durchhalten" (Conzelmann, *Mitte der Zeit*, 87); see the entire chapter dedicated to

analysis of the adversative particle alone but rather more from conclusions adopted in his study on the eschatology of the third Gospel. Luke may have been the first to consciously de-eschatologize the message of Jesus in order to interpret it as a history of salvation. In this way, he would have avoided any temporal presence of the kingdom whether in the church, in Christ, or in the Spirit, by relegating it beyond history.[33] Luke would be the first to have consciously appealed to the gift of the Spirit in order to solve the problem of the delay of the Parousia.[34]

The question of the eschatology of the New Testament at present stumbles over the great ambiguity of vocabulary and, more than anything else, over the diversity of concepts regarding time and history.[35]

Lukan eschatology (ibid., 87–127), and his articles "Lukasanalyse" and "Gegenwart und Zukunft in der synoptischen Tradition," esp. 288–93.

33. "An identification of Kingdom and Spirit is impossible for Luke [Eine identifizierung von Reich und Geist ist bei Lukas unmöglich]" (Conzelmann, *Mitte der Zeit*, 106).

34. According to Conzelmann, Mark feels already unconsciously drawn to eliminate the impatient waiting for the Parousia, but Luke is the first to consciously propose the solution. "Luke is the first to make this deliberate appeal to the phenomenon of the Spirit as a solution of [sic] the problem of the Parousia. Instead of possessing such knowledge, the disciples are called to be witnesses before the world, a task for which they are enabled by divine power [Als *erster* beruft sich Lukas *bewusst* auf das Geistphänomen zur Bewältigung des Parusieproblems. An die Stelle solchen Wissens tritt die Existenz als Zeugen vor der Welt, zu der die Jünger durch die göttliche Kraft befähigt sind]" (*Theology of St. Luke*, 136; *Mitte der Zeit*, 127). His chapter on the eschatology of Luke claims precisely to verify this conscious reflection of Luke, going beyond the idea of the permanence of unrelated planes, which Wellhausen attributes to Luke (*Mitte der Zeit*, 88). Later Conzelmann ("Gegenwart und Zukunft," 292) recognizes that in Mark there are also vestiges of a differentiation between the time of Christ and subsequent time, but assumes that these facts are neither conscious nor reflected.

35. See Cullmann's "Parusieverzögerung und Urchristentum" and the chapter "Heil als Geschichte" in his *Heil als Geschichte* for an explanation of the state of the question in contemporary exegesis (see also "Prolegómenos," ch. 3 in *Heil als Geschichte*, and Mollat, "Judgement dans le Nouveau Testament"). Adler (*Erste christliche Pfingstfest*, 153–55) rejects the supposed tension between the Spirit and the Parousia suggested by Michaelis, (*Täufer, Jesus, Urgemeinde*) and Loisy (*Actes des Apôtres*). Schweizer ("Gegenwart des Geistes," in a Dodd FS) corrects Dodd's expression "realized eschatology," suggesting instead "anticipated eschatology." See also Cadbury, "Acts and Eschatology" (in the same FS); Borgen, "Eschatology and Heilsgeschichte"; Grässer, *Problem der Parusieverzögerung*; Smith, "Eschatology of Acts"; idem, "History and Eschatology"; Bartsch, "Problem der Pausieverzögerung"; Robinson, *Weg des Herrn*; Ellis, "Present and Future Eschatology"; Salas, *Discurso escatológico prelucano*; Kerrigan, "Sensus plenior"; Bourke, "Jour de Jahvé en Joël." Practically speaking, the interpretations are divided between the tendency of Albert Schweitzer, reinterpreted by Bultmann, and the tendency of Dodd (consequent, existential, or realized eschatology).

However, Conzelmann's study presents the question directly as an exegetical one. A critique of his study leads to the acceptance, not only of many of Conzelmann's valuable observations, but also, of the tripartite scheme of the history of salvation that has been emphasized in the work of Luke. However, upon closer examination, the point of the forced schematization of Conzelmann's thesis is more visible—in one part, it banishes those facts in Matthew and Mark that are similar, and in another, it forces those texts in Luke, which are discordant, to fit Conzelmann's model.[36] The schema of the history of salvation is valid, but it is not exclusive to Luke, nor is it the key principle of his work.[37]

The attempt to suppress any Lukan reference to the actual presence of the kingdom turns out to be especially hasty in view of, for example, these texts: "But if it is by the finger of God that I cast out demons, then the kingdom of God has come to you" (Luke 11:20); "The kingdom of God is not coming with things that can be observed; nor will they say, 'Look, here it is!' or 'There it is!' For, in fact, the kingdom of God is among

---

36. Haenchen, in his review of *Mitte der Zeit*, notes that the kingdom of God is truly *sichtbar* [visible, apparent, obvious] in Christ, and not simply *sehbar* [able to be seen]. He also notes that the age of the church is not predominantly a time of persecution, but of the triumph of salvation. However, I would concur with his statement that "The time of the Spirit and the Church is in no way that of the Kingdom of God [Die Zeit des Geistes und der Kirche keineswegs die des Gottesreiches ist]" (160).For extensive later recensions of this interpretive method see León-Dufour, "Redaktionsgeschichte"; Rasco, "Conzelmann y la Historia salutis"; Rohde, *Redaktionsgeschichtliche Methode*, 125–44; Oliver, "Lucan Birth Stories"; and Flender, *Heil und Geschichte*, 113f.

37. In reality, the two great periods in the history of salvation continue to be the promise and the fulfillment of the messianic period. We can see this illustrated in two very significant texts: Luke 16:16, "The law and the prophets were in effect until John came; since then the good news of the kingdom of God is proclaimed, and everyone tries to enter it by force"; and the naturalness with which Acts 7:17 sees history divided into two parts, "But as the time drew near for the fulfillment of the promise . . ." This is not to say that three periods cannot be established. Baer (*Heilige Geist*, 76–77; see also 108) has already observed this tripartite division: "If we find in Heb 1:1f. the contrasting of only two salvation periods, even so, a clear three-part salvation history is present in the work of Luke, even if this notion is also nowhere directly pronounced [Wenn wir in Hebr 1,1s die gegenüberstellung nur zweier Heilsepochen finden, so liegt im Lukaswerke eine deutliche Dreigliederung der Heilsgeschichte vor, wenn dieser Gedanke auch nirgends unmittelbar ausgesprochen ist]."What is not apparent is that these three epochs can be stylized to the point of being presented as the expression of a theological concept. From the moment that times after Jesus are alluded to, a different stage is automatically suggested, without this necessarily revealing a special theological interpretation.Strecker (*Weg der Gerechtigkeit*, 238–42) found this same tripartite division in Matthew and also, albeit in a less distinct form, in Mark.

you" (Luke 17:20–21; 9:27; 10:9, 11). Conzelmann dedicates very little attention to the exegetical analysis of the eschatology of Acts,[38] which, given this work's limited theme of the Holy Spirit in Acts, is lamentable. I admit that the writing of a history of the post-Easter church supposes a postponement of the Parousia, but it cannot be concluded a priori that this excludes in the same way any form of eschatological actualization. Conzelmann's interpretation of the Spirit as a substitute for the kingdom in Acts 1:8 would be possible in this isolated text, but not probable. First of all, the assistance of the Spirit would not be a concept original to Luke as Conzelmann claims. The Synoptics have each related the promise of Jesus to the help of the Spirit for testimony before tribunals.[39] They suppose, therefore, a time when they would need a strengthening of character by means of the Spirit. The evasion of Christ, who responds to a question concerning the moment of eschatological fulfillment with ethical advice, is likewise not original. The apocalypse of Mark 13 contains a similar question (v. 4), ethical advice (vv. 5, 9), and the promise of the help of the Spirit (v. 11). This time will be extended until the gospel is preached to all people (v. 10) and will be sufficiently lengthy to allow for battles, wars of kingdoms and of races, earthquakes, and famines.[40]

The promise of Acts 1:8 concerning the power of the Spirit for testimony does not contain the entire interpretation of Jesus concerning the sending of the Spirit, and, therefore, we cannot deduce from this one text the function of the Holy Spirit in Acts. Having just promised them the sending of the Spirit as a baptism in the Holy Spirit, and, in the face of the inopportune question by the disciples, Jesus shifts their attention

---

38. Evidently, Acts does not expect an immediate Parousia, but this does not eliminate the belief of living in the end times, in the times of the fulfillment of the Promise. Texts can be examined that deal with the fulfillment of the Promise, of the resurrection of Christ, and with all such exhortations as "save yourselves from this corrupt generation" (2:40). The lack of clarity is interesting in the second discourse of Peter (3:12–26) concerning events between the fulfillment of the prophecies in the life of Jesus and his second coming. [See also "Erzählrahmen und der Skopus der zweiten Petrusrede" in Wasserberg, *Aus Israels Mitte*, 225. –Ed]

39. See secs. 1.1 and 5.3.

40. In a certain sense, the Spirit substitutes for the immediate integral possession of the kingdom, but this concept finds its origin already in Jesus. On the other hand, in order to justify the name of provisional substitute, the Spirit would have to demonstrate that, upon the arrival of the kingdom, that substitute would lose its reason for being. If the substitute remains, we are not dealing with a provisional substitute, but with a true foretaste.

from a useless curiosity (also beyond human capacity) to the practical effects of the gift of the Spirit. Peter interprets the Pentecostal gifting announced in 1:8 as the distribution of the gift that Christ had received in his exaltation (2:33), and Peter promises it to all those who are baptized, even though they are not called to be witnesses. The author places special interest on establishing the equality of the gift received by Cornelius with the Pentecostal gift, but, evidently, this does not have to do with a gift that makes him a witness.[41] Acts 1:8 is, therefore, not the key text for interpreting the gift of the Spirit in Acts. More important is the baptism in the Spirit and the citation of Joel in 2:17–21. (This latter text, as will be seen, has an eschatological meaning.) However, if Jesus replaces the expectation of a falsely envisioned kingdom, announcing a gift that pertains to the true, definitive kingdom, it cannot be said that this gift is a provisional substitute for the kingdom, but rather a foretaste.

Conzelmann has referred very briefly to the citation of Joel 2:28–32. He recognizes in the prophecy an eschatological meaning, but Luke

---

41. The author places special emphasis on limiting the mission of testimony to the apostles, and only as an exception is it expanded to include Paul and, in a certain sense, Stephen. [This concept of the limiting of testimony to the 12 apostles from among the 120 disciple-believer-witnesses, and to other selected characters, is not detected, for example, by Weinel, *Wirkungen des Geiste*; Gunkel, *Wirkungen des heiligen Geistes*; Schneider, *Apostelgeschichte*; or Fitzmyer, *Acts of the Apostles*. Rather, Luke most probably expects readers to understand Acts 1:8 to apply individually to all characters who are employed in the rhetorical vein of examples and precedents with respect to Spirit reception.

Here, then, Haya-Prats might appear at first glance to be overly influenced in his concept of "limiting the mission of testimony" by the prevailing theological/ecclesiological theory of the "apostolic age" ("Pfingstzeitalter" or "apostolische Zeitalter"), which lies in the formative background of both Conzelmann's interpretive theory of various epochs and of von Baer's imaginative introduction and imposition of narratively disruptive epochal devices, which Haya-Prats does not adopt as a fixation for interpretation. Therefore, the editor welcomes Haya-Prats' clarification of his concept, wherein he observes that "The testimony that Luke attributed exclusively to the apostles is the testimony about the life, death, and resurrection of Jesus. It is a historical testimony about the events they have attended and is a testimony that could be called a constitutional foundation. Something similar occurs in a wedding; there are many witnesses, but only those who sign the marriage document are legally considered witnesses. Luke also describes a testimony for all Christians, but it is testimony of faith, not face-to-face, which is our life or our death, which guarantees that Jesus is the Christ of God. Many pagans embraced Christianity seeing 'how they love.' In ch. 5 we study the various aspects and the development of testimony presented in the book of Acts." (This clarification is based on private communication with the author.) —Ed.]

would have de-eschatologized it in his application.⁴² He admits, nevertheless, that the reading ἐν ταῖς ἐσχάταις ἡμέραις is more likely, in spite of the fact that Haenchen prefers μετὰ ταῦτα, which would be more favorable to Conzelmann's thesis.⁴³ It appears to be of little consequence in Conzelmann's conclusions that Luke retouched every phrase of his sources in the Gospel in order to eliminate the eschatological aspect and instead introduced, without any clear motive, the expression "in the last days" where one would only have read "after that." Probably the phrase does not indicate an imminent hope of the Parousia, but perhaps Conzelmann's prejudice is in the confusing of the imminence of the Parousia with the arrival of the eschatological times. Luke could have softened those terms that suggested an imminent consummation, but could have accepted at the same time the commencement of a completely different age already conceived of by the prophets as the end times.

The prophetic eschatology appears to have split into two periods: *a beginning* of the eschatological period with the coming of Christ (or perhaps with his exaltation and the outpouring of the Spirit) and *a fulfillment* by the great day of the Lord. The same text, Joel 2:28–32, distinguishes two periods, even though it does so without specifying their duration: (1) the filling of the Spirit in the messianic days "before the day of the Lord arrives, [and (2)] a day great and terrible."⁴⁴ To consider eschatological those days prior to the great day of the Lord, or to refuse them this term, could be merely a question of terminology. In fact the Pentecostal story calls them "the last days."⁴⁵ If we consider the content

42. Conzelmann, *Mitte der Zeit*, 88.

43. Conzelmann, *Apostelgeschichte*, on Acts 2:17, 28–29. The reasons given by Mussner ("In den letzten Tagen") in favor of such a reading are convincing: the accommodation to the text of Joel ("after that") can be adequately explained as a work of a scholarly copyist. However, the introduction of a new formula would be less explicable as a change initiated by copyists, while it would be normal in an author that narrates the coming of the Holy Spirit as a sign of the fulfillment of the Promise. The prophet starts from a period of tribulation, and for this reason says "after that," while the Pentecostal story starts with the outpouring of the Spirit, making it a mistake to say "after that," which would not signify "after the coming of the Spirit," but rather after a period that had not been specifically mentioned or identified.

44. Cullman has demonstrated the double aspect of NT eschatology that comprehends the "now" and the "not yet." The "anticipated eschatology" of Schweizer has this same sense (see his "Gegenwart des Geistes").

45. It is probable, however, that the Pentecostal story had a predominantly eschatological tone that Luke did not correct when incorporating it, but neither did he continue its use in the collecting of his work (see sec. 4.3). Luke is interested in demonstrating

more than the eschatological term itself, we see as well that the essence of the day of the Lord had already entered into history with the presence of salvation. A philological or philosophical scruple should not prevent understanding this eschatological term in the same sense that it is understood by Luke.

The eschatological value of the citation of Joel rests not only in the term employed but, before anything else, in the finality of the christological-messianic discourse of Peter and in the thesis of the entire book concerning the salvation of the Gentiles. The gift of the Spirit is in Acts the sign that the fulfillment of the promise has commenced, and, therefore, is the proof that Jesus has been exalted as Messiah. The gifting of the Spirit to Cornelius (as with the gifting at Pentecost) is the sign that the uncircumcised have been incorporated into the true people of God and are inheritors of the Promise.

I recognize that the gift of the Holy Spirit in Acts has predominantly utilitarian-historical effects, whether kerygmatic or ethical: an impulse to testimony and evangelization, wisdom, and fearlessness. This is natural, since Luke wishes to present the development of the church and sees in it a sign of divine assistance. Nevertheless, Luke knows also some of the rapturous effects that anticipate celestial fullness—joy, glossolalia as exultant praise—and the reader can see at the very least in these joyous gifts a confirmation of the divine presence.[46]

The utilitarian-kerygmatic aspect of the gift of the Holy Spirit appears clearly in the giving of the Spirit to Jesus at the Jordan. The joyful eschatological aspect appears in his exaltation as Messiah and, in an anticipatory mode, in the so-called Jubilation hymn (Luke 10:21). Perhaps it is possible to advance a step further and arrive at the deduction that the joyful, eschatological aspect is more important, even in Acts, than

the incorporation of the Gentiles into the true people of God. This means, in biblical language, participation in the messianic-eschatological people. However, Luke would not express this spontaneously in eschatological categories that would not pertain to his original situation, unless forced by his sources. In part, Conzelmann would be right to show that Luke avoids eschatological vocabulary, but that appears to result from unselfishness with regard to a terminology that is increasingly less comprehensible, more than resulting from any opposition to its theological concept. Luke respects many of the eschatological expressions of his sources. It is true that he softens the aspect of imminent realization, but he does not arrive at the place of suppressing all of the eschatological sense as Conzelmann claims to demonstrate. (See also sec. 8.1 on the prophetic gift in its kerygmatic and life-bringing sense.)

46. Part 2 of this study examines "The Effects of the Holy Spirit" in detail.

the utilitarian-historical aspect, in spite of the author's insistence on the latter, owing to the practical character of his work. Joel's prophecy refers to the joyful aspect of the gift of the Spirit, since it supposes a time of triumph, and the outpouring of prophecy necessarily removes its didactic purpose in order to allow unselfish praise of God. If this gifting of the Spirit serves as a guarantee of the messianic age, it is not given as an arbitrarily established sign but as the exterior exuberance of the messianic blessings already received. The reception of the Spirit in the exaltation of Jesus should surpass the reception at the Jordan, and it does not appear that it should be reduced to the faculty of transmitting the Spirit as helper. Throughout the book joy-bringing effects are encountered. It would not be too bold to say that the dynamic effects are applications of the eschatological gift to historical circumstances.

To summarize, *the Promise* refers to the collected blessings announced for the messianic age. *The kingdom*, on the other hand, is a less defined term in Acts, which represents the collected message of Jesus. The Holy Spirit is one of the gifts of the Promise—not exactly the gift of reconciliation or sanctification of the people, but a gift of superabundant power—both a sign and, at the same time, an increase of the participation already attained in the Promise. This gift is manifested in prophetic charismata, but it is not confined to these manifestations. The vacillation in Luke between Christ and the Spirit as fulfillment of the Promise could have as its foundation a vacillation between the fundamental eschatological fulfillment in the Spirit—now only anticipated—and the initial fulfillment in the work of Christ.

The eschatological or temporal aspect of the gift of the Spirit depends on the tendency to see the fulfillment of the Promise and of the kingdom in history or in a *merely* eschatological situation. In reality, there can be little doubt that the principal part of the Promise had begun to fulfill itself in history, because it is the essence of the Christian message. However, the importance attributed to the hope of an immediate Parousia has been converted into an unquestionably eschatological criterion for an exegetical school, and according to this criterion it shapes and classifies the books of the New Testament. As for the gift of the Holy Spirit, it has always been considered as an obviously eschatological gift. However, Conzelmann had wished to find in the answer of Jesus concerning the kingdom (Acts 1:8) a confirmation for his theory regarding the historization of Luke. The gift of the Spirit would be a temporal substitute owing to the delay of the purely eschatological kingdom. However, the gift of the Holy Spirit had been prophesied by Joel as an eschatological gift, as Conzelmann himself recognizes. The Pentecostal story does not de-eschatologize this citation, but rather emphasizes its eschatological character with the correction "in the last days," which corresponds perfectly with the application of the prophecy to the experience of the Spirit. Peter can admonish his audience to "save yourselves from this corrupt generation" because the final extraordinary sacrifice for salvation had commenced prior to the arrival of the great day of the Lord.

To avoid entanglement in a mere question of terminology—whether eschatological or historical—I have endeavored to examine whether the gift of the Spirit had only temporal effects or whether it presented atemporal characteristics. Naturally, the comparison cannot be established on equal footing since the revelation does not try to describe the future but only indirectly allows it to be inferred. As a criterion of the temporal gift, I have established the dynamic character of ethical behavior or of a kerygmatic impulse. As a criterion of the atemporal gift, presented in history, I have considered the selfless aspect, the merely joyful one. Jesus promised a baptism in the Holy Spirit which Luke interpreted as Pentecost, the coming upon Cornelius, and equally the coming upon every group that is baptized. In all those cases, the joyful expression of glossolalia predominates, as tangible exultation in the gift received and a response of selfless praise to God. The interpretation of Pentecost as power for testimony is a particular restriction for the apostles (not valid for Cornelius, nor for those who are baptized), probably added by Luke to the Pentecostal story.

In the collecting of Acts, Luke insisted preferentially on the dynamic aspect of the gift of the Spirit (already presented by Jesus in speaking of persecutions). However, Luke does not claim to diminish the joyful aspect of the Pentecostal story that is consciously imitated in the case of Cornelius and in certain transitional verses (9:31; 13:52). Christ received in his exaltation the Spirit as the fulfillment of the Promise (2:33). It is difficult to prove in a historical book that the Spirit is the anticipation of that which is to come, but it would be impossible to prove exegetically that the gift of the Spirit in Acts is a provisional substitute that would lose its reason for being at the end times.

The gift of the Holy Spirit is not a provisional substitute, but rather a true foretaste. Schlatter has already seen "the arrival of the Holy Spirit as the first sign of that for which the disciples waited, the coming of Christ";[47] and more recently Lohse has presented this as "a piece of the realized eschatology itself."[48]

---

47. Schlatter, *Geschichte der ersten Christenheit*, 16; "die Ankunft des Hl. Geistes als erstes Anzeichen für das von den Jüngern erwartete Kommen des Christus."

48. Lohse, "Bedeutung des Pfingsberichtes," 436; "ein Stück sich verfwirklichende Eschatologie." [Cantalamessa (*Mystery of Pentecost*, 11) presents this realized eschatology in observing that "After Pentecost, when the coming of the Holy Spirit completely relocated the axis of their thoughts from themselves to God, behold, we see them forming a 'community . . . of one heart and one mind' (Acts 4:32) among themselves. . . . The new language that they learned and that everyone comprehends is the language of humility." —Ed.]

4

The Holy Spirit's Mode of Action

4.1 Invasive Irruptions and Complementary Influences

IN REGARD TO THE mode of the Spirit's action, two divergent sets of texts are relevant. At times the action of the Spirit appears as an exterior intervention in the life of the community, imposing his decisions directly or speaking through ecstatic prophets that serve to echo his warnings. In these passages, the Spirit appears to intervene at the level of historical action, replacing human decision as a boss who momentarily assumes the responsibilities of his subordinates. When these interventions are decisive, they can be attributed exclusively to the Spirit. When they are mere announcements, they are relayed through a prophetic oracle. It is difficult to label this anomalous collection of the Spirit's interventions. They might be called *invasive irruptions*.[1] In another series of texts, human activity predominates though the author notes that such activity results from an impulse of the Holy Spirit. I call this mode of action a *complementary influence* to underscore that the primacy of the action is attributed to the person that acts, while the impulse of the Spirit is presented as a complementary cause. Three fundamental levels of texts may be considered: the event as a news reporter might verify it, the historical interpretation of the author, and the expression that he has selected to underscore a specific aspect of it.[2]

---

1. Though begging for greater elaboration, we may call them exterior or impersonal interventions, inbreakings in the timelines of history, and direct actions of the Spirit.
2. Although we cannot enter here into the complex question of the historical value of Acts, we can note certain discrepancies in details that do not agree completely with

The invasive irruptions predominate in the Pauline cycle of Acts, both in their anticipation before the Jerusalem Council and also in their full development afterward. In the first part, these invasive irruptions occur only in the narrative of the eunuch and in Peter's vision preparing him for his encounter with Cornelius: "the Spirit said" (8:29; 10:19 = 11:12) and the more anthropomorphic "the Spirit of the Lord snatched Philip away" (8:39). We note that neither of these texts uses the term *Holy Spirit*. As we will see in a more detailed study of these texts,[3] they deal with narratives incorporated by the author but which he chose not to rework, perhaps to avoid conforming them to his concept of the Holy Spirit. Paul's first missionary journey is attributed directly to an intervention of the Spirit: "While they were worshipping the LORD and fasting, the Holy Spirit said, 'Set apart for me Barnabas and Saul for the work to which I have called them.' . . . So, being sent by the Holy Spirit . . ." (13:2, 4). The expression used by the author has eliminated all human intervention in order to emphasize beyond all doubt the absolutely divine origin of Paul's mission.

If we ask how the author perceived this event, we can by no means think in terms of an anthropomorphic dialogue. The event deals clearly with a charismatic intervention by means of a prophetic oracle, such as are abundant in the Pauline cycle. The context clearly demonstrates that the circumstances are decidedly at odds with this decision of the Spirit. It does not deal with a human decision endorsed by the Spirit but rather

---

their respective contexts or with other NT facts or even with the rest of the book of Acts. At times this can be attributed to the author's faithfulness to diverse sources, but on other occasions they appear in his discourses (1:19 and 15:20), even in key passages in which Peter and Stephen cite from the Septuagint where these deviate from the Hebrew text. The more serious difficulties are found in the chronology and in the account about Paul. See sec. 1.1, n. 19; concerning the discourses, see Dupont, *Études*, 41–56; Grässer, "Apostelgeschichte in der Forschung"; Guthrie, "Recent Literature on Acts," 38–39. In general, the defense of the historical accuracy is in inverse proportion to the theological value that is ascribed to the book of Acts. Even so, a truly historical value can be maintained in spite of the fact that the details are redacted as a function of the interpretation of the event (Haenchen, *Acts*, 98–103 = *Apostelgeschichte*, 88–93). The articles by Dibelius, collected in *Aufsätze zur Apostelgeschichte*, are of special interest. [See the English translation of *Aufsätze* in the bibliography. —Ed.]

[The historical value of Luke's presentation continues to be a subject of interest, as illustrated by the following studies: Hemer, *Book of Acts*; Gill and Gempf, eds., *Book of Acts*, vol. 2; Bauckham, ed., *Book of Acts*; Marguerat, *First Christian Historian*; Alexander, "Preface to Luke-Acts." —Ed.]

3. See secs. 2.5 and 8.3.

with an inbreaking of the Spirit that changes the course of events. With respect to the verifiable determiner of the Pauline mission, there is no lack of interpretations that propose some human motive. Knox suggests that it could be a consequence of the disagreement between Peter and Paul.[4] What interests us is that, beyond the motives that may be mixed into this decision, the author has seen the intervention of the Holy Spirit and has wished to emphasize it as much as possible in his expression.

There is a greater probability of encountering a human motive in the hindrances that caused Paul to change his course for Greece: ". . . having been forbidden by the Holy Spirit to speak the word in Asia. When they had come opposite Mysia, they attempted to go into Bithynia, but the Spirit of Jesus did not allow them" (16:6–7).[5] Nevertheless, Luke's pausing to clarify whether this concerns a vision such as the Macedonian one (16:9), like those experienced in the journey to Jerusalem, internal premonitions, illnesses, or local rivalries,[6] seems to be contrary to the author's intention not to have been interested in the mechanism of revelation, but rather to attribute the event to the Holy Spirit. Such is Dibelius' insightful observation: "it is important simply to point out, that godly power guides the writings of the apostles."[7] We can say the same about the journey to Jerusalem: "And now, as a captive to the Spirit, I am on my way to Jerusalem" (20:22).[8] The redaction of these texts in order to eliminate all human mediation leaves the Holy Spirit not simply as a direct participant in the action, but as the singular agent that moves the game pieces.[9]

The action of the Spirit upon the presbyters of Ephesus appears in a similar way: "Keep watch over yourselves and over all the flock, of which the Holy Spirit has made you overseers, to shepherd the church of God"

---

4. Knox, *Acts of the Apostles*, 90.

5. Concerning the Spirit of Jesus see sec. 2.3.

6. Haenchen (*Acts*, 488 = *Apostelgeschichte*, 427) in commenting on this passage makes reference to Gal 4:13 and 1 Thes 2:18. [While here Luke does not say what activity of the Spirit was involved in this guidance ("*Wie der Geist die Verkündigung verhindert, sagt Lukas nicht*"), Jervell (*Apostelgeschichte*, 416–17) posits a "concrete" revelatory activity of the Spirit, equivalent in discernable impact with a vision or inspired prophetic speech. —Ed.]

7. "[W]ichtig ist nur zu zeigen, dass göttlicke Macht die Schritte des Apostels lenkt" (Dibelius, *Aufsätze*, 170; Haenchen, *Acts*, 483–87 = *Apostelgeschichte*, 423–27).

8. See sec. 4.2.

9. Certain variants to 19:1 and to 20:3 can also be seen: "the Spirit said to him."

(20:28). Evidently, a human intervention is assumed in this text also, but this is eclipsed by the divine origin of the election. Schweizer suggests an automatic attribution of the ecclesial decisions—perhaps hierarchical—to the Holy Spirit. It appears more likely, though, that it deals with a case similar to that already cited in the origin of Paul's mission, in which the Spirit is manifested charismatically.

Another group of texts manifest these messages from the Holy Spirit through a prophetic oracle. However, the less than personal presence of the prophet places these texts with this first series of external interventions of the Holy Spirit. Agabus predicts by means of the Spirit the famine that would come (11:28); also the other prophets from Tyre speak to Paul by means of the Spirit (21:4). These expressions, in spite of presenting the prophets as subjects of the action and including the Spirit in the subordinate expression διὰ τοῦ πνεύματος,[10] designate an equivalent situation, as Agabus expresses with a more solemn attribution, "Thus says the Holy Spirit" (21:11; with double article),[11] and Paul avers that "the Holy Spirit testifies to me in every city" (20:23).[12]

The *complementary influence* of the Spirit is found in only two texts in the Pauline cycle of Acts: ". . . Paul resolved in the Spirit . . . to go on to Jerusalem" (19:21). Many interpreters believe that the text refers to the spirit of Paul; however, the attribution to the Holy Spirit seems more in keeping with the overall origin of the trip and is equally admissible grammatically, as we will see later in a more detailed study.[13] Less important is the text that refers to the blindness of Elymas for its character of imitating Peter's miracles. The expression has been taken from the prophetic formulas of the Pentecostal story: "Paul, filled with the Holy Spirit, looked intently at him and said . . ." (13:9–10).[14]

The *complementary influence* of the Holy Spirit is, on the other hand, characteristic of the first part of Acts. The Holy Spirit is given (5:32; 8:18;

10. This expression is examined in sec. 4.2.

11. Haenchen (*Acts*, 602 = *Apostelgeschichte*, 533) sees in this expression a sense similar to the "oracle of Yahweh" of the OT prophets.

12. Wikenhauser (*Apostelgeschichte*, 233) comments, "Yet the Holy Spirit said in advance on every stage of his journey through the prophetic mouth of gifted Christians that chains and hardship awaited him there [Sagt ihm doch auf jeder Station seiner Reise der Heilige Geist durch den Mund prophetisch begabter Christen voraus, dass ihn dort Fesseln und Drangsale erwarten]."

13. See sec. 4.2.

14. They can also be seen in the variants of 18:5 and 26:1: "also trustful in the Holy Spirit and filled with consolation [confidens et in spiritu sancto consolatione repletus]."

11:17; 15:8) or poured out (2:17, 18, 33; 10:45) upon the disciples that receive him (1:8; 2:38; 8:15, 17, 19; 10:47; 19:2) in fullness (2:4; 4:8, 31; 6:3, 5; 7:55; 9:17; 11:24; 13:9, 52). This fullness of the Spirit gives the disciples exultant speech (2:4b; 4:20), but the historical person is always the responsible subject of the action. It is the disciples who are the witnesses (even though they are so through the power of the Holy Spirit, 1:8) and who speak the word of God with fearlessness (4:31), as Peter and Stephen spoke full of the Holy Spirit before the Sanhedrin (4:8; 6:10; 7:55). The author attributes the wisdom and faith of Stephen to the Holy Spirit (6:3, 5), along with the faith of Barnabas (11:24) and the fearlessness of Peter (4:13, 31). But they are presented as *acting with their diverse human characteristics*, such as the vehemence of Stephen in debate and the conciliatory understanding of Barnabas.

This same personal actuation of the individual under the influence of the Spirit is characteristic of the Gospel of Luke with respect to Mark and Matthew in the sayings on the Spirit's help before tribunals. Mark 13:11 says openly, "[F]or it is not you who speak, but the Holy Spirit." Matthew 10:20 softens this expression somewhat stating, "[F]or it is not you who speak, but the Spirit of your Father *speaking through you*" (emphasis added). Luke 12:12 supposes that the one speaking is the disciple, even though he is repeating the teachings of the Spirit, "for the Holy Spirit *will teach you* at that very hour what you ought to say" (emphasis added), and in a similar manner, even though attributed to Christ, Luke 21:15 affirms, "[F]or I will give you words and a wisdom that none of your opponents will be able to withstand or contradict." The similarity of Luke 21:15 with Acts 6:10 is noteworthy: "But they could not withstand the wisdom and the Spirit with which he spoke." The impulse of the Spirit is as decidedly internal and assimilated for Stephen as the wisdom.[15] It deals with a gift of God, but not with a gift that breaks through the surface of history changing the course of events, but rather with an internal gift that prompts and complements human decisions.

In the same way, we encounter the violent expression of Mark 1:12, "And the Spirit immediately drove [ἐκβάλλει] him out into the wilderness," softened by Matthew 4:1, "Then Jesus was led by the Spirit into the wilderness." The parallel text in Luke maintains the verb in the passive (ἤγετο), but the Spirit is not in the genitive agent as in Matthew, but in a circumstantial complement: "Jesus, full of the Holy Spirit, returned

---

15. See sec. 7.1.

from the Jordan and was led by the Spirit [ἐν τῷ πνεύματι] in the wilderness" (Luke 4:1).¹⁶ In Mark the Spirit is the subject of a violently active verb, in Matthew he is a genitive agent of a preferably persuasive verb, and in Luke he is a circumstantial complement of the cause (or of an instrumental cause). The passive term in Luke 4:1 (ἤγετο) is actually a theological passive, attributed in a general way to God. In Luke 4:14, a very similar expression is repeated, underscoring the primacy of Jesus' action, an action that is complemented by the action of the Spirit: "Then Jesus, filled with the power of the Spirit, returned to Galilee [ἐν τῇ δυνάμει τοῦ πνεύματος]." (This characteristic of a complementary causal reappears in the term ἔχρισεν that Acts 10:38 and Luke 4:18 apply to the gifting of the Spirit to Christ. It is above all typical of the more often repeated Pentecostal expression.)

In the Pauline cycle of Acts, external and consuming inbreakings of the Holy Spirit are normal, while that which is characteristic of the first part—the Pentecostal block—is the complementary nature of the causal action of the Spirit.¹⁷ I have called this action of the Spirit a *complementary influence* in order to avoid the misunderstandings that the designation *internal influence* could suggest, though the latter is in itself perhaps more appropriate. In effect, the Spirit is given, poured out by God, and received by the disciples, who feel it bursting forth in their interior in the form of wisdom, fearlessness, and charismatic faith, which are manifested as personal characteristics even though they are stirred up by the Holy Spirit.

The next section examines some of the circumstances of these expressions used by Luke to refer to the action of the Holy Spirit.

---

16. See sec. 4.2.

17. In dealing with the testimony of the Holy Spirit in sec. 5.4, we will speak of the direct testimony of the Spirit as distinct from testimony of the disciples that is prompted by him, which we could call indirect testimony of the Spirit. Both types of testimony appear in an important text, "And we are witnesses to these things, and so is the Holy Spirit whom God has given to those who obey him" (5:32). However, this direct testimony has nothing to do with that which I have called an *invasive irruption*. It is expressed fundamentally in the charism of glossolalia and only has power in light of prophecy: Joel 2:28–32 for Pentecost, Acts 11:16 for the baptism in the Holy Spirit of Cornelius, and Acts 15:15 for other prophecies in James' discourse.

4.2 The Spirit in Circumstantial Expressions

As seen in the preceding section, the action of the Holy Spirit is frequently expressed in Acts by means of a circumstantial complement. The expression διὰ (τοῦ) πνεύματος (ἁγίου) occurs in four texts in Acts (1:2; 4:25; 11:28; 21:4),[18] where the author frequently avails himself of the construction of διά with a genitive.[19] Its sense is one of mediation (time, place, or cause), but it may also signify a principal cause.[20] The lack of an article in the first two texts is not peculiar but characteristic of well-known classical Greek and even more so in the New Testament as a Semitism or an imitation of the Septuagint.[21]

In 1:2, there occurs an influence of Christ on the disciples—through teaching or election—by means of the Holy Spirit. It is not easy to determine how this influence by means of the Holy Spirit is carried out. It does not appear probable that the author refers to an action of the Spirit in the disciples prior to Pentecost; therefore, it is more likely referring to the Spirit that has descended upon Jesus at the incarnation and at the Jordan. However, it is very probable that this text arises from a later interpolation.[22] The text 4:25 presents an overloaded form that originated in a later addition or in an unfortunate translation from the Hebrew: ὁ τοῦ πατρὸς ἡμῶν διὰ πνεύματος ἁγίου στόματος Δαυὶδ παιδός σου εἰπών. Haenchen proposes as later additions τοῦ πατρὸς ἡμῶν and πνεύματος ἁγίου, with which the original would be "You ... who said by the mouth of your servant David."[23] This is the customary expression in speaking of inspiration of the Scriptures (3:18, 21). Koch proposes the existence of a double διά in the text of 4:25, as a translation of the Hebrew b^e of which the first expresses the principal cause and the second designates the instrument that it uses.[24] Only two other times does the expression διὰ τοῦ πνεύματος occur: "Agabus stood up and

---

18. In two other texts, it is the Holy Spirit who speaks (subject) by means of David (1:16) and Isaiah (28:25).

19. Matthew uses this construction 25 times, Mark 11 times, Luke 15 times, Acts 51 times, Paul 198 times, Hebrews 40 times, and John 15 times.

20. BDF n. 223; the originator is probably also denoted by διά instead of the agent (Zerwick, *Biblical Greek*, nn. 113–14).

21. See sec. 1.2, n. 30.

22. See sec. 8.3, n. 36.

23. *Acts*, 226 = *Apostelgeschichte*, 184–85.

24. Koch, *Geist und Messias*, 53.

predicted by the Spirit that there would be a severe famine" (11:28), and in the same way, referring to other prophets, "Through the Spirit they told Paul not to go on to Jerusalem" (21:4b).[25] Neither of these two texts uses the complete expression *Holy Spirit*; however, the commentaries support the reference as evident. In effect, the same Agabus prophesies once again with an expression that leaves no room for doubt: "Thus says the Holy Spirit . . ." (21:11). And Paul himself acknowledges that "the Holy Spirit testifies to me in every city that imprisonment and persecutions are waiting for me" (20:23).

With regard to the expression *the Holy Spirit*, it is impossible to give it the sense of a mere causal instrument manipulated by the prophets. Wikenhauser considers practically equivalent the expressions "through the Spirit [durch den Geist]" and "compelled, urged (or guided) by the Spirit [vom Geist getrieben]."[26] In 1 Cor 1:9, the expression "God is faithful [δι' οὗ ἐκλήθητε] . . ." occurs, in which διά certainly designates the principal and unique cause. The same text of 21:11 ("thus says the Holy Spirit") that assures us of the reference to the Holy Spirit in the two texts at hand (11:28; 21:4) obliges us also to see the same Spirit as author of the message. Therefore, the expression has in essence been understood in a broader sense and not in its more restricted grammatical meaning. The author tries to say that the Spirit was shown by means of the prophet but, by accepting this as the subject of the action in a concrete narrative, has included the action of the Spirit in this subordinate instrumental expression. The expression διὰ (τοῦ) πνεύματος (ἁγίου) is found in two texts in the first part (of which one is probably interpolated and the other corrupted) and in another two texts referring to Paul's itinerations that require a painstakingly precise expression. It appears, therefore, that we are not dealing with an expression that Acts considers appropriate for the action of the Spirit, even less, the author of the overarching structure of the book.

The expression ἐν πνεύματι ἁγίῳ is, above all, characteristic of the sayings regarding the baptism of the Holy Spirit (Matt 3:11; Mark 1:8; Luke 3:16; John 1:33; Acts 1:5; 11:16). Luke 4:1 employs this expression when Jesus goes to the desert: "Jesus, full of the Holy Spirit, returned from the Jordan, and was led by the Spirit [ἐν τῷ πνεύματι] in the

---

25. See sec. 5.5, n. 65.

26. Wikenhauser, *Apostelgeschichte*, 135 (commentary on 11:28). Bover y Oliver and Burgos (*Sagrada Biblia*) translates it "movidos por el Espíritu [moved by the Spirit]."

wilderness." And in a very similar expression, "Then Jesus, filled with the power of the Spirit, returned to Galilee" (Luke 4:14).[27] In Acts, we encounter this expression only one time apart from the two references to Spirit baptism: "Paul determined in the Spirit to go . . . to Jerusalem" (19:21). The interpretation of this text has been much discussed. The expression τίθεσθαι ἐν πνεύματι can be equivalent to "make a decision." However, in this case it probably expresses a determination made by the Holy Spirit (i.e., under the influence of the Holy Spirit). The intention of the author is to present this journey to Jerusalem as initiated by the Holy Spirit. For that reason, the Holy Spirit is to be interpreted as the active agent in the text of 20:22 ("as a captive to the Spirit").[28] It would be strange if, on one hand, the Holy Spirit repeatedly shows Paul the persecutions that he can expect in Jerusalem (20:23 and 21:11, *Holy Spirit* with the double article) and, on the other hand, the decision has been made by Paul in his own spirit, and he feels equally captive in his own spirit without telling us why or by whom.

In this Pauline cycle of Acts, the circumstantial complements referring to the Spirit, equally in the dative without a preposition (20:22) and with the preposition ἐν (19:21), as in the genitive with διά, refer to the Holy Spirit. It is probable that the redactor of this cycle avoided using the complete term *Holy Spirit* in circumstantial expressions, yet opted to use it when dealing with the agent subject: 16:6 (genitive agent with a simple article and an inserted adjective; 20:23, 28; 21:11).[29] The preposition ἐν with a dative is frequently translated in occidental languages using the

---

27. Some codices add in Luke 10:21 the preposition ἐν. We find other texts in the dative with ἐν referring to the Spirit in Matt 12:28; 22:40; Mark 12:36.

28. Lake-Cadbury (*Beginnings* 4:244) have doubts regarding both texts. Zerwick, *Analysis Philologica*) interprets both to refer to the spirit of Paul, 19:21 as a Semitism and 20:22 as a dative of relation. Haenchen (*Acts*, 568 = *Apostelgeschichte*, 503) interprets the first (19:21) as a decision of Paul (he cites Bauer's *Wörterbuch* on τίθεσθαι ἐν πνεύματι) and the second (20:22) as the Holy Spirit. We have already seen other texts that, in spite of a lack of an adjective, refer to the Holy Spirit. [For discussion of similar active agency in Acts, see Mainville, *L'Esprit*, 308–16. —Ed.]

29. The motive for the lack of an adjective may merely be stylistic, or perhaps in certain cases it may suppose a certain irresolution in the author himself. In 19:21 and in 20:22, it is evident that the author thinks ultimately of an intervention by the Holy Spirit, but it is not nearly so clear that the expression used underscores this intervention instead of emphasizing the firmness of Paul's decision. In 11:28 and 21:4, it appears that the writer has avoided the complete term, *Holy Spirit*, because of the subordinate construction with a preposition.

preposition *with*, which is called the associative use of the expression.³⁰ This association is naturally imprecise, but it alludes to a certain causal influence by the associated term. We have already seen that Luke 4:1b, "by the Spirit," would equate to Luke 4:14, "with [or *in*] the power of the Spirit." In the second case, the preposition *with* does not designate something that is added on but rather a shared cause that potentiates the action. On the other hand, Acts 4:1 and Luke 2:27 are not habitually translated "with the Spirit" because this would suggest a mere passive companionship, but the sense is the same.

In Luke 1:17, we find a very significant example referring to John the Baptist: "With the spirit and power of Elijah (ἐν πνεύματι καὶ δυνάμει Ἡλίου) he will go before him"; that is to say, moved by the same spirit and force that drove Elijah. Matthew 9:34 offers us another interesting example with a personal term in the association, ἐν τῷ ἄρχοντι τῶν δαιμονίων ἐκβάλλει τὰ δαιμόνια, which evidently alludes to a form of power imparted by the prince of demons. The causality indicated by this associative use of the expression is of an influential type; that is to say, of something that is received by the agent person and contributes to his action, yet continues being characteristic and personal. It is neither possible to determine in a unanimous manner to what degree the influence is decisive, nor whether it is conceived of in a materialistic or spiritual form. Therefore, the expression ἐν τῷ πνεύματι alludes to a causal influence of the Spirit, assimilated by the person in such a way as to preserve the characteristic nature of his or her action. This expression, however, is not prevalent in the Gospel of Luke or in Acts, which only utilize it twice and once respectively, apart from the baptism sayings. We encounter with greater frequency the similar expression of the dative without a preposition. Also, the dative without the preposition frequently has the value of a circumstantial complement of cause; that is to say, of a complementary cause. In certain passages that refer to the Spirit, but without the adjective, doubt remains as to whether they are dealing with a causal dative or with a dative that substitutes in Hellenism for the accusative of relation.³¹ The causal sense would favor the reference to the Holy Spirit, while the sense of relationship or determination would favor the reference to the spirit itself.

---

30. BDF nn. 219–20. Zerwick, *Biblical Greek*, nn. 64, 116–19. See other significant examples in Matt 6:7; Mark 5:2, 25; Rom 8:9.

31. Zerwick, *Biblical Greek*, nn. 53, 58.

We encounter a dative with a causal value in Luke 10:21, ἠγαλλιάσατο τῷ πνεύματι τῷ ἁγίῳ, and in Acts 6:10, "But they could not withstand the wisdom and the Spirit with which he spoke [ᾧ ἐλάλει]." We encounter a relational dative in Luke 1:80 referring to the Baptist, "The child grew and became strong in spirit." Other cases are doubtful. Acts 20:22 can be translated "captive to the Spirit" or "captive in spirit" according to whether one interprets a causal dative or a relational dative.[32] In the same way, 18:25 leaves unclear the pathos of Apollos as "ardently by the Spirit" or "ardently in [or *of*] spirit."[33]

As a circumstantial complement of substance of the verb χρίω, we find in 10:38 the dative without a preposition applied to the consecration of Jesus: ". . . how God anointed Jesus of Nazareth with the Holy Spirit and with power."[34] The Holy Spirit is presented as a circumstantial complement of substance in the Pentecostal formula that is repeated constantly, with minor variants, in the entire first part of Acts: ἐπλήσθησαν πάντες πνεύματος ἁγίου (2:4).[35] This expression does not require a particularly complicated grammatical analysis as previous expressions did. It does require, however, an interpretation of the rich content of this fullness. This fullness can only be known through the effects that it produces (the focus of pt. 2). The important thing at the moment is to note the mode of action of the Spirit that is revealed in this pentecostal expression.

The author mentions the fullness of the Spirit evidently as a cause of the disciples' actions, even though both events are only linked with a joining conjunction. Only in 2:4b is the same Spirit explicitly presented as the source from which proceeds the exultant words of the disciples. This fullness proceeds, as we shall see, not only from the ecstatic word but also from the reasoning of the wise and from fearlessness. The mode of the Spirit's action through an interior fullness coincides with the sense

---

32. Zerwick, *Biblical Greek*, n. 53; idem, *Analysis Philologica* on 20:22. See also n. 11 above.

33. The fact that he is not baptized is not a true difficulty for his possessing the Holy Spirit. We will address the problem of Apollos and the disciples of Ephesus in sec. 6.4. A summary can be seen of the diverse interpretations in Haenchen, *Acts*, 554–57 = *Apostelgeschichte*, 489–92.

34. BDF n. 155:6.

35. In the same way, in all of the dependent series: 4:8, 31; 9:17; 13:9, 52; and with the adjective: 6:3, 5; 7:55; 11:24. Only 4:31 employs the article and the construction of the inserted adjective.

of a complementary cause that we have seen in the dative both with and without the preposition ἐν. It appears that the union of the two principles of action, the human and the divine, is so close and intimate that, if the complete term *Holy Spirit* is not mentioned, it is debatable whether the text refers to the human spirit or to the Holy Spirit. In 6:3 and 10, the author supposes, evidently, that Stephen is full of the Holy Spirit that assists him with his testimony before the tribunal. However, this does not exclude the possibility that the author of these texts thinks, consciously or unconsciously, in a more general and ambiguous sense of the spirit. In the same way, I have presented the determination of Paul with respect to his journey to Jerusalem (20:22) as an ambiguous case, perhaps the author does as well.[36]

In these circumstantial expressions, those who act are the disciples, but their action does not proceed solely from themselves. Their action has been stimulated and empowered by the Holy Spirit, which is presented as a supernatural means (ἐν πνεύματι), as fullness or anointing. The first part of Acts leaves us to understand that no important testimony of the disciples exists that has not been compelled by the Spirit. This compulsion may be conceived of as a renewed sensation of the presence of the Spirit. Acts, however, does not attempt a psychological description but a theological attribution to the Holy Spirit of certain historical events.

4.3 Evidence of Diverse Concepts

Comparing the two modes of the Holy Spirit's action in Acts—namely overpowering inbreakings and complementary influences—with the diverse grammatical formulations and with the most compact redactional blocks of the book yields a notable correspondence. However, this correspondence is neither clear nor evident, and there exists a considerable series of exceptions that can be explained in terms of clearly external motives but which blur the lines of symmetry. These observations confirm the hypothesis proposed in sec. 1.3; however, the complexity of the theme would require a specialized study to fully explore. Presented here are mere observations at the periphery of our study, noting as well significant similarities with respect to the presentation of the Spirit by the

---

36. See n. 12 above.

author of the Pentecostal story and that of Luke 1–2 and between the principal author of Acts and that of the third Gospel.

With reasonable precision, the action of the Holy Spirit in the Pentecostal story is conceived of as a complementary influence and is described using circumstantial expressions. Certainly, there is no lack of exceptions to this generalization, but they appear to be marginal. In Acts 1:8, the Holy Spirit is encountered in an expression of the genitive absolute as subject of a verb of movement. This verse does not deal, as such, with the subject of an overpowering inbreaking, such as described in sec. 4.1, but rather as a manner of indicating that his coming in 1:16 relates to the inspiration of Scripture and is completely marginal to the narrative and is taken from the topics of the period. Nor does 2:4b refer to an overpowering inbreaking. Perhaps, I should add also to the group of Pentecostal texts 5:32, even though it is separated by the narrative of Ananias and Sapphira. In this verse, the Spirit appears as the subject of a predicate that indicates a qualified presence more than an action. Circumstantial expressions also occur in 1:2 (doubtful); 1:5; 2:4a; 2:17, 18; 4:8; 4:25 (very doubtful); and 4:31.

Less precision exists in those stories that segment the progress from Pentecost to the central block of the Cornelius–Jerusalem Council material. The author of the material has evidently adapted somewhat diverse stories. The episode of Stephen preserves the style of the Pentecostal fullness, using, however, the adjective in place of the passive participle (6:3, 5; 7:55). The story of the Samaritans is expressed in an imprecise way— "received/receive the Holy Spirit" (8:17, 19) and "gift of God," (8:20)— and presents a diverse use of the verbal tenses. The mention of the Spirit as the subject of a passive verb breaks the monotony of the other two occurrences in the accusative in the adjoining verses. The Spirit that speaks to Philip (8:29) and to Peter (10:19 = 11:12) is a vestige of an older story that only just fits with the conception of the Pentecostal Holy Spirit. In the narrative of Cornelius, the use of the double article prevails, both with the subject and with the direct object. The conception of the Spirit, however, is presented persistently as identical to the Spirit of Pentecost. Certainly, no overpowering inbreakings occur, even though the Spirit is the subject of an intransitive verb of movement (10:44 = 11:15).

In the Pauline cycle of Acts, it is evident that the overpowering inbreakings of the Spirit predominate. The construction as grammatical subject is only slightly predominant (13:2; 16:7; 20:23; 20:28; 21:11;

and 28:25, a marginal citation of the inspiration of the Scriptures). We encounter the logical subject of the action, albeit in the genitive agent, in 13:4 and in 16:6. In spite of the prepositional expression, I have recognized an overpowering inbreaking of the Spirit in 11:28 and 21:4. Nevertheless, I have also found two examples of complementary influence with circumstantial expressions (19:21 and 20:22). The full range of colors, from complementary influence to the overpowering inbreaking, occurs. The religious density and descriptive freshness of the first narratives testify to a still living experience, expressed literally in a biblical style. The Cornelius narrative is more preoccupied with demonstrating its identification with Pentecost than with an active description of the manifestation of the Spirit. The Pauline cycle in Acts frequently introduces the Spirit as a *deus ex machina* and in repeated situations that can only have importance globally. These mentions of the Spirit appear to be used to confirm the divine origin of the act (just as visions and prophetic oracles are used) more than a lived experience. This use of the Spirit may be especially suggested by the imitation of the first part of the work. Regarding the conception of the Spirit, the second part varies a great deal from the original impulse of the first, due to a variety of sources or a variety of redactors.

The true mode of the Holy Spirit's action is that which predominates in the first part and which I have called a complementary or internal influence. It deals with a divine principle that provokes the activity of the human principal, empowering that human principal in an extraordinary manner, but without suffocating or distorting it. The human is the true subject of attribution for the historical action. But the sacred writer reveals, in the quality and the intensity of the action, the signs of a divine influence that is attributed to the Holy Spirit. This influence over the actions of persons is never attributed in Acts to angels, nor to other spirits, nor to the δύναμις, but only to the Holy Spirit.

This complementary influence is more clearly manifested with circumstantial expressions, which are encountered primarily in the Pentecostal story. It can also be expressed as a subject of actions, which may be called intermediate because they do not refer to actions that are verifiable at the historical level. For example, the Holy Spirit comes upon Cornelius and causes him to speak in tongues, but He does not speak for himself as the first mission of Paul claims to emphasize. This type of intermediate action is that which predominates in the central structure of Acts and is expressed by the double article accompanying the subject or the direct object (just as in the Lukan narrative of the baptism at the Jordan). However, in the second part of Acts, even though the preference for the subject and the double article is maintained, true inbreakings of the Spirit which overpower the activity of the human person occur.

There are, then, two modes of the Holy Spirit's action according to the book of Acts: (1) overpowering inbreakings that appear to act directly at the historical level of events and (2) the internal influence that is limited to complementing human action. This leads, naturally, to two interpretations of events, one more open and the other more nuanced by realism and theology. It is this latter which predominates in the entire first part, the more religiously dense part of the book. Consequently, the more genuine mode of the Holy Spirit's action, according to Acts, is an influence that complements human action.

4.4 Indications of a Proper Personality

The proper personality of the Spirit is an important aspect of the dogmatic theology on the Holy Spirit. However, this theme affects no more than marginally a theology of the book of Acts since it does not appear likely that the author was aware of this problem. I believe that the reader would not have proposed the question if it had not been raised by other testimonies of the dogma. Once the question is legitimately raised, it demands a reflection on the book of Acts in order to discover the possible indications that the progressive homogeneity of the revelation has been left in the conscious or unconscious thought of the writer of Scripture.

The Holy Spirit is evidently an intervention of God. The citation of Joel 2:28, which is a key to the entire Pentecost story, is expressed unequivocally, ἐκχεῶ ἀπὸ τοῦ πνεύματός μου, and the Spirit of which is spoken in Acts is the same πνεῦμα Θεοῦ that we find throughout the Old Testament tradition. If Luke has characterized him with the adjective ἅγιον (infrequent in the Old Testament), he has done so to fix it as a proper name signaling its importance. The Holy Spirit descends from above, from the Father, and consecrates Jesus as Messiah-Prophet (Luke 1:35; 3:22; 4:18; Acts 10:38). If Jesus sends the Spirit upon the disciples (Acts 2:33),[37] this deals specifically with reflecting toward the earth the

37. [Mainville's thesis, *L'Esprit*, retains a focus on Acts 2:33 throughout. Her conclusions (321–40) are consistent (unlike Lampe, "Holy Spirit") with activities of the Holy Spirit being understood as emanating from a spiritual person. —Ed.]

gift that he himself received from the Father in the moment of his exaltation. The inspiration of the Scripture is attributed interchangeably either to God or to the Holy Spirit, a sign that it refers to the one God in the speaking of the Holy Spirit. The parallelism between "to lie to the Holy Spirit" (5:3) and the following verse, "You did not lie to us but to God" (5:4), has been noted frequently. It deals with a confirmative indication but one of which an indisputably true value is not required. The author of Acts would not have had a problem in saying that to lie to an angel would be to lie to God, because he considered from whom the angel came.

Another important indication that the Spirit is God is deduced from the superiority that he has with respect both to angels and to the δύναμις.[38] But all these indications are unable to add more light to the evident clarity of the presentation that the author himself makes, especially in the theophanies at the Jordan and at Pentecost. The Holy Spirit is the Spirit of Yahweh, and his manifestations demonstrate a personal decision of knowledge and of love, of this there is no doubt. The problem is in determining at what point in Acts the Holy Spirit is conceived of as one sent from God with an independent personality. Lampe does not find in Luke the attribution to the Spirit of a true personality: "St. Luke follows the Old Testament in his conception of the nature of the divine Spirit. In his writings the Spirit is still, generally speaking, a non-person; it is the mode of God's activity in dealing with man and the power in which he is active among his people."[39] Imschoot[40] and Koch[41] distinguish three gradations in the manner in which the New Testament conceives of the nature of the Holy Spirit: (a) as a divine force; (b) as a literary personification (to this group belong Acts 4:25; 8:20; 13:2, 4; 20:28); and (c) as a true person (in Acts found only in 15:28).

This division appears to be formed from the metaphysical point of view, according to the level of certainty that the text offers that its author thought of something more than a literary personification. I prefer to maintain, as much as possible, the unity—or unities—of a

---

38. See ch. 2.

39. Lampe, "Holy Spirit," 163. [However, Lampe observes that the "Spirit comes to be thought of as something more than a divine energy" (161), concluding that Luke's "theme of the activity of the Spirit in relation to the birth, life, death, and exultation of the prophet 'like unto Moses' and in the origin, life, and mission of the apostolic Church is impressive and ably worked out" (200). —Ed.]

40. Imschoot, "Geist Gottes," 538–39.

41. Koch, "Geist," 451–52.

conception that is encountered in each book. In Acts, we have noted a Pentecostal concept that remains close to the Old Testament concept. The central concept, which should be dealt with as a whole, laying aside the fact that some texts can prove it better than others, is the concept of the second part.

We will first examine those isolated texts that are frequently cited to demonstrate the personhood of the Spirit, and we will see that in reality they do not prove this notion, not even Acts 15:28 (the only text that van Imschoot and Koch accept). Afterwards, I will attempt to analyze Luke's thought, as much as it is possible for me to do so, without worrying about the personal/impersonal dilemma. I will attempt to clarify a concept that is at times confusing, since the author's thinking evolves with regard to this concept.

The texts that are habitually cited in order to prove the personal concept of the Spirit in Acts are rather weak when considered in their immediate contexts. That the inspiration of Scripture is attributed to the Holy Spirit (1:16; 4:25; and 28:25) is no proof of the independent personality of the Spirit. The author could have thought of the Holy Spirit as a manifestation of the person of Yahweh himself, to whom is attributed the inspiration of Scripture. The attribution to the Holy Spirit is precisely one of the stereotypic formulas in pre-Christian Judaism on the inspiration of Scripture that is evidently attributed to Yahweh.[42] These texts would be sufficient to prove the divinity of the Holy Spirit, but it would be difficult to demonstrate from them his independent personality. However, it should be borne in mind that Luke does nothing more than simply repeat expressions used in reference to a theme that touches only marginally (and does not directly affect) his narrative.

To turn to texts such as 8:29; 10:19; 13:2–4; 16:6–7; 20:22–23; 20:28; and 21:11[43] is to avoid the true conceptualization of the Holy Spirit in Acts and to present the texts that demonstrate an external intervention of the Spirit as proof of his personal actuation. To anthropomorphize these texts goes too far; from the reports that the Spirit snatches up Philip, speaks to Peter, or places obstacles in the way of Paul's plans, it cannot be deduced that the Spirit is anything more than a literary device, without pretensions of presenting him as a personified concept. Also, it is common to cite the text of 15:28, "it has seemed good to the Holy

---

42. See sec. 8.1, n. 3.
43. Renié, *Actes des Apôtres*, 30; Ceuppens, *Sanctissima Trinitate*, 122–24.

Spirit and to us," but in reality this text refers to the testimony that God has shown favor to the Gentiles by sending upon them the Spirit as he did at Pentecost. This text is supported practically by 15:8, where the author has constructed the entire Cornelius narrative in order to justify the crucial decision to admit the Gentiles into the church. It does not address, therefore, a decision that the Holy Spirit made together with the apostles during the Jerusalem Council. The coming of the Holy Spirit upon Cornelius was the unique decision of the Holy Spirit or, more precisely, testimony to the decision of God. In a certain sense, this text attributes the decision to both the Spirit and God. However, we should not try to force an equality between the decision of the Spirit and that of the disciples.[44] A similar case can be seen in the appeal of Peter: "And we are witnesses to these things, and so is the Holy Spirit whom God has given to those who obey him" (5:32); even though in reality the Spirit is more the testimony than the witness.[45] Ananias' and Sapphira's resistance to the Holy Spirit could also be considered an indication of the personhood of the Spirit. However, it should be kept in mind that Stephen accuses the Sanhedrin of resisting the Holy Spirit, just as their predecessors had done, and this phrase does not appear to suggest a greater degree of independent personalization of the Spirit than that which appears in the Old Testament. Isaiah himself had spoken of those who grieve the holy spirit of Yahweh (Isa 63:10, with a double article). All in all, just as in the preceding texts, we take note of an insistent tendency toward personalization that goes beyond a mere literary device.

One difficulty could be raised by the Pentecostal expression ἐπλήσθησαν πνεύματος ἁγίου and in general by the circumstantial expressions that we have classified as the most characteristic of Pentecost.[46] These expressions create the impression of an impersonal gift, of a mere assistance by Yahweh, of a divine force that is communicated to people.

---

44. With regard to the structure of Acts, see sec. 8.4. The author presents the episode of Cornelius as a central argument in support of the admission of the uncircumcised.

45. See ch. 5, particularly sec. 5.4.

46. [These expressions contribute to the view of some scholars that the activity of the Spirit in Luke-Acts (and of course elsewhere in the NT) supports the concept of an interactive person. See the works cited in n. 5 of the Editor's Foreword to this volume; also Welker, *Gottes Geist*, 259–313; and Elbert, "Paul of the Miletus Speech," 267, who questions J. Jervell's notion of the Spirit as "impersonal force." The concept of interactive person is not necessarily that of an "independent personality" so much as one reflected in the author's "Spirit of Jesus." —Ed.]

With respect to the independent personality of the Spirit, it is probable that the first Pentecostal story contains less awareness than the general author of Acts. In examining these texts, we have the impression that we are expecting them to respond to a sketch of a personal or impersonal Spirit that was not in the mind of the author. At the conclusion of the evolution of the concept of the Spirit, we still do not know how best to resolve the personal/impersonal dilemma. But the author does not share in this dilemma; rather he is only the heir of a concept of the Spirit whose importance appears to have been made great by certain words of Jesus and by the charismatic experience of his communities. The author's most important texts proclaim the gift of the Spirit himself promised by the prophets, without adding any conscious correction.

A thought that is already encased in a writing is unable to respond to an ulterior problem; that would indicate a continuance of thought. We can find indications that this thought follows a line that leads to personification, but we cannot throw these texts out of joint with a question that they never proposed. If we truly wish to understand these texts, we must begin to walk with them from their own point of origin. Only after we have come to understand the authors' ways of thinking will we be able to propose an answer to our own question, one which will approximate how the authors themselves would have answered it.

Luke has come across diverse expressions for designating the Spirit of God: πνεῦμα Θεοῦ, Κυρίου, Θεῖον (Job 33:4), καινόν (Ezek 11:19 and 36:26), ἀγαθόν (Ps 142:10; Neh 9:20), and above all an ample series of determinations of the spirit by means of the genitive: συνέσεως (Deut 34:9; Sir 39:6), παιδείας (Wis 1:5), σοφίας (Wis 7:7), χάριτος καὶ οἰκτίρμου (Zech 12:10), κρίσεως καὶ . . . καύσεως (Isa 4:4), and the seven gifts of Isaiah 11:2 (Septuagint). The Qumran,[47] Matthew,[48] and Paul[49] have all continued using this scattering of names. However, Luke almost always uses (τὸ) πνεῦμα (τὸ) ἅγιον. And when he wanted to specify the Spirit's activity, he does not say πνεῦμα σοφίας, but rather

---

47. These differences are addressed in sec. 1.1. With regard to the diversity of these identifying names in Qumran, see Coppens, "Don de l'Esprit."

48. Matt 3:16; 10:20.

49. Here are some examples, though they are by no means exhaustive: πνεῦμα Θεοῦ: Rom 8:9, 14; 1 Cor 2:14; 3:16; 6:11; 7:40; and 12:3; Κυρίου: 2 Cor 3:17 and 2 Tim 4:22; with a genitive that designates its effect: Rom 1:4; 8:15; 11:8; and Eph 1:17. Also the term *Holy Spirit* is used twelve times (see sec. 1). 1 Thes 4:8 and Eph 4:30 are also notable, "And do not grieve the Holy Spirit of God . . ."

πνεύματος καὶ σοφίας (6:3, 10) and πνεύματος ἁγίου καὶ πίστεως (6:5; 11:24). Luke employs the same term whether he is addressing a manifestation of glossolalia, the testimony of Peter (4:8), fearless evangelization (4:31), or when he is addressing faith, wisdom, or joy. This persistence in the use of the same term, *Holy Spirit*, indicates that the author is not thinking of an indeterminate force of God that produces this or that effect according to that which fits and that is only defined through such effects. The author appears to think in terms of a self-determining power of God that produces diverse effects although contained within a fixed spectrum.

By comparing the diverse means by which God acts, it is apparent that Luke distinguishes carefully between the message given by means of an angel or the δύναμις or one given by means of the Spirit. The following scale may be established:

(a) The δύναμις is an energy with its source in God that realizes transformations of a physical order such as healings (4:33; 6:8; 10:38). It appears, however, to differ only in intensity from a true human δύναμις (3:12; 4:7). Evidently, it does not deal with any emanation from Yahweh, but does perhaps preserve something of the concept of natural, mysterious powers, in this case given by God. It is very significant that Luke has only expressed this power with an article in the case of Simon the Magician, who was considered to be a personification of the mysterious prevenient forces of God ("This man is that power of God which is called Great," 8:10, with a double article). Luke also speaks about the power of the Holy Spirit (1:8). I would not go so far as to say that here the power has the same sense as in other texts. Nevertheless, it does not fail to have a certain physical aspect that is ultimately dependent on the Spirit, ". . . until you have been clothed with power from on high" (Luke 24:49).[50]

(b) The angel represents an emissary, a person totally distinct from the divine being, charged with an anthropomorphic transmission of a divine message by means of dialogue or a physical intervention in events. The importance of the message may be great, but in such cases the angel simply announces a direct action of God. The action of the angel is in no way comparable to God's action.[51]

(c) The action of the Spirit is less material than that of the δύναμις and less anthropomorphic than that of an angel. It is always much more

50. See sec. 2.1 and also the conclusions in sec. 4.3.
51. See sec. 2.2.

important than either of them and on a determined scale of effects can almost be mistaken for the action of God. This could indicate that this refers to an intervention by Yahweh himself. We can note, however, that Luke employs another series of expressions in order to refer to a direct action of Yahweh.

(d) The exaltation of Jesus should be to τῇ δεξιᾷ οὖν τοῦ Θεοῦ (2:33). His saving power manifested in exorcisms, which demonstrates the presence of the kingdom, finds its origin ἐν δακτύλῳ τοῦ Θεοῦ (Luke 11:20) or in the hand of the Lord. Both the right hand and the finger or hand of God designate the intervention of Yahweh in a more immediate manner than the intervention by means of the Spirit.[52]

These indications appear to demonstrate that Luke goes beyond a mere anthropomorphic personification of the Spirit in his narratives, and it is with this same concept that Luke represents the Spirit as a particular, precise, and constant manner of God's acting, but in a certain sense without God acting for himself as when he acts with his right hand or his finger. God anoints the Messiah with his Spirit and gives him the Spirit in order to pour it out on his disciples, but raises him with his own right hand. Another indication of independent personality, even though more unconscious in Luke, can be seen in the important role that the Spirit begins to play with respect to Christians. Even though Luke never expresses the necessity for the gift of the Spirit, evidently he understands it to be the gift of the promise fulfilled in them. In fact, he presents it as a normal experience for the communities and as a key question that serves as proof for Paul of the Ephesians' faith (19:2–3).

We can discover in the three important steps of the Christian life a correspondence to the action of the three persons of the Trinity. The Father offers salvation directing a person to Jesus and calling him to faith. Jesus bestows salvation by means of the invocation of his name and baptism. The possession of the Spirit is the gift that crowns the work of salvation, whether in its dynamic earthly aspect or in its joyful eschatological aspect. The initiative is attributed to the Father, the realization to Jesus, and the unfolding and fulfilling joy to the Holy Spirit. I do not claim with this understanding to arrive at any logical conclusion. It only addresses indications of the growing personification of the Spirit. It will not be through the conception of the Spirit that a richness of monotheistic faith with a plurality of persons will be arrived at. This understanding

---

52. See sec. 2.1.

takes the step of being prepared for faith in the divinity of Christ. Only to the extent that we are conscious of the equality of Jesus and the Father is a Trinitarian reflection possible. At this point it must be recognized that the Christology of Acts does not come to the point of clearly proposing equality between Jesus and the Father, and it frequently presents a nuance of subordination.[53]

In conclusion, I accept as fundamental the position of Jacquier: "Nothing allows us to respond clearly to the question of whether the Holy Spirit was designed as a person or whether it was viewed as a cornerstone impersonal, sent by God or coming from him."[54] I believe, however, that there are sufficient indications, although not actual proofs, to suggest something more. Knox suggests incidentally a personification similar to that of Wisdom in the wisdom books, but he addresses only an approximate correspondence.[55] With respect to the personality of the Holy Spirit, Acts finds only a dim reflection of personhood that can only be fully understood in the light of later developments. But these developments are lacking to a certain degree in the expressions used in this book. The only thing that can be said with confidence is that, in Acts, a notable progress toward the personification of the Holy Spirit, which goes beyond mere literary personification, is manifested. The constant attribution of a well-determined series of important interventions in the history of salvation appears to reflect a mind that conceives of the Spirit practically as a subject of attribution, divine and distinct in a certain manner from Yahweh, even though Acts does not directly introduce the problem of the distinction between the two.

---

53. See Dupont, *Études*, 105–15.

54. "Rien ne nous permet de répondre nettement à la question si l'Esprit-Saint était conçu comme une personne ou s'il était regardé comme un élement impersonnel, envoyé par Dieu ou venant de lui" (Jacquier, *Actes*, ccix).

55. Knox, *Acts*, 92. See Goitia, "Noción dinámica del pneuma," who believes that the personality proper of the Spirit is found nowhere else but in John. Also, del Moral encounters it in the first part of Peter in his article "Sentido trinitario."

PART TWO

The Effects of the Holy Spirit

5

Testimony and Evangelization

5.1 Presentation of the Theme

PART 1 DEFINED THE reality identified in Acts as the *Holy Spirit*, contrasting it to other divine interventions and promises. Part 2 examines the effects attributed to the Spirit. The work of the Holy Spirit that is most emphasized in Acts is that of *testimony*.[1] We find it explicitly attributed to the Spirit in the book's key passages. The narrative opens with the promise of Christ that will serve as a prophetic program for the events that follow: "But you shall receive power when the Holy Spirit has come upon you; and you will be my witnesses in Jerusalem, in all Judea and Samaria and to the ends of the earth" (1:8). The author presents here, in a global manner, the entire activity of the apostles as a testimony under the impulse of the Holy Spirit.

With the promise of Pentecost fulfilled, the activity of the apostles begins to unfold, described at times as *testimony* and more frequently as *evangelization*. An awareness of the extent to which these two concepts correspond as well as the explicit and implicit dependence of each concept on the Spirit is needed. For now, observe two passages from

---

1. With respect to testimony in Acts, see Casey, "Μάρτυς"; Strathmann, "μάρτυς"; Cerfaux, "Témoins du Christ"; Rétif, "Témoignage et predication missionaire"; Michl, "Geist als Garant"; E. Günther, "Zeuge und Martyrer" (where he summarizes his work *Martys Geschichte des eines Wortes*); Menoud, "Jésus et ses témoins"; see also von Baer's observations in *Heilige Geist*, 98–108; Trocmé, *Livre des Actes*, 65–70; Brox, *Zeuge und Märtyrer*, esp. the first and second parts; La Potterie, "Notion de témoignage"; idem, "Paraclet" (examined in his *La vie selon l'Esprit* [see too de La Potterie and Lyonnet, *Christian Lives by the Spirit* —Ed.]); Comblin, *Témoignage et l'Esprit*, on Luke and John.

the Pentecostal context: "And we are witnesses to these things, and so is the Holy Spirit whom God has given to those who obey him" (5:32), and "they were all filled with the Holy Spirit and spoke the word of God with boldness" (4:31). The relationship between the Holy Spirit and testimony reappears explicitly at the climactic moment of the book—when the gospel of Christ is delivered to the Gentiles: "And God, who knows the human heart, testified to them by giving them the Holy Spirit, just as he did to us" (15:8). In these texts, the complexity of the notion of testimony is already apparent. The Spirit is promised as a power that enables testimony to the ends of the earth. This testimony is more frequently designated as *evangelization*. (Peter, however, distinguishes proper testimony from a direct testimony of the Spirit.) This complexity of the notion of testimony in Acts, and in the later books of the New Testament, is an indication of the urgency with which this new concept is elaborated. Its importance is paramount for the new generations that would not have known Christ.[2] Menoud perceives *testimony* as the unifying principle in Luke-Acts ("Jésus et ses témoins").[3]

Before studying the relationship between the Holy Spirit and testimony in Acts, it seems useful to provide an overview of all the texts that deal explicitly with testimony. I do not wish to enter into the extensively problematic issues surrounding testimony but only to concentrate on

---

2. Acts mentions testimony thirty-eight times, of which twenty-nine are in the Christian religious sense. This concept developed when it became necessary to reflect on and justify the means by which the word of God had been transmitted. John gives *testimony* a particular theological sense. In the Gospel of John, the idea of *testimony* appears forty-seven times, seventeen times in his epistles, and nineteen times in Revelation. On the other hand, in the Synoptics it appears six times each in Matthew and in Mark, of which four in Matthew and five in Mark have a profane or vulgar sense. In Luke it appears seven times, of which five have a profane sense. The first uncertain steps toward an evolving theme leave footprints that are difficult to reconcile. Congar ("Saint-Esprit et le corps apostolique réalisateurs," 26 n. 7) lamented the lack of detailed study on the theme.

3. Luke would have wanted to show that the foundation of the church is Christ and the apostles; immediate witnesses who were especially chosen by God for this mission. In his Gospel, Luke had spoken of Christ; he would have, therefore, needed to complete his idea with a second book on the testimony of the apostles. So too, Brox (*Zeuge and Märtyrer*, 43): "Within the Lukan Theology, the firmly set outlook of the disciples plays a decisive role. It is a somewhat key idea in the understanding of the Lukan portrayal of the beginnings of Christianity [Innerhalb der lukanischen Theologie spielt eine ganz bestimmte Anschauung vom Zeugen eine entscheidende Rolle. Sie ist in etwa ein Schlüsselbegriff zum Verständnis der lukanischen Darstellung der Anfänge des Christentums]."

the influence that the Holy Spirit exercises over the theme as a whole. I have collected the various texts that deal with testimony together on one table where the person who offers the testimony and the content itself are indicated.[4] Even though we will not go extensively into this problematic topic with respect to the technical details of the expressions considered, I have considered (as a way of basic orientation) the recipients of the testimony and the vocabulary employed in each case. In the table, the references to *testimony* in the profane sense are not included,[5] neither is the relationship with the vocabulary of *evangelization*, which would have enlarged the table excessively. The following three observations explain the table: (a) First, we observe that the subjects that testify are the apostles, preferably as a group. This also applies to Paul in the second part and even refers to Stephen. In the biblical language, we should not be surprised that God himself appears as a subject who testifies. Nevertheless, the express mention of the Holy Spirit as a subject who testifies will require a separate section in order to consider a particular aspect of testimony that I believe is of great importance for our understanding of the work of the Spirit in Acts.

(b) With respect to the object of testimony, there is evidently an evolution that is not haphazard but which is propelled by the same expansive force of testimony. The first object of testimony is the risen Christ. It is in this sense that 1:8 should be understood, "you will be my witnesses," but this emphasis appears especially evident in Acts in 2:32; 3:15; 5:32; 10:41; and most notably 4:33, "With great power the apostles gave their testimony to the resurrection of the Lord Jesus . . ."

Testimony extends from the very beginning of Jesus' life. The indecisiveness in 1:22 is notable, in which a new witness is required to have accompanied Jesus from his baptism by John; nevertheless, it is specified that "one of these must become a witness with us to the resurrection." In 10:39, Peter presents himself before Cornelius as one of the "witnesses to all that he did both in Judea and in Jerusalem," in order expressly to add the testimony of the resurrection with the full guarantee of those "who ate and drank with him after he rose from the dead" (10:41). In the same discourse before Cornelius, Peter passes directly from historical testimony (*Tatsachezeuge*) to confessional testimony (*Wahrheitszeuge*

---

4. See the table at the end of this section.

5. See 6:3; 10:22; and 22:12 in the sense of a good reputation; 6:13; 7:58; 22:5; and 26:5 with a legal sense. I also omit three passages that refer to the OT (7:44; 10:43; 13:22).

or *Bekennerzeuge*): "He commanded us to preach to the people, and to testify that he is the one ordained by God to be judge of the living and the dead" (10:42).

In the second part, the testimony of Paul refers directly to the redemptive plan: the messiahship of Christ (18:5), the penitence and faith in Christ (20:21), the announcement of the grace of God (20:24), and the plan of universal redemption through the death and resurrection of Christ (26:22–23), different aspects of a single reality that can be summarized as testimony about the kingdom of God (28:23) or about the Lord (23:11). This application of the object of testimony to the truthfulness of testimony led *in practice* to an assimilation of testimony and evangelization. Generally, they deal with the same situation that can be considered either testimony or *kerygma*. The preaching of Peter is at one and the same time both testimony and evangelization, even though the nuance of testimony predominates. However, as we move away from the earliest days, the evangelistic aspect begins to predominate. The preaching of Paul is a typical case of this gradual prevailing of evangelism. Cerfaux has proposed a rather precise distinction between these two aspects. *Testimony* would be offered before Jewish communities (preferably in Jerusalem, but also in the mixed communities of the Diaspora) and pertains most appropriately to the Twelve. *Evangelization* would designate the transmission of the message to the Gentiles. Rétif, on the other hand, has shown that these two categories cannot be neatly contrasted in this way without a forced reading of certain passages.[6]

It appears clear that the mission of the witness has a particular significance in Acts that should not be forgotten (1:21–22; 10:41; 13:31–32). However, it should be recognized that Acts has not been able to maintain the exclusivity of these terms. Menoud has emphasized the value of the mission that distinguishes the witness (μάρτυς) from the mere spectator of the events (αὐτόπτης). More artificial is his designation of Paul and Stephen as witnesses.[7]

An incipient theological interpretation can be seen in the theme of testimony that does not evolve harmoniously. Early on, one could refer

---

6. See the articles by Cerfaux and Rétif cited in n. 1 above. This theme is further explored in sec. 5.2.

7. See Menoud, "Jésus et ses témoins." A greater arbitrariness actually results from proposing testimony and evangelization as divergent activities, as in Comblin, *Témoignage et l'Esprit*.

to testimony before tribunals. Luke would understand it in a more positive sense as an evangelization that is qualified by the special mission of the messenger. Later on, the importance of the testimony of blood is imposed, obscuring the positive aspect that Luke had developed. With respect to the influence of the Holy Spirit, sec. 5.2 examines the texts that refer to positive testimony and to evangelization.

(c) As to the use of vocabulary, the prevalence of the substantive μάρτυς is notable, and its application is exclusive, in the first part, to the Twelve. In the election of Matthias, this exclusivity is set out with careful deliberation (1:22, 24). Peter distinguishes between the people and the apostles "chosen by God as witnesses" (10:41). Paul himself, according to Acts 13:31–32, distinguished between the testimony of the apostles and his own evangelistic mission. In the second part, the title of *witness* is extended to include Paul and Stephen.

In order to study the relationship between the Holy Spirit and testimony, the material is divided into the following sections: Sec. 5.2 examines the relationship to testimony that we can call *ordinary* or *continuous*, which is announced as a program of the book in the promise of Christ and which, practically, is mixed with evangelization. Sec. 5.3 examines the cases of testimony before tribunals that represent a line of thinking that is very characteristic of the Synoptics. Secs. 5.4 and 5.5 deal with a very distinct aspect of testimony, namely, the testimony that the Spirit himself gives directly, as something distinct from the testimony that he brings by means of the apostles. Sec. 5.6 summarizes the findings.

"Testimony" in Acts

Verse	Subject	Object	Audience	μά–ρτυς	μαρτυρέω	διαμαρ–τύρομαι	μαρτ–ύριον	μαρτυρία
1:8	Apostles	Risen Christ	Universal	*				
1:22	Apostles	Resurrection	Universal	*				
2:32	Apostles	Resurrection	Jews	*				
2:40	Peter	(Repentance/Salvation)	Jews		*			

Verse	Subject	Object	Audience	μά—ρτυς	μαρτυρέω	διαμαρ—τύρομαι	μαρτ—ύριον	μαρτυρία
3:15	Apostles	Resurrection	Jews	*				
4:33	Apostles	Resurrection	Jews				*	
5:32	Apostles/H.S.	Resurrection/Salvation	Jews	*				
8:25	Peter & John	Word of the Lord	Samaritans			*		
10:39	Apostles	Life of Jesus	Cornelius	*				
10:41	Apostles	Resurrection	Cornelius	*				
10:42	Apostles	Jesus as judge	Cornelius			*		
13:31	Apostles	Jesus	People (Jews)	*				
14:3	God	Message of Grace	Iconiumites		*			
15:8	God	God's acceptance of Gentiles	Jews/Gentiles		*			
18:5	Paul	Jesus=Messiah	Jews			*		
20:21	Paul	Penitence/Faith	Jews/Greeks			*		
20:23	Holy Spirit	Tribulations	Paul			*		
20:24	Paul	Gospel	Jews/Gentiles			*		
22:15	Paul	Seen and heard	Universal	*				
22:18	Paul	Jesus	Jews					*
22:20	Stephen	Jesus	Jews	*				

Verse	Subject	Object	Audience	μά-ρτυς	μαρτυρέω	διαμαρ-τύρομαι	μαρτ-ύριον	μαρτυρία
23:11	Paul	Jesus	Jerusalem/Rome		*	*		
26:16	Paul	Things seen/to be shown	Gentiles	*				
26:22	Paul	Messiah/Resurrection	Universal		*			
28:23	Paul	Kingdom of God/Jesus	Jews			*		

5.2 The Holy Spirit and Evangelism

We have just seen that the object of testimony coincides with the object of evangelism. Testimony and evangelism are two aspects of the same reality.[8] In the words of Rétif, *kerygma* is testimony informed by a mission.[9] Acts applies two derived verbs from the terminology of testimony to the evangelistic action of Paul: διαμαρτύρομαι and παρρησιάζομαι. This true inseparability of testimony and *kerygma* obligates us to treat them together in their relationship to the Holy Spirit. Rétif is right when he says that confusion results when two concepts that are aspects of the same reality are strictly separated.[10] Acts attributes the evangelistic impulse to the Spirit, just as it attributes testimony to the Spirit.

8. See in sec. 5.1 the discussion of the object of testimony, and the bibliography provided above in n. 1. See also Asting, *Verkündigung des Wortes*, esp. 336–47 and 599–615; and the interesting note by Reicke, "Zum Begriffe Martys," 52, which underscores the correspondence in many passages between testimony and evangelism (Luke 11:48; 21:13; 24:48; Acts 1:8; 4:3; 22:18); Boer, *Pentecost and Missions*; López-Gay, *Espiritu Santo*. [Re: this contemporary relevance of evangelism and mission, see too "Applying Luke-Acts" in Stronstad, *Prophethood of All Believers.* —Ed.]

9. Rétif, "Témoignage," 163.

10. Rétif ("Témoignage," 156) comments on the exclusivist position of Cerfaux with respect to testimony with the following observation: "Excesses of interpretation of this kind are perhaps due to the fact that we dissociate the word from the object in scriptural reality without considering the object in its concrete dimension. From there we focus

Von Baer dedicates a chapter to the theme "The Holy Spirit and Missions Proclamation" ("Der Heilige Geist und die Missionsverkündigung"), in which he presents the Spirit as "The Driving Force and Road Signs of Proclamation" ("Triebkraft und Wegweiser der Verkündigung"), recognizing in it the principal work of the Holy Spirit in Acts: "He did not wish *in the first place* to give an exhibition of souls from the moral-religious renewing power of the Spirit, but the outward in appearance of the power the fearless spirit of Missions, that the proclamation of the exalted Lord is poured out in the world. This is *the baseline* that Luke pursued in the second part of his outline."[11] Schweizer also joins the aspects of testimony and evangelism, by attributing them to the Spirit: "In particular, however, the preaching of the disciples is ascribed to the Spirit. This is a divine miracle, though it is preaching to a hostile world which persecutes the preachers."[12] I do not agree, however, with the second part of the quote, as it appears to me that Luke focuses more on an optimistic and expansive testimony, without emphasizing the enmity of the hearers, even though it evidently exists.

In order to analyze the diverse situations in which Acts relates evangelism with the Spirit, I begin by noting the vocabulary employed. I have already pointed out the vocabulary of *testimony* and now will look

---

only on the examination of the word, without remembering that the object may arise and exist without the word being pronounced. Thus, in this case, there is de facto in the Scripture some kerygma where the technical word is not reported, and even testimonials without the word [Les excès d'interprétation de ce cenre viennent peut-être du fait qu'on dissocie trop le mot et la chose d'une réalité scripturaire sans assez l'envisager au concret. De là vient qu'on s'attache uniquement à l'examen du mot, sans assez de souvenir que la chose peut se presenter et exister sans que le mot soit prononcé. Ainsi, dans le cas qui nous occupe, il y a de fait dans l'Ecriture des kérygmes où le mot technique n'est pas rapporté, et de meme des témoignages sans le mot]." With respect to the correspondence between testimony and evangelism, I would cite St. Thomas (*ST* III, q. 55, art. 1:2): "By this is the resurrection of Christ made plain, the lives of the witnesses of the resurrection . . . this moreover is the testimony publicly supported by public prediction [Illi, quibus manifestata est resurrectio Christi, fuerunt resurrectionis testes . . . hoc autem testimonuim ferebant publice praedicando]."

11. "Nicht ein Seelengemälde von der sittlich-religiösen Erneurungskraft des Geistes will er *in erster Linie* geben, sonder die nach aussen hin in Erscheinung tretente macht des unerschrockenen Missionsgeistes, der die Verkündigung von dem erhöhten Herrn in die Welt hinasträgt. Das ist *die Grundlinie* die Lukas im Aufriss des zweiten Teiles verfolgt" (Baer, *Heilige Geist*, 98; emphasis added).

12. Schweizer, "πνεῦμα," 408.

briefly at the vocabulary of *kerygma*:[13] (a) κηρύσσω and its semantic group designates a first announcement like an official proclamation of the message; (b) εὐαγγελίζομαι, λαλέω τὸν λόγον are the more general verbal ideas; (c) and the group διδάσκω refers to the later instruction of the believers. The terms for *evangelization* multiply at the beginning of Acts 8, in which the more or less official missions begin.

In the general presentation of the theme, as previously noted, the key text for the entire book is *the promise of the Spirit*, which initiates testimony from Jerusalem unto the ends of the earth (1:8). The author of the book employs here, just as he did in the third Gospel, the geographic plan as a literary construct of the theological content. It deals, therefore, with a clearly redactional phrase that expresses the intention of the author to place all of the work of the apostles (especially their outreach to the Gentiles) under the impulse of the Spirit. Peter alludes to this mandate/promise of Jesus in his discourse with Cornelius: "He commanded us to preach to the people and to testify that he is the one ordained by God as judge of the living and the dead" (10:42). We note the variants in both texts: Peter interprets the promise as an order, unfolds the idea of testimony in testimony and announcement of the message, and reduces perhaps the universal program ("to the ends of the earth") to refer to the Jewish people (τῷ λαῷ). This final variation could serve to emphasize the need for the testimony of the Spirit so that Peter inaugurates with Cornelius the baptism of the Gentiles. Truly, the impulse of the Spirit was necessary to open up evangelism to the Gentiles.

The same manifestation of the Spirit at Pentecost has the character of a universal promulgation of the message. Luke had wished to represent all the people of the entire earth with the insertion of a brief catalogue. But still he is dealing with Jewish devotees and proselytes from the Diaspora, established now in Jerusalem κατοικοῦντες, and they are not going to disperse as immediate proclaimers of the Gospel. The universal expansion would commence with the persecuted Hellenists and would only be inaugurated by the case of Cornelius. The Pentecostal manifestation of tongues as of fire is a symbol of the proclamation of the message that would begin immediately with the discourse of Peter. Nevertheless, I believe that this Pentecostal gift has a greater magnitude than the impulse for testimony-evangelism, as will become apparent later in our study.

13. See Friedrich, "κηρύσσειν, κτλ," 703–14.

The author sets a series of scenes in the initial post-Pentecostal period in Jerusalem in order to demonstrate this testimony-evangelism. The impulse of the Spirit is evident, although implicit, in the discourse of Peter on the day of Pentecost (2:14–39). Allusions to the underlying force of the Spirit are apparent in the introductory formula: "But Peter, standing with the eleven . . . raised his voice and addressed them [ἐπῆρεν τὴν φωνὴν αὐτοῦ καὶ ἀπεφθέγξατο αὐτοῖς] . . ." (2:14). The interpretation of all that followed as the infusion of the Spirit (2:17, 33) refers perhaps more directly to glossolalia, but we do not have the right to restrict the concrete and immediate character of the words "this that you both see and hear."[14] Peter's discourse appears to form part of the manifestation of the Spirit as the prophecy that interprets the preceding glossolalia.

Among the references to testimony or to proclamation of the message in the first days of Pentecost, some lack an explicit allusion to the Spirit (3:15; 4:2, 17; 5:20, 42).[15] Others make an implicit allusion by way of a certain characteristic term: "With great power [δυνάμει μεγάλῃ] the apostles gave their testimony to the resurrection of the Lord Jesus" (4:33).[16] Peter also appears to allude to the irresistible force of the Spirit when he declares: "Whether it is right in the sight of God to listen to you rather than to God, you must judge; for we cannot keep from speaking about what we have seen and heard" (4:19–20).[17]

---

14. [For discussion of this phrase from 2:33 in its narrative context, see Menzies, *Development*, and Mainville, *L'Esprit*, passim. Similar to Haya-Prats at this juncture is Keener's (*Spirit in the Gospels and Acts*, 200) observation that "Acts 2 is programmatic for the church in Acts. The church is a missionary church in the rest of Acts because they waited first to receive divine enablement. Luke's narrative examples in Acts 2 of prophetic inspiration in speech and longer-range witness of lifestyle presents his readers with the ideal model for Spirit-empowered Christianity, a lifestyle intended to display the character of the coming kingdom." —Ed.]

15. 5:20 attributes to an angel the exhortation to continue the proclamation of these words of life.

16. Concerning the association of δύναμις and Spirit see 1:8, "you will receive power when the Holy Spirit has come upon you"; sec. 2.1 is devoted to the relation between the two concepts. Acts 4:33 specifies the impulse of the Spirit that has just been described in 4:31, even though they belong to different contexts. The proclamation of the word that 4:31 mentions as an effect of the coming of the Spirit cannot correspond to more in this period than to the apostles themselves cited in 4:33 with regard to the aspect of testimony.

17. See sec. 2.1.

These references to testimony and to the proclamation of the message express situations that are similar to others that are explicitly attributed to the Holy Spirit. At the end of the community's public prayer "they were all filled with the Holy Spirit and spoke the word of God with boldness" (4:31). This text refers to the apostles, for until deacons were selected no one else was thought of as a proclaimer of the word. It referred, therefore, to a fresh burst in the activity of the Spirit that had already begun and that extended at least throughout the entire time spent in Jerusalem. Concerning the deacons associated with the work of the apostles, we are told that they were men full of the Holy Spirit and wisdom,[18] and that Stephen appears to be irrefutable, so that his adversaries could not resist "the wisdom and the Spirit with which he spoke" (6:10).

Acts 8 initiates the period of evangelistic expansion. In it, kerygmatic terms are multiplied, while those referring to testimony diminish. In all of these chapters, until Paul's missions commence, we find no attribution to the Holy Spirit other than that which is cited in Peter's discourse before Cornelius in which he alludes to the mandate/promise of Christ.[19] In the narratives of the activity of Paul in the second part of Acts, we find few references to the Spirit, and even these are in a less dense style than those at Pentecost. First of all, we know that Ananias was sent to Paul "so that you may regain your sight and be filled with the Holy Spirit" (9:17), but it is never explicitly apparent that his activity derives from that fullness. We can find an allusion in the application of the term μάρτυς (22:15; 26:16) and derivative verbs (18:5; 20:21, 24; 22:18; 23:11; 26:22; 28:23), but it is evident that the vocabulary has lost

---

18. Haenchen (*Acts*, 271 = *Apostelgeschichte*, 223–24) interprets wisdom in the sense of "Praktische Lebensklugheit" (lit. "practical life cleverness," or common sense), but in v.10 he necessarily recognizes its true sense of profound religious knowledge and expressive force. Even though the first intent of the election of the seven was table service, the intention of the author in inserting it into the work appears to be the extension of the message to include the Hellenists and Samaritans through the work of Stephen and Philip. In that case, it appears most probable that he has interpreted the wisdom of the deacons in light of the function of the next work of evangelism. See sec. 7.1.

19. The intervention of the Spirit that snatched Philip away and deposited him in Azotus, from which point he continued on his evangelistic journey (8:39–40), can be interpreted as an impulse for evangelizing these cities. However, due to the similarity between this spirit and the angel mentioned in 8:26, and because of the singular character of this inbreaking so discordant with the Pentecostal style, I prefer not to have this allusion in mind; see sec. 2.2.

the technical force of the first part of Acts. We find, nevertheless, certain specific texts that reveal the impulse of the Spirit for evangelism. This impulse is given, in accordance with the style of the second part, in the form of missions. "While they were worshipping the Lord and fasting, the Holy Spirit said, 'Set apart for me Barnabas and Saul for the work to which I have called them.' . . . being sent out by the Holy Spirit . . . they proclaimed the word of God in the synagogues of the Jews" (13:2–5). The Holy Spirit impeded evangelization in certain regions, while evidently directing it toward others (16:6–7);[20] in Jerusalem Paul testified, saying, "as a captive to the Spirit, I am on my way to Jerusalem . . . if only I may finish my course and the ministry that I received from the Lord Jesus, to testify to the good news of God's grace" (20:22, 24).[21]

In summary, the promise of Jesus (1:8) refers to the impulse of the Spirit for testimony and for evangelism, though more directly for testimony. Perhaps, one could add that as such it refers to evangelism in so far as it has a part in testimony. At least all of the texts that relate to the Spirit and evangelism retain some aspect of testimony. The author sees this promise fulfilled in the activity of the apostles, those who he sees as obligated to add other proclaimers of the word, ideally in respective concentric circles, each one more open than the last. As the narratives progress, the activity of the Spirit gradually disappears and becomes more conventional. This is probably not an intended effect but is drawn from the documents used in redacting the book.[22]

5.3 Testimony before Tribunals

Section 1.1 illustrates that the assistance of the Spirit before tribunals is one of the Synoptic teachings concerning the Spirit, but that Luke reserved its development for his second book. Most significantly, our attention is called to the similarity between Luke 21:15, "for I will give you words and a wisdom that none of your opponents will be able to withstand or contradict," and Acts 6:10, "But they could not withstand the wisdom and the Spirit with which they spoke." Nevertheless, we note that, in Acts, testimony before tribunals is an occasional circumstance of the overwhelming testimony that the Spirit compels through the apostles.

---

20 See the interpretation of those passages in secs. 4.1 and 4.2.

21. It is not certain that the Spirit mentioned in 20:22 is the Holy Spirit. See sec. 4.2.

22. See sec. 5.3.

In fact, this testimony before tribunals has hardly any of the tremendous and apocalyptic character of the Synoptics. Although the entire book of Acts develops to the rhythm of persecutions, testimony ordinarily acquires a triumphant and expansive air, very distinct from the almost defiant character that the Synoptics attribute to it.[23] Practically, we encounter only three references to the assistance of the Spirit before tribunals.[24]

The episode of Stephen clearly develops within the style of the Synoptics with respect to testimony offered before tribunals. Stephen, "full of faith and the Holy Spirit" (6:5), argues with such an extraordinary ardor that his adversaries "could not withstand the wisdom and the Spirit with which he spoke" (6:10). Having been dragged before the Sanhedrin, he offers his discourse under the inspiration that transfigured him so that "his face was like the face of an angel" (6:15). The decisive act of his testimony appears expressly as an effect of the Spirit: "But filled with the Holy Spirit, he gazed into heaven and saw the glory of God and Jesus standing at the right hand of God. 'Look,' he said, 'I see the heavens opened and the Son of Man standing at the right hand of God!'" (7:55–56). These words provoke the fury of his judges and Stephen's execution, just as similar words by Jesus (Luke 22:19) provoke his definitive sentencing.

There are two other cases of testimony offered before tribunals under the impulse of the Spirit. Peter before the Sanhedrin experienced a new filling of the Holy Spirit (4:8) and proclaimed openly the resurrection of Jesus and his salvific mission. Faced with the threats of the Sanhedrin, *the community* offered up its prayer: "And now, Lord, look at their threats, and grant to your servants to speak your word with all

---

23. The commentaries are not in agreement concerning the interpretation of testimony in Matt 10:18; 24:14 and Mark 13:11. It could have a condemnatory sense as in Mark 6:11, "shake off the dust that is on your feet as a testimony against them," or simply one of an official and solemn proclamation. Brox (*Zeuge and Märtyrer*, 28–31) underscores the prevalence in Matthew and Mark of apocalyptic hostility. Luke 21:13 changes the sense of the phrase since it no longer refers to a testimony for the Gentiles but rather to an occasion for the apostles to give testimony. Haenchen, in his review of *Die Mitte der Zeit*, emphasizes, *contra* Conzelmann, the triumphal character in Acts of the spreading of the gospel.

24. The second part presents various scenes of Paul before various tribunals with a clear confession of his faith. At times the term *testimony* is explicitly used, as in 23:11, which speaks of his judgment before the Sanhedrin. In a more general manner, he is called a *witness* before the Jewish and Gentile people (22:15), "both small and great" (26:22). The vocation of testimony is attributed to Christ without mention of the Holy Spirit. But we can also attribute it to the work of the Spirit with regard to his sending him to evangelize and directing his itinerary.

boldness ... and they were all filled with the Holy Spirit and spoke the word of God with boldness" (4:29, 31). The texts cited demonstrate two characteristic forms in which the help of the Spirit in the face of trials is manifested: boldness and wisdom. Παρρησία has remained a characteristic expression of the influence of the Holy Spirit. The description of Pentecost calls attention in an impressive way to the contrast between the timidity of the disciples who were shut up in the house and the liberty with which they began to proclaim the word of the exaltation and the message of Jesus.[25] In Peter's discourse we come across the term παρρησία in what appears to be an almost incidental aside: "I may say to you confidently of our ancestor David that he both died and was buried ..." (2:29). Nevertheless, it does not appear that this allusion to the liberty of the word by Peter is casual, since it corresponds perfectly to the situation of the discourse. Little in the way of boldness is required in order to call to remembrance the death of David, but certainly a very special impulse from God is necessary in order to proclaim in front of the very people that had crucified him only fifty days previously that Jesus has been raised from the dead by God and exalted as the Messiah. The denotation of *boldness* in παρρησία refers, therefore, to the entire spirit of Peter, and it is probable that its rather strange location results from the abbreviation of a discourse that was written earlier. We encounter this same term referring to the spirit of Peter and John that disconcerts the members of the Sanhedrin (4:13). In this text, the παρρησία, besides its principal meaning of freedom of expression, alludes to a certain wisdom, as the express contrast with ἀγράμματοί ("unschooled") suggests. Before the threat of the Sanhedrin, the community asked of the Lord boldness of speech in order to proclaim the message and that he intervene with wonders (4:29). We observe in the petition a difference between the manner in which they hope to receive boldness and the manner in which the wonders that are considered to be interventions by the hand of God are realized. The prayer is accompanied by a new com-

---

25 Παρρησία retains in Acts its classic sense of "openness, outspokenness, freedom of speech" (le tout-dire, le franc-parler, la liberté de langage). In the Gospel of John, it means "openly" (ouvertement) in contraposition to "in secret" (en secreto); in the Epistle to the Hebrews and in those of John it designates confidence in God that allows one to speak without fear. See Joüon, "Divers sens de παρρησία." See also Scarpat, *Parrhesia*, esp. 81 on its sense in Acts ("courage" [coraggio]) and the summary (105); Jaeger, "Parrhesia et fiducia." [See too BDAG, 630–31; and Danker, *Lexicon*, 273. —Ed.]

ing of the Holy Spirit, but the author only designates speaking "the word of God with boldness" (4:31) as an effect of this coming. In the following summaries, the author adds that the apostles gave their testimony with manifestations of great power (4:33) and with great signs and wonders (15:12), but he avoids expressing any relationship of these events with the Holy Spirit.

We only come to encounter this term in the end of the book with the spread of evangelism to Rome: μετὰ πάσης παρρησίας ἀκωλύτως (28:31), evidently alluding to the triumphal completion of Jesus' commission, "you will receive power when the Holy Spirit has come upon you and you will be my witnesses . . . to the ends of the earth" (1:8).

Acts uses the verb παρρησιάζομαι more frequently in the Pauline cycle (9:27, 28; 13:46; 14:3; 18:26; 19:8; 26:26) with the same sense of proclaiming the gospel with liberty. However, we find no passage which explicitly relates this term with the action of the Holy Spirit. Acts 14:3, "speaking boldly for the Lord [παρρησιαζόμενοι ἐπὶ τῷ κυρίῳ], who testified to the word of his grace by granting signs and wonders to be done through them," appears to allude to 4:29–31, but the liberty of speech is not related to the Spirit but rather to the Lord (the construction with ἐπί has a nuance that is closer to *confidence*) and does not make a distinction between the derivation of this confidence and the origin of the signs and wonders.[26]

Few passages use the substantive παρρησία, but it occurs in texts that are of central importance in the structure of the book. Its meaning alludes more directly to the aspect of testimony than to that of evangelism. Its dependence on the influence of the Holy Spirit is evident in 2:29; 4:13; and 28:31, although it is only explicit in 4:31. The verb παρρησιάζομαι only occurs in the Pauline cycle and denotes also the aspect of testimony and evangelism, although with a predominance of the former, and does not appear to have been closely related to the impulse of the Spirit, although a general dependence on the Spirit could be supposed in that he directs Paul's activity.

The other aspect, perhaps more original but now somewhat eclipsed, is the wisdom that the Holy Spirit places on the lips of the witness that is interrogated by religious and civil authorities, but also upon

---

26. 18:26 refers to Apollos, but this does not clearly indicate whether his freedom of expression is attributed to the Holy Spirit (since the mention of the Spirit in 18:25 is very ambiguous) or to the instruction that he received in the way of the Lord.

the pastors of the diverse communities (6:3).²⁷ Luke expressly notes in the case of Stephen irrefutable wisdom (6:10), an eloquent discourse that reveals the direction of Israel's history and, above all, an illumination in the decisive moment that allows him to see Christ exalted to the right hand of God—the object of his testimony (7:55). In order to show the amazement of the Sanhedrin as a result of Peter and John's action, Luke inserts a phrase that at first glance appears superfluous, "... when they ... realized that they were uneducated men, they were amazed ..." (4:13). This allusion to the commonness of the apostles is not accidental but serves to contrast the wisdom of their answers, making apparent an assistance from that which is greater. For the disciples of Christ, one of the gravest problems had been confronting knowledge and the prestige of the religious authorities as they struggled to introduce a radically new interpretation of the Scriptures. John had not been the first to attribute to the Holy Spirit a mission of teaching. According to the Synoptics, the concern of the disciples in being hauled before tribunals is not so much fear as finding an adequate response. The promise of Jesus refers directly to the content of the answer: "When they bring you before the synagogues, the rulers, and the authorities, do not worry about how you are to defend [ἀπολογήσησθε] yourselves or what you are to say; for the Holy Spirit will teach [διδάξει] you at that very hour what you ought to say" (Luke 12:12).²⁸

As earlier noted, the texts that speak of the aid of the Spirit before tribunals are, strictly speaking, few in number and have a marginal value in Acts. The boldness of Peter in his Pentecostal discourse has more to do with a positive sense of testimony and an evangelistic nuance than with the negative aspect of testimony before tribunals. The boldness of Paul in Rome in particular has a totally positive sense, and he expressly lacks opposition (ἀκωλύτως). Testimony before tribunals and earthly authorities only has importance in Acts if we understand it in a broad sense, being much more positive and associated with evangelism.

The perspective of the book is very distinct from our own. The author still did not know of an apologetic based on the blood of the

---

27. The relationship between wisdom and the Holy Spirit is addressed in sec. 7.1.

28. See Mark 13:11 in a context of apocalyptic confusion that begins with the warning, "Beware that no one leads you astray" (Mark 13:5). See also Luke 21:15, "I will give you words and a wisdom that none of your opponents will be able to withstand or contradict." The parallel text in Mark 10:19 has the same sense.

martyrs,[29] nor does he take refuge in a disdainful and pessimistic dispute with the environment of the world. His apologetic is one of a convert, which calls attention to the uncontrollable expansion of the word of God (28:31) as proof of the dynamic subjugation by the Spirit. This Spirit, according to the prophecy of Joel, is the sign of salvation granted to the messianic people.

5.4 The Unmediated Testimony of the Holy Spirit

The preceding sections demonstrate how the Holy Spirit assists the apostles in their testimony, whether with that testimony which we have called ordinary and that functions *practically*, much the same as evangelism, or with the particular circumstance of testimony before religious or civil tribunals. In both cases, the intervention of the Spirit is indirect, occurring by means of the Spirit's enabling of the apostles. It was they who offered testimony under the impulse of the Spirit. The hearers would have been able to discern the presence of a supernatural force through the wisdom and extraordinary boldness of these unschooled men. This impulse of the Spirit to cause the apostles to testify could be considered also as testimony of the Spirit himself, but an indirect testimony or one that is mediated through the apostles. We find other texts in which Acts attributes direct testimony to the Holy Spirit, an unmediated manifestation of his presence, without the need to be actualized through the apostles. The apostles in the cases that follow are not the testifying subjects, but rather the recipients who benefit from it, whether this unmediated testimony of the Spirit is manifested in them or in others. Therefore, this section addresses that which we may call the unmediated testimony of the Holy Spirit himself.[30] Peter himself explicitly distinguishes his own testimony—offered, no doubt, under the action of the Spirit—and the direct testimony of the Holy Spirit himself: "We are witnesses to these things, and so is the Holy Spirit whom God has given to those who obey

---

29. Stephen is not called a witness because he dies, but rather he dies because he is a witness, according to the well-known statement by Strathmann, "μάρτυς," 494. [On Stephen and his speech, see "Die Rede des Stephanus (7,1–53)" in Pesch, *Apostelgeschichte*, I, 241–60. —Ed.]

30. This unmediated testimony should not be confused with the overpowering inbreaking (sec. 4.1). In unmediated testimony, such as will be discussed, the Spirit is not presented in an anthropomorphic form. His gifts produce an exaltation that testifies to his presence, but this is only a sign that must be interpreted in light of the Scriptures through the mediation of the church.

him" (5:32). In the decisive moment at the Jerusalem Council, Peter appealed to the direct testimony of the Spirit that had led to the baptism of Cornelius: "And God, who knows the human heart, testified to them by giving them the Holy Spirit, just as he did to us" (15:8).[31] These are the two texts that mention explicitly the testimony that is given by the Holy Spirit himself. We see other equivalent situations in which an unmediated manifestation of the Spirit serves as a guarantee or divine testimony.[32] When Peter appeals to the prophecy of Joel to interpret the wonder that all had heard and seen, he presents implicitly this outpouring of a prophetic Spirit as testimony in favor of the exaltation of Christ and of the formation of a messianic eschatological people.

The unmediated testimony of the Spirit must be expressed with a proper sign, perceptible by those to whom it is intended. In the case of Cornelius, this sign was the glossolalia that is encountered repeatedly in Acts as a sign of the initial comings of the Spirit.[33] (We will deal later in this section with other characteristic manifestations of his secondary comings.) Glossolalia occurs on the day of Pentecost,[34] in the imparting

---

31. This text requires a more formal clarification. The subject who gives the testimony is the Father (ὁ Θεός), so it appears that it is not the Spirit who testifies, but rather the Spirit *is* the testimony given by the Father. It should be noted that in addressing the election of the Gentiles to form part of the people of God, the action had to be attributed to the Father and not to the Spirit. Furthermore, when the testimony presented is a person, he likewise received the title of *witness*. In other words, God gave the Gentiles the guarantee of their election by giving them, as a testimony, the Holy Spirit, who in his turn gave his testimony by means of glossolalia.

32. Testimony here does not have the technical sense limited to the life and resurrection of Christ but would include God's entire plan of salvation. In the case of Cornelius, the verb "to testify" also does not maintain the technical sense of testimony found in the opening chapters.

33. I use the expression "initial comings" to refer to the manifestation of the Spirit among new believers in order to distinguish these from other manifestations or intensifications of his presence in those who have already received him, and I refer to those as "second comings." A typical case of a second coming of the Spirit is the filling that Peter received before the Sanhedrin (4:8).

34. Is it glossolalia or the gift of tongues? The Pentecostal wonder has been amply discussed since there are evidences of the two charisms in the story. We understand by glossolalia a type of ecstatic prayer, a hymn of praise to God in unintelligible sounds or a type of supernatural *Esperanto* (Trocmé, *Livre des Actes*, 201–6). The gift of tongues would properly be the charismatic faculty of improvising a discourse in a foreign language that is unknown to the speaker. Glossolalia manifested in the primitive communities is well attested to in 1 Cor 14. The accusation of the apostles being intoxicated appears to agree with the Pauline description. However, the text in Acts speaks of foreign languages and refers to each person understanding them in their own language.

of the Spirit to the Samaritans (according to what can be inferred from the attitude of Simon the Magician, 8:15–17), on the Spirit's coming upon Cornelius (10:46), and finally with the baptism and laying on of hands of the Ephesian disciples (19:2–6).[35] Two other passages very probably allude to glossolalia as an unmediated testimony of the Spirit. One of these has already been addressed in sec. 3.1, that is, 2:38, "Repent, and be baptized every one of you . . . and you shall receive the gift of the Holy Spirit." We could say that the entire context is determined by the citation of Joel and, therefore, that the gift of the Spirit refers primarily to the prophetic gift that is promised there, a prophetic gift that Peter interprets in his discourse as divine testimony to the inauguration of the eschatological age.[36] The other text is less specific: "we are witnesses to these things, and so is the Holy Spirit whom God has given to those

---

Lyonnet, ("Glossolalia Pentecostes eiusque significatione") interprets this to refer to a charismatic glossolalia and at the same time to an interpretation that occurs in well-disposed hearers. With regard to our theme of the relation of the Spirit to testimony, I would see any of these interpretations as equally possible; however, I prefer that of glossolalia. The allusions in Acts to strange tongues could be a symbolic interpretation by the author to emphasize the universalism of the new message, similar to the traditions of the proclamation of the law at Sinai in diverse languages. [However, that no "parallel" between the first Jerusalem Pentecost and the giving of the law at Sinai was intended is argued by O'Toole, "Acts 2:30 and the Davidic Covenant of Pentecost." —Ed.] Among the extensive bibliography on this theme are the selected following articles: Behm, "γλῶσσα"; Cerfaux, "Symbolisme attaché"; Davies, "Pentecost and Glossolalia"; Lohse, "Bedeutung des Pfingstberichtes"; idem, "πεντηκοστή"; Richtstätter, "Glossolalie im Lichte der Mystik"; Dupont, Études, 85–93; idem, "Première Pentecôte chrétienne." Almost all of the commentaries are in the habit of making an excursus on the theme; see, for example, Jacquier, Wikenhauser, and Haenchen. [Barrett (Acts, I, 116) argues that it would be a mistake to suppose that glossolalia was a single uniform phenomenon that always occurred in the same form. —Ed.] Section 8.1 discusses glossolalia in relation to the prophetic gift.

35. In 10:46 and 19:6 the adjective ἑτέραις with the expression γλώσσαις λαλεῖν "has only weak versional support" (BDF, 480 [3]).

36. For a commentary on the text see secs. 3.1 and 6.4. [As to the Lukan intention that 2:38 probably refers to the gift of the Holy Spirit as evidenced by glossolalia, Haya-Prats has the support of no less than Calvin himself, cf. Commentariorum Joannis, I, 30. The French theologian René Laurentin, having surveyed the relevant scholarship (Lyonnet, Jacquier, and Dupont, for example), correlates the gibes of the mockers in Acts 2:13 with Paul's description of uninitiated people or unbelievers at 1 Cor 14:23. He notes that "Our contemporary experience confirms the view of the better exegetes that the glossolalia of Pentecost (Ac. 2) is the same as the glossolalia mentioned in other passages of Acts and in 1 Corinthians 12:14. It is an inspired, disinterested, mysterious prayer of praise, not an intelligible communication in a foreign language. It is a charism given by the Spirit" (Laurentin, Catholic Pentecostalism, 230 n. 50). —Ed.]

who obey him" (5:32). The text does not say how the Holy Spirit gives his testimony, but the phrase τοῖς πειθαρχοῦσιν αὐτῷ appears to allude to new Christians, to those for whom Acts claims the charismatic experience of glossolalia.³⁷

The only instance of an initial coming of the Spirit that does not mention glossolalia would be the case of Paul (9:17). There are those, however, who note that the author passes rather quickly over these first moments of Paul's conversion. He cites the miracle and baptism but without describing the gifting of the Spirit that we know of indirectly from Ananias who was sent "so that you may regain your sight and be filled with the Holy Spirit" (9:17). It is likely that, because this scene took place in private, it did not include the charism of glossolalia as would be appropriate in assemblies of the community. The author, who finds no descriptive details of the coming of the Spirit in this scene—or for whom they appear inappropriate for a scene with an individual—is content with a simple allusion, and so reserves his pen strokes for the account of the scales that fell from Paul's eyes. It could also be the case that he will consciously avoid a direct mention of the giving of the Spirit to a convert that is not accompanied by the typical charismatic manifestations in order to avoid offending the weak.

The secondary comings of the Spirit, that is to say, his manifestation in those who have already received him, are also accompanied by external phenomenon as signs of his presence. In a certain sense, it may be considered a reassuring testimony for those who receive it and for those who witness it, but Acts never applies to these secondary comings the idea of testimony. It is necessary here to list these indications, for without these related aspects the presentation of the unmediated testimony of the Spirit would remain incomplete.³⁸ First of all, these secondary comings produce a sensation of overflowing fullness equal to the initial comings of the Spirit. The same Pentecostal verb (ἐπλήσθησαν) serves to describe the impulse of Peter before the Sanhedrin (4:8) and the impulse normally received by the community in prayer (4:31). In the community, there are men who enjoy the respect of all (μαρτυρουμένους) as being "full of the Spirit and of wisdom," from among whom the deacons are chosen (6:3).

---

37. We may deduce this from 19:2, 7 (the Ephesian disciples). Probably it is assumed in the Samaritan passage (8:14–20) and in the promise of Peter (2:38).

38. It is useful at this point to remember again the methodological observation by Rétif ("Témoignage," 163), cited in n. 9 of sec. 5.2.

Special emphasis is given to Stephen, "a man full of faith and the Holy Spirit" (6:5), and Barnabas, "a good man, full of the Holy Spirit and faith" (11:24). The same community is filled with (ἐπληροῦντο, 13:52) the joy of the Spirit.[39] Paul is filled with the Holy Spirit (13:9) and prophesies the punishment of Bar-Jesus (that would be brought about by the hand of God, 13:11). Evidently, this fullness that manifests itself in wisdom, in boldness and in joy, in solemn moments and in the ordinary life of the community, must also have a confirming effect on the community, similar to that of glossolalia.

We also find a text that appears to establish a similar relation between comforting fullness in the community and its outward action: "the church . . . had peace and was built up. Living in the fear of the Lord and in the comfort of the Holy Spirit, it increased in numbers" (9:31).[40] It is not easy to determine precisely the sense of the text. The first part refers to the interior progress of the church. Being edified and walking in the fear of the Lord are terms that are already familiar in this sense. The verb πληθύνω means to multiply and, in the middle voice, to multiply itself and to spread itself.[41] Therefore, the second part refers to the spreading of the church and agrees perfectly with the listing unto Judea, Galilee, and Samaria. The question is, in what sense is this spreading attributable to the strengthening of the Holy Spirit (τῇ παρακλήσει τοῦ ἁγίου πνεύματος ἐπληθύνετο)? Παράκλησις has the original

---

39. This is one of the more obvious cases in which the conjunction expresses a hendiadys: the joy of the Holy Spirit. Per our discussion of the use of tenses (sec. 3.2), the manifestation of the Spirit is not described in the imperfect. This tense corresponds better to the effects of the Spirit. 13:52 does not claim to say that they were filled gradually with the Spirit, but rather with the joy of the Spirit.

40. The translation of this text (9:31) comes up against a complicated structure and with an indeterminate sense of some terms. Here are some possible translations: Bover y Oliver and Burgos (*Sagrada Biblica*), ". . . and with the breath that the Spirit infused they were multiplied [. . . y con el aliento que infundía el Espíritu Santo se iba multiplicando]"; Leal (*Sagrada Escritura*), ". . . being multiplied by the impulse of the Holy Spirit [multiplicándose con el impulso del Espíritu Santo]"; Renié (*Actes*), "and with the assistance of the Holy Spirit they were multiplied [et par l'assistance du Saint-Esprit elles s'accroissaient]"; Cerfaux (in his contribution to the Jerusalem Bible), "and they were fulfilled with the consolation of the Holy Spirit [et elles étaient comblées de la consolation du Saint-Esprit]" (in a note Cerfaux proposes "they were multiplied [elles croissaient]" and the terms "assistance" and "with the encouragements" [grâce aux encouragements]); Haenchen (*Acts*, 330 = *Apostelgeschichte*, 278), "and they were multiplied by the comfort of the Holy Spirit [und sie wurde vom Trost des heiligen Geistes vermehrt]."

41. This is the sense in all of the texts in Acts: 6:1, 7; 7:17; 12:24.

sense of calling someone close to oneself (παρακαλέω), from which comes the judicial sense of *advocate* or *lawyer* (παράκλητος). From this comes the more general sense of a consolation and a comfort that gives security. Also, it is used in charismatic language in the sense of exhortation that derives more directly from the use of the verb. The substantive παράκλησις is found four times in Acts and twice in Luke. In 13:15 the synagogue officials in Antioch of Pisidia invite Paul to bring some words of comfort (or of exhortation?). In 15:31 it is used to designate the message of the Jerusalem Council. In 4:36, Barnabas is given the name Son of Consolation.[42] In these three texts, the sense can be equally consolation or exhortation. In the two texts in the Gospel, however, the sense is clearly that of comfort. Simeon was "looking forward to the consolation of Israel, and the Holy Spirit rested on him" (Luke 2:25), a synthesis of the messianic promises for the poor of Yahweh. For that reason, Luke warned the wealthy: "But woe to you rich, for you have received your consolation [παράκλησιν]" (Luke 6:24).[43]

It appears, therefore, that παράκλησις in our text signifies a consolation, or better, a comfort.[44] And within this meaning it has more in

---

42. The character of Barnabas stands out more by means of his goodness and understanding that encourages every good initiative than by means of his oration. He gives away his possessions generously in order to meet the needs of the community (4:36), becomes a protector of Mark when he is beset by Paul's intransigence (15:37–40), and, most of all, being sent to Antioch, he recognized "the grace of God, he rejoiced, and he exhorted them [παρεκάλει] all to remain faithful to the Lord with steadfast devotion; for he was a good man, full of the Holy Spirit and of faith" (11:23–24).

43. [As to this παράκηλσις ("comfort," NIV) at 6:24, Schürmann (*Lukasevangelium, I*, 338) observes firmly that this saying addresses the misguided comfortable satisfaction of the present. —Ed.]

44. Jacquier (*Actes*) translates it "with the consolation [par la consolation]," but in an additional note he adds "invitation, encouragement, call, exhortation, consolation; it could have here the sense of call" [invitation, encouragement, appel, exhortation, consolation; il est possible qu'il ait ici le sens de appel]." Lemonnyer ("L'Esprit Saint Paraclet") rejects the sense of "consolation" as a deviation introduced around the fourth century, defends the sense of "exhortation," and believes that testimony and *paraclesis* are two aspects of evangelism and works of the apostles but also of the Holy Spirit directly. Lemonnyer cites numerous texts in the NT, the majority of which have an imprecise sense, but he does not cite Luke 2:25 and 6:24, which would not have the sense of the translation "exhortation." I believe that they do not refer to exhortation but to the results of exhortation, which is comfort; the provoking of dormant internal energies. I believe that the translation "exhortation" supposes an internal intervention of the Spirit in non-believers, calling and exhorting them to receive the exhortation of the apostles. For this internal action among non-believers there is not the smallest foundation in Acts. The call to faith is attributed to the Father. This action of the Spirit

common with the text of Simeon (because it mentions the Holy Spirit) than the partial consolation that Paul, Barnabas, and the Jerusalem decree were able to contribute. When the text is understood in this way, we conclude that the church multiplies due to the Holy Spirit who fortified it with the experience of possessing the messianic blessings. The messianic consolation is the external overflow of the security of the covenant with God. This consolation necessarily reinforces the efficacy of the word, both by means of the exaltation of the apostle and by means of the guarantee of authenticity that it offers the hearers. In the consolation of the Spirit, we have a case—even though it is difficult to interpret—in which the security and joy that the Spirit gives serve as confirmative testimony for those who possess it and for those who perceive it.

Perhaps, other gifts of the Spirit should also have been considered as comforting testimony for the favored ones and for the community. Such would be the charismatic faith of Stephen ("full of faith and the Holy Spirit,"6:5) or perhaps others not explicitly related to the Spirit, such as the κοινωνία. Since I have given here a sufficient idea of the testifying aspect of these experiences of the Spirit, I prefer to leave the study of these other themes for sec. 6.2 where they will find a more appropriate setting.

5.5 Characteristics of the Unmediated Testimony of the Holy Spirit

We will continue a while longer with the unmediated testimony of the Holy Spirit himself, in part because it has been less studied, but mostly because it will help us understand the action of the Spirit more intimately. We will focus on three characteristics: (a) confirmative testimony for believers, (b) confirmation through means of a discernible experience, and (c) manifestations of the plans of the Father.

(a) *Confirmative testimony for believers*. It is easy to verify that the *unmediated* testimony of the Holy Spirit is always directed to believers.[45]

---

would only result from a very imprecise translation of παράκλησις as "exhortation" and still needs to pass over the sense of exhortation of a prayer by means of his words to the direct exhortation of the Spirit without words. Renié in his commentary on the Pirot Bible expressly follows Lemonnyer. [Haya-Prats' analysis here is quite harmonious with Danker's conclusions in *Concise Greek-English Lexicon*, 268. —Ed.]

45. I am not referring to the testimony of the apostles offered under the influence of the Spirit.

Evidently, this is the case with respect to the apostles at Pentecost. That same day, in his discourse, Peter promised the gift of the Holy Spirit to those who converted and were baptized in the name of the Lord Jesus (2:38). Also, among the Samaritans and Ephesians, glossolalia appears after faith manifested at baptism (19:6). The faith of Cornelius is mentioned explicitly in 15:9, where the aorist καθαρίσας indicates a time prior to the giving of the Spirit: "God . . . testified to them by giving them the Holy Spirit . . . and in cleansing their hearts by faith he has made no distinction between them and us" (15:8–9). This priority of initial faith with respect to the coming of the Spirit and the treatment of the relation between the two is further developed in sec. 6.3. (It is highly doubtful that the mention of the Spirit in the activity of Apollos refers to the Holy Spirit. In any case, it would not deal with an influence of the Spirit prior to faith, since Apollos is understood by Luke to be a believer, albeit only partially informed.[46])

Only at Pentecost is glossolalia publicly manifested[47] with the explanation that it is an unmediated testimony of the Spirit. We note, however, that Peter does not present it as an apologetic testimony that endorses the resurrection, as will be done, though, with the miracle of the lame man at the temple (4:10, 21).[48] Glossolalia will be a sign only for those who readily receive Joel's prophecy. Only to these will it be disclosed that the Messiah has entered into full possession of the Spirit and now pours out this Spirit on his new people (2:33). The unmediated testimony of the Spirit does not have, therefore, an apologetic sense as a miracle may have. Glossolalia is a charisma, but it is not properly speaking a miracle, as are healings. Luke presents glossolalia as the typical manifestation of the Spirit, while avoiding attributing healings to him.[49]

46. See Schweizer, "Bekehrung des Apollos"; and sec. 6.4.

47. Glossolalia and the rest of the exultant manifestations of the Spirit have a place in the ritual of initiation—baptism and the laying on of hands—or in the community meetings. They do not have, therefore, an apologetic character for those who are not initiates, who it would be difficult to imagine being present in such meetings. Traces of this reservation remain in the veiled formulas that allude to the Eucharist and perhaps also, in another aspect, in 5:13, "none of the rest dared to join them," even though it refers still to the meetings on Solomon's porch.

48. ". . . this man is standing before you in good health by the name of Jesus Christ of Nazareth" (4:10). Also, it appeals to the guarantee of miracles in 2:22, ". . . Jesus of Nazareth, a man attested to you by God with deeds of power, wonders, and signs that God did through him among you."

49. See sec. 2.1.

The mission of the Spirit in Acts is not apologetic, nor is it the preparation of faith. The Spirit is manifested as a gift granted to believers. His testimony can be nothing more than a confirmation for a later maturing in faith. The extraordinary faith of Stephen and Barnabas is a charisma of the Holy Spirit, though it does not deal with initial faith but rather with an apostolic and pastoral maturation of faith.[50] The testimony that the Spirit initiates through the apostles is a kerygmatic testimony. The unmediated testimony of the Holy Spirit is directed to believers as a confirmation and maturing of their faith.

(b) *Confirmation through discernible experience.* John and Paul refer, as does Acts, to a testimony of the Holy Spirit that offers confirmation to believers. The difference between their writings and Acts is that they write in a time of reflection in which the Spirit has become an object of teaching and faith, while the narratives in Acts bear the seal of the early days in which the Spirit was not an object of teaching but of experience.[51] John speaks of this testimony among the promises made during the last supper, referring to the Spirit: "When the Advocate comes . . . he will testify on my behalf" (15:26). The context shows that this is referring to an internal confirmation for the apostles in their battle with the world, that is to say, with the same theme of testimony before tribunals but expressed in a more theological and transcendent form.[52] John describes as an abstract promise the aid of the Spirit that Acts describes in various concrete circumstances. Both agree in recognizing this assistance of the Spirit as a testimony which attests to the disciples. John considers it from within, presenting it as an internal teaching without words, a sense of security or a remembrance.[53] However, Acts views it externally, expressed in the form of impulses, of boldness, of wisdom, and of joy.[54]

---

50. The Holy Spirit and faith will be further discussed in sec. 6.3.

51. Gunkel, *Influence*, 13–14 = *Wirkungen*, 4.

52. See the commentary on these promises by La Potterie, "Le Paraclet," in *La vie selon l'Esprit*, and esp. pp. 96–101. [See the English translation in La Potterie and Lyonnet, *Christian Lives*. —Ed.]

53. ". . . will teach you everything, and remind you of all that I have said to you" (John 14:26); see 16:13–15.

54. John focuses more on the threatening tension of the fight with the world, raised to the point where its significance is more theological than anecdotal. Acts, on the other hand, describes the powerful expansion of the gospel, and its testimony has an eminently kerygmatic and optimistic sense.

Paul's thought concerning the testimony of the Spirit appears to be more remote. He also refers to it in a way that is favorable to believers as a confirmation of their faith. But the content of this testimony is neither an indeterminate teaching, as in John, nor concrete impulses as in Acts. The Spirit, according to Paul, testifies to us of the impalpable reality of our divine sonship: "It is the very Spirit bearing witness with our spirit that we are children of God" (Rom. 8:16).[55] It is not within the scope of our study to consider how this testimony is known, but we can imagine that Paul would certainly not be referring to glossolalia, upon which he looked with considerable caution (1 Cor 14). The most prominent difference between the unmediated testimony of the Spirit to which Acts refers and that mentioned by Paul and John is that the first is essentially concrete, historical, experiential, and verifiable through the senses, whereas the testimony of the Spirit according to Paul and John is a theological truth, more an object of faith than of experience. Naturally, Acts interprets the experiences sensorially. The experience of Pentecost is interpreted in light of Joel's prophecy and that of Cornelius by means of the remembrance of Christ's promise concerning the baptism of the Spirit. Every extraordinary event requires an interpretation, but this is presented in Acts as occurring spontaneously. It is sensory experience that matters most in the story.[56]

We see in Luke's collection *the sensory data* that he describes for us in the manifestations of the Holy Spirit. We note first of all the frequent use of the verbs *to see* and *to hear*. At Pentecost a mighty rushing wind is heard, the apostles' speaking in tongues is heard, and tongues as of fire that spread out among them is seen. Peter speaks in realistic terms of this gifting of the Spirit: "having received from the Father the promise of the Holy Spirit, he has poured out this *that you both see and hear*" (2:33; emphasis added). In the coming of the Spirit upon the community in prayer, the structure in which they found themselves meeting was

---

55. See Gal 4:6, "that you are children is shown in that God has sent the Spirit of his Son into our hearts, crying, 'Abba! Father!'" (author's translation). This explanatory sense of ὅτι appears preferable to the causal sense "because you are children . . . has sent . . ."

56. If the description of such experiences has been amplified literarily—which seems highly probable—the value that the author attributes to the verifiability of such interventions of the Holy Spirit appears all the more evident. A typical case of literary expansion could be the imprisonment of Paul in Philippi with the earthquake and subsequent conversion of the jailer (16:19–40).

once again shaken (4:31). Simon the Magician, an expert in dazzling demonstrations, *saw* that by the laying on of the apostles' hands the Holy Spirit was given (8:18) and was prepared to purchase this ability, which was doubtless more spectacular than his own skills. The glossolalia of Cornelius is such strong evidence that it overcomes the indecision that Peter harbored even after the visions and the words of the Spirit. In the same way, it overcame the prejudices of his companions from Joppa and those present at the Jerusalem Council. The verifiability of such manifestations seems a natural assumption in Paul's questioning of the Ephesian disciples as to whether they had received the Holy Spirit. The author adds that with the laying on of Paul's hands the Holy Spirit came upon them and they spoke with tongues and prophesied.[57] The reaction of bystanders underlines the sensory character of such manifestations of the Spirit. This reaction is (1) bewilderment before the unfamiliar and (2) amazement before a superior, uncontrollable force. Acts employs the verb θαυμάζω in an intransitive form (2:7 and 4:13), which means to remain amazed and bewildered.[58] Συγχύνω in the passive form (2:6) expresses a state of internal agitation when confronted by contrary elements.[59] Διαπορέω in the middle voice has the same sense of agitation and internal confusion in which one turns first one way, then another, without encountering a solution.[60] Ἐξίστημι in the middle voice (2:7, 12; 10:45) has the sense of remaining outside of oneself.[61] These terms

---

57. The evidence of the wonders is typical of the style of Acts. The healing of the lame man is γνωστὸν σημεῖον, πᾶσιν . . . φανερόν (4:16). Peter saw a vision clearly (φανερῶς) around the ninth hour of the day (10:3).

58. Zorell, *Lexicon*, "stupeo" (amazing); Bertram ("θαῦμα, κτλ") signals the frequent use that the Synoptics make of this verb as a call to readers to take into account the extraordinary nature of the wonder. [Danker (*Lexicon*), "be extraordinarily impressed." —Ed.]

59. The sense of the passive form is found very realistically described in 19:32, "Meanwhile, some were shouting one thing, some another; for the assembly was in confusion, and most of them did not know why they had come together [συγκεχυμένη]." Equally in 21:31, "While they were trying to kill him, word came to the tribune of the cohort that all Jerusalem was in an uproar [συγχύνεται]." Zorell, *Lexicon*, cites this text (2:6) expressly with the sense of exciting confusion. [Danker (*Lexicon*), "confused and confounded." —Ed.]

60. See 5:24, "they were perplexed about them, wondering what might be going on" (διηπόρουν περὶ αὐτῶν); 10:17, "Now while Peter was greatly puzzled about what to make of the vision that he had seen . . ." (διηπόρει).

61. Zorell (*Lexicon*), "excessum mentis patior, insanio"; Zerwick (*Analysis Philologia*), "egredior ex me prae stupor." [Danker (*Lexicon*), "be amazed, be overwhelmed." —Ed.]

apply equally to human reactions to other divine interventions, such as healings or wondrous acts. Notably, the manifestations of the Holy Spirit in Acts are as highly verifiable as the case of a wondrous healing, as Acts attributes great importance to the sensory experience of the manifestations of the Holy Spirit, in contrast to Paul and John. This propensity in Luke is inexplicable by earlier known principles and is, thus, a primary principle of its own right. In Luke, it emerges as a spontaneous tendency. It is better understood by remembering Luke's situation.

Already in the Old Testament, the sensory character of the gift of the Spirit predominates, as we have seen concerning the gifting of the Spirit to the elders (Num 11; see sec. 3.2). The Pentecostal story, with its roots in Joel, had formidable influence over Luke, whether the story came as an oral tradition or, more likely, as a written story. This story begins with a sensory event in which the exaltation of the believers is contrasted with their timidity during the passion of Jesus—a timidity now conquered. Their reflection on this sensory event led them to discover the fulfillment of the prophecy of Joel concerning the outpouring of the Spirit in messianic times and with it a confirmation of their faith. The story resembles, as does Luke 1–2, a hymn of contemplative description. Paul, on the other hand, does not refer to the manifestations of Pentecost in his letters. Rather, he distrusts exterior manifestations of the Spirit and, instead, refers to the prophecies of the Spirit as a moral renewal. In order to justify the overcoming of circumcision and the law, he turns to theological/scriptural reasons, without invoking the experience of the Spirit in Cornelius' house. Neither has John made use of the Pentecostal story, in spite of having insisted on the promises concerning the Spirit. Furthermore, he has referred discretely to a Passover imparting of the Spirit devoid of sensory manifestations (John 20:22–23). Luke thinks in terms of historical facts more than he does speculative arguments. As a convert, he feels impressed by the tangible exultation in the communities and, more than anything, of the extraordinary spread of the gospel among the Gentiles. In this extraordinary phenomenon, he finds the fulfillment of Jesus' promises, as the Pentecostal story had interpreted the prophecy of Joel as the exultation of the first Jerusalem community. In the same way, he feels that these extraordinary events are able to confirm the faith of his converted brothers. The case of Cornelius is typical, which Luke has developed as a grand argument for the incorporation of the uncircumcised into the true messianic people of salvation.

The importance of the sensory aspect of the gift of the Spirit has, therefore, its origin in the more diffuse Old Testament concept that is clarified in the Pentecostal story. Luke would have assimilated easily this tendency that accommodates itself so thoroughly to his personal experiences, as it does to the confirmative finality and historical style of his work. It does not appear that we need to look for any other reasons for this sensory aspect. Rather, one would need to look in the theologies of Paul and of John and ask why they have not insisted on these experiences of the Spirit.

(c) *Manifestations of the plans of the Father.* The unmediated testimony of the Holy Spirit offers believers confirmation by means of his sensory manifestations in concrete situations. But we can still go a step further and describe in these diverse situations a constant object. The Holy Spirit in all of those instances that can be called first comings (as at Pentecost, as in the case of Cornelius, as in the incorporation of each Christian[62]) guarantees a divine pleasure with those who receive him.[63] We can see that this testimony, by means of the Spirit, to such a divine pleasure appears in the critical moments in a change of religious ethos, be it personal or collective. Pentecost signals, according to Acts, the beginning of the messianic age, which is to say, the shift from the age of the promise to the time of realization.[64] The manifestation of the Spirit confirms the new way taken, making God's pleasure obvious since he poured out his Spirit upon the new people. The new way has been adopted by faith in the message and in the resurrection of Christ. The manifestation

---

62. See 2:38; 5:32.

63. This testimony guarantees that one has entered into the messianic, eschatological people (see ch. 8).

64. If the tripartite division is preferred, I suggest the phase from the time of Christ until the time of the church. The dispersing of the Spirit, whom the Messiah had received at his exaltation, signals the beginning of the messianic work, the new people of God. [These general theological observations by Haya-Prats as to how one might see or not see various periods in the text of Luke-Acts do not at all intrude vigorously into his exegesis of the text, as they do in von Baer's *Heilige Geist* and in subsequent uncritical imitations of von Baer's intrusive tripartite epochal divisions. In this overly simplistic and narratively divisive scheme—probably a product of ecclesial "apostolic age" confinement tendencies in the Reformed tradition—no Lukan characters can experience legitimate and lasting salvation during the earthly ministry of Jesus. Luke 7:36–50, for example, is never mentioned by von Baer. Such significant texts illustrating salvation during the earthly ministry of Jesus are antithetical to the exegetical imposition of artificial divisions, just as other examples of salvation experience which are portrayed in Acts cannot be subjected to exegetical confinement in an "apostolic age" (*Pfingstzeit*) division. —Ed.]

of the Spirit confirms that this faith is agreeable to God. The same may be said of the manifestation of the Spirit in new groups that are added to the community. In the case of Cornelius, we can discern two aspects. The manifestation of the Spirit reveals the pleasure of God resulting from the conversion that took place in Cornelius. But also this is an indication for Peter that God desires the admission of the uncircumcised into baptism. That which for Cornelius was a testimony of the first coming of the Spirit (that is to say, divine confirmation of his conversion to the faith) is for Peter a testimony of the second manifestation of the Spirit (that is to say, an impulse to act in a different manner).

The experience of the Spirit that I have called *second comings* does not simply confirm with a passive joy the faith received, but rather it always signals the achievement of a new activity. It is this experience of the Spirit that compels the perilous testimony of Peter and Stephen before the Sanhedrin (4:31 and 7:55) which presses them to evangelize in spite of the threats made: "and they were filled with the Holy Spirit and spoke the word of God with boldness" (4:31). If the deacons Philip and Stephen are associated with the work of evangelism, it is because they are men filled with the Holy Spirit, and Stephen in particular would argue with the irresistible force of the Spirit (6:10). In the second part of the book, it is also the Spirit who puts Paul on the scene (13:2, 4) and guides his itineraries by means of prophetic oracles (11:28; 20:23; 21:4, 11) or by means of various impediments (16:6, 7; 20:22). The preceding chapter examined these forms of the Spirit's manifestation. Now I am interested in emphasizing that such manifestations are for Paul an indication of the plans of God.[65]

65. Such indications of the Holy Spirit were not precise orders but rather insinuations through persons, feelings, and circumstances that needed an interpretation. Paul did not allow himself to be diverted from his journey to Jerusalem, in spite of the prophets of Tyre who "through the Spirit . . . told Paul not to go on to Jerusalem" (21:4). Naturally, it is unlikely that the Holy Spirit would inspire this warning contrary to what Paul himself felt: "And now, as a captive to the Spirit, I am on my way to Jerusalem" (20:22). Dupont in his contribution to the Jerusalem Bible understands this to mean that the Spirit allowed them to know the sufferings that awaited Paul and that the prophets tried to dissuade him because of the affection they had for him. It does not appear that one has to take account of all of the details down to the last letter and then try to find a way to harmonize them. It appears rather that the passage is dealing with a religious exaltation in which it is necessary to discern what comes from God and what is human resonance with the message. In the prophets' intentions to dissuade Paul from his journey to Jerusalem, Conzelmann (*Apostelgeschichte*, 121; commentary on 21:4, 12) sees the liberty that is left to the prophets and most of all the intention of

The most important text that presents the activity of the Spirit as a sign of the plans of God is precisely the culminating point of the thesis of the book of Acts, the hinge upon which the church turns toward the Gentiles: "For it has seemed good to the Holy Spirit and to us to impose on you no further burden than these essentials" (15:28). This text appears difficult only if we try to reconstruct the scene to fit our own concerns and try to discover the forms by which the appearing of the Holy Spirit was manifested. However, if we trust the author of the book who has arranged the scenes in order to arrive at the proclamation of his thesis, it is clear that the appearance of the Spirit has been manifested in the case of Cornelius, and so insistently repeated, by the intent of the author.[66] The apostles recognize that testimony of the Spirit signals God's new plans with respect to the Gentiles, and they proclaim it for the entire church with the authority of the mission that Christ had confided in them.

5.6 Summary

The principal effect of the Holy Spirit, according to Acts, is *testimony*, as seen in the most significant passages in the book: the promise of Christ formulated as the program for the entire book (1:8), the use made of Pentecost interpreted in the light of Joel's prophecy (Acts 2–5), and the Cornelius complex (10–11), which led to a decisive point in the Jerusalem Council (15:8, 14, 28). The sense of testimony in the texts is not completely consistent. We have distinguished two large groups of texts: the first gathers the references to the testimony that the Spirit initiates through the apostles, while the second refers to the testimony offered directly by the Holy Spirit himself. The first appears as testimony

---

the author to underscore Paul's fearlessness: "Paul must work it out himself, but he says yes to his free destiny [Paulus muss ziehen; aber er bejaht sein Schicksal frei]" and "The disciples should also not, perhaps, become characterized as having so little faith. Luke wants simply to demonstrate the free readiness of Paul to suffer for the faith [Die Jünger sollen auch nicht etwa als kleingläubig charakterisiert werden; Luke will einfach die freie Bereitschaft des Paulus zum Leiden für den Glauben vorführen]."

66. The apostles also see the approving appearance of the Spirit in the entire narrative that Barnabas and Paul relate concerning their evangelistic activity: "The whole assembly kept silent and listened to Barnabas and Paul as they told of all the signs and wonders that God had done through them among the Gentiles" (15:12). However, the author has synthesized the decisive reference in the episode of Cornelius that James himself mentions in the key phrase of the entire book: "Simeon has related how God first looked favorably on the Gentiles, to take from among them a people for his name" (15:14). See sec. 8.5.

by the apostles motivated by the Spirit, because Luke, unlike Mark and Matthew, emphasizes the personalities of those who are moved upon by the Spirit. The testimony of the apostles is normally exercised by means of evangelism. Testimony and evangelism are two aspects of the same apostolic activity. The promise of Christ regarding the help of the Spirit in giving testimony (1:8) is interpreted by Peter as a method of evangelism (10:42) and by Luke himself as the program that arranges the various steps of the proclamation of the word until it arrives at Rome where it is announced "with all boldness and without hindrance" (28:31). Testimony before tribunals, which was the origin of the theme of testimony among the Synoptics, is reduced to a marginal theme in Acts. The author does not participate in the defensive Jewish pessimism that sees in testimony a defiance of the powers of the surrounding world. Luke sees with great optimism the expression of the word of God among the brothers, and considers testimony, received by the apostles from the Pentecostal Spirit, to be the driving force for evangelism.

The direct testimony of the Spirit indicates a reflection over certain wondrous events, such as glossolalia and prophecy. This reflection, though, takes place in close proximity to the events, virtually merging with them and contributing to their intelligibility. They do not have to do with a theological interpretation, as is the case with Paul and John, but with a kerygmatic presentation of the events, as that realized by the Synoptic Gospels. In describing these wondrous phenomena, and even more in interpreting them by means of discourses and biblical references, Luke has presented them as the testimony of God on behalf of his new messianic people.

The testimony that God gives on behalf of the Gentiles, sending them the Holy Spirit that is manifested in glossolalia, is identical to the testimony that he gave on behalf of the disciples at Pentecost. This testimony is interpreted in the light of Joel's prophecy, just as it comes to be interpreted in the light of baptism in the Spirit.

The direct testimony of the Spirit appears to me to be more decisive in Acts than the indirect testimony that takes place through the apostles. The direct testimony of the Spirit appears most often in a solemn form in decisive moments. It can be assumed also to be normally experienced by all of the new members of the community in the exultant form of glossolalia, and also throughout the life of the community in the experience of an overflowing joy. This direct testimony of the Spirit is always a sensory experience that confirms the faith of those who are already believers. At times, it serves as a decisive sign for knowing the plans of God concerning the community in concrete circumstances, opening unsuspected directions in evangelization.

Christian vocabulary concerning testimony did not develop along the tentative tracks established by Luke. It has developed in only one aspect, perhaps the most marginal one, but one that is dramatically tangible and decisive for the primitive church. The testimony of blood has largely eclipsed the richness of the theme of testimony in Acts and in the entire New Testament.

6

The Beginning of the Christian Life

6.1 Interpretations of the Exegetes

From a moral-biblical perspective of theology, the question arises about the influence of the Spirit on Christian conduct, which is the origin of this entire study. Such influence is one of the great Pauline themes. Now this being so, does the book of Acts, which contains the grand Pentecost narrative and that of the first Christian communities and which dedicates half of the work to the activity of Paul, fail to recognize the influence of the Spirit on Christian conduct? An initial reading of the exegetes leaves the theme rather confused. Some, crediting the impression of the book as a whole, affirm such influence of the Spirit. They assume his sanctifying presence in baptism, and they attribute to it the exemplary conduct of the first community described in the summaries in the first part of the book. Other exegetes submit the texts to painstaking analysis, dissolving completely the relation of the Spirit to Christian life. Rereading such exegetes attentively, though, warns us of a series of reservations that they themselves have seen fit to formulate. It would be difficult to divide the commentaries into two distinct groups because one has the impression that the difference between them consists in little more than the shifting of emphasis, and the degree to which this takes place varies widely from one chapter to the next within the same commentary.

Haenchen, a highly meticulous commentator, believes that Acts presents baptism as a normal means of conferring the Spirit: "[Luke] presents the Spirit as the gift which every Christian receives at baptism...."[1] "These form the preconditions for baptism, and in baptism the Spirit is bestowed. It is the Spirit which is the essence of Christian baptism and distinguishes it from John's."[2] Equally, he attributes to the Spirit the religious life of the community: "But Luke saw also another effect of the Spirit in the fact that the throng of believers were of one heart and soul ... there was no division among them."[3]

Dodd expresses the same meaning as Haenchen, although in a more general character study,[4] as does Lampe in his article "The Holy Spirit in the Writings of St. Luke." Lohse affirms explicitly the influence of the Holy Spirit on the life of the community referred to in the summaries: "Therefore, it is no chance arrangement, but rather a well thought out plan; Luke allows the whole Pentecost story to flow as a description of the life of the first Church, which draws its strength from the Spirit (2:24–47)."[5]

A tendency exists for some to see in the Pentecost narrative a parallel with the proclamation of the law at Sinai and, consequently, a presentation of the Spirit as the new law of the community.[6] Usually predominating, however, is a denial of the unity of the influence of the Holy Spirit in the Christian life according to Acts. But such denial always comes expressed with limitations. Schweizer summarizes the theme: "Luke thus shares with Judaism the view that the Spirit is *essentially* [emphasis mine] the Spirit of prophecy. This stops him from explicitly attributing to the πνεῦμα both the χαρίσματα ἰαμάτων on the one side and strongly ethical effects like the common life of the early

---

1. Haenchen, *Acts*, 92. "Einmal nämlich stellt er den Geist als die Gabe dar, die jeder Christ bei der Taufe empfängt [n.: Apg 1:5, 8; 2:4, 38]" (*Apostelgeschichte*, 83).

2. Ibid., 94. "Damit sind die Vorbedingungen für die Taufe gegeben, in welcher der Geist verliehen wird. Er macht, im Unterschied von der Johannestaufe, das Wesen der christlichen Taufe aus" (*Apostelgeschichte*, 84).

3. Ibid., 232. "Aber Lukas verstand es auch als Geistwirkung, dass die Menge der Gläubigen ... ein Herz und eine Seele war" (*Apostelgeschichte*, 190).

4. Dodd, *Predication apostolique*, 77–78.

5. "Deshalb ist es keine zufällige Anordnung, sonder überlegter Plan, dass Lukas die ganze Pfinstgeschichte in eine Schilderung des Leben der ersten Gemeinde, die aus der Quelle des Geistes ihre Kraft schöpft, ausmünden lässt (2:24–47)" (Lohse, "Bedeutung des Pfingstberichtes," 432).

6. See sec. 8.5, n. 55.

Christian community on the other."⁷ And with a similar expression, he ends by saying: "Only on the margin do we find formulae in which the Spirit is generally understood as dwelling continually in the individual or the community."⁸

Schweizer also cites von Baer in support of his view, whose thoughts can be summarized as follows: "Mission rather than moral renewal is the gift of the Spirit according to Lk. . . ."⁹ This reference, though, can only be understood to refer to the final goal of the work of the Spirit, since von Baer tends to exaggerate the range of the action of the Spirit and attributes the Christian life concretely to it in various texts: "But there are also other characteristics that indicate Spirit possession and are situated along the lines of the ethical-religious new creation of men (cf. Acts 19:2)."¹⁰ "Also brotherly love is a fruit of the Holy Spirit . . ."¹¹ With respect to baptism, von Baer identifies *Wassertaufe* (water baptism) with *Geistestaufe* (Spirit baptism).¹²

Schnackenburg does not find in Acts any influence by the Spirit on moral life, which would be a characteristic introduced by Paul: "Paul is the first to consider the Spirit of God as the driving force of the ethical life."¹³ Wikenhauser nuances the comparison further: the work of the Holy Spirit is not exhausted in the charismata. His principal influence is in the promotion of evangelism, but on one point he is distinguished from Paul's teaching: "Acts does not contain a clear and unambiguous

---

7. Schweizer, "πνεῦμα," *TWNT* 6:407 [409] (see also 410 [412]). [Haya-Prats' stress from the *TWNT* reads as follows: "Lukas teilt also mit dem Judentum die Anschauung, dass Geist *im Wesentlichen* [emphasis mine] Geist der Prophetie ist. Das hindert ihn, einerseits die χαρίσματα ἰαμάτων anderseits stärker ethisch geprägte Wirkungen wie das Gemeinschaftsleben der Urgemeinde diret auf das πνεῦμα zurückzuführen." A fresh translation of this *TWNT* quote is provided above. —Ed.]

8. Ibid., 408.

9. Ibid., 409; "Nicht sittliche Erneuerung, sonder die Mission ist für Lukas die Gabe des Geistes" (*TWNT* 6:407 n. 500, referring to von Baer, *Heilige Geist*, 108.) Von Baer's exact text is quoted in sec. 5.2.

10. "Es hat aber auch andere Merkmale gegeben, die den Geistesbesitz verraten haben und auf den Gebiet der sittlich-religiösen Neuschaffung des Menschen liegen (vgl. Apg 19, 2)" (Baer, *Heilige Geist*, 179).

11. "Auch hier ist die Bruderliebe eine Frucht des Pneuma Hagion . . ." (ibid., 104).

12. Ibid., 180. This text is cited in sec. 6.4(a).

13. "Erst Paulus betrachtet den Gottesgeist als treibende Kraft des sittlichen Lebens" (Schnackenburg, *Sittliche Botschaft des Neuen Testamentes*, 134).

clue to suggest that the religious and ethical life of the Christian is connected with the possession of the Holy Spirit."[14]

Gunkel's interpretation appears to me to be more thoroughly worked out and more in harmony with the results obtained from the present direct study of the texts.[15] I present it now as a synthetic vision to be kept in mind during the extensive analysis of the texts that I shall be presenting in the sections that follow. According to Gunkel, "We may not state, therefore, that the activities of the Spirit are indifferent to the moral-religious sphere. There are spiritual revelations that occur in this area. But the everyday religious acts of the ordinary Christian are not perceived as gifts of the Holy Spirit. Where the moral and religious aspects are regarded as pneumatic, there is always a heightening of the commonplace. Incidentally, when we speak of the Spirit we are thinking less of these activities than of prophecy, glossolalia, and so on, which do not directly pertain to the area under discussion."[16] In this paragraph, Gunkel deals with the direct relationship of the Spirit with certain moral manifestations. In the following section, it is assumed that many of the manifestations ordinarily attributed to the Spirit naturally have an indirect repercussion in the moral life of Christians.[17] Therefore, according to Gunkel, frequent indirect repercussions exist in the life of Christians, but a direct action of the Spirit also exists that strengthens in an extraordinary manner that moral ethos.

All exegetes agree in admitting to at least a degree of relationship of the Spirit with the Christian life in the book of Acts, even though it is only a rather blurred point at the edges of the Lukan focus, "ganz

14. "Sie [Acts] enthält keine klaren und unzweideutigen Anhaltspunkte dafür, dass das religiöse und sittliche Leben der Christen mit dem Besitz des Hl. Geistes in Zusammenhang stehe" (Wikenhauser, *Apostelgeschichte*, 102).

15. Gunkel, *Influence of the Holy Spirit* (*Wirkungen des heiligen Geistes*). Schweizer ("πνεῦμα," 412) expressly rejects this solution; however, he then proposes a somewhat similar one: "No doubt it would be wrong to ascribe only extraordinary religious effects to the Spirit. Nevertheless, according to Luke, the Spirit gives only the power which enables the believer to discharge a special task, to express his faith in concrete action."

16. Gunkel, *Influence*, 18. "Wir dürfen also nicht sagen, dass die Wirkungen des Geistes dem Gebiete des sittlich-religiösen gegenüber indifferent seien. Es giebt Geistesoffenbarungen, welche in dies Gebiet fallen. Aber die Gewöhnlichen religiösen Funktionen des einfachen Christen werden nicht als Gaben des heiligen Geistes empfunden. Wo Sittliches and Religiöses für pneumatisch gehalten wird, da ist es stets eine Steigerung des Gewöhnlichen. Übrigens denkt man, wenn man vom Geiste spricht, viel weniger an derartige Wirkungen, als an solche wie Prophetie, Glossolalie u. a. welche dem gesprochene Gebiete nicht unmitelbar angehören" (*Wirkungen*, 9).

17. Ibid.

am Rand" (very much on the edge), according to Schweizer's expression. This point has remained eclipsed by the clarity and brilliance of the purely charismatic aspect that predominates in Acts. In turn, the Lukan conception of the Spirit has remained essentially forgotten by a world that believes it to be de-charismatized and that has found in Paul a more moralistic and mystic concept of the Spirit. It is worth the effort, though, to return to the concept of the Spirit that the narrator of Pentecost has formulated and the aspect of it that has been attributed to the moral impulse of the community. The preceding chapters examine Luke's general concept of the Spirit and his principal effect in relation to a testimony of Christ, followed with that which naturally follows in the book of Acts. This chapter and the next examine the small and somewhat murky point in the setting of Acts that constitutes the relationship between the Spirit and the moral life of Christians. Necessarily, the point is clarified with a degree of relief that is not found in the whole. A final reflection takes into consideration the required proportions and explains, somewhat, this preference of Luke for the extraordinary.

This chapter considers whether there is a relationship between the Holy Spirit and the beginning of the Christian life. The next chapter examines the relationship that the Spirit may have in the development of the Christian life.

6.2 The Process of Conversion

The beginning of the Christian life is designated at times with a general expression such as πιστεύω (believe), but on other occasions it appears somewhat less ordered in its diverse aspects. The precision of these aspects and their mutual relationships would merit a separate work.[18] However, in general terms they can be presented in this order: the apostles proclaim the resurrection of Jesus and his value as savior, culminating in an exhortation to repentance (μετανοέω) and conversion (ἐπιστρέφω). Repentance-conversion represents the subjective part of the person in his or her negative aspect of renouncing the best of his or her thought and action. The positive aspect of conversion is the faith that accepts Christ and his message as the only means of salvation. This faith finds its

---

18. See the interesting article by Dupont, "Repentir et Conversion"; idem, "Conversion dans Actes"; Schnackenburg, "Typen der Metanoia-Predigt"; Michiels, "Conception lucanienne de la conversion." [See too George, *Études sur l'oeuvre de Luc*, 351–68; Talbert, "Conversion in Acts." —Ed.]

formal expression in water baptism that officially incorporates a person into the new salvation community. Conversion-faith-baptism leads to the forgiveness of sins or, expressed positively, opens the door to life (ζωή). In connection with baptism, the ritual of the laying on of hands was practiced from the beginning and normally led to the manifestation of the gifts of the Spirit, particularly glossolalia and prophecy.[19]

The whole of this process of salvation, and most especially the first calling to God, is attributed directly to God (ὁ θεός): "For the promise is for you, for your children, and for all who are far away, everyone whom the Lord our God calls to him [Κύριος ὁ θεὸς ἡμῶν]" (2:39); "and as many as had been destined for eternal life became believers" (13:48); "And day by day the Lord added to their number those who were being saved" (2:47). These texts refer to an obvious principle as will become apparent in the texts that will be cited in various sections that follow. Together with this prior action by God that reaches the person at the most intimate level, "The Lord opened her [Lydia's] heart to listen eagerly to what was said by Paul" (16:14). Luke insists on presenting the virtues exercised by persons. Lydia was "a worshipper of God" (16:14). Tabitha, who will be favored by Peter with the wonder of resurrection, is a woman "devoted to good works and acts of charity" (9:36). Cornelius is a "God-fearing man" (10:2, 22), whose piety and gifts to the poor has earned him a place of honor in the estimation of the Jews (10:22), and his constant prayer appears to play an important role in the grace that God shows to him: "Your prayers and your alms have ascended as a memorial before God" (10:4). Aware of this event, Peter exclaims, "I truly understand that God shows no partiality, but in every nation anyone who fears him and does what is right is acceptable to him" (10:34–35).[20]

Luke has connected the initiative of God to another initiative taken by man without seeing any problem in doing so. It is God who directs Peter and Cornelius, but they had prepared themselves with prayer. We could say that Luke sees the lesser virtues as human merits and that he reserves for God the greater expressions of grace, be it opening the heart of Lydia to the faith (16:14) or sending an angel or his Spirit.

19. "Belief in Jesus (or in his Name), baptism, the remission of sins, the laying on of Apostolic hands, and the reception of the Spirit seem to have formed a single complex of associated ideas, any one of which might in any single narrative be either omitted or emphasized" (New, "Name, Baptism," 134). There are, however, more essential aspects, while others appear to be their customary complement.

20. These religious attitudes are the focus of secs. 7.1–3.

Before beginning a study of each aspect of the process of conversion, it would be useful to have access to a list of the texts in Acts that relate, at the very least, to two of these aspects. I present them briefly in the following footnote.[21]

(a) *Repentance* is presented as the human response to the salvation message or at least as its negative aspect of renouncing the life of sin. It is frequently expressed using the imperative form. For this reason, it should not seem strange that repentance is never attributed to the Holy Spirit. However, we do encounter some passages that consider repentance to be a gift from God, although they generally emphasize the objective aspect of repentance or, to be more precise, the possibility of repentance. In its expression as a gift, repentance is invariably attributed to the Father

---

21. The following column headings indicate the diverse elements mentioned in each text: Repentance, Faith, Baptism in the name of Jesus, Forgiveness of sins or equivalent restoring of life, receiving the Holy Spirit, and the Laying on of hands:

ELEMENTS OF THE PROCESS OF CONVERSION IN ACTS

Acts	Repentance	Faith	Baptism	Forgiveness	Receiving HS	Laying on Hands
2:38	*		*	*	*	
3:19	*			*		
5:31	*			*		
5:32		(*)			*	
8:16–17			*		*	*
8:22	*			*		
8:36		*	*			
10:43		*		*		
10:47			*		*	
11:17		*			*	
11:18	*			*		
11:21	*	*				
15:9		*		(*)		
18:8		*	*			
19:2–6	*	*	*		*	*
20:21	*	*				
22:16		*	*	*		
26:18	*	*		*		

(ὁ θεός). We can call to mind certain texts, such as, "God exalted him at his right hand as Leader and Savior, so that he might give repentance to Israel and forgiveness of sins" (5:31), in which the objective sense is highlighted. In the case of Cornelius, penitence could refer to the final, concrete result, but it could also be the case that what caused the Jews to marvel was God's having given the Gentiles the possibility of repentance that leads to life (11:18).

The case of Lydia could suggest that God also supplies the subjective act of repentance: "the Lord opened her heart . . ." (16:14). However, in this case the text has more to do with faith than with repentance. The text mentions none of the typical words for repentance and the action of God is to incite her to listen to the words of Paul. On the other hand, even supposing the generality of sin that must be pardoned by faith, Acts does not insist on repentance when the person does not have an immediate consciousness of sin, as in the case of Cornelius and that of Lydia. Therefore, that which God worked in Lydia appears to be the opening up of faith.[22]

(b) *Forgiveness of sins* is a work of God realized in Christ, as we have just seen in the citation of 5:31 and equally well in 3:26: "he sent him first to you, to bless you by turning each of you from your wicked ways." In order for a man or woman to receive this pardon, it is necessary that he or she repent: "Repent therefore of this wickedness of yours, and pray to the Lord that, if possible, the intent of your heart may be forgiven you" (8:22). The forgiveness of sins is received by means of faith. Acts 2:38 relates forgiveness with baptism, "Repent and be baptized . . . so that your sins may be forgiven," and 22:16 relates baptism with faith, "Get up, be baptized, and have your sins washed away, calling on his name." However, almost all of the relevant texts point to faith as the means by which forgiveness of sins and an inheritance or eternal life is received. For the rest, baptism is the formal expression of faith.

A number of texts point to forgiveness or salvation by means of faith: "Everyone who believes is set free from all those sins" (13:39);

---

22. See Dupont, *Études*, 421–57. Peter brings about repentance among the Jews by forcing them to take note of their solidarity in the condemnation of Jesus and among the Gentiles by reproaching them for their idolatry. In the case of Cornelius, he omits an explicit mention of conversion because there is no immediate circumstance of sin, but he does not fail to remind them of the general problem of sin by proclaiming to them that "everyone who believes in him receives forgiveness of sins through his name" (10:43).

"Believe on the Lord Jesus, and you will be saved, you and your household" (16:31). Paul is sent to the Gentiles "to open their eyes . . . so that they may receive forgiveness of sins and a place among those who are sanctified by faith in me" (26:18). We will see other similar texts dealing with faith in the next section, in particular 15:9, the text that gives the most complex account of the purification of Cornelius.

We have found nothing to indicate that Acts attributes forgiveness of sins to the Holy Spirit. The variant of the second petition of our Father that some manuscripts present—"send your Holy Spirit and purify us"— is uniformly rejected. Lohymeyer notes that the use of the possessive "your Holy Spirit" is foreign to Luke.[23] The sections that follow will demonstrate that the gift of the Holy Spirit presupposes faith and usually baptism; that is to say, it presupposes the forgiveness of sins. This serves as a confirmation that Luke does not relate the Holy Spirit to the forgiveness of sins.

In contrast to this concept in Acts, we should remember that we find already in the Old Testament certain passages that attribute salvation to the Spirit. There is an expressed preference for the Spirit's positive aspect which produces a new life, but at times the texts refer explicitly to the aspect of purification: ". . . once the Lord has washed away the filth of the daughters of Zion and cleansed the bloodstains of Jerusalem from its midst by a spirit of judgment and by a spirit of burning" (Isa 4:4). Isaiah 32:15–16 expresses this idea less directly but with the same basic sense. Much more specific are the texts in Ezekiel that refer to a new heart that God will place in his people: "A new heart I will give you, and a new spirit I shall put within you. . . . I will put my spirit within you, and make you follow my statues and be careful to observe my ordinances. . . . [Y]ou shall be my people, and I will be your God" (Ezek 36:26–28; and in the same sense Ezek 11:19).

Luke has made reference to Isa 61:1 in order to place the evangelizing work of the Messiah under the action of the Spirit: "The Spirit of the Lord is upon me, because he has anointed me to bring good news to the poor" (Luke 4:18a). In contrast, he does not make use of Isa 11:2, which describes the six gifts of the Spirit given to the Messiah.

Of the passages that use the expression *Holy Spirit*, Isa 63:11 *almost* presents the sanctifying sense. Wisdom 1:5 and 9:17 could refer to sanctification, but by means of a spirit of wisdom that could as easily be

---

23. Lohmeyer, *Vater-unser*, 185–92.

understood in terms of a prophetic spirit. The text that gives the most precise reference to the sanctifying Holy Spirit is Ps 51:10–12, "Create in me a clean heart, O God, and put a new and right spirit within me. Do not cast me away from your presence, and do not take your holy spirit from me. Restore to me the joy of your salvation, and sustain in me a willing spirit."[24] The Qumran sect attributes to its members, at least to a certain extent, the possession of the spirit that purifies and creates new life, referring to it as a holy spirit, a spirit of sanctification, of justice, of truth.[25] Paul develops this aspect of the sanctifying Spirit as one of the principal lines of his theology. The negative aspect of purification is much less developed and in each case appears in connection with baptism: "But you were washed, you were sanctified, you were justified in the name of the Lord Jesus Christ and in the Spirit of our God: (1 Cor 6:11). The Spirit is given as a seal in the baptism of every Christian and is a filial Spirit (Rom 8:9, 16; Gal 4:6) that dwells in the Christian as in a temple. Everything that proceeds from the Christian will no longer be in the flesh but in the Spirit; "living in the Spirit" and "living in Christ" are frequently equivalent formulas, which is to say, there is no precision in the attribution of the new Christian life to Christ or to the Spirit. John places in sharp relief the need to "be born of the Spirit" and has presented the giving of the Spirit as a power for pardoning sins. Acts does not adopt any of these interpretations of the work of the Spirit, but instead prefers to remain tied to the fundamental Old Testament concept of the prophetic Spirit that governs the people's journey, poured out now in the fullness announced by Joel. Furthermore, Acts omits the sanctifying aspect of the Spirit already initiated in the Old Testament but which has not been recognized by Jesus. Luke attributes to Jesus the entire work of salvation, and to the Spirit, the extraordinary exultation whether expressed in praise or apostolic impulse.

6.3 Faith and the Holy Spirit

The relationship between *faith* and the Holy Spirit needs greater attention. The majority of texts present faith as a state that necessarily precedes the receiving of the Spirit, but not all of the relevant texts are clear and, most important, given their narrative style, they do not expressly

---

24. See Schweizer, "πνεῦμα," 383–86.
25. Coppens, "Don de l'Esprit."

state the necessity of faith as a precondition. However, we find texts that appear to attribute the faith of Stephen and Barnabas to the Holy Spirit. As we will see, though, these texts refer to a distinct quality of faith.

We begin with the reference of Peter, "And we are witnesses to these things, and so is the Holy Spirit whom God has given to those who obey him" (5:32). The participle πειθαρχοῦσιν is in the present tense because it expresses a proper name for the believer,[26] but from its sense we can see that it refers to a situation prior to the gifting of the Spirit. In effect, the Spirit is given to believers and it is evidently supposed that he is not given to unbelievers, because in that case the Spirit would lose all its value as testimony that Peter has just invoked. In addition to this testimony of the Spirit is, in all probability, the gift of glossolalia that in the early community was a typical manifestation for believers. We will see that this gift of faith is also attributed to Cornelius when he receives the testimony of the Spirit.

In the narratives that describe the falling of the Spirit upon Cornelius,[27] we find three mentions of faith, and it will be necessary to pause in order to examine them in greater depth. Owing to the use of the participle, the text of 11:17 contains various grammatical imprecisions that demand clarification: "If then God gave them the same gift that he gave us when we believed in the Lord Jesus Christ. . . ." (a) The first difficulty is in determining to whom the participle πιστεύσασιν refers.[28] We can say that, whether explicitly by means of a grammatical agreement or implicitly in a comparison with the disciples, the text refers to the faith of Cornelius. The same conclusion can be deduced from the context, which emphasizes the welcome that Cornelius accorded both the announcement of God and the words of Peter, and from the explicit mention of his faith in the parallel narrative in chapter 15, to be analyzed shortly.

26. Zerwick, *Biblical Greek*, n. 371.

27. [From a narrative perspective, see U. E. Eisen's discussion of "Die Petrus-Cornelius-Erzählsequenz" and "Grenzüberschreitung und Extrempunkt" in her *Die Poetik der Apostelgeschichte*, 169–87. —Ed.]

28. In their respective commentaries at 11:17 Preuschen and Conzelmann understand αὐτοῖς to refer to the family of Cornelius, so that they have understood certain manuscripts to add ". . . not giving the Holy Spirit to those that had believed in him." Wendt, on the other hand, sees πιστεύσασιν as referring to ἡμῖν, which is the dative that immediately precedes it. Jacquier makes it agree grammatically with ἡμῖν, but logically with both datives. Bauernfeind and Haenchen consider it simply to refer to both. [Similarly, G. Schneider also suggests that πιστεύσασιν possibly refers to αὐτοῖς and to ἡμῖν.—Ed.]

(b) Given that this text deals with the faith of Cornelius, we still need to clarify the temporal value of the participle in relation to the principal verb. In our case, the aorist refers to an action clearly distinct from the principal verb and, thereby, indicates an action prior to it. The same sense results from the comparison with the disciples in whom faith certainly preceded the giving of the Spirit. (c) We can further clarify the value of the participle, which could be either temporal or causal. It appears that the context authorizes a slight causal-occasional or conditional tone that could be translated "since we had believed" or "given that . . . ," since faith is the occasion or the condition by which God bestows the Spirit and not a merely fortuitous event that preceded it.

In the words of Peter before the Jerusalem Council (15:7–9),[29] we have two mentions of faith that it will be necessary to consider within the structure of the paragraph: "My brothers, you know that in the early days God made a choice among you, that I should be the one through whom the Gentiles would hear the message of the good news and become believers. And God, who knows the human heart, testified to them by giving them the Holy Spirit, just as he did to us; and in cleansing their hearts by faith he has made no distinction between them and us" (15:7–9). In the text are two aorist participles. Δούς indicates an action simultaneous with the principal verb, even though the giving of the Spirit is the mode by which God gives testimony. Καθαρίσας, on the other hand, expresses a preceding action of its principal verb, which is to say that God, having purified by faith the hearts of the Gentiles, made no distinction between them and the disciples, giving them the Holy Spirit equally. If καθαρίσας is simultaneous with the principal verb, the sense would be that God made no distinction between one and the other in purifying them by faith. This may true, but the intention of the paragraph is to affirm the equality of the gift of the Spirit repeatedly in the three parallel stories,[30] which is the only similarity that has been offered by Peter as a testimony and which he would also offer as an argument in the council. Peter would have no solid evidence to affirm the purification of the Gentiles by faith if he has not deduced it to be a supposed precondition for the reception of the Spirit. The point that is discussed in the council is precisely the purification of the Gentiles without the

---

29. [From a narrative perspective on this scene, see Eisen, "Erzählung vom so genannten Apostelkonzil." —Ed.]

30. The three parallel stories are found in 10:44–48; 11:15–18; 15:7–11.

necessity of circumcision.³¹ But Peter is not able to content himself with simply affirming it but maintains that it is proven by the testimony of the Spirit. As he comes to understand that placing the burden of the law on the Gentiles would be to tempt God, he concludes that "On the contrary, we believe that we will be saved through the grace of the Lord Jesus, just as they will" (15:11). In the same sense, James concludes that "Simon has related how God first looked favorably on the Gentiles to take from among them a people for his name" (15:14).

The structure of the paragraph remains perfectly balanced. In it we can appreciate two distinct moments in the plan of God:

a. A first moment of election or purification by faith.
b. A second moment of public testimony to their election.

The text of 15:7–9 may be outlined as follows: A-B-A:³²
My brothers, you know that

A. God chose me so that . . . they would become believers
B. And God testified
   by giving them the Holy Spirit, just as he did to us
   and He has made no distinction between them and us
A. cleansing their hearts by faith

Putting it all together then, the argument that Luke has placed in the mouth of Peter is the following: It is necessary to admit the Gentiles into baptism and into the community without imposing the law on them, because the contrary would be to tempt God who has testified to having purified them by faith and having made them his people. This testimony consists in the giving of the Spirit, just as he did to those at Pentecost.

Grammatically, we cannot dispense with the possibility that the purification by faith occurred simultaneously with the giving of the Spirit, even though it appears to have happened prior to that gifting. The context, however, indicates clearly the priority of faith. The action of the Spirit testifies to the election of the Gentiles, and there is nothing to indicate that

---

31. Καθαρίσας connotes a certain sense of legal purification that is very much at home in this passage since it seeks to overcome the horror that the Jews have in admitting into the community the Gentiles, whom they consider to be an impure people. Faith purifies them, not in an exterior manner, but profoundly in their hearts.

32. The outline of these verbs in the original would be ἐπίστασθε ὅτι . . . ἐξελέξατο ὁ Θεὸς . . . πιστεῦσαι (15:7); καὶ . . . ἐμαρτύρησεν . . . δοὺς τὸ πνεῦμα τὸ ἅγιον (15:8); καὶ οὐθὲν διέκρινεν . . . τῇ πίστει καθαρίσας (15:9).

this occurred by means of purification. One one hand, the testimony supposes, at least logically, the thing that is testified to. On the other hand, purification by faith is clearly in harmony with all of the texts cited in the preceding section on the forgiveness of sins by means of faith.[33]

The more complicated text containing Paul's question to the Ephesian disciples can be understood in the same sense. "Did you receive the Holy Spirit when you became believers?" (19:2). The aorist participle, πιστεύσαντες, has here a sense of priority since the action is distinct from the principal verb. Paul would suppose, therefore, faith as a condition for receiving the Spirit.[34]

I have mentioned in the first part of this section the distinct cases of Stephen, "a man full of faith and the Holy Spirit" (6:5) and of Barnabas,

---

33. La Potterie, *Vie selon l'Esprit*, 151–53, 31–63. In citing this text (15:7–9), de La Potterie has followed an explanation that attributes to the Spirit the faith that Cornelius needed in order to be baptized. This supposes two interventions by the Spirit, one that gives faith prior to the baptism and the other after this that acts as a sign that perfects faith by means of testimony. I believe that, in Acts, there is nothing that would allow us to defend a first intervention of the Spirit that would produce faith in those who receive it. The Spirit always appears as the gift which is a sign of its reception. Faith is produced spontaneously through the hearing of the word of God, probably because God "opens the heart" of the hearers. The call to salvation is invariably attributed in Acts to God. See sec. 6.2.

34. This aorist participle can also be considered as an ingressive aorist that would denote the same initiation of faith and may be translated "upon embracing faith." It would deal in this case with an approximate simultaneity, without claiming to indicate a relation between the Spirit and faith. At the very least, it is certain that the Spirit is not prior to faith, and the difference in action between receiving and believing assumes that the two are not treated as simultaneous.

[C. B. Williams, in his *Participle in the Book of Acts*, determines from context that 540 of 588 (or 91.83 percent) refer to antecedent action with respect to the main verb, 4.25 percent refer to identical action, and 3.91 percent being doubtful as to their time relation to the principal verb. He characterizes πιστεύσαντες (19:2) from context as antecedent (39), not as coincident or simultaneous. P. Elbert ("Observation on Luke's Composition") shows that the question in 19:2 is structured in contextual Lukan style for application to disciple-believers. Spirit-reception here, as Haya-Prats observes, is contingent upon existing belief or faith, the participle expressing a *different* and temporally antecedent action from that of the principal verb. For the Lukan Paul, the participial action of belief is antecedent to the main verbal idea of receiving the Spirit. A grammatically more reflective translation would be, "Did you receive the Holy Spirit since you believed?" or "Did you receive the Holy Spirit, having believed?" In this regard, the narrative similarity of Christian disciples receiving the gift of the Holy Spirit as portrayed with respect to believers in Acts 19:1–2 with the narrative at 2:38 and 8:15,16, is observed by Wasserberg, *Israels Mitte-Heil für die Welt*, 258; Jacquier (*Actes*, 260) also connects 8:16 to 2:38. —Ed.]

"a good man, full of the Holy Spirit and of faith" (11:24). We understand from these that faith and the Spirit do not simply appear randomly coordinated in these phrases but that faith is the expression by which the fullness of the Spirit is manifested in them. They deal, therefore, with faith encouraged by the Holy Spirit.[35] This faith, however, is not the faith with which we first begin to believe and which is the common inheritance of every Christian. These passages have to do with a faith that distinguishes Stephen and Barnabas from the rest of the community. In the case of Stephen, this faith could be manifested as wisdom and persuasiveness with which he defended the message of God (6:10) or, perhaps, as the wondrous works he performed (6:8) by a charismatic faith that moves mountains (Matt 17:20; Luke 17:6). The profound faith of Barnabas is seen most clearly in its comprehensive character in discerning the plans of God in new situations that are somewhat confusing, such as that which occurred in the community at Antioch in which Gentiles had entered (11:20, 23–24).

In conclusion, the faith that initiates the Christian life is never attributed to the Holy Spirit in Acts. Rather, it appears to be a precondition for God giving the gift of the Spirit. The presence of the Spirit at times activates this faith which precedes it, lending it a charismatic intensity that sets apart certain favored individuals from among the community.

The study of these texts has demonstrated for us the precision and accuracy of Gunkel's observations: "In Acts it can be considered obvious that belief and the moving of the Spirit are distinct events. Indeed, only the believer can receive the Spirit, but it is therefore still not the case that he who has faith is also in possession of the Spirit (cf. particularly Acts 8:12–17)."[36] Evidently, what he rejects is that Spirit reception is an absolutely necessary consequence, and not that, in fact, every Christian might receive the Spirit, as Paul's question to the Ephesians supposes. Continuing with this same quote, "Faith originates through preaching. The Spirit is imparted, usually by means of the laying on of hands. . . .

---

35. See sec. 7.1 on the selection of the seven.

36. Gunkel, *Influence*, 17. "In der Apostelgeschichte gilt es als selbstverständliches, dass gläubig werden und vom Geiste ergriffen werden verschiedene Vorgänge sind. Zwar nur der Gläubige kann den Geist empfangen, aber deshalb ist noch nicht, wer den Glauben hat, auch schon im Besitze des Geistes (cf. besonders Acts 8:12–17)" (*Wirkungen*, 6–7).

The reception of the Spirit is therefore also a witness of God of the preceding faith (15:18f; 11:17)."[37]

Referring to the faith of Stephen, Gunkel spoke of an extraordinary gift: "In the first two cases (6:5 and 11:24) it is a matter of a special vitality of faith, which only certain special of the pardoned have, such as in 9:31 and 13:52, which speak of specific acts of perseverance in faith, namely those which follow."[38]

The results of this study of faith and the Spirit are in complete harmony with the Lukan conception of the Spirit. The Spirit is given to the messianic people as the fruit of a salvation that has already been initiated, even though it is not completed in the Day of the Lord, and it serves as a confirming testimony that they are members of this salvation community which is the beginning of the kingdom of God.

6.4 Baptism and the Holy Spirit

The initiating faith of the Christian's life is a necessary prerequisite for the coming of the Spirit. The biblical texts locate this faith in a moment prior to the coming of the Spirit, although the sequence can be more logical than temporal. No text presents the reception of the Spirit by unbelievers, and if we take these texts in their full force, they deny such a possibility, which would be a counter-testimony.

The texts that refer to baptism display very different characteristics. (a) First of all, it is important to avoid equating *baptism in the Spirit* with baptism in the name of Jesus. I will address the latter more extensively in this section. Among those texts that refer to baptism in the name of Jesus, we find various references to (b) baptism without any mention of the giving of the Spirit (8:38, the baptism of the eunuch; 16:15, of Lydia; 16:33, of the jailer; and 18:8, of the Corinthians); (c) one delayed case of the giving of the Spirit, which took place by means of the ritual of the laying on of hands (8:16); (d) two cases in which the giving of the Spirit precedes baptism (Cornelius and the apostles); and (e) two cases

---

37. Ibid. "Der Glaube entsteht durch die Predigt; der Geist kommt hernieder, gewöhnlich unter Handauflegen... Der Geistesempfang ist also ein Zeugnis Gottes für den vorhandenen Glauben (15:8ff.; 11:17)" (*Wirkungen*, 6–7).

38. Ibid., 17–18. "Es handelt sich an beiden ersteren Stellen (6:5; 11:24) um eine besondere Energie des Glaubens, welche nur bestimmten besonders Begnadigten eignet, ebenso wie 9:31; 13:52 von einem besonderen Beharren im Glauben geredet wird, nämlich dem unter Verfolgungen" (*Wirkungen*, 7).

in which the giving of the Spirit and baptism appear to be simultaneous (2:38 and 19:2–3).

The classification of texts alone demonstrates that the imparting of the Spirit in Acts is not intimately associated with water baptism. I do not know if such a dependency would have occurred to me were it not for a circumstance that lies outside of the book itself, namely, the teaching of the Catholic tradition.[39] The problem has been introduced into the book of Acts from outside, building on the imprecise nature of 2:38 and on the apparent proximity of baptism and the Spirit.

For the analysis of the texts, I will follow the order of previous classification.[40]

(a) *Baptism in the Holy Spirit.* The book of Acts mentions three classes of baptism: the baptism of John, the baptism of the Holy Spirit, and baptism in the name of Jesus (with either an explicit or implicit formula). These deal with realities that are very different and which only coincide in a certain eschatological preparation. We can start with a basic cataloging of the texts:

John's baptism: 1:5; 10:37; 11:16; 13:24; 18:25; 19:3–5
Spirit baptism: 1:5; 11:16
Baptism in Jesus' name:
    Explicitly: 2:38; 8:16; 10:48
    Implicitly: 2:41; 8:38; 9:18; 16:15, 33; 18:8; 19:5; 22:16

The baptism of John is clearly contrasted with the baptism in the Spirit (1:5; 11:16) and with the baptism in the name of Jesus (18:25, Apollos; 19:3–5, the Ephesian disciples). It is a baptism of repentance that prepares the way for faith in the Messiah (19:4) and that, therefore, is situated in a phase that precedes the giving of the Spirit to which it contributes. We can dispense, therefore, in our study with the baptism of John.

The baptism of the Spirit could have been identified with the baptism that the disciples began to practice beginning at the Day of Pentecost

---

39. [Sullivan, "Baptism," also challenges the teaching of Catholic tradition that the gift of the Holy Spirit is automatically coincident with water baptism. —Ed.]

40. See the commentaries on 8:16 of Haenchen (*Acts*, 300–308 = *Apostelgeschichte*, 250–59), Conzelmann (53–55); Wikenhauser (98); New, "Name, Baptism"; Baer, *Heilige Geist*, 153–82; Bardy, *Saint-Esprit en nous*, 100–108; Lampe, *Seal of the Spirit*; Davies, *Spirit, Church*; Best, "Spirit Baptism"; Alonso-Díaz, "Hasta qué punto los elementos"; Bieder, *Verheissung der Taufe*, esp. 124–39; Wilkens, "Wassertaufe und Geistesempfang." See also the works cited in the following footnotes.

(2:41) and with which Jesus had entrusted them, according to a possibly subsequent reference in Mark 16:16 (and that includes a Trinitarian formula according to the text of Matt 28:19, which is perhaps also subsequent). Neither the Synoptic Gospels nor Acts nor John nor the Christian writers have understood it in this way. It could be said that the Synoptics as well as John have limited themselves to transmitting the prophetic promise of the Baptist without having sought its interpretation in any concrete realization. Certainly, they had not thought that it would reach its fulfillment with the baptism that the disciples received from Jesus during his public life. John is the only one to mention this baptism (3:22; 4:1–3), but he locates categorically the giving of the Spirit after the glorification of Jesus (7:39).

The repetition of the saying of John the Baptist presents a grand stabilizing formula (Matt 3:11; Mark 1:8; Luke 3:16; John 1:33; Acts 1:5; and 11:16).[41] However, only Matt 3:11 and Luke 3:16 mention the baptism with fire. Chevallier believes that the original expression of the Baptist would have been "in spirit and in fire" but that the term *spirit* would refer to a mighty breath as in Isa 11:4 and in Ps 2:12, messianic passages that were heavily utilized in the early community (see also Isa 4:4). The evangelists would have added the adjective, understanding it as the "Holy Spirit" according to Jesus' teachings. With the change of meaning, the mention of fire makes less sense, so that it disappears from some texts.[42]

This explanation appears probable. The associating of the Holy Spirit with baptism could have come spontaneously with the manifestation of the Holy Spirit in the baptism of Christ, which, according to the more primitive tradition, is a scene that pertains equally well to the ministry of the Baptist. If Luke mentions fire in the Gospel (3:16) and does not mention it in Acts (1:5 and 11:16), I believe that it could be that the Gospel attributes the phrase to the Baptist, while in Acts it is attributed to Jesus. With the Baptist, an eschatological purification can be attributed to baptism by means of fire, while in Acts the purification is not apocalyptic, nor is it attributed to the Spirit but rather to the name of Jesus by means of faith. We can deduce the importance of the saying in

---

41. The reading of the preposition ἐν πνεύματι in Mark 1:8 is probable.

42. Chevallier, *L'Esprit et le Messie*. See Baer, *Heilige Geist*, 159–63; Margoliouth, "Baptizing with Fire"; Edsman, *Baptême de feu*; Imschoot, "Baptême d'eau et baptême"; Best, "Spirit Baptism"; Turrado, "Bautismo 'in Spiritu Sancto et igni'"; Alonso-Díaz, "Bautismo de fuego anunciado." [See also Charette, "'Tongues of Fire.'"—Ed.]

the tradition from its persistent use. The same formal rigidity of the expression could suggest a lack of a true assimilation of the idea. With the lack of a concrete realization, the expression *baptism in the Holy Spirit* fell into disuse, perhaps to avoid confusion with the baptismal ritual, which came very quickly to be connected with the giving of the Spirit.

Acts is the only book in the New Testament that presents clearly a concrete application of the baptism in the Spirit. In the narrating of a solemn imparting of the Spirit at Pentecost and of its repetition in the new members of the community, we find the concrete situation that could correspond with the baptism in the Holy Spirit. There is no doubt that Acts has interpreted the baptism in the Spirit as the Pentecostal gift: "you will be baptized with the Holy Spirit not many days from now" (1:5). Even more significant is the fact that Luke still considers the pouring out of the Spirit on Cornelius to be a baptism in the Spirit, even though he must give a somewhat forced interpretation to the quoted text, extending to the Gentiles the promise that Jesus had made to the disciples and extending noticeably the very concrete time period "not many days from now."[43]

Von Baer, however, has interpreted the baptism in the Spirit as the giving of the Spirit in water baptism: "Baptism as a true sacrament, as it has come to us out of the Pauline letters, is also found in Acts, where one is ready to deal with it not only as a water baptism, but also simultaneously as a Spirit baptism."[44] I do not believe that this opinion explains either of the two references to the baptism in the Spirit that we read in Acts.[45] We will see, furthermore, that Acts never says that the Spirit is given by means of water baptism (in the name of Jesus). The baptism of John was with water, while the baptism that Jesus promises is in the Holy Spirit. The contrast is between the use of the human ritual and a direct action by God. This is not to say that opposition exists between these

---

43. Luke does not hesitate to vary certain circumstances when he narrates the same event, as for example in the conversion of Paul. The saying concerning the baptism in the Spirit attributed to the Baptist in Luke 3:16 is attributed to Christ in Acts 1:4 (see Haenchen's commentary on this text).

44. "Die Taufe als reales Sakrament, wie sie uns aus den paulinischen Briefen bekannt ist, findet sich auch in Acta, so weit es sich nicht nur um eine Wasser-sonder auch gleichzeitig um eine Geiststaufe handelt" (Baer, *Heilige Geist*, 180).

45. [Here, Haya-Prats is in agreement with Kim regarding baptism in the Spirit; see in Kim's *Geisttaufe*, "Geistmitteilung an die neubekehrten Samaritaner" (171–86) and "Geistausgießung auf die Heiden" (186–208). —Ed.]

two modes. Peter, in the case of Cornelius, drew the opposite conclusion, that is, that not only does the baptism in the Spirit not permit one to dispense with the ritual of baptism, but on the contrary it obliges one to grant such a ritual.

The baptism of John was intended for purification, and baptism in the name of Jesus was intended for the forgiveness of sin, but we do not find this purifying aspect with the baptism in the Spirit, which is of a distinct order. Baptism in the Spirit is for Acts the outpouring of the Pentecostal gift. It can be verified to be independent from baptism in the name of Jesus and should be understood in accordance with the Lukan characteristics of the Pentecostal Spirit.

(b) *Baptism without the giving of the Spirit.* This group of texts in which a baptism without any mention of the giving of the Spirit is described has no polemical value for determining the relationship between the two aspects. Certain codices amend the text of the eunuch's baptism (8:39), having the Holy Spirit descend upon him: "when they came up out of the water, the Holy Spirit fell upon the eunuch and the angel of the Lord snatched Philip away." The correction attempts to avoid the physical intervention of the Spirit, which is foreign to Luke. Such a correction is highly improbable critically, but in addition it introduces the new difficulty of attributing to the baptism administered by Philip the giving of the Spirit which has been expressly denied in the preceding passage in Samaria.[46] In Paul's baptism (9:18), there is an indirect mention of the giving of the Spirit, since Ananias is sent "so that you may regain your sight and be filled with the Holy Spirit" (9:17). Nothing indicates to us, however, at what point Paul received the Spirit.[47] Others have asked why Apollos was not baptized (18:24–28). This passage is very suggestive, perhaps because of the same lack of precision regarding the facts that it contributes and because of the traces that it reveals of a distinct concept. I do not believe that a clear conclusion can be taken from this story, nor does it follow with certainty that the spirit mentioned refers to the Holy Spirit. The case of Cornelius has shown us that, for Luke, the possession of the Spirit did not dispense with the reception of baptism.[48]

---

46. I have spoken about the strange character of this material intervention by the Spirit and its probable priority in sec. 2.2.

47. Fascher, "Taufe des Paulus."

48. Schweizer, "Bekehrung." See also the preceding note.

(c) *The giving of the Spirit without baptism.* The case of the Samaritans baptized by Philip (Acts 8) demonstrates explicitly the separation of baptism and the giving of the Spirit. The latter, connected with the ritual of the laying on of hands,[49] appears for the moment to be beyond the abilities of Philip. This situation is so self-evident that no commentary has dared to deny it. Traditionally, this text has been used as a foundation for the sacrament of confirmation. It has been thought to claim a distinction between the charismatic gift of the Spirit transmitted by the laying on of Peter's hands and the gift of the Holy Spirit received at baptism. Certainly this text does not deny that in the baptism administered by Philip the Samaritans could have received the Holy Spirit in an interior, invisible, sanctifying form. Acts never speaks of such a presence of the Spirit and, consequently, neither does it deny it.[50] We can know from a primitive tradition of the gift of the Spirit in baptism and, therefore, may assume it *in the historical case* of the Samaritans, but we may not assume it *in the mind of the author* of this story.

(d) *The giving of the Spirit preceding baptism.* Even more significant is *the coming of the Spirit* in the case of Cornelius, which caused Peter to decide not to withhold baptism. Those who defend an attribution of the gift of the Spirit to baptism recognize in this passage the freedom of the Spirit to blow where he wills. Naturally, this is a case of the exception which proves the rule that will occur in any theory, because the Spirit is also not tied here to the laying on of hands. However, the exception illustrates the possibility of such comings by the Spirit. We have seen that, without exception, there is not any case in which the Spirit descends upon unbelievers. However, he can descend, in rare exceptions, on those who are not baptized, as in the case of Cornelius, of the apostles themselves, and perhaps of Apollos. This indicates that the Spirit's relation with baptism is external and somewhat accidental, while his relation with faith appears to be more internal and necessary. Faith may be considered as an internal and necessary condition for the giving of the Spirit, and perhaps we might interpret it using philosophical categories as a type of cause or contributing cause. Baptism, on the other hand, would only be an exterior condition that is generally required.

---

49. Coppens, *L'imposition des mains*; Oulton, "Holy Spirit, Baptism."

50. Some interpret the joy of the Samaritans (8:8) as a sign that they had received the Spirit in baptism; however, joy is not exclusive to the presence of the Spirit, but is a sign of the messianic blessings. See sec. 7.1.

(e) *Two apparent cases of simultaneity* (19:1–7 and 2:38). Paul's question to the disciples of Ephesus gives the impression that the giving of the Spirit was commonly attributed to the baptism in the name of Jesus. When those disciples say that they had not even heard about the Holy Spirit, Paul begins to have suspicions concerning the authenticity of the baptism that they had received, so he asks, "Into what then were you baptized?" (19:3).[51] The objection of this text is only apparent, since we do not need to attribute the giving of the Spirit to baptism, but rather it is sufficient to suppose the custom of receiving the Spirit concurrently with baptism without there existing between the two a direct, intimate relationship. This second interpretation prevails as the story continues.

The narrator has distinguished perfectly the two moments in the incorporation of the Ephesian disciples: ". . . they were baptized in the name of the Lord Jesus. When Paul had laid his hands on them, the Holy Spirit came upon them, and they spoke in tongues and prophesied . . ." (19:5–6). The separation of the two moments is highlighted even more starkly by the change from the passive form ἐβαπτίσθησαν to the active form that introduces a change of subject, καὶ ἐπιθέντος αὐτοῖς τοῦ Παύλου χεῖρας. It is highly probable that the change of subject is intentional in order to emphasize that the laying on of hands was an office of Paul, while baptism would have been conferred by one of his companions.[52] At the very least, the distinction of the two rituals is perfectly framed. This difference has already been demonstrated in the passage with the Samaritans. In the baptism of the Ephesians, therefore, we find only the appearance of simultaneity. In reality, it is assumed that the Spirit is given subsequent to baptism.[53]

The other text that appears to attribute the giving of the Spirit to baptism is the promise of Peter in his Pentecost discourse: "Repent, and be baptized every one of you in the name of Jesus Christ so that your sins may be forgiven; and you will receive the gift of the Holy Spirit. For the

---

51. Käsemann, "Johannesjünger in Ephesus"; see also the conclusions that Lohmeyer deduces from this passage in *Vater-unser*, 188–92; Baer, *Heilige Geist*, 158, 177–78. [See also Shepherd, "Apollos and the Ephesian Disciples" in his *Narrative Function of the Holy Spirit*, 224–30. —Ed.]

52. We know from 1 Cor 1:14 that Paul was not in the habit of administering baptism.

53. [On the episode of Spirit reception by the Ephesian believer-disciples (as Luke describes them), see in Kim, *Geisttaufe*, "Struktur der Ephesusjüngerepisode," "Kohärenz," and "Komposition der Ephesusjüngerepisode druch Lukas" (210–13). —Ed.]

promise is to you . . ." (2:38-39). The interpretation of this text has been much discussed as being the key text by those who see in Acts an attribution of the Spirit to baptism. Among those exegetes, many give scant attention to the concept of the Spirit as sanctifier.[54] In order to prove the attribution of the Spirit to baptism in this text, or in order to reject it, commentators have presented three types of arguments: syntactic construction, vocabulary, and relation with other texts. With respect to the syntactic construction of 2:38, Jacquier,[55] Elfers,[56] and Beasley-Murray[57] believe that the conjunction καὶ λήμψεσθε is a case of a καὶ consecutive whose use is especially frequent following an imperative.[58] In this case, the sense would be: "repent and be baptized so that you will receive the Holy Spirit." Adler accepts the same syntactic value for a καὶ consecutive but interprets the thought of the text in a distinct way, placing it in the future: "repent and be baptized so that you will *afterward* receive the Holy Spirit."[59]

This triple conjunction — repentance, baptism, and the Spirit — is a unique case, since normally only repentance and baptism are associated. Kittel believes that we are dealing with an error in punctuation that should be corrected in this sense: "repent and be baptized each one of you in the name of Jesus Christ for the forgiveness of your sins. And you will receive the gift of the Holy Spirit, for to you is the promise. . . ."[60]

---

54. I have used in my study of 2:38 important material collected by Fr. B. Russel, OFM, in a work at the seminary that has not been published, completed at the Pontifico Instituto Bíblico de Roma. I have selected various titles from his extensive selected bibliography. The following authors, for example, appear to consider the Spirit a *baptismal gift*: Loisy, *Actes des Apôstres*; Jacquier, *Actes*; Büchsel, *Geist Gottes*; Oepke, "βάπτω"; Elfers, "Gehört die Salbung mit Chrisma"; Renié, *Actes*; Schnackenburg, *Heilgeschehen bei der Tauf*; Bultmann, *Theologie des Neuen Testament*; Haenchen, *Acts of the Apostles* (*Apostelgeschichte*); Beasley-Murray, *Baptism in the New Testament*, esp. 104-22. The following authors, for example, appear to consider the Spirit a *post-baptismal gift*: Lake, "Baptism"; Kittel, "Wirkungen der christlichen Wassertaufe"; Coppens, *L'imposition des mains*, and his contributions to *Dictionnaire de la Bible, Supplément*, Baptême Suppl. 1:871-924; Confirmation Suppl. 2:120-53; Adler, *Taufe und Handauflegung*; Leal, *Hechos de los Apóstoles*; Wikenhauser, *Apostelgeschichte*; La Potterie, "L'onction du chrétien"; Glombitza, "Schluss der Petrusrede"; Ysebaert, *Greek Baptismal Terminology*.

55. Jacquier, *Actes*, 82-83.

56. Elfers, "Gehört die Salbung," 335.

57. Beasley-Murray, *Baptism*, 107-8.

58. BDF, 442(2).

59. Adler, *Taufe*, 27-28.

60. Kittel, "Wirkungen der christlichen Wassertaufe," 37-38.

With this interpretation, the connection between baptism and the Spirit would remain very imprecise.

Ysebaert has made a particular study of the baptismal vocabulary of the New Testament[61] and demonstrates that the terms used by Luke with respect to the giving of the Spirit (λαμβάνω, δωρεά, δίδωμι, πίμπλημι) are not baptismal terms. My analysis of δωρεά in sec. 3.1 demonstrates that Acts refers to the same Holy Spirit, although attending directly to the charismatic manifestation which attests to its impartation. It did not address, however, the sanctifying Spirit, but rather the Spirit as anticipated, eschatological gift.

I attributed more strength to the comparison of 2:38 with the remainder of the texts on the Holy Spirit that are found in Acts. It is true that no text—neither that which refers to the Ephesian disciples nor that which refers to the Samaritans—proves that the Spirit is not given at baptism. Neither do I intend to say that Acts denies any impartation of the Spirit at baptism. From those texts, it is at the very least possible to deduce that the impartation of the Spirit spoken of in Acts is not directly confirmed to be part of baptism.[62] If the writer of Acts had known of a filling by the Spirit at baptism, he would have treated it as a gift of the Spirit that is distinct from that which is spoken about in the rest of the book. But we have no indication to affirm that the writer knew of this other gift of the Spirit, just as we have no positive indication that allows us to deny it. The only thing that we can say is that the writer has not spoken to us concerning this other gift of the Spirit that is received at baptism.[63]

The collecting of the texts as I have classified them demonstrates that the gift of the Pentecostal Spirit occurs both prior to and subsequent to baptism, which attests to its internal and direct independence. This does not prevent the existence of an *external relationship* that sees in baptism a condition that is *ordinarily* a prerequisite.

---

61. Ysebaert, *Greek Baptismal Terminology*, 266–68.

62. [Schweizer ("πνεῦμα," 414) observes in this vein that "A far more significant point is that precisely in Acts the freedom of the Spirit is strongly emphasised [die Freiheit des Geistes stark unterstrichen wird (*TWNT* 6:411)]. The Spirit is not tied to baptism." —Ed.]

63. Wilkens ("Wassertaufe und Geistesempfang," 29) has observed that Luke dissociates the coming of the Spirit upon Jesus from the act of baptism (compare Luke 3:21 with Mark 1:10 and Matt 3:16).

I recognize that these arguments of the interpretation of a text based on the work as a whole carry with them the danger at times of suppressing a theme simply because it is not repeated elsewhere in the work. Nevertheless, as far as it is possible for us to interpret an author's text, it is not possible to deduce an entire line of thought that is distinct from that ordinarily expressed in the work, supporting it with only a single very doubtful text that can be explained perfectly well by following the work's line of thought.

I believe, therefore, that the gift of which Peter spoke in his Pentecostal discourse refers to the charismatic manifestation of the Spirit in testimony to the possession of the Spirit as the initiation of the messianic fulfillment of the kingdom of God, and that this gift is not intimately connected in this text with baptism but only in an external manner as a gift that usually follows. This gift is not given in order to strengthen the believers in their testimony to their faith, but is a spontaneous exuberance springing from the participation of the messianic people in salvation (i.e., in the kingdom of God). Therefore, in Acts the idea that every believer is called to give testimony is expressly excluded. The gift of the Spirit is not given for something but is a foretaste of anticipated fulfillment, although as a consequence it serves as a guarantee of belonging to the messianic people. Only those who are called to a special work are promised the dynamic aspect of the Spirit's help.

7

The Development of the Christian Life

7.1 "Filled with the Holy Spirit"—The Election of the Seven

IF, AS ILLUSTRATED IN the last chapter, the book of Acts does not speak of the intervention of the Holy Spirit at the commencement of the Christian life, an obvious question is, does the Spirit exercise any influence in the *development* of the Christian life? In chapter 5, we saw that the Spirit acts as the impulse for testimony and evangelization. Such an impulse does not pass through the disciples without effect but filters through their consciousness, saturating them with wisdom and fearlessness. It was not the Spirit that spoke in them but rather they themselves who spoke under his impulse, confronting threats and punishments. Luke has a special interest in correcting in this way those sayings transmitted by Mark and Matthew.[1] Wisdom and fearlessness are, therefore, effects of the Holy Spirit but also personal attributes manifesting in the development of the disciples' lives.

We have already explored the theme of fearlessness and partially that of wisdom,[2] because they formed part of the theme of testimony. We will not repeat this discussion, but it was necessary to call attention to its importance in preparation for discussing the present theme. In this section, we will analyze other passages that are more characteristic of

---

1. See secs. 1.1, 4.1, and 5.3. Recall that Luke 12:12 and 21:15 highlight the personal action of the disciples, in contrast with Matt 10:20 and Mark 13:11.

2. See sec. 5.3.

the religious-moral aspect that we will now study, even though they are connected to extroversion leading toward evangelization.[3] We will focus, therefore, on three groups of texts that, at least at first glance, appear to demonstrate an influence of the Spirit on the moral ethos of Christians. Section 7.1 analyzes the expression "full of the Holy Spirit and of faith [or wisdom]," which is practically exclusive to the story of the election of the seven. Section 7.2 analyzes the religious life of the Jerusalem community described in the summary passages. In sec. 7.3 we will study the action of the Spirit placed in sharp relief by human resistance. We will add in sec. 7.4 a summary that includes the two sections of this chapter.

The story of the election of the seven uses the expression "full of the Holy Spirit and of faith [or wisdom]," more than once. This use of the adjective πλήρης with a positive religious sense is practically unique to Luke. The apostles asked the Hellenists to elect "seven men of good standing, full of the Spirit and of wisdom" (6:3). Among those, Stephen emerges as "a man full of faith and the Holy Spirit" (6:5) who, precisely because he was "filled with the Holy Spirit, gazed into heaven and saw the glory of God and Jesus standing at the right hand of God" (7:55). The case of Barnabas may be considered as an extension of the same group of seven. He also acts as an intermediary between the Jewish and Hellenist communities in Jerusalem and is presented as "a good man, full of the Holy Spirit and of faith" (11:24).

The good reputation of those who were selected—faith, wisdom, and goodness being attributed to them in connection with their being full of the Spirit—suggests an influence by the Spirit in the area of Christian conduct. We must, however, examine each text to understand the significance and the extent of the relationship with the Spirit that the author attributes to them. To this end we will study: (a) the use of the adjective πλήρης; (b) those terms that serve as its objects; (c) the significance of these texts within the larger plan of the author; and finally, (d) we will then gather the results and draw some general conclusions.

---

3. It is impossible to establish a precise separation between the outward aspect of the Spirit (testimony and kerygma) and the more personal and interior aspect. The two are completely interdependent. The impulse toward testimony penetrates to the personal attitude, and the attitude of joy and enthusiasm reverberates in the growth of the community. In an analytical reflection, the two aspects may be considered separately but only if we do not forget their actual unity.

(a) *The use of the adjective.* The adjective πλήρης is used infrequently in the New Testament. Of the sixteen times that we encounter it, the two texts in Matthew[4] and the two in Mark[5] carry a pedestrian sense that is, to an extent, physical. In 2 John 8 and Luke 5:12, it has a similar though metaphorical sense. Only in two texts in the second part of Acts does it have a negative moral sense ("full of all deceit and villainy" [13:10] and "filled with rage" [19:28]). The remaining ten texts have a positive religious-moral sense, and we see the term applied to Jesus, who is "full of the Holy Spirit" (Luke 4:1) and "full of grace and truth" (John 1:4), and to others in the first part of Acts (6:3, 5, 8; 7:55; 9:36; 11:24).[6] The adjective πλήρης is constructed with a material genitive, with only one genitive in the two texts of the Gospel of Luke (4:1; 5:12); with two

---

4. Matt 14:20; 15:37.

5. Mark 4:28; 8:19.

6. In the Septuagint, we find the adjective πλήρης more frequently, as much in the sense of a physical degree (especially in the book of Numbers) as in a metaphorical sense (full of days, a full heart, a house full of every good thing) or with a morally negative sense (full of sin or deceit) and in a religiously positive sense (the land is full of the mercy of Yahweh or of his glory). Below is a brief outline of the sense in which πλήρης, πίμπλημι, and πληρόω are used in the NT.

	Sense	Matthew	Mark	Luke	John	Acts	Paul	Gen. Ep.	Revelation
πλήρης	Physical	2	2						
	Metaphorical			1				1	
	Moral neg.					2			
	Moral pos.			1	1	6			
πίμπλημι	Physical	1		1					
	Metaphorical	1	1	7		1			
	Moral neg.			2		3			
	Moral pos.			3		5			
πληρόω	Physical	1		(1)	1	1	1		
	Metaphorical	12	3	8	11	10	5	1	1
	Moral neg.	1			1	1			1
	Moral pos.	2		1	3	4	17	2	

The Septuagint uses πίμπλημι frequently also with religious-positive objects (joy in Ps 125:2; spirit in Prov 15:4; and holy spirit in Sir 48:12 in Codex Alexandrinus). Also, it uses πληρόω and fairly frequently (especially when referring to the Spirit of God) ἀναπληρόω, which the authors of the NT rarely use and never in reference to the Spirit.

of the texts in Acts (7:55, ὑπάρχων δὲ ... and 19:28, γενόμενοι); and with two genitives in John 1:4 and in six texts in Acts.[7]

The clarification of the precise relationship between both genitive objects of the adjective remains. This pairing of objects or of adjectives is frequent in Luke.[8] It is not easy to determine through formal grounds the exact relationship between the two members of certain parallel modes. However, considering the majority of the examples, it may be said that they are not equivalent members duplicated for mere similarity of sound but that they complete and clarify one another. One of the terms is usually more general and is made more concrete by the other. I see no indication of significance to the first or second place in this double object.[9] In those texts that refer to the Holy Spirit in the story of the election of the seven, it appears clear that the other object indicates the manner in which the fullness of the Spirit will be manifested. In order to elect seven delegates "full of the Spirit," the community had to

---

7. Following is an outline of the use of the construction of the following terms. First of all, I provide the total for the texts, without specifying other constructions such as the absolute form, which can be deduced based on the total for the constructions specified here.

	Sense	Matthew	Mark	Luke	John	Acts	Paul	Gen. Ep.	Revelation
πλήρης	TOTAL	2	2	2	1	8		1	
	1 mat. gen.			2		2			
	2 mat. gen				1	6			
πίμπλημι	TOTAL	2		13		9			
	1 mat. gen.	2		6		8			
	2 mat. gen.					1			
πληρόω	TOTAL	16	3	9	15	16	24	3	2
	mat. dat.			1			2		
	1 mat. gen.					3	2		
	2 mat. gen.						1		

8. See Morgenthaler, *Lukanische Geschichtsschreibung*, 1:23. See, for example, Luke 2:25, 52; 21:15; 23:50; Acts 3:14; 7:10; 9:36; and 10:2, 22, 35, 38.

9. In 6:5, the order is "faith and the Holy Spirit," while in 11:24 the terms are inverted, "The Holy Spirit and faith." The same thing occurs in 6:3 and 6:10 with respect to wisdom and the Spirit.

perceive this fullness through an external manifestation. The expression "full of the Spirit and wisdom" indicates in reality a single perceivable quality, namely wisdom. Acts does not wish to use the expression "spirit of wisdom" because it wishes to emphasize that it is not referring to a series of impulses or helps from God in a disconnected form but of the sending of the Holy Spirit who, always the same, will produce diverse effects or manifestations. It deals with electing men in whom the presence of the Spirit is manifested in a particular manner through wisdom. The term directly required is wisdom, but the author is not able to conceive of it in isolation from its source, which is the Holy Spirit.

This same cause-and-effect relationship between objects is confirmed clearly in the other pairings of Spirit/wisdom that are found in the same story. The adversaries are unable to resist "the wisdom and the Spirit with which he [Stephen] spoke" (6:10). Evidently, this does not refer to resisting the Holy Spirit directly. The controversy is with Stephen, but the profundity of his answers reveals to the sacred author that Stephen did not speak in his own natural ability but was saturated with supernatural wisdom that for the recorder of these sacred events is a gift of God by means of the Holy Spirit. Apparently, Luke has presented Stephen as a realization of the promise of Jesus concerning the assistance of the Spirit in the face of earthly powers. Luke 12:12 attributes it to the teaching of the Spirit and Luke 21:15 to Jesus, "[F]or I will give you words and a wisdom that none of your opponents will be able to withstand or contradict."[10] It appears that the pairing of faith/Spirit in Acts 6:5 and 11:24 would have to be interpreted in the same cause-and-effect relationship. The sense in which faith should be understood will be further addressed later, but it appears that faith is equally a manifestation of the gift of the Spirit. Or, if one prefers, faith is the gift given by the Spirit, who in his turn is called the gift of God because he anticipates the possession of the fullness of the kingdom of God and because he is always ready to assist believers in their times of need.

Similarly, a cause-and-effect relationship is found in the object relationship between the two members of the expression "and the disciples were filled with joy and with the Holy Spirit" (13:52). The Spirit

---

10. See in n. 1 the sections where I have explained these texts. [In this contextual vein, so too Soards, *Speeches in Acts*, 44; Luke's presentation of Stephen, contrary to human powers of reasoning, demonstrates that salvation is only available in Jesus (see Kilgallen, "Speech of Stephen"). —Ed.]

is the cause of the joy, and the joy is the manifestation of the possession of the Spirit. We find a relationship between objects leading to a more concrete understanding, perhaps through a manifestation but not through a cause-and-effect relationship, in the expression "devoted to good works and acts of charity" (9:36). The acts of charity are demonstrations, perhaps one could say manifestations, of good works, but one can by no means say that they are the effects of good works. An additive, complimentary relationship of nuances can be found frequently in passages that contain qualifying adjectives: Jesus is "holy and righteous" (3:14); Cornelius "a devout man who feared God" (10:2) and who is "upright and God-fearing" (10:22); Peter came to understand that for God "anyone who fears him and does what is right is acceptable to him" (10:35).[11]

An additive complementary relationship would be, in my opinion, the sense of the anointing of Jesus "with the Holy Spirit and with power" (10:38) since, according to reasons cited in sec. 2.1, the power is consciously separated by Luke from being among the works of the Spirit. The anointing with the Spirit refers to the proclamation of the message, and the power refers to the confirmation of the message by means of wonders. Each aspect complements the other, so that they function together as a unit in the prophetic mission of Jesus. One formal expression leaves open the possibility that the relationship between objects is one of cause-and-effect, of manifestation or more complete understanding, or of an additive relationship. It is the coherence of the larger theme, though, that leads me to prefer the last of these formal possibilities.

I conclude, therefore, that the use of the adjective πλήρης with a double material object in the genitive and with a positive religious sense is a Hellenistic formula. The story of the election of the seven applies it preferentially to the Holy Spirit, giving to the other object a sense of effect or of a manifestation of the fullness of the Spirit.

(b) *The objects of the adjective.* The objects of the adjective πλήρης and of the verb πίμπλημι in a positive religious sense are reduced, practically, to the Holy Spirit, wisdom, faith, joy, power, grace (or favor), and perhaps also to the goodness of Stephen. The paired relationship with the Spirit is found only with wisdom, faith, and joy. Wisdom is

---

11. We find an object relationship through the addition of a new nuance in Luke 2:25, "righteous and God fearing"; 2:52, "Jesus increased in wisdom and in years, in divine and human favor"; and 23:50, Joseph was a "good and righteous" man.

applied in biblical language to the man who has received an extraordinary knowledge of the plans of God, which shapes his own conduct.[12] Luke employs it in this sense in the infancy of Christ (Luke 2:40, 52).[13] In our texts, wisdom is a gift that is used directly toward testimony, both in its negative sense of overcoming worldly powers and in its positive sense of evangelization. The wisdom required in the election of the seven is an eminently pastoral charisma. Haenchen defines it as ". . . religious wisdom and the capacity to express it persuasively."[14]

Faith is one of the most abundant and rich concepts in the New Testament. I believe, however, that these texts have more of an Old Testament sense of faith that places confidence in the extraordinary power of God and in his intervention on behalf of his people.[15] We encounter this sense clearly in Acts 14:9, "seeing that he had faith [πίστιν] to be healed. . . ."[16] Certainly this does not refer to the act by which one begins to believe in Jesus, as this would not be a sign for distinguishing Stephen (6:5) or Barnabas (11:24) from the larger community. I have already dealt sufficiently with initial faith in sec. 6.3. The faith of Stephen and Barnabas appears to indicate a pastoral gift very similar to wisdom, but instead of emphasizing the cognitive profundity that made Stephen irrefutable, it would refer in particular to extreme confidence in the wondrous intervention of God. It is probable, even though in reality we have no certain indication to confirm it, that the faith of Stephen comes to be declared through the continuation of the story, "Stephen, full of grace and power, did great wonders and signs among the people" (6:8).

---

12. See Wilckens, "σοφία," 514: "σοφία here epitomizes a pious manner of life which shapes the character and which finds expression in early and astonishing knowledge of the Law. . . . Luke portrays Stephen similarly in Ac. 6:3, 10 except that here πνεῦμα is used as well as σοφία, so that his wisdom of speech is shown as a divine gift."

13. Wisdom is found frequently associated with δύναμις (Matt 13:54; Mark 6:2; 1 Cor 1:24) and with the Spirit (Eph 1:17; Col 1:9).

14. *Acts*, 271, commentary on 6:10. ". . . die religiöse Erkenntnis und die Fähigkeit, sie überzeugend auszusprechen" (*Apostelgeschichte*, 223–24). On the other hand, he believes 6:3 deals with "wordly prudence" (262) ("praktische Lebensklugheit," 216). The next subsection examines the purpose of the election of the seven and their integration into the work, a purpose that is pastoral, not practical, administration.

15. Bultmann ("πίστις," 206) observes: "In the OT and Judaism . . . the sense of 'trust' is combined with faith. The same is true in the NT as well. This sense is especially prominent where the influence of the OT and Jewish tradition is strong."

16. Zorell, "πίστις," *Lexicon* 1(2). [Danker, *Lexicon*, 285 (believing response to divine outreach). —Ed.]

On the other hand, the faith of Barnabas, of a more passive and welcoming temperament than that of Stephen or Paul, is recognized in the confidence with which he recognizes the intervention of God and with which he encourages the perseverance of the Gentiles who were recently converted in Antioch. Wisdom and faith, in the story of the election of the seven, designate extraordinary gifts that serve to distinguish the seven elect. But it should not be thought that only seven members of the community possessed these gifts, because the number seven was chosen for other external motives.[17] The *goodness* of Barnabas is perhaps also related to the fullness of the Spirit, even though it falls outside of the two-part construction "for he was a good man, full of the Holy Spirit and faith" (11:24).[18]

The *joy* of Barnabas also has a relationship, though not very precise, with the Holy Spirit: "When he came and saw the grace of God, he rejoiced, and he exhorted them all to remain faithful to the Lord with steadfast devotion; for he was a good man . . ." (11:23–24). Probably the cause of the joy is the presence of salvation among the Gentiles, while the action of the Spirit would fall more directly on the pastoral action of Barnabas, (comparing παρεκάλει in 11:23 with παρακλήσει in 9:31). However, a very precise division does not appear to be made in this text between cause and effect, and in a certain sense the Spirit may be considered as the subjective, internal cause that makes Barnabas rejoice at the spread of salvation among the Gentiles. Joy is attributed to the Spirit more clearly in another text with a double object: "And the disciples were filled with joy and with the Holy Spirit" (13:52). This joy at being expelled from Antioch is very similar to that of the apostles for having been insulted for the cause of the name of Jesus (5:41). Both cases have to do with an aspect of the Spirit's assistance before earthly powers, although there is no express allusion to such a promise.[19]

---

17. Concerning the number seven, see Gächter, "Sieben," esp. 149–50.

18. Joseph of Arimathea was a "good and righteous man" (Luke 23:50), and his compassionate attitude bears a certain resemblance with that of Barnabas. We encounter the distinct nuance in Jesus' praise for the "good and trustworthy servant" (Luke 19:17; cf. Matt 25:21) and in the more generic saying, "the good person out of the good treasure of the heart produces good" (Luke 6:45; cf. Matt 12:35). A more transcendent reflection on goodness is indicated in Jesus' response, "Why do you call me good? No one is good but God alone" (Luke 18:19; cf. Matt 19:17 and Mark 10:18).

19. Acts 5:41 evidently participates in the Pentecostal impulse, even though it is attributed explicitly to the Holy Spirit. We see, therefore, that joy is attributed to the Holy

We can affirm that joy is one of the effects of the Holy Spirit. However, recalling other descriptions of joy that have been given us by Luke, even using the same terms (χαρά, χαίρω), we see that it is not an effect exclusive to the Spirit. We find the joy of the brethren over the release of Peter (12:14), the joy of the Gentiles that hear the message of Paul and receive it by faith (13:48), the joy of the brethren at hearing of the conversion of the Gentiles (15:3), and of the converts at the reading of the message from the Jerusalem Council (15:31). Two passages that refer to joy following baptism have been interpreted as a sign of the first presence of the Spirit:[20] Acts 8:8 refers to the activity of Philip in Samaria and 8:39 to the joy of the eunuch after his baptism. It does not appear, however, that a solid foundation exists for making such a deduction. Luke does not speak to us of the gift of the Spirit in baptism, and it is not possible to deduce this teaching from this remote, problematic allusion.

Joy is a consequence of the presence of the messianic blessings and in particular of salvation.[21] The joy attributed to the Holy Spirit is not the joy common to every believer but is a special manifestation in order to provide testimony—in its negative sense of resistance before tribunals (5:41), or in the positive sense of evangelization (11:24 and 9:31), or as an especially intense state of the anticipated fruition of the fullness of the kingdom, as we will see in our study of the term ἀγαλλίασις.[22]

(c) *The larger plan of the author.* It is highly probable that the story of the election of the seven was already well established when it came to Luke, even though it would be very difficult to determine which are the original expressions and which arise from his adaptation. In order to understand the sense of the texts, it would be advisable to analyze, as much as possible, the intention of the event in the independent story and the purpose attributed to it by Luke in the general conception of

---

Spirit explicitly on various occasions (13:52), implicitly on others (5:41 and 11:23), but still on others it is clear that the author had not thought to attribute it to the Holy Spirit but rather to other immediate causes. This warns us that we should not fix our hermeneutical classifications too firmly but keep them elastic and porous. Regarding the messianic sense of joyous exultation, see Bultmann, "ἀγαλλίασις," 19–21.

20. Oulton, "Holy Spirit, Baptism," 238–39.

21. See Luke 1:14, 28; 2:10; 6:23 (beatitudes); 10:20, "but rejoice that your names are written in heaven"; 13:17; (15:5, 7, 10, joy for the sinner that has repented); 19:6 (Zacchaeus); 19:37 (the disturbance during the triumphal entry into Jerusalem); and 24:41, 52 (the Easter appearances).

22. See sec. 7.2.

his work.²³ Gächter has shown in minute detail that the incident of the service to the widows does not correspond to the solemnity of the larger scene.²⁴ The consecration of the seven (6:6) and the evangelistic activity that is expressly attributed to Stephen and Philip allow us to see that it is not a mere beneficent activity but rather the pastoral problem of the Greek-speaking group.²⁵ It is not the Hebrews that denounce Stephen

23. See Haenchen, *Acts*, 264–69 = *Apostelgeschichte*, 218–22; Schumacher, *Diakon Stephanus*; Cadbury, "Hellenists"; Grundmann, "Hellenistische Christentum"; idem, "Apostel zwischen," esp. 113–14; Klausner, "Jewish Christianity and Gentile Christianity" in his *From Jesus to Paul*, ch. 5; Menchini, "Discorso di Stefano Protomartire"; Gächter, "Sieben;" Förster, "Stephanus und die Urgemeinde," passim; Trocmé, *Livres des Actes*, 183–91; Simon, *St. Stephen and the Hellenists*; Bihler, "Stephanusbericht"; idem, *Stephanusgeschichte im Zusammenhang*; Barnard, "Saint Stephen"; Rinaldi, "Stefano." See also sec. 8.3 and Cullmann, "L'opposition contre le temple."

24. Gächter, "Sieben": "The entire complex of measures taken and above all the sacramental consecration are clearly directed to the area of spiritual-religion, in actuality to the area of ministry [Der ganze Komplex der getroffenen Massnahmen und vor allem die sakramentale Weihe zielten eindeutig auf das Gebiet des Geistlich-Religiösen ab, auf das Gebiet der Seelsorge im eigentlichen Sinn]" (140); ". . . the Hellenist portion of the believers appoint official leaders from their own ranks, that they might work among the Hellenists as helpers and representative of the twelve [. . . dem hellenistischen Teil der Gläubigen aus ihren eigenen Reihen amtliche Leiter zu bestellen, die als Gehilfen un Vertreter der Zwölf unter den Hellenisten wirken sollten]" (143); "One of the principal tasks of the seven should be the proclamation of the word of God within the community, and with it was also inevitably connected the faith proclamation to those outside [Eine der Hauptaufgaben der Sieben sollte die Verkündigung des Wortes Gottes innerhalb der Gemeinde sein, und Damit war unvermeidlich auch die Glaubensverkündigung nach aussen verbunden]" (144). Gächter believes that this has to do with the creation of a college or association that today we would call Episcopal, "with the fullness of consecration power [mit der Fülle der Weihegewalt]." Through other indications from Acts can be seen the creation of another Episcopal college for the Hebrews that would corresponded to the πρεσβύτεροι introduced in 11:30 with no explanation. The author is thinking of certain limitations of jurisdiction at the outset of the activity of such colleges.

25. Cadbury believes that Ἑλληνισταί as Ἕλληνες designates the Gentiles. He assumes that already in Pentecost some Gentiles were converted. It would not have to be, therefore, a progressive opening that culminates in the conversion of Cornelius, or at least this progression would not be systematic or linear. "On the contrary, all were represented at the Day of Pentecost" (Cadbury, "Hellenists," 65, 68). Trocmé (*Livre des Actes*, 189), on the other hand, cites three passages in Acts 6:1; 9:29 and 11:20 in which the term Ἑλληνιστής appears and concludes that "it is an imprecise term that is applicable to a common characteristic in different circumstances. This characteristic could not be the Greek style of living, which the Jewish adversary of Stephen and Paul held in horror; it has to be the Greek language [il s'agit d'un terme imprécis qui s'applique à un trait commun à des milieux divers. Cette caractéristique ne saurait être la vie à la grecque, que les adversaires juifs d'Etienne et de Paul considéraient certainement

but rather the Hellenists themselves (6:9). In the same way, it was the immediate persecution of the apostles (8:1) and of other pious men that followed the burial of Stephen that forced Philip to depart (8:4–5), along with others from Cyprus and Cyrene (11:19–20). The dispute of the service of tables constitutes no more than the initial anecdote in the story. It is difficult to determine to what extent this was the historical motive or the pretext for the institution of the seven.[26] We can say that, in the story, the service of tables does not constitute the purpose of the institution. The author claims to narrate the official establishment of a group of Hellenist overseers to a level immediate below that of the apostles.

In this plan of the story, wisdom and faith, as gifts of the Holy Spirit, evidently have a pastoral aim. The seven elected ones were already distinguished for their zeal in testifying and in evangelization and for their profound interpretation of the message of Jesus in contrast with other interpretations that were more in keeping with Jewish traditions. The institution of the office of the seven officially sanctions the pastoral primacy of these charismatic expressions. Luke has seen in this story a first step toward the evangelization of the Gentiles, which constitutes the thesis of his work. The Hellenists continue to preach among the Greek-speaking Jews, but are now open to the language (and in part also to the way of thinking) of the Gentiles. Persecution, particularly, will lead them to evangelize in Samaria (Philip), Phoenicia, Cyprus, and Antioch (11:19).

The section that extends from the episode with Stephen until the Jerusalem Council presents more obvious signs of the redaction that distorts some narratives in order to insert other information.[27] (Section 8.5

---

avec horreur; c'est donc la langue grecque]." That there exists among the Hellenists a majority of Greco-Roman observers does not eliminate the possibility that there exists another group, probably not Christian, of a conservative passion that provokes persecution (6:9; 8:1, 3; and 9:29). [For discussion of these and other details, see also Schneider, "Stephanus, die Hellenisten und Samaria." —Ed.]

26. We could be dealing with the pretext that specified other less important complaints of the Hellenists, who would perhaps not know Aramaic well and would feel neglected or who were not in agreement with certain traditional Jewish practices. It could also be that the situation is reduced to a question of serving tables, but afterward the seven took on pastoral importance in the community. Whatever the case, the first editor has supplemented the anecdote about the serving of tables.

27. See Cerfaux, "Composition de la première partie"; Jeremias, "Untersuchungen zum Quellenproblem"; Grundmann, "Hellenistische Christentum,"; Sahlin, *Messias und das Gottesvolk*, 351–70; Trocmé, *Livre des Actes*, ch. 6.

examines Luke's structure in greater depth.) As will be demonstrated, Luke has taken the story of the election of the seven as a justification for the evangelization of the Hellenists and even the Gentiles. However, given the importance of the event that he wishes to justify, neither this justification nor the vocation that Paul received from Christ is sufficient, so he prefers to attribute it to Peter, who is in turn compelled by the testimony of the Spirit. The decision is officially sanctioned by the calling of the Jerusalem Council. Luke has accepted the sense of the story of the election of the seven, even though he has separated it into two parts, as a first approach to the Gentiles and as an extension of the case of Cornelius.

The sense of the wisdom and faith of the seven and in particular of Philip (and equally of Barnabas) is eminently kerygmatic. Perhaps the purpose of attending to the internal difficulties of the community is less prominent than in the story. That is to say, Luke emphasized the evangelistic sense over the pastoral sense.

(d) *General Conclusions.* I conclude this study of the expression "full of the Holy Spirit and of faith [or wisdom]" in the story of the election of the seven by noting the following characteristics. The fullness of the Holy Spirit is something observable that distinguishes certain members of the community, qualifying them to be elected as equally responsible as the apostles. This fullness is manifest in wisdom, faith (probably as a charismatic confidence), and perhaps in the goodness and joy of Barnabas. These qualities are special gifts, but they do not appear directly as wonders. Their purpose is evangelistic and pastoral, and they are expected to be permanent to the point that they are the basis for the designation of an institutional office. These gifts are shared by diverse members of the community, but not by everyone. The fullness of the Spirit manifested in wisdom, faith, joy, and goodness has a dynamic outward purpose for the edification of the community and for evangelization, but it concurrently holds them to a personal ethical-religious lifestyle, conforming behavior with the sense of the message (wisdom) to the point of converting it into spiritual interior joy, even when they suffer persecutions for their proclamation or when they risk their very lives.

Luke has attributed to the Holy Spirit the extraordinary kerygmatic dynamism of the communities and has not stopped to develop the influence of the Spirit in the religious-ethical life of every believer. However, he has left us indications that the influence of the Spirit, precisely because it respects the person, motivates primarily the personal spiritual perspective of the charismatics.[28] Acts has not avoided attributing these ethical-religious effects to the Spirit, as it has avoided attributing to him wonders and healings, because these interior sensations would not be a major participation in salvation (that comes only from Christ) but rather an extraordinary activation of the salvation forces already acquired. Joy, faith (as wisdom and as confidence), and goodness have been received initially through Christ, but their extraordinary intensification (whether in an order of fullness or a kerygmatic order) results from the influence of the Holy Spirit.

7.2 Religious Life According to the Summaries of Luke

By way of the election of the seven, we have examined the fullness of the Spirit in certain members of the community in order to see if the author relates it with the practice of the Christian life. Now, we take the opposite tack. We will take the summary statements in which the author typifies the Christian life in order to see if we discover any allusion to the presence of the Spirit in them. The summaries of Luke have stimulated an abundance of literature.[29] The author uses them to articulate two narrations, returning attention to the community and affirming its continual progress. Beginning with Dibelius, it is commonly conceded that Luke composed the summaries generalizing cases from individual contexts because of a lack of more precise data. Though their historical importance can be somewhat relative, the value of these summaries for understanding the perspective of the author is critical.

---

28. [This observation by Haya-Prats bears on the current discussion of religious experience. For reasons why religious experience is considered suspect by some, despite the importance given to it in Scripture and tradition, see O'Connor, *Pentecostal Movement*, 267–79. Congar moved the conversation along with respect to the OT and NT; see Congar, "Holy Spirit in the 'Economy'" (for Acts material with interaction with Haya-Prats, cf. 44–49). See too, Kurz, "Servant in Isaiah"; Tibbs, *Religious Experience*, passim. —Ed.]

29. A good synopsis can be seen in Haenchen, *Acts*, 190–96 = *Apostelgeschichte*, 152–58; Trocmé, *Livre des Actes*, 40; Wikenhauser, *Apostelgeschichte*, 72. The following articles are especially interesting: Lake, "Communism of Acts"; Cadbury, "Summaries in Acts"; Cerfaux, "Composition;" idem, "Première communauté chrétienne"; Jeremias, "Untersuchungen zum Quellenproblem"; Dibelius, *Aufsätze*, 15–16, 111–12; Benoit, "Remarques sur les 'summaries'"; Zimmermann, "Sammelberichte der Apostelgeschichte."

In the first part, three grand summaries are highlighted that describe the religious life of the community: 2:42–47; 4:32–35; and 5:11–16.[30] There are other isolated verses that present the same generally reflective character. Because of their brevity, they have been classified as "stops" placed by Luke periodically throughout the narrative. Such stops refer to the dispersion of the community and are like refrains (as found in Greek epic poems) to the dispersion of the gospel "unto the ends of the earth."[31] These stops generally express the growth of the community with an impersonal formula, equivalent to the theological passive. However, 9:31 refers, as we have already seen, to the comforting of the Holy Spirit.[32]

The three grand summaries present a very unfortunate literary structure that Benoit attributes to the interference of an earlier redactor.[33] We encounter three themes in these passages, each one dominant in one of the summaries but also intermixed with the dominant themes of the other two summaries. Harnack has attempted to explain this by means of his theory of two sources. Cadbury recalls the Lukan technique of the repetition of the same theme. Jeremias and Cerfaux attempt to distinguish those verses that are original to the written sources from those added by Luke. If a summary in a written source existed, it appears that it would be found in the second summary in Acts, in chapter four. For our part, it will suffice to study the three themes of the summaries through their use of vocabulary, examined successively as (a) the religious life of the community, (b) the giving up of material goods, and (c) the admiration provoked by the wonders that the apostles worked.

(a) *The religious life of the community* occupies the place of honor in the first summary, 2:42–47, and is repeated as an allusion interspersed in 4:32 and in 5:13.[34] This life is characterized by perseverance

---

30. The precise limits of each summary vary according to the delineating criteria used by the various commentators: Cerfaux identifies 2:42–47; 4:32–35; and 5:11–16; Zimmermann ("Sammelberichte," 76) has the first summary beginning at 2:41.

31. It is difficult to identify precisely all the verses that should be considered as brief summaries that repeat the refrain of the spread of the community. The following are commonly cited: 1:14; 4:4; 5:5b; 5:42; 6:7; 9:31; 11:21; 12:24; 13:48–49; 13:52; 16:5; 18:8; 19:10, 20; 28:31.

32. I have already dealt with 9:31 in sec. 5.4, and I will return to a more ample discussion of the theme of the spread of the community through the impulse of the Spirit in ch. 8.

33. Benoit, "Remarques sur les 'summaries,'" 7–10.

34. To the bibliography already cited above in n. 29 above with regard to the

(προσκαρτεροῦντες),³⁵ an attribute typical of the second generation that has seen the Parousia deferred indefinitely. This perseverance applies to four realizations: the teaching of the apostles, the community (κοινωνία), the breaking of bread, and prayer. It is not our concern to determine the full scope of these four expressions but rather to understand in what sense we can relate them to the influence of the Spirit. The teaching of the apostles is never related directly to the Spirit. Only indirectly, as a complement to evangelization, can teaching be found in Acts as being derived from the impulse of the Spirit. The temper of the believers to persevere in this teaching appears to be even less related to the Spirit. Nor does the act of the breaking of bread appear to be related to the Spirit. However, in 2:46 the aspect of the demonstration of joy, ἐν ἀγαλλιάσει, is added, which presents certain points of contact with the Spirit.

Luke 10:21 tells us that Jesus "rejoiced in the Spirit" (ἠγαλλιάσατο). In the infancy narratives, rejoicing appears in the context of the manifestations of the Spirit, even though it does not depend directly on them (1:14, the promise of the rejoicing of Zechariah at the birth of John; 1:44, the joy of John in his mother's womb; 1:47, the rejoicing of Mary; Acts 2:26 applies rejoicing in Ps 15:9 to the messianic sense of the resurrection of Christ). Rejoicing is, therefore, a messianic fruit, a complement of the gift of the Spirit and at times precedes that gift. However, we cannot conclude that the presence of this rejoicing necessarily supposes an attribution to the action of the Spirit. Rejoicing appears to overflow from the first moment in which the presence of the messianic gifts are perceived. Rejoicing in the Holy Spirit would be a more intense degree. We obtained the same result in our study of the term *joy*.³⁶

---

summaries may be added the following: Haenchen, *Acts*, 230–35 = *Apostelgeschichte*, 187–92; Hauck, "κοινός"; Thorton, *Common Life*, passim; Dupont, "Communauté des biens"; Schweizer, *Geist und Gemeinde*; Menoud, *Vie de l'Eglise naissante*. [See too Pesch, "Gemeinsame Leben der Gläubigen," "Güter gemeinschaft der Gläubigen," and "'Zeichen und Wunder' der Apostel" in his *Apostelgeschichte I*, 128–33, 179–94, 204–208, respectively. —Ed.]

35. Acts uses this term six times, twice with the sense of recurring faithfulness, whether it be Simon the Magician toward Philip or the servants of Cornelius. Paul prefers the term ὑπομονή but also employs προσκαρτερέω four times; Rom 12:12 and Eph 6:18 refer to it with regard to prayer.

36. See sec. 7.1. Bultmann, "ἀγαλλίασις."

The term κοινωνία, "communion with" or "participation in," includes various aspects that are emphasized to a greater or lesser degree in diverse passages. One can know of communion by means of the Eucharist or by means of the collection made for the needs of the poor, from the sharing of material goods or for the agreement in thought and unity of desire resulting from the teaching of the apostles.[37] Menoud and Dupont interpret this passage as a community of spiritual life that is expressed in the ease of sharing individual goods when others in the community have need of them. This interpretation is solidly supported in Luke's own expansions that refer to the sale by part of the community of their own goods in order to provide for the needs of the poor in the community, and also by the mention of καρδία καὶ ψυχὴ μία (4:32).[38] There is no indication that Luke considers this communion to be an effect of the presence of the Holy Spirit. It is true that, in the narrating of the life of the community after Pentecost, a general influence of the gift of the Spirit may be supposed in each new development of the community. Perhaps this is the thought that guides a highly regarded author like Haenchen when he affirms, "But Luke understood this also as Spirit-effect, that the multitude of believers . . . was one heart and one soul."[39] Von Baer also tends to derive all activity from the Spirit, both of Christ and of the community after his solemn reception of the Spirit at the Jordan and the believers' at Pentecost. Other authors have expressed themselves in the same way.[40]

37. Dupont ("Communauté") summarizes the diverse interpretations of the term κοινωνία. An abundant bibliography exists on this term: Carr, "Fellowship"; Scott, "What Happened at Pentecost?"; idem, "Fellowship or κοινωνία"; Wood, "Fellowship"; Campbell, "Κοινωνία and Its Cognates," esp. 374–75; Seesemann, *Begriff* κοινωνία *im Neuen Testament*, esp. 87–92 on Acts 2:42; Lyonnet, "κοινωνία de l'Eglise primitive."

38. The commentaries are in agreement that a mere sharing of material goods is not referred to, although the action of Barnabas (4:36–37) is presented as a generous selflessness, and the sin of Ananias consists of lying and not of retaining the field or its full price as Peter expressly says (5:4). Other indications demonstrate the existence of other more necessary things that had to be maintained by the community or of others who possessed the houses where the community met. Cerfaux (*Recueil* 2:150–52) and Dupont ("Communauté," 518–19) have pointed out that the original Greek for the expression πάντα κοινά represents the ideal of friendship and not a communal regimen. It deals fundamentally with an intimate communion of souls that were disposed to share their material goods in order to offer succor to needy brothers.

39. *Acts*, 232. "Aber Lukas verstand es auch als Geistwirkung, dass die Menge der Gläubigen . . . ein Herz und eine Seele war" (*Apostelgeschichte*, 190).

40. See sec. 6.1.

Thorton studied "the communion of the Holy Spirit" in the following texts: "the grace of the Lord Jesus Christ, the love of God, and the communion [κοινωνία] of the Holy Spirit be with all of you" (2 Cor 13:13); "any sharing in the Spirit [εἴ τις κοινωνία πνεύματος]" (Phil 2:1); and "those who have shared [μετόχους] in the Holy Spirit" (Heb 6:4). He asks whether these deal with the communion of the entire community produced by the action of the Holy Spirit, or of the participation (= communion) of the entire community *in* the same Holy Spirit. Compare this text with the passage that interests us in Acts 2:4 that, for him, evidently deals with the κοινωνία of the Holy Spirit. Now then, this κοινωνία refers to the sharing in common of one's own goods, which goes beyond the mere giving of alms or material goods.[41] Thorton opts for an interpretation of the κοινωνία as participation ("sharing") in the Spirit that in turn leads to communion ("fellowship") among Christians: "The essence of the κοινωνία was a life shared in common. In Acts, it is described by reference to a gift of the Spirit outpoured and received. The common object was the gift of the Holy Spirit as imparted to the disciples. . . . The author of Acts would have agreed that 'the κοινωνία' to which he refers in 2:42 is not to be distinguished from 'the κοινωνία of the Holy Spirit' of which Paul wrote in 2 Corinthians 13:14 or from 'κοινωνία πνεύματος' at Philippians 2:1."[42]

Thorton's interpretation does not bear in mind the context. This essential element of the life of the community would not be found easily situated in the midst of an enumeration such as that found in 2:42. Even more difficult to explain would be its grammatical dependence on προσκαρτεροῦντες that indicates an active attitude of perseverance. Perseverance is perfectly understood in the teaching of the apostles, in the practice of the breaking of bread, in prayer, and in both spiritual and material openness to brothers, but perseverance would not be understood in the context of the participation in the gift of the Spirit that is rather a passive event. Also, the Pauline idea of participation in one single Spirit itself is foreign to Acts.[43] For Acts, it deals with an equal

41. Thorton, *Common Life*: "The whole of this section of Acts is occupied with showing that the κοινωνία was something altogether new, originated by an act of God. It came into being (in its full form) through the descent of the Holy Spirit upon the disciples at Pentecost" (6). "For him [Luke] the gift of the Spirit was by far the most momentous and characteristic of the things shared in common . . ." (74).

42. Ibid., 75.

43. 1 Cor 12:13, "For in the one Spirit we were all baptized . . ."

gift, τὴν ἴσην δωρεὰν . . . ὡς καὶ ἡμῖν (11:17), that testifies to divine election, anticipates its fulfillment, or influences in decisive evangelistic situations, but there is no indication of a mystic union of believers in the Spirit. Neither does it appear that the Spirit is indispensable for every believer. Rather, it is a normal experience in the communities, but the author assumes that it may be lacking in isolated persons.[44]

With respect to the second alternative of Thorton's interpretation—that the communion is caused by the Holy Spirit—it is more easily reconciled with the context, but there is no indication that demonstrates perseverance in communion as an effect of the Spirit. The task consists specifically in examining the indications that it would be possible to discover this thought implicit in Luke. Without any such indications, affirmation is not justifiable. In this passage, it remains highly problematic whether Luke attributes to the Spirit the union of the community. A smaller group had felt equally united prior to Pentecost, but perhaps in this summary something more extraordinary exists that Luke has seen as an influence of the Spirit. This situation is possible and even probable but is by no means certain.[45]

Further, perseverance applies to *prayers* (προσευχαῖς, 2:42). In 2:46–47, they are presented again as "day by day . . . they spent much time together in the temple . . . praising God [αἰνοῦντες]." According to 5:12, "they were all together on Solomon's porch." Is there in these expressions some vestige that attributes perseverance in prayer to the impulse of the

---

44. See sec. 3.1, and esp. the summary of ch. 3. See also the difference between Paul's and Luke's concepts of the Spirit in sec. 1.1.

45. [Perhaps a little more sympathy to the probability of Thorton's suggestion that the fellowship of which Luke writes in the first summary statement (2:41–47, including prayers [προσευχαῖς, 2:42]) is attributable in his mind to Pentecostal events may be gleaned from Laurentin's insights and descriptions relative to Acts 2:4 in *Catholic Pentecostalism*, "Glossolalia from the Religious Viewpoint," 79–83. The section is quite compatible with fellowship and with common glossolalic prayer, as is his interpretive comment (87): "How could a large crowd hear distinctly a hundred or so people (cf. Ac. 1:14–15) who were all speaking at once? The whole account becomes more intelligible if we relate it to our contemporary experience of tongue speaking. The 120 disciples now inspired by the Spirit, emerge from the upper room. Their tongue speaking is a collective glossolalic prayer. The impressive musical harmony of this praying arouses the enthusiasm of a crowd of Eastern pilgrims, and the enthusiasm spreads rapidly through the crowd. Despite the language barrier, the pilgrims recognize an inspired celebration of 'the marvels of God,' as they assert in 2:11. Some confirmation of this interpretation is afforded by the fact that some in the crowd are perplexed or outright ironic and even sardonic, 'They have been drinking too much new wine' (2:13)." —Ed.]

Spirit? A study conducted earlier on the relation between prayer and the Holy Spirit as seen by Luke has already brought us to the following conclusions. Two types of prayer can be considered in Luke. The first may be called ordinary prayer and is expressed using the verbs of supplication προσεύχομαι, αἰτέω, and δέομαι and their corresponding nouns, along with the cultic verbs λειτουργέω, εὐλογέω, and ὑμνέω. None of these verbs appear as an action caused by an impulse of the Holy Spirit. However, the temper of man is frequently described prior to the manifestation of the Spirit.[46] It is notable that Luke is the only Gospel writer that presents Christ as being in prayer at the Jordan at the descent of the Spirit upon him (Ἰησοῦ βαπτισθέντος καὶ προσευχομένου, Luke 3:21)[47] and that mentions the Spirit in the promise of Jesus ("how much more will the heavenly Father give the Holy Spirit to those who ask him," Luke 11:13), where Matt 7:11 is content with the general term ἀγαθά.[48]

The second type of prayer may be called joyful or rejoicing prayer and is expressed by the verbs μεγαλύνω, εὐλογέω, δοξάζω, αἰνέω

---

46. Luke presents the salvific manifestations in an atmosphere of liturgical and private prayer—the announcement to Zechariah (Luke 1:8, 10, 13), the baptism of Christ (Luke 3:21), the transfiguration (9:28; neither Mark 9:2 nor Matt 17:2 mentions the prayer), the selection of the apostles (Luke 6:12), and the primacy of Peter (Luke 9:18), being on the latter two occasions the only one to cite the preceding prayer of Christ. Another prayer of Christ that he alone shows use (Luke 5:16) and the prayer for Peter in Luke 22:32 are also exclusive to Luke, as is the prayer in Gethsemane (Luke 22:40, 44–46). Exhortation in prayer and the doctrine concerning the form of prayer is found in Luke 6:28; 10:2; 11:1, 2, 9–10, 13; 18:1, 10–11; 19:46; 21:36. The texts in which Christ lifts up his eyes to heaven, both in benediction and in thanksgiving, can also be added. Acts presents the apostles in prayer awaiting the gift of the Spirit (1:14) and the community persevering in prayer (2:42) and petitioning for boldness before the threats of the Sanhedrin (4:24, 31). We see prayer that God would guide the apostles in their selection of a replacement (1:24), accompanying the laying on of hands in order to impart the Holy Spirit (8:15) or any type of ecclesiastical mission (6:6 and 13:3), prayer prior to experiencing a miraculous healing (9:40 and 28:8), and prayer for the forgiveness of sin (8:22, 24). There is the prayer of Ananias and of Paul (9:11) and the prayer of Peter and Cornelius (10:2, 4, 9, 30–31; 11:5), prayers that prepare the way for both of these conversions so decisive for the church, prayer for Peter during his imprisonment (12:5, 12), prayer as a custom of Paul (16:25; 22:17) and of the Pauline communities (14:22; 16:13, 16; 20:36; 21:5). The apostles considered their most important obligation the preaching of the word and prayer (6:4).

47. Cf. Matt 3:16; Mark 1:10; John 1:32.

48. Concerning the supposed petition of our Father with respect to the sanctifying Spirit, see sec. 6.2.

and ἐξομολογέω. Frequently, it is pronounced with a greater intensity of voice, φωνῇ μεγάλῃ, ἐπαίρω τὴν φωνήν[49] and is situated in the context of spiritual joy, χαρά, ἀγαλλίασις, and μακάριος. This joyful prayer is always fruit of a supernatural manifestation that could be the gift of the Holy Spirit, the message of an angel, an announcement of salvation, or the manifestation of the salvific force of God through a miracle. It interests us here especially to recall the texts in which the manifestation of the Spirit leads to this joyful prayer: "Elizabeth was filled with the Holy Spirit and exclaimed with a loud cry, 'Blessed are you among women, and blessed is the fruit of your womb'" (Luke 1:41-42); "Zechariah was filled with the Holy Spirit and spoke this prophecy: 'Blessed [εὐλογητός] be the Lord God of Israel . . .'" (Luke 1:67). The hymn of Simeon (Luke 2:25-35) is a similar case, even though the terms are not as explicit.[50] In the life of Christ, we find the hymn of praise to the Father that Luke 10:21 (in contrast with Matt 11:25) presents as joyous in the Spirit: "At the same hour Jesus rejoiced in the Holy Spirit and said, 'I thank you Father . . .'"

In the book of Acts, we find the term μεγαλύνω preferred for expressing this ecstatic prayer of praise to God: "How is it that in our own languages we hear them speaking about God's deeds and power? [τὰ μεγαλεῖα τοῦ θεοῦ]" (2:11). We have already interpreted the gift of glossolalia as a prayer of rejoicing.[51] The term ἀποφθέγγεσθαι (2:4) also expresses the sense of rejoicing. The brethren of the circumcision marveled that "the gift of the Holy Spirit had been poured out even on the Gentiles, for they heard them speaking in tongues and extolling God [μεγαλυνόντων τὸν θεόν]" (10:45-46). In the case of the Ephesian disciples, glossolalia came together with prophecy (19:7) and should be designated as rejoicing prayer.[52] We note that, in Acts, when the Spirit is manifested in benefit to the community of believers, it is as a foretaste of the bountiful contemplation of the definitive possession of the kingdom.

Having in mind this brief synthesis of the relation of the Holy Spirit with Christian prayer, we can ask if any allusion to the Spirit can be

49. Κράζω and κραυγή could designate spiritual intensity but also human passion; cf. Luke 1:42; Acts 23:9.

50. Also, the Magnificat could be considered as a song of rejoicing in the Spirit although the text does not say so explicitly.

51. See secs. 5.4 and 8.1.

52. See sec. 8.1 for prophecy specifically.

found in the prayer mentioned in the summary statement in 2:41–47. Of the two terms used in this passage, προσευχή (2:42) indicates perseverance in ordinary prayer, as I have just indicated. The same expression is used in 1:14 ("All these were constantly devoting themselves to prayer"), precisely in the context of anticipating the Holy Spirit. In 10:4, 30–31, the term designates the prayer of Cornelius prior to meeting Peter. In all of the other passages, communal or private prayer and regimented or spontaneous prayer are all expressed equally.[53]

The second term employed, αἰνοῦντες (2:47), expresses the idea of a rejoicing prayer but may be occasioned by any type of salvific intervention and not only the action of the Spirit. The only time that it is repeated in Acts, it refers to the joyful praise of the lame man who was recently healed (3:8, 9), with a similar sense in Luke 2:13, 20 and 19:37. We find the parallel text to that which we cited (2:47) in Luke 24:53, καὶ ἦσαν διὰ παντὸς ἐν τῷ ἱερῷ αἰνοῦντες καὶ εὐλογοῦντες τὸν θεόν, where the rejoicing refers to participation in the salvific blessings that has already begun but which was still not completed with the gift of the Spirit.

(b) The second theme of the summaries, the *disinterest in material goods* that predominates in 4:31–35, has already been discussed in considering the term κοινωνία. In the entire description employed in this respect, we find not the smallest indication that could be examined in order to uncover an allusion to the Holy Spirit.

(c) The third theme of the summaries refers to the *extraordinary action of the apostles* that causes amazement and admiration among the people. This theme predominates throughout the summary in 5:11–16, but we also find it in the other summaries in verses 2:43 and 4:33. This extraordinary action is manifested in the great signs that they work (τέρατα καὶ σημεῖα, 2:43 and 5:11–12a, 15–16), arousing a great fear (2:43 and 5:11, 13), and in the great power (δυνάμει μεγάλῃ, 4:33) with which they give their testimony, earning them the esteem of all (χάρις τε μεγάλη, 4:33). As demonstrated, τέρατα καὶ σημεῖα (wonders and signs) are not attributed to the action of the Spirit.[54] However, testimony and boldness are clear effects of the impulse of the Spirit; it is enough for Luke just to mention them for the reader to recall the active presence of the Spirit. Now then, if Luke in the relating of a summary of the life

---

53. See the citations in n. 46 above; almost all of those texts use προσεύχομαι.
54. See sec. 2.1.

of the community mentions an activity that evidently derives from the gift of the Spirit, would we not have to assume that the other activities mentioned in the same summary also proceed from the same gift?

The mention of *testimony* is located in the second summary (4:32–35), that is to say, in the most important one from which the first probably originates and that which is perhaps found in the written source. This summary is actually somewhat distorted like the others, but it is possible that its original form can be limited to verses 32 and 33 and that the remainder is an addition intended to prepare the way for the Ananias and Sapphira episode. It is precisely in these two more primitive verses that we find the spiritual communion, the disinterest in material goods by a portion of the community, and the testimony of the apostles (note the change of subject) with the great admiration that it occasions.

The summaries provide a transition between two concrete stories that lend to the events a more generalized sense of time and space. Their goal is not to contribute new information and even less to introduce a totally new theme with a minor allusion. Therefore, the author has not claimed to attribute the religious life of the community, described in the summary, to the impulse of the Holy Spirit. Nevertheless, there still remains the possibility that without making any explicit claim, since he wrote a history of the spread Christianity rather than an admonition, the author in his conception would attribute to the Spirit this religious life of the community. This conception in the foundation of his thinking could have appeared spontaneously in those summaries in which the author is less directly connected to the events and could reflect more of his own thought. It does not appear, though, that this is the case in this summary. The change of the subject indicates the union of two distinct thoughts in the summary: all of the believers lived in a true communion of spirit, and the apostles for their part fulfilled the mission of testimony that had been entrusted to them. Luke reflects in these two lines of thought the characteristic of the community in its two strata. He does not claim to add anything to either of these characteristics but presents them at a single glance. What we know about each of them will come from other passages where they are spelled out expressly. With regard to testimony, we know that it is an effect of the Spirit. With regard to the union of the believers around the apostles and especially for prayer, we know that it is a tendency of the community extending back to the day of the Lord's ascension.

In conclusion, the analysis of the three summaries of the life of the community has not revealed any serious indication that Luke attributed this religious life to the Holy Spirit. Three terms appear to express allusions to the Spirit (κοινωνία, προσευχή, and αἰνέω), but a more detailed examination shows that these terms never appear related to the Spirit. We find a greater probability of an allusion to the Spirit in the term ἀγαλλίασις, but in the majority of the passages, it does not appear as an effect of the Spirit but rather as a consequence of participation in the messianic gifts. The only clear allusion to the Holy Spirit in the summaries is the mention of the testimony of the apostles. However, the change of subject that distinguishes the life of the community and this testimony demonstrates that it deals with the summary of two distinct effects and gives us no right to suppose the same origin for the life of the community as that for the testimony of the apostles.

I recognize that the actual placement of the entire first summary invites an extension of the influence of the Pentecostal Spirit to encompass the life of the community.[55] However, it would have no more basis than this general impression. This dislocation that the summaries have suffered could offer as much in favor as it could against such an attribution. Luke has not avoided absolutely the attribution of this life of the community to the Spirit as he has avoided completely attributing exorcisms and healings to it. One could almost say that the actual placement of the summaries favors such an attribution, but we are not able to deduce with any conviction that such is Luke's intention. Comparing it with the homogeneity of the Lukan conception of the Spirit, there is no difficulty in attributing to the Spirit the ethical-religious ethos of the Jerusalem community, since it deals with a situation of zeal and extraordinary generosity and with a communal life that was already initiated before Pentecost.

The result of the study of the summaries is, therefore, along the same lines as the interpretation of the story of the election of the seven, even though the indications provided by the summaries are much less positive than the expression "full of the Holy Spirit and wisdom."

---

55. See Lohse, "Bedeutung des Pfingstberichtes."

7.3 Resisting the Holy Spirit

In the investigation of the possible influence of the Holy Spirit upon the moral life of the believers according to Acts, a series of contrasting passages remain to be examined. Acts presents two cases of resistance to the Holy Spirit: (a) the lies of Ananias and Sapphira and (b) the opposition of the Sanhedrin. To these cases could be added (c) the reference to blasphemy against the Holy Spirit that Luke interprets in his Gospel in a manner that is different from either Mark or Matthew. The resistance of these persons presupposes a prior action of the Spirit upon them. So, if such resistance is a sin (perhaps the major sin) that closes the doors of salvation, is the Spirit's action of a directly salvific character? The answer does not necessarily have to be in the affirmative, but it is necessary to examine this series of texts as it relates to the Spirit and the moral life.

(a) *The case of Ananias and Sapphira* (5:1-11). The commentators feel understandably perplexed when faced with this story,[56] which is in evident contrast with the evangelistic spirit.[57] Neither is Peter the most likely person to act in this manner, especially with regard to the rather capricious question he puts to Sapphira (5:8). Some have claimed to find similar cases elsewhere in the New Testament, but it needs to be recognized that neither the threatening of Simon the Magician (Acts 8:20-24), nor the blinding of Elymas (Acts 13:10-11),[58] nor the case of the incestuous relationship in Corinth (1 Cor 5:1-5) has the same character of absolute condemnation. It is even more difficult to determine if the case is presented as the so-called blasphemy against the Holy Spirit. Certainly it would not be blasphemy in the sense that Mark understands it, as Ananias does not attribute the action of Jesus to a demon. Von Baer believes that blasphemy against the Holy Spirit according to Luke consists in denying Christ after having received the Spirit that initiates

---

56. See Haenchen, *Acts*, 236-41 = *Apostelgeschichte*, 192-98; Trocmé, *Livre des Actes*, 197-200; Reicke, *Glaube und Leben*, 87-97; Menoud, "Mort d'Ananias et de Saphira"; D'Ales, "Nota a Acts 5:3."

57. See Matt 18:15-17 and Luke 17:3 on fraternal correction. The parables about mercy may also be recalled, the constancy of sown discord until the hour of harvest, the behavior of Christ toward Judas and with Peter himself.

58. The blinding of Elymas appears to be a transposition of the case of Paul, and Peter's cursing of Simon the Magician is perhaps reminiscent of the punishment of Ananias. In any case, the punishment is very distinct, and it assumes, as in the case of Simon the Magician, that there is a hope of pardon.

testimony, but he rejects the similarity of the case of Ananias with blasphemy against the Spirit since there is no denial of testimony.[59] It deals, therefore, with an isolated case in the New Testament.

The style of the narration, both in its way of thinking and in the use of certain terms, denotes an extensive influence from the Old Testament, especially of the punishment of Achan narrated in chapter 7 of Joshua.[60] All in all, the Old Testament has supposed in many of its pages these thundering punishments resulting from God's wrath. It is difficult to conceive of a similar punishment in the New Testament. Jacquier attempts to explain it, following in the footsteps of St. Jerome and St. Augustine, as an exemplar punishment given at the founding of the church. St. Augustine adds that the mercy of God is able to save them for the next life.[61] It is still incomprehensible that the moving of God would return, though, to a pedagogy of fear, when it has just been expressed plainly in the mercy of Jesus.

The degree of the sin's seriousness does not consist in the holding back of a portion of the money but rather in the lie of appearing to hand over all of it (additionally, it reveals a lack of confidence in God's providence). There are no reasons for assuming, as Jacquier and others have done, a provoking of the Holy Spirit that motivated the apostles to see if Peter noticed the shortfall.[62] Trocmé (*Livre des Actes*) believes that Ananias claimed to have entered into the group of the perfect ones, in the style of the Qumran community, but without running the risk of renouncing everything. Schmitt develops this similarity with Qumran extensively.[63] Haenchen believes that such similarities are very vague, since, for example, the punishment at Qumran for a similar fault would have been a return to novice status and a period of penitence.[64]

---

59. Baer, *Heilige Geist*, 136–47.

60. This exemplifies an influence of a way of thinking and not exactly a repetition of a formulated outline. Trocmé (*Livre des Actes*) sees only a remote similarity with passages such as Lev 10:1–5 and Deut 23:23. In Josh 7, we encounter the infrequent ἐνοσφίσατο. Below, I will add a probable similarity with Isa 63:10–14. A similar case is cited in Sahlin (*Messias und Gottesvolk*, Exkursus 4, 370–73), dealing with a repentant dead person at the feet of his accuser, but here the victim was innocent.

61. See Jacquier's commentary on 5:1–11, especially on v. 10 (*Actes*, 155).

62. E.g., ibid. on 5:9 (155).

63. Schmitt, "L'Église de Jérusalem."

64. Haenchen, *Acts*, 241 = *Apostelgeschichte*, 197.

I believe that Menoud ("Mort d'Ananias et de Saphira") has taken the correct approach by reversing the terms of the problem: it is not that they died because they had sinned, but that the community has sought an explanation for the death of this married couple; that is to say, given that they have died, that is a sign that they have sinned. Not all of the process that Menoud imagines in the formation of this story, however, is convincing, and least of all that a vulgar death, even if it was the first after Pentecost, had required such an explanation on the part of the community. Perhaps it can be explained more easily as a case of an especially terrifying death, and perhaps it was experienced by less committed members of the community. The event has been interpreted as a punishment of God from the perspective of the first community, still more firmly grounded in the Old Testament than in the New.[65] Acts has picked up this edifying anecdote in order to illustrate the selflessness of the community, without seeing in it any contradiction with the supposed sharing of all goods that in reality it never claimed to reveal. It seems strange that Luke has incorporated this anecdote into his work, when in his Gospel he has given indications of a predisposition toward sinners and of gentleness in dealing with women. However, it should not be forgotten that he is also the only writer that has assigned curses to the rich as part of the blessing of the poor.

As for the two references to the Spirit, it should be asked when they were introduced into the narrative. The conception of the Spirit does not appear to be the same as that of Pentecost. At the very least, it supposes a later reflection that has transformed the excessive dynamism of Pentecost into a veiled presence of the Spirit, whether it be in the apostles or in the activities of the community. Nevertheless, the emphatic expression of the double article used to designate the Holy Spirit suggests a reference to Pentecost, but we have already seen that this is not necessarily an indicator of great value.[66] It appears probable that Luke encountered in the primitive story the reference to the *Spirit of the Lord* that was preserved in 5:9. In adapting the narrative for his work, Luke interpreted this reference as *the Holy Spirit* (as it has remained in 5:3), correcting perhaps an earlier mention of the Spirit of the Lord.

---

65. See Luke 13:1–5, "Or those eighteen who were killed when the tower of Siloam fell on them—do you think that they were worse offenders than all the others living in Jerusalem? No, I tell you."

66. See sec. 1.2.

Looking at a number of similar passages that could have served as a basis for the pre-Lukan author for editing this anecdote, I have found a surprising correlation with Isa 63:10–14, "But they rebelled and grieved his holy spirit [τὸ πνεῦμα τὸ ἅγιον αὐτοῦ]; therefore he became their enemy; he himself fought against them. Where is the one who brought them up out of the sea . . . ? Where is the one who put within them his holy spirit [τὸ πνεῦμα τὸ ἅγιον] . . . ? Like the cattle that go down into the valley, the spirit of the LORD [πνεῦμα παρὰ Κυρίου] gave them rest. Thus you led your people, to make for yourself a glorious name." In this passage, we encounter the use of the expression *Holy Spirit* with a double article, followed by the expression *Spirit of the Lord*, as in the story of Ananias (5:9), except that in Isaiah the preposition is inserted. The text of Isa 63:10–14 explains better than do other parallels in the Old Testament the sense of our story. It deals with the grieving and provoking of the Holy Spirit that God has poured out at Pentecost in order to guide his messianic people.[67]

In the Jerusalem Council, Luke employs once again the expression *to tempt God*, which is rare in the New Testament: "Now therefore why are you putting God to the test by placing on the neck of the disciples a yoke that neither our ancestors nor we have been able to bear?" (15:10). Furthermore, James expresses the sense of the giving of the Spirit to Cornelius in a way that is similar to that of the apostles: "Simeon has related how God first looked favorably on the Gentiles, to take from among them a people for his name" (15:14).

Tempting God, according to Acts, means placing human obstacles in the way of the Spirit who directs the messianic people. In the case of Ananias, the impediment is the falsification of the procedure that is supposedly encouraged by the Spirit. In the Jerusalem Council, the obstacle would be the insistence on circumcision with which the Spirit himself had dispensed. In Isaiah, the impediment is the sins of the people.

The similarity of the story of Ananias with the passage in Isaiah, and the ways that it is reminiscent of the Jerusalem Council implies that it was Luke himself who included the reference to the Holy Spirit in

---

67. The story of Achan (Josh 7:1–26), which appears to have been a great influence in the redaction of our text, also does not use the phrase *tempting God*. The typical use of *tempting God* refers to the murmuring of Israel in the desert; see Exod 17:1–7; Num 14:22; Deut 6:16; 9:22; 33:8; Pss 78:18, 41, 56; 95:9; 106:4; 1 Cor 10:9; Heb 3:8. See also Jdt 8:12; Wis 1:2; Sir 18:23; Mal 3:15; Num 27:14.

the episode of Ananias. Still, whether Luke has found this formulary expression or whether he has done nothing more than simply adapt it, it is evident that he has found in it an application of his conception of the Spirit. This probably refers, as I have said, to a secondary application or reflection but one that is in harmony with its fundamental intention.

(b) *The opposition of the Sanhedrin.* Stephen accused the members of the Sanhedrin, saying, "You stiff-necked people, uncircumcised in heart and ears, you are forever opposing the Holy Spirit, just as your ancestors used to do" (7:51). Once more we find in this text the typical Pentecostal expression with the double article to designate the Holy Spirit. But this is clearly a post-Pentecostal story and this expression is not surprising. However, the resistance that is attributed to the members of the Sanhedrin supposes an action by the Spirit upon them, and it is this action that we are interested in specifying. The context allows us to see clearly that the resistance of the Sanhedrin coincides, specifically, with their being hardened by Stephen's testimony and, generally, by that of the apostles. The action of the Holy Spirit, with which they collide, is the impulse that he gives to the apostles for testimony. There is not, therefore, any evidence to support a certain resistance to the internal calling of the Spirit to the members of the Sanhedrin, which would be totally foreign to Acts' way of thinking.[68]

Even more foreign to Acts is the result of the comparison that Stephen establishes between the members of the Sanhedrin and preceding generations. Stephen assumes that those in the past had also resisted the Holy Spirit, even though the expression remains implicit. The reference to the condemnation of the prophets makes it sufficiently clear that resistance to the Spirit had been confirmed by the rejection of the prophets inspired by him. Acts refers on three occasions to the Spirit that inspired the prophets.[69] Acts does not establish any difference between the Spirit that inspired the prophets who were resisted by those in earlier generations and the Spirit whom the members of the Sanhedrin are now resisting. Both cases may be expressed with the emphatic use of the double article. For Acts, there exists no such clear division in the giving of the Spirit as that which has been expressed in John 7:39, "[F]or as yet there was no Spirit, because Jesus was not yet glorified." Pentecost

---

68. See the sec. 6.3 concerning initial faith and sec. 6.2 concerning the call to conversion.

69. See Acts 1:16 and 28:25 with the double article; also 4:25.

signifies for Luke the outpouring upon all of the people the same Spirit that had been bestowed already on the leaders and prophets. The action of the Spirit assumed in the accusation of Stephen turns out to be an impulse for testimony to Christ as the foundation for being incorporated into the messianic people.

(c) *Blasphemy against the Holy Spirit.* Even though this theme does not pertain to the book of Acts, it will be useful to consider it here, at the very least as a complement to the theme of resisting the Spirit. Luke detaches this saying from the context found in Mark, who refers to it with regard to the accusation that Jesus expels demons with the power of the prince of demons: "but whoever blasphemes against the Holy Spirit can never have forgiveness, but is guilty of an eternal sin—for they said, 'He has an unclean spirit'" (Mark 3:29–30). Matthew (12:31) appears to harmonize Mark and Luke. He has respected Mark's context but has eliminated his final explanation. Luke has placed the saying about blasphemy against the Holy Spirit between exhortations to confidence and testimony in future persecutions: "but whoever denies me before others will be denied before the angels of God. And every one who speaks a word against the Son of Man will be forgiven; but whoever blasphemes against the Holy Spirit will not be forgiven. When they bring you before the synagogues, the rulers, and the authorities, do not worry ... for the Holy Spirit will teach you at that very hour what you ought to say" (12:4–12).

Mark relates the sin against the Spirit to the accusation of the scribes against Christ. Luke appears to reserve this sin for a future time and directs it only to the disciples who deny Christ, probably after having received the Spirit that motivates them to testimony. Von Baer and Lagrange believe that these divergences assume two distinct sources for Mark and Luke or that they include two distinct sayings of Christ.[70] Von Baer understands blasphemy against the Spirit, according to Luke, as the resistance to the Spirit that urges testimony: "Just as the prophet cannot deny his God, in the same way, this is the worst sin for Christians, who, having already received the Spirit of Jesus Christ, deny their Lord when in great distress."[71] The sin against the Son of Man would consist

---

70. See Baer, *Heilige Geist*, 136–47; Lagrange, *Commentaire à l'Évangile de Luc*, note on Luke 12:10, p. 355.

71. "Wie der Prophet nicht seinen Gott verleugnen kann, so ist es auch die schwerste Sünde für einen Christen, der doch den Geist Iesu Christi empfangen hat, diesen seinen Herrn auch in der grössten Not zu verleugnen" (Baer, *Heilige Geist*, 147).

in rejecting the earthly Christ. The sin against the Spirit would be rejecting Christ after having received the Spirit. This division appears doubtful, but even more so the consequences that result from it: Peter sinned against the Son of Man, but not against the Spirit because he had not yet received him. Neither had the members of the Sanhedrin sinned against the Spirit, because they had not received him. Ananias had received the Spirit but had not denied the Son of Man. The exegetes and commentators confess their vexation when confronted with these and a few other texts that deal with unforgivable sin.[72] Luke and Matthew have somewhat softened Mark's expression. It remains doubtful that the resistance of the Sanhedrin can be interpreted as blasphemy against the Spirit by means of rejecting his testimony given through the apostles. The story in Acts might incline us toward this understanding, but the context of the Gospel of Luke appears to refer only to the disciples.

For my part, it is enough to confirm that blasphemy against the Spirit is related, according to Luke, with testimony offered under the Spirit's influence. Resisting this testimony that comes from the Spirit is a grave sin, just as proclaiming it in the face of resistance establishes the virtues of boldness and wisdom. The sin consists perhaps in rejecting absolutely the plans of God, his saving intervention in history, whether these plans are communicated with internal impulses or by means of the testimony of his messengers.

In conclusion, although only with a sufficient degree of probability, the three cases of resisting the Spirit—Ananias, the Sanhedrin, and blasphemy—signify an opposition to the plans of God in the history of salvation. Ananias and Sapphira resist not so much the Spirit that confirms the authority of the apostles as they do the Spirit that imparts a new dynamic of generosity in the community. Their disloyalty threatens to retard the development of the salvific work (just as to demand circumcision is to tempt God by making more difficult the entrance of the Gentiles who have been blessed with the testimony of the Holy Spirit). In a certain manner, it may be supposed that the Spirit motivates the generosity of the community, but the author does not concentrate so much on the generosity as an effect of the Spirit as he does on the impulse to practice this generosity in a notable way. The resistance of

---

72. See 1 John 5:15–17; Heb 12:16–17; and esp. Heb 6:4–8 and 10:26–31 which relate unpardonability with the possession of the Holy Spirit, even though they only list it as one of the gifts that may be possessed.

the Sanhedrin to the preaching of the apostles and to the discourse of Stephen is a resistance to the Holy Spirit, just as earlier generations had resisted the Holy Spirit by resisting the prophets that led the people of God toward a messianic salvation. Blasphemy against the Holy Spirit could be interpreted, in this same sense, as a resistance to the saving plans of God testified to directly and indirectly by the Spirit.

These resistances by human beings assume an action of the Holy Spirit. This intervention may fall into the category of the religious-moral life of the community, but first and foremost it appears to consist of the guidance of God's people through the historic stages of salvation marked out by God.

7.4 Summary and Conclusions

The analysis in this chapter has been slow, fragmented, and has at times drawn on the subtleties of terms more than on concrete realities. For this reason, and in order to deal here more specifically with the theme that I proposed, it is appropriate to pause and assemble an ample summary that contributes a unified and carefully constructed vision with concrete conclusions. I do not propose, therefore, to introduce any new ideas but rather to set out a synthesis and, where possible, to place in sharp relief the arguments and the conclusions developed in the chapter. Section 6.1 presented the tendency of some exegetes to attribute every aspect of the new environment of the first communities to the Pentecostal Spirit, from testimony-evangelization to sanctification and healings. Another more analytical tendency takes note of the fact that Luke expressly avoids attributing healings and exorcisms to the Spirit and, at the very least, makes secondary the Spirit's influence over the Christian ethos of the community. For my part, I would adhere to Gunkel's formulation: the Spirit does not appear in Acts to be indifferent to the religious ethos of the community. It tells of religious behaviors that are indirectly, or even directly, instigated by the Spirit. These behaviors always have some aspect of the charismatic, of the reviviscence of the religious life that is already possessed.

In order to analyze the texts that possibly connect the Spirit and the Christian life, we must distinguish between the period of the *initiation of* and the period of the *development of* the Christian life. In the beginning of the Christian life, we have seen that *neither conversion nor the forgiveness of sins* (sec. 6.2) is attributed to the Spirit, but rather to the Father. Nor is the *initiation of faith* a work of the Spirit (sec. 6.3). On the contrary, the coming of the Spirit presupposes faith. God gives the Holy Spirit to those who obey him (5:32), to those who have believed (11:17), and to those who have been purified already by means of faith (15:9). The Spirit strengthens, however, to an extraordinary degree the faith of Stephen and Barnabas, always with a directly pastoral-kerygmatic goal but also with repercussions that penetrate their ethical character.

Section 6.4 examined the relationship between the Holy Spirit and water baptism according to the book of Acts. The problem has been introduced into the book from without. In reality, only an imprecise relationship between the two themes, and two rather unspecific texts, have given occasion to interpret in Acts a gift of the Spirit at baptism. Above all, a study of Baptism in the Spirit has shown us that it refers to the Pentecostal gift of the Spirit without any direct relationship to the ritual of baptism. The case of the Samaritans, in which the gift of the Spirit was brought about much later than baptism, and the case of Cornelius, in which the gifting of the Spirit precedes baptism, demonstrate clearly the internal independence of the Spirit with respect to the ritual of baptism. The two texts that give occasion for relating the Spirit to baptism are the story of the Ephesian disciples (19:1–7) and the promise of Peter in his Pentecostal discourse (2:38). The situation of the Ephesian disciples is very unclear, but the story expressly attributes the gifting of the Spirit to the laying on of hands. It deals with a different ritual, introduced syntactically with a change of subject that probably corresponds also to a change of minister in the celebration of these rituals.

The interpretation of 2:38 is much discussed. Generally, it has been seen as a promise of the gifting of the Spirit by means of water baptism. Certainly, the text establishes a certain continuity between baptism and the imparting of the Spirit. However, the internal relation between the two appears to be an effect of the projection of our own categories acquired in the Christian tradition. The syntactical analysis of the text shows us no more than an inference—καί consecutive—that could very well be extrinsic. I have not wanted to insist on arguments based on vocabulary because it appears to me that they lack sufficient range to define the exact value of the terms. I prefer the argument (see sec. 6.4) taken from Kittel's new punctuation ("Wirkungen der christlichen Wassertaufe"), which restores the bi-member style of the conversion-baptism expression and distances its connection with the Spirit. It appears that a decisive argument is the coherence with the other baptismal texts in Acts that have already been examined, where the gifting of the Pentecostal Spirit is not attributed to baptism, even though it generally occurs after the baptismal ritual. The precedence of baptism is not an essential requirement as is the requirement of faith. Acts at no point denies an outpouring of the Spirit at baptism, but such an outpouring would be distinct from the Pentecostal outpouring, which is the only gifting of the Spirit to which Acts refers. In other words, Acts neither affirms nor denies another class of outpouring of the Spirit, but we have no right to attribute it to the book.

By way of conclusion to this first stage, we can say that the Spirit, according to Acts, exerts no influence either in the forgiveness of sins or in the beginning of the Christian life. On the contrary, the Spirit is given as a fruit of faith to those who already participate in this life. In the second stage corresponding to the *development* of the Christian life, I focused on the theme that affects moral theology, examining evidence that Acts attributes to the Spirit any influence over the Christian ethos of the first communities. I focused the study concretely on the three reports that the book gives of the life of the early community: the election of the seven, the religious life described in the summaries, and the resistance to the action of the Spirit. The story of the *election of the seven* (6:1–7) and the reference to Barnabas (11:24) (sec. 7.1) have preserved the expression "full of the Holy Spirit and faith [or wisdom]." This faith and wisdom are effects of the Spirit, as is clearly apparent in the irrefutable wisdom of Stephen (6:10), which is clearly related to the promise of Christ that "the Holy Spirit will teach you at that very hour what you ought to say" (Luke 12:12). Wisdom appears in the biblical texts as an eminently pastoral gift, emanating from a religious transformation of the person. Something similar could be said about faith that appears here to have the sense of extraordinary confidence in the salvific intervention of God, including the effects of wondrous acts. This confidence is a religious attribute typical of Israel and of Christianity. It appears that the goodness of Barnabas also is related to the Holy Spirit. The sense of the texts, according to the intention of the story concerning the election of the seven, and according to the book's overall plan, serves to highlight further the pastoral purpose of wisdom and faith.

This study reveals a charisma that is eminently kerygmatic-pastoral, but founded on the religious-moral transformation of the person blessed with it. Luke more or less, in contrast to Mark and Matthew, emphasizes personal action under the influence of the Spirit. These pastoral *charismata* are manifested permanently and to an extraordinary degree in certain members of the community. Slight indications are also found that the number of those favored is not limited to the seven elected ones whose names are given to us in the story. The study of the expression "full of the Holy Spirit and of faith [or wisdom]" shows us, therefore, that the wisdom and faith of Stephen, along with joy and boldness, are attributed to the Holy Spirit and are interpreted as an extraordinary activation of the faith and messianic blessings already received from God by means of Jesus.

Section 7.2 analyzed the religious life described in the summaries. Starting with the use of vocabulary, we attempted to discover if Luke alluded to an intervention of the Spirit in order to uncover the religious proceedings of the community. The terms ἀγαλλίασις (2:46) and χαρά signal participation in the messianic blessings, one of which is the possession of the Spirit manifested in the charismata of glossolalia, wisdom, and joy in the midst of persecution. This exultant joy could be a fruit of the Spirit but could also be a fruit of the more general participation in the messianic blessings. From the use of this term, we are unable to deduce an attribution to the Spirit of the entire religious temper of the community, even though on certain occasions a special demonstration of this ethical-religious temper is attributed to the Holy Spirit. The term κοινωνία (2:42) does not designate a participation in the Holy Spirit himself, as Thorton (*Common Life*) proposes. It signifies a common union of hearts that leads to the sharing of one's own goods with believers in need. We do not find any serious indication that this communion is brought about by the action of the Spirit. In a certain sense, it had already begun with common prayer (ὁμοθυμαδόν) prior to Pentecost.

Neither is the prayer that is cited in 2:42 (προσευχαῖς) attributed to the Spirit. On the contrary, προσεύχομαι, αἰτέω, δέομαι, and other more cultural verbs designate the normal human prayer that prepares the way for the coming of the Spirit or for a salvific intervention by God: "how much more will the heavenly Father give the Holy Spirit to those who ask him" (Luke 11:13). This prayer prior to the salvific manifestations[73] is one of the characteristics of Luke with respect to the parallel

---

73. [Haya-Prats seems hard to follow here with his odd (and uncharacteristically quick) characterization of Luke's description of the zenith (or *Zeilpunkt*) of Jesus' in-

passages in Mark and Matthew and, also, with respect to John. There exists, however, an extraordinary prayer caused by the presence of the Spirit or, at times, by salvific interventions of God. This extraordinary prayer is expressed using the verbs μεγαλύνω (more appropriate for prayer in the Spirit) ἐξομολογέω, ἀποφθέγγομαι, and other verbs that refer rather to the rejoicing that is excited by other salvific manifestations, such as δοξάζω, αἰνέω, and εὐλογέω. In the description of the life of the community, we find the verb αἰνέω (2:47), but it appears to refer in a general manner to the recognition, by means of the new life, of those who participate. We cannot deduce from this verb an intervention of the Spirit.

In the third constituent theme of the summaries, we encounter a certain allusion to the intervention of the Spirit. It deals with the term μαρτύριον (4:33) in one of the verses that appears to be oldest in the summaries. This allusion to the Spirit seemingly implies that, in describing the life of the community, the author implicitly attributes such behavior to the influence of the Spirit. However, within the summary, the step from an attribute of the community to an exclusive characteristic of

---

structions to his disciples on prayer as referring to prayer "prior to the salvific manifestations." Perhaps this is best understood as stemming from the probable tangential influence of von Baer's dogmatic employment of arbitrary temporal epochs, which, to his credit, Haya-Prats does not adopt as an interpretive tool. The demand of the first of von Baer's arbitrary anti-narratival divisions is that no person during the earthly ministry of Jesus experiences salvation; accordingly, for example, Luke 7:36–50 does not appear in von Baer's thesis, as it would be an unharmonious element of his first supposed epoch. Other obvious narrative contradictions to this simplistic divisional hypothesis are similarly overlooked and ignored, while 11:13 is essentially dismissed as a problematic redaction (Baer, *Heilige Geist*, 152).

How could Jesus intend disciples in his earthly ministry to pray for the gift of the Holy Spirit when they supposedly did not have genuine faith? How could Luke possibly think that disciples in the later ministry of the heavenly Jesus should pray for the gift of the Holy Spirit? Von Baer's anti-contextual dismissal of 11:13 via his pseudo-epochal perspective leads to anti-narrative presuppositions which then require a negative answer to these questions—false questions that are not raised by Luke or by anything in his portrayal of Jesus. At this juncture (and others), Luke's considered portrayal of Jesus (both earthly and heavenly) in history is decidedly at odds with von Baer's artificial imposition of narratively disruptive epochal constraints and their false interpretive demands. Fitzmyer (*Luke*, 2:916), for example, is of course correct to observe that "Here [11:13] Luke makes Jesus speak of the gift to be given in the Period of the Church (24:49; Acts 1:4, 7–8)." While duly citing several of von Baer's observations, Haya-Prats certainly does not follow von Baer in his pseudo-epochal hermeneutic, as do a few later embellishments that are not substantive in view of their adoption of this narratively false underpinning. —Ed.]

the apostles demonstrates the juxtaposition of the facts mentioned. Luke generalizes or repeats in the summaries that which he has already mentioned in the individual stories in order to make a transition with the sensation of distance and time. But each one of these facts retains in the summaries the value that it had in its original narrative. I do not believe, therefore, that the mention of the testimony of the apostles, evidently under the influence of the Spirit, authorizes extending this influence to the common life or to individual prayer in the same summary.

Section 7.3 examined the action of the Spirit starting with the contrasting aspect of human resistance: (a) the sin of Ananias and Sapphira appears to be in opposition to the Spirit who is directing the formation of the new community. It does not deal with opposition to the hierarchy but rather to the saving plans of God that are realized spontaneously in the community. Similarly, Peter thinks that for the hierarchy to require circumcision of the Gentiles would be to tempt God, contrary to the practice confirmed by the testimony of the Holy Spirit. The sin consists in resisting the Spirit who directs the historic march of God's people. This is, therefore, the true action of the Spirit, even though his influence is made concrete, in this case urging people to exceptional zeal and selflessness. (b) The sin of the Sanhedrin is in its opposition to the new historical direction of salvation announced by the apostles, even as earlier generations had opposed the guidance of the prophets. The action of the Spirit is, therefore, the leading of the people of God in both the Old and New Testaments. (c) Perhaps blasphemy against the Holy Spirit can be explained in this sense: it involves a positive resistance to the salvific plan of God, realized in Christ, but manifested by the direct and indirect testimony of the Holy Spirit.

As a conclusion for the entire chapter, we deduce that Acts does not attribute to the Holy Spirit the origin of the Christian life nor the religious-moral behavior of the community, but that it does, in an incidental way (implicit but sufficiently clear), attribute to him an extraordinary empowerment of the Christian life.

The Spirit intensifies existing faith in exceptional circumstances and makes it break in as profound and irresistible wisdom, as confidence, boldness, joy, ecstatic doxology, and probably also as goodness, loyalty, and a complete disinterest in material goods. This impulse of the Spirit leading to the extraordinary practice of religious-moral behavior is integrated into a clearly human activity. We observed it in our study of the mode of the Spirit's activity (ch. 4), in the contrast between Luke and certain parallel texts in Mark and Matthew, and also in some characteristic expressions in Acts. Now we see it confirmed by the possibility of people resisting the influence of the Holy Spirit. It has to do, therefore, with human activities for which they are clearly responsible, but the intensity of such activities are an apparent sign that we are not dealing with merely human actions but with an accompanying intervention of God that the Old Testament attributes to the Holy Spirit.

I have not felt the need to address the precise limits between that which is ordinary and extraordinary. It is not that the Spirit cannot intervene in the ordinary life of the Christian but rather that Luke does not attribute this activity to him. Nor are we dealing with a metaphysical analysis of cause and effect, but with a theological interpretation of historical events. Even though the activity of the unique God is indivisible in its origin; nevertheless, in the New Testament it appears already to be attributed to three distinct origins. *Luke attributes to the Holy Spirit that which he conceives of as extraordinary in the formation of the messianic people.*

Luke has inherited his conception of the Spirit from the predominant conception of the Old Testament that sees the intervention of the Spirit of Yahweh in the decisive moments of the people's history. Luke, an older convert, feels proud of his entrance into the messianic people, confirmed by his joyous experience of the Spirit. Luke sees in this experience the outpouring of the gift of the Spirit announced by the prophet Joel and reaffirmed by the Baptist and by Jesus himself in the promise of the baptism in the Spirit. For this reason, he takes advantage of every report of these experiences of the Spirit—perhaps without importance for Mark, Matthew, Paul, and John—and he gives them a place of importance through the full force of his description, unrestrained by minor scruples over minor incidental details, as displayed by the varied iterations in his own stories.

It appears highly probable that Luke had known other traditions that attributed sanctification to the Spirit, be it the negative aspect of purification or the positive aspect of the creation of a new sanctified life. Already in the Old Testament some passages are found that have this sense: Isa 4:4; 32:15–16; Ezek 11:19; 36:25–28; and with the term *Holy Spirit* in Wis 1:5 and 9:17; and especially in Ps 51:10–12. The Qumran texts demonstrate that this aspect of the sanctifying Spirit continues to live among certain groups of Jews; however, it appears to be in inverse proportion to the prophetic impression of the Holy Spirit. Why has Luke not continued in this direction that had been vaguely initiated by the Old Testament, collected by Qumran, and fully adopted by Paul? I can propose two motives that appear to have influenced Luke.

The first motive could be the historic apologetic style of Acts. Luke does not start, as Paul and John do, from a new life, a mystic background from which all Christian works proceed. Such a conception supposes a second stage of reflection that starts from the interior plane in order to explain exterior events. Luke maintains it in a single stage of theological-historical reflection that thinks from the event to the superior cause. For him the prophetic experiences are a manifestation of the Spirit given by God to a community in testimony of having granted them salvation, incorporating them through faith into the messianic people. As a Gentile convert, Luke feels proud of his incorporation into the new messianic people. In order to confirm this new dimension of the people of God, Luke prefers to narrate the prophetic experiences of the community and the dynamic unstoppableness of the spread of the gospel, confirmed with various citations from the Scriptures and with the approval of the apostles. Luke attributes the origin of such prophetic experiences and of evangelistic dynamism to the Spirit promised by Jesus and sent on Pentecost.

A second motive could be the Greek clarity and precision more characteristic of the historian than of the philosopher or the theologian. Luke reserves for Jesus all that refers to salvation, including the exorcisms and healings that Mark and Matthew attribute to the influence of the Spirit. Paul, in attributing the divine Father-Son relationship to the Spirit, creates a certain amount of confusion between the action of the risen Christ and that of the Spirit in believers. On the other hand, Luke attributes to the Spirit only that which is, in the broadest sense, prophetic communication, that is to say, the extraordinary intervention of God in order to give direction to his people, be it in manifesting his designs or in encouraging his leaders or any believer in decisive circumstances.

8

The Prophetic Direction of the People of God

8.1 The Spirit and the Prophets—The Prophetic Gift

THE WORK OF THE Spirit places testimony-evangelization in sharp relief in Acts. We have seen that other aspects develop around this theme, such as testimony before tribunals and the direct testimony of the Spirit that confirms the believers. We also saw that the Spirit is not indifferent to the religious-moral sphere but that he only intervenes to strengthen it in extraordinary cases. Through these activities we discovered a less explicit trajectory but one which gives cohesion to these interventions of the Spirit. We can say that the impulse to evangelization and testimony, the extraordinary moral charisms, and the manifestation of the unforeseeable plans of God are interventions through which the Spirit directs the new People of God in decisive moments.

Gewiess has fittingly summarized this impression of cohesiveness produced by reading the book of Acts:

> In summary it should be said that Acts, true to its purpose, shows us frequently the importance and the intervention of the Holy Spirit with respect to every believer and his behavior, as well as that participation that he has in the testimony to Jesus, in the spreading of the Gospel, and in the founding, development, and direction of the kingdom. One need only think of the place that the Spirit of God occupies with respect to the people of Israel who, according to the Old Testament way of thinking, were under his particular direction and received from him, through their leaders,

decisive influences for their destiny. From this can be deduced how he formed among the believers the consciousness of being the people of God, the true Israel.[1]

I believe that Luke has understood the assistance of the Spirit for testimony-evangelism from a fuller perspective. The beginning of this trajectory as preparation for the messianic times is naturally less developed than the central point of testimony, but we will see that those preparatory beginnings are sufficiently attested to. In this chapter, the diverse elements will converge, giving us a synthesized vision of the action of the Spirit as a prophetic direction of the messianic people. It will not deal with an analysis of texts, which has in large part already been done, but with appraising their mutual relations in a coordinated vision.[2]

Section 8.1 analyzes how Luke attributes to the Holy Spirit the inspiration of the prophets who had sustained the people in their messianic hope. When the messianic age arrived, this prophetic gift of the Spirit would be poured out on all of the people, both in its restricted sense of prophecy and in its complete sense. Section 8.2 examines how the Holy Spirit consecrated Jesus initially so that he could fulfill his messianic mission, i.e., as Messiah, finally in full possession of the eschatological Promise. Sections 8.3 and 8.4 analyze the hierarchical means and the charismatic means that the Spirit uses to direct the community, focusing on the intervention of the Spirit in the breaking away of the Gentile Christians with respect to the Mosaic law. Section 8.5 proposes a structure for Luke's work centered on the three great inbreakings of the Spirit in the formation of the new people of God. The attribution of the prophetic gift to the Spirit is a common theme throughout the

---

1. Gewiess, *Urapostolische Heilsverkündigung*, 95.

2. I offer here the bibliography that has served to provide the general shape of this chapter: Causse, "Mythe de la nouvelle Jérusalem"; idem, "Pélerinage à Jérusalem; Sahlin, *Messias und das Gottesvolk*; Schmitt, "Église de Jérusalem"; Conzelmann, *Mitte der Zeit*, 128–57; 193–210; Congar "Saint Esprit et le corps apostolique réalisateurs." The journal *LumVie* dedicated issue 10 (1953) to "L'Esprit et l'Église," with articles by Spicq, "Saint-Esprit, vie et force de l'Église primitive"; Paissac, "Don de l'Esprit au chrétien"; Congar, "L'Esprit-Saint dans l'Église"; Chenu, "L'Expérience des Spirituels"; Grangette, "Esprit Saint et communauté chrétienne." Poelmann, "L'action de l'Esprit Saintu salut," in an issue of *LumVit* dedicated to "Je crois au Saint-Esprit"; Lampe, "Holy Spirit in Writings of St. Luke"; Boismard, "Revelation de l'Esprit-Saint"; Bonnard, "L'Esprit Saint et l'Église"; Chevallier, *L'Esprit et le Messie*; Dupont, *Études*, 361–66, 393–419; Dahl, "People for his Name"; idem, *Volk Gottes*; Winter, "Miszellan zur Apostelgeschichte"; Flender, *Heil und Geschichte*, 111.

Scriptures. Specifically, the frequency with which it appears has contributed to a series of nuances that spread a degree of confusion with regard to the theme. This section attempts to clarify the diverse aspects related to the Spirit in the book of Acts.

Messianic Prophecies

The inspiration of the prophets was unanimously attributed to the Spirit of God. In Jewish commentaries, the Holy Spirit has come to be identified, practically, with the spirit of prophecy.[3] Luke shares with both the Old and New Testaments the attribution of the prophets' inspiration to the Spirit, concretely expressed in the inspiration of David (Acts 1:16 and 4:25) and of Isaiah (Acts 28:25).[4] Acts knows that the Holy Spirit has directed the people of God from antiquity, by means of the prophets, up to the messianic salvation, even though this idea is not at all original with it. The originality of Luke is in the infancy narrative in his Gospel in which the Spirit (whose long absence the rabbis have lamented) breaks in through Elizabeth, Zechariah, John, and Simeon (1:15, 41, 67; and 2:25–27) in order to predict the imminent arrival of the Messiah.[5] We have noted the similarity of Luke 1–2 with the story of Pentecost both in its expression and in its surroundings.[6] If Luke has incorporated these stories, he has had no difficulty in recognizing the same Holy Spirit acting prior to the coming of Messiah. Luke does not say as John does that

---

3. Str-B (2:127–28) observes that "As is evident to the rabbis, Judaism equated the Holy Spirit with the God-Spirit of the God of prophecy or the expression of wisdom. One realizes various things from that, such as that the Targum has restored the Old Testament 'Spirit of God' or 'Spirit of Yahweh' or 'holy Spirit' simply by means of the term 'Spirit of Prophecy.' One is permitted to say, therefore, without further details being required, that the rabbinic scholars overall, in those cases where the connection is not important, understand by those terms the Spirit of Prophecy or the prophetic gift [Wie selbstverständlich dem rabbin. Judentum die Gleichsetzung des heiligen Geistes mit dem Gottesgeist der Prophetie oder der Weissagung gewesen ist. Erkennt man besonders daraus, dass die Targumin das alttest. 'Geist Gottes' oder 'Geist Jahve' oder 'heiliger Geist' einfach durch 'Geist der Prophetie' wiedergegeben haben. Man darf deschalb ohne weiteres voraussetzen, dass die rabbin. Gelehrten überall da, wo der Zus. hang nicht nötig, an den Geist der Prophetie oder der Prophet. Begabung verstanden haben]." See also Barrett, *Holy Spirit and the Gospel*, 107–12; 122–25; Sjöberg, "πνεῦμα," 381–83.

4. See also Acts 7:51–52.

5. The rabbis lamented the disappearance of this spirit of prophecy, even though great rabbis were mentioned who were said to be worthy of having received it (see Str-B 2:129). An allusion is also found in 1 Macc 9:27.

6. See sec. 4.3.

"for as yet there was no Spirit, because Jesus was not yet glorified" (John 7:39). That which is characteristic of Pentecost is not the first acting of the Spirit in history, but rather his outpouring that signals the beginning of the end times.

With respect to the expression with double articles, we have noted that they are equally lacking in the Pentecostal story, in that of Stephen, and in that of the Samaritans. On the other hand, we encounter the double article in the attribution to the Holy Spirit of the prophecies of David and Isaiah.[7] Acts recognizes, therefore, the intervention of the same Holy Spirit in the inspiration of the prophets that announce the messianic salvation.

Predictions in Daily Life

In the second part of Acts, prophecies abound as short-term predictions that refer to situations of only relative importance to the community. We come across itinerant prophets like Agabus, who predicts by the Spirit the famine that causes the collection and the return of Paul to Jerusalem, (11:28), or the imprisonment of Paul: "Thus says the Holy Spirit" (21:11 with a double article). We have already referred to the curious case of the prophets who, by means of the Spirit, told Paul that he should not go up to Jerusalem (21:4).[8] Acts also speaks occasionally of other prophets, even though it does not mention an intervention of the Holy Spirit: 11:27; 13:1; 15:32; and 21:9 (the four daughters of Philip).

The texts that have mentioned the Holy Spirit all pertain to a complex of manifestations of the Spirit that give direction to Paul's travels, whose value for the conception of the Holy Spirit in Acts appears to be very limited.[9] Even though these texts follow the line of the decisive intervention of the Spirit on behalf of the people of God; nevertheless, in order to minimize it, they remove religious density from it.

The Kerygmatic Sense of the Prophetic Gift

The prophet is a proclaimer of the message of God. His teaching is more than mere moralizing, as it calls to mind and makes more profound the fundamentals of the people's faith. Jesus is the great Prophet who had

---

7. See sec. 1.2.
8. See sec. 5.5, n. 65.
9. See esp. sec. 4.3.

come and to whom it is necessary to listen in order to obtain salvation (Acts 3:22–23; Deut 18:15–19). The coming of the Holy Spirit upon him (Luke 3:22) is interpreted by Luke as consecration for evangelization (Luke 4:18). Because of the importance of this theme, all of the next section is dedicated to it. The original sense of the prophecy of Joel 2:28–32 appears to exclude this kerygmatic aspect of the gift of prophecy, since its universal outpouring among the people makes this kerygmatic aspect practically useless and impossible. In a certain sense, everyone who proclaims his or her mystic experience of God has much to teach others, not concerning the message of salvation but rather as a follow-up message of a fruitful-contemplative type for those already initiated.

In the actual redaction of Pentecost, two themes exist that respond to the two interpretations of the prophetic gift spoken of in the citation of Joel. Peter applies the citation of Joel to the glossolalia of the disciples. This does not have a kerygmatic goal,[10] but neither does it have one in the case of Cornelius or in that of the Ephesian disciples. It deals with an irrepressible and selfless outpouring of joy and praise unto God, i.e., Spirit baptism. However, Luke interprets Pentecost as an impulse to testimony and evangelization, with the interpretation of Pentecost as Spirit baptism (1:5) being added to the interpretation of it as an impulse to testimony-evangelization (1:8). However, this latter sense is restricted to the apostles and progressively to new, specially chosen groups, while the primary sense of Pentecost continues to be for all believers. Therefore, in Acts, the prophetic gift announced by Joel is primarily a charismatic experience of God expressed publicly. Only secondarily has it been interpreted by Luke as a prophetic gift in its kerygmatic dimension, but this aspect remains restricted to the apostles.[11] At Pentecost, all receive

---

10. Glossolalia is addressed in sec. 5.4; see especially nn. 34 and 36 there (also sec. 7.2, n. 45). Conzelmann (*Apostelgeschichte*, 67), commenting on Acts 11:15, writes, "Speaking in tongues is, for Luke, identical with prophecy [Zungenreden ist für Lk mit Prophetie identisch]."

11. [Haya-Prats clarifies his expression of restrictions here and elsewhere in this chapter, as noted in an editorial comment in n. 33 below. The tendency to theologically restrict selected prophetic experience and impulses to apostles within dogmatics is best understood as due to the influential legacy of the Protestant Reformation with its reaction against Catholic claims of the miraculous and the concretizing of an "apostolic age" (also dubbed the "Pentecostal age" [*Pfingtszeit*]) wherein these effects were generally confined. On the other hand, Haya-Prats, writing in the Catholic faith tradition, is quite delicate, flexible, and nuanced when engaging such established "apostolic age" notions and fine tuning, perhaps with a level of sophistication that may be difficult to appreciate.

the promised eschatological gift that Jesus received in his exaltation, but only the apostles received the kerygmatic gift that Jesus received at the Jordan.

Prophecy as Exultant Doxology

As demonstrated, the gift of prophecy announced in the citation of Joel has a prevailing sense of exultant proclamation of the greatness of God. The story of Pentecost does not make concrete the realization of the visions or the prophetic gift. It does not claim to offer details but rather a global comparison of the Pentecostal situation, which was scandalous for some, with the promise of the outpouring of the prophetic gift. Without claiming an exact correspondence, we can say that Peter interprets glossolalia as the prophetic gift announced for the end times. Glossolalia consists of a type of exultant prayer, more or less intelligible, that proclaims the greatness of God (2:11). Also, in the story of Cornelius a correspondence exists—perhaps equivalence—between glossolalia and exultant doxology: "[F]or they heard them speaking in tongues and extolling God" (10:46). Something similar to this is said of the Ephesian disciples, that upon receiving the Holy Spirit they spoke in tongues and prophesied. The prophetic gift announced by Joel is interpreted by Peter as glossolalia and specifically as exultant praise of God. Cornelius receives the same gift that is given at Pentecost—the outpouring of the prophetic gift announced by Joel—and it is interpreted as glossolalia and exultant prayer. The Ephesians, who evidently receive the same gift, speak in tongues and prophesy.

It appears, therefore, that the prophetic gifts in the most important texts in Acts have the sense of exultant doxology and of a type of mystical prayer with a community character. It refers to a gift that is more joyful than it is dynamic-utilitarian.

The Full Sense of the Prophetic Mission

Diverse senses of the prophetic gift emerge: messianic predictions, predictions in ordinary life, and exultant doxology. An aspect that is less

---

Haya-Prats is not claiming here—against considerable narrative information—that only the twelve apostles received the gift of the Holy Spirit at the first Jerusalem "Pentecost" and that the rest of the 120 disciple-believer-witnesses just experienced salvation there, as in some "apostolic age"-fixated Protestant interpretation that is still erroneously repeated today under the guise of Lukan theology. —Ed.]

clearly spelled out in Acts would be prophecy as the transmission of a message or teaching from God. The Pentecostal discourse of Peter could be interpreted as the prophecy that interprets glossolalia or the gift of tongues (per 1 Cor 14), but in Acts we have little evidence for such an interpretation. Reflecting on the diverse aspects of the prophetic gift and on the sense of the action of the Holy Spirit in Acts, we discover a similarity that, even though it is not expressed in any text and perhaps would not even be explicit for Luke, explains the coherent and profound sense of the actions of the Holy Spirit.

Luke feels tied to the Old Testament concept. The Spirit that had been in Moses was shared with the seventy elders and transferred to Joshua in order to govern the people. From the time of the monarch, the Spirit is especially manifested through the prophets. The prophet feels carried away by the Spirit and penetrates into a sacred place of knowledge concerning the plans of God but also feels immediately and equally sent forth to proclaim this message before the people or the king.[12] There exist, therefore, two moments in the prophetic gift: the contemplative moment and the missional moment. The prophet continues as an extraordinary intermediary between God and his people. His mission breaks out when the religious, moral, or political posture of the people deviates from Yahweh's designs, perhaps as the placing of Moses as intermediary between God and his people has remained divided into two formal, distinct functions: the *ordinary* leadership of the people that will lead eventually to the monarchy, and the *prophetic* function charged with proclaiming and stimulating the execution of Yahweh's designs in the most critical circumstances.

In Acts, we do not find prophets in this full sense of the prophetic mission, but neither does it deal with a sense that has remain antiquated. Acts has recognized the fullness of the prophetic mission in Jesus and records twice the announcement of Deut 18:15, applying it expressly to Jesus: "Moses said, 'The Lord your God will raise up for you from your own people a prophet like me. You must listen to whatever he tells you. And it will be that everyone who does not listen to that prophet will be utterly rooted out from the people'" (Acts 3:22–23; see Acts 7:37 and

---

12. See Neher's interesting study, *L'essence du prophétisme*, esp. the introduction and the first chapter of the second part on the Spirit and the word in Hebrew prophecy; Iglesias, "Profetes del Nuevo Testamento."

Deut 18:15–19).[13] The Holy Spirit that impels this full mission of the Old Testament prophets, among which the Baptist still belongs (Luke 1:15, 17; 16:16), has consecrated Jesus for his messianic work (Luke 3:22; 4:18; Acts 10:38).

After Jesus' exaltation, the Spirit is sent to the disciples as continuers of the evangelistic work. However, not even the apostles themselves assume the prophetic mission in its full sense. They enjoy a series of charisms from the Spirit, but the critical decisions of God do not come through them. Nor are they announced by a prophet as in Israel's history. The Holy Spirit manifests himself (naturally through persons by means of glossolalia) as testimony to God's designs. The Holy Spirit impels the prophetic mission in its full sense in the Old Testament and in Christ, but beginning with Pentecost he appears to take on for himself the fullness of the prophetic mission. He fulfills this prophetic mission, imparting diverse prophetic gifts of preaching, of the impulse to testimony and evangelization, and of exultant doxology. But he reserves the manifestation of God's designs in extraordinary circumstances, giving testimony by means of his charismatic gifts.[14] Christ will continue as the great Prophet announced by Moses. After him exist no prophets in the full sense of that calling, but only in partial aspects. All of the people prophesy when they participate in certain moments of exultant doxology. On the other hand, prophets exist in the sense of predictions in daily life (all of these texts are found in the Pauline cycle in Acts). The prophetic ministry in its complete sense remains exclusive to Christ. The disciples participate only in certain aspects of it. And the Holy Spirit, without the necessity of any connection with intermediaries (though always by means of persons), assumes the prophetic mission in its full sense.

---

13. See Daniélou, "Christ prophète"; Lampe, "Holy Spirit in Writings of St. Luke," passim. [See too Panagopoulos, "Urchristliche Prophetie"; Ellis, "Prophecy in the New Testament Church"; Reiling, "Prophecy, the Spirit"; idem, "Role of the Christian Prophet"; Hill, "Prophets and Prophecy"; Stronstad, *Prophethood of All Believers*, passim. —Ed.]

14. By understanding the prophetic gift in this complete sense, it is not problematic for us to admit with Schweizer that Luke shares with Judaism the concept of the Spirit as prophetic spirit. However, the expression lends itself easily to misunderstanding. It is certain that Luke continues in the same line of the prophetic spirit and does not pass on to the sanctifying Spirit; however, the field of interventions of the Spirit has developed under the teaching of Jesus and the experience of the communities in both the magnitude and mode of his interventions. See Schweizer, "πνεῦμα," 409.

Conclusions

Luke certainly attributes to the Holy Spirit the inspiration of certain Old Testament messianic prophecies and the announcement of the immediate coming of the Messiah in the infancy narratives of his Gospel. The second part of Acts attributes to the Holy Spirit predictions and oracles that are relatively important in the daily lives of the communities. This type of prophetic gift, although also taken from Old Testament models, appears to have less religious density than the interventions of the Spirit in the first part and also less than many of the prophetic manifestations from the Old Testament. The giving of the Holy Spirit at Pentecost is expressly considered to be an outpouring of the prophetic gift among the people. The prophetic aspect, mentioned by Joel and picked up by Acts, does not appear to be kerygmatic but rather to be an equivalent to glossolalia, which I have called exultant doxology. However, it is probable that Luke adapted the Pentecostal story to the evangelistic mission of the apostles, and in this adaptation the prophetic gift may also have a kerygmatic aspect.

Reflecting upon the diverse data in the book of Acts, it appears that we can deduce that Luke limits to Jesus the prophetic ministry in its fullest sense. Believers would receive the prophetic gift in its abundant sense of exultant doxology. The apostles would receive additionally the kerygmatic aspect. But the full sense of the manifestation of God's designs in the salvation history of his people would be assumed by the Holy Spirit himself. The manifestation of the plans of God is realized in the first part through persons, at times allowing them to control their actions, while at other times manifesting them by means of extraordinary phenomena, such as glossolalia, that do not burst directly into the plane of human decisions. Only in the second part can one speak of impersonal inbreakings of the Holy Spirit. With this density of meaning, it can be said that the Holy Spirit in Acts is a prophetic Spirit, the same Spirit that compelled the Old Testament prophets. Nevertheless, the data of Acts surpass considerably the Old Testament understanding of the Spirit of God. Even taking only the information of Acts at an earlier stage of our reflection, the conception of the Spirit has been notably enriched, although it continues in the principal trajectory of the Old Testament.

The community of the book of Acts is a people of prophets because the Messiah has poured out the Holy Spirit upon them. It is exactly this that

Moses had wished for: "Would that all the LORD's people were prophets, and that the LORD would put his spirit in them!" (Num 11:29).

8.2 The Spirit and the Messiah

The critical data that contributes to the Lukan concept of the relationship between the Spirit and the Messiah must be handled in a synthetic manner. The majority of this data is found in the Gospel. In Acts, we find only two texts that refer to the Spirit and the Messiah: 10:38, which refers to the baptism of Jesus, whom "God anointed . . . with the Holy Spirit and with power," and 2:33, which refers to the exaltation of Christ. We will deal with these texts in a chronological order.[15] The intervention of the Spirit in the incarnation of Jesus (Luke 1:35) is a text that is difficult to interpret and appears to be of a distinct nature from every other Lukan reference to the Spirit. It is very probable that Luke and Matthew have taken this information from a primitive tradition. This aspect of the intervention of the Spirit can be coupled with the Lukan perception, but it does not proceed from it.[16] Sahlin summarizes the diverse interpretations that have been given to the action of the Spirit in this Lukan passage into three basic classifications: (a) a supernatural substitution of the generative force; (b) a creative force; and (c) the promise of divine protection.[17] He rightly rejects the first as a concept that is totally foreign to Judaism. He also rejects the second, which in his judgment is possible but has been distorted by mystic interpretations and supposes a virginal

---

15. See the bibliography in n. 2 above, esp. Sahlin, *Messias und Gottesvolk*; idem, *Studium zum dritten*; Chevallier, *L'Esprit et le Messie*; Koch, *Geist und Messias*; Goitia, "Noción dinámica del pneuma"; La Potterie, "L'onction du Christ"; Tatum, "Epoch of Israel," which defends the idea of a preceding story that Luke has undertaken as preparation for the epoch of Christ.

16. See also Minear, "Luke's Use of the Birth Stories"; issue 21/4 (1966) of *BK* is dedicated to the childhood stories of Jesus by Luke, with articles by Schürmann, "Aufbau, Eigenart"; Voss, "Christusverkündigung der Kindheitsgeschichte." Roover, "L'Exégèse patristique"; Laurentin, *Structure et théologie de Luc 1-11*, 13-18, believes that Luke has only slightly reworked this story in order to incorporate it into his Gospel because it pertained to his own Johannine atmosphere. There exists, therefore, a homogeneity of thought, and one sees only traces of it in Luke in stylistic reworkings, perhaps due to the task of translation. I present a summary of diverse interpretations of this text because of its special difficulty, even though it is not truly integrated into the Lukan concept of the Spirit.

17. Sahlin, *Messias und Gottesvolk*, 123-36; 186-99.

concept that he believes to have been refuted earlier.[18] The text would be reduced, therefore, to promising divine protection in relation to Exod 40:34 and Isa 4:2–6.

Barrett insists on the biblical tradition of the creative force of the Spirit, presenting abundant citations: "From these passages we learn then that in the OT the Spirit appears to act creatively only in relation to the primal creation of the world and man, and in the redemption of the people of God."[19] This aspect has been preserved more in Hellenism than in Palestinian Judaism. It admits also to a later contact with the Greek way of thinking about the generative intervention of the gods. A suggestion that appears interesting is the relation of this passage with the baptism of Jesus: "The authors of the infancy narratives perceived that which, as we shall see, was set forth in another form in the baptism narrative. The ministry of Jesus could only be properly explained on the basis of the OT, and this involved both the messiahship of Jesus and the work of the Holy Spirit."[20] Chevallier notes that the progressive parallelism, with respect to the conception of the Baptist, comes to interpret the action of the Spirit as a more radical empowering of the Messiah than the filling of John. Concerning how this took place, the angel responded with the divine mystery, alluding perhaps to Isa 49:2, "in the shadow of his hand he hid me."[21] Feuillet understands both the ἐπισκιάσει of 1:35 and the dove at the Jordan to allude to the beginning of Genesis in which the Spirit covered the waters as though incubating them with creative power. Jesus is the point of departure for a new creation and Luke emphasizes this, proposing a genealogy from Christ back to Adam immediately after his baptism.[22] Laurentin accepts the allusion to Exod 40:35, where he discovers two complementary manifestations, one of the tent that expresses transcendence and the other that penetrates the tabernacle and manifests the immanence of God. Also in Luke 1:35 there is a creative action of the Spirit upon Mary of the type found in Gen 1:1 and an internal presence of God in Mary that would initiate the conception of the Son of God, with which the expression διὸ καὶ recovers all of its causal force. The overshadowing also has a weaker

18. Ibid., 125–26.
19. Barrett, *Holy Spirit*, 20; see all of ch. 2.
20. Ibid., 24.
21. Chevallier, *Esprit et le Messie*, 84–92.
22. Feuillet, "Marie et la nouvelle création"; idem, "Messianisme du livre d'Isaïe."

sense in the Scripture, but the context as a whole leads to this more complete interpretation. The lack of an article is a Semitism as in 1:25.[23] I do not believe it probable that the δύναμις has in this passage a superior significance to the πνεῦμα. The action of the Spirit does not appear to be limited to a radical fulfillment in the Messiah, as seen in Mary's conception, whether it is *creative* in nature or a *mystery*, as Chevallier proposes. There is an agreement among the commentators in seeing the most radical empowering of the Messiah as a principal effect of the Holy Spirit in Luke 1:35. The disagreement is over a complementary action of the Spirit upon Mary and the fertile, creative, or simply mysterious manner in which the action is catalogued. Even though Luke is far from the realism of Matt 1:18, εὑρέθη ἐν γαστρὶ ἔχουσα ἐκ πνεύματος ἁγίου, he also refers to the action of the Spirit directly upon Mary ἐπὶ σέ, from which a holy seed will be engendered (διὸ καὶ τὸ γεννώμενον ἅγιον) that will be called the son of God. Framing this passage within the Lukan concept of the Spirit, we see that the action of the Spirit upon the Messiah is fully in line with the messianic consecration at the Jordan, only duplicating it in anticipation. Because of this aspect, it is probable that the text is drawn from the same way of thinking but not from the same author. The action of the Spirit upon Mary, whether it is creative or fertile, is foreign to the Lukan concept, although not to that of the Old Testament or to Hellenism. As said at the beginning, the text is adapted to the Lukan concept but does not come from it.[24]

The coming of the Holy Spirit upon Jesus at the Jordan (3:22) is one of the fundamental facts of the primitive tradition. Luke has scarcely reworked the story, but he has left his characteristic mark on it: he has presented Christ in prayer, has made less tangible the corporal appearance of the dove, but has given greater realism to the coming of the Spirit, deleting the term εἶδεν found in Matt 3:16 and Mark 1:10. Evidently, the story signifies, in the tradition, the empowerment of the Spirit that the Messiah would receive. The story has been envisioned in the light of the more relevant messianic texts from the tradition (Isa 42:1; 61:1). Although, the symbolism of the dove has not been explained

---

23. Laurentin, *Structure et théologie de Luc 1–11*, 73–79. See also Lyonnet, "Récit de l'Annonciation."

24. [For discussion of this tradition in the context of Luke's portrayal, see too Fitzmyer, "Virginal Conception"; idem, "Infancy Narrative" in *Gospel According to Luke* 1:302–448. —Ed.]

with sufficient certainty, the interpretation that correlates the dove with the people of God is suggestive (see particularly the Song of Songs, "my dove, my perfect one," 5:2; see 2:14; 5:12; 6:8).²⁵ The manifestation of the Spirit would not correspond to the nature of the Spirit but rather to the work that he comes to promote, in this case the convocation of the messianic people. Luke has placed in sharp relief the messianic sense of the scene by the Jordan via the anticipation of the discourse of Jesus at the synagogue in Nazareth with the citation from Isa 61:1. Evidently, the statement "Today this scripture is fulfilled in your hearing" (Luke 4:21) refers to the coming of the Spirit that Luke has just narrated.²⁶

The text of Acts 10:38 employs the term ἔχρισεν, alluding explicitly to Luke 4:18, at the beginning of Jesus' public life. The phrase καὶ δυνάμει, which this text adds, appears to indicate the cause of the healings: "That message spread throughout Judea, beginning in Galilee after the baptism that John announced: how God anointed Jesus of Nazareth with the Holy Spirit and with power; how he went about doing good and healing all who were oppressed by the devil, for God was with him" (Acts 10:37–38). This text confirms the importance of the baptism of Jesus in the primitive kerygma.

Von Baer has emphasized the importance of the passage at the synagogue in Nazareth, but exaggerates it to the point of attributing to the influence of the Spirit all of the activity of Christ during his life, including exorcisms and healings.²⁷ De La Potterie has shown that the anointing of Jesus in Luke 4:18 and Acts 10:38 refers to his prophetic consecration to announce the good news. His establishment as Messiah-King is confirmed through his exaltation. A marked parallel exists between the

---

25. See Sahlin, *Studien zum dritten Kapitel*, 102–5; Feuillet, "Symbolisme de la colombe". Chevallier (*L'Esprit*, 57–67), on the other hand, confirms with fresh arguments the proposal of Abbott (*Letter to Spirit*, 106–35) attributing the mention of the dove to a corruption of the Hebrew text of Isa 11:1 that had been quickly corrected in other texts. Traces of this textual corruption may be found in John and in the *Gospel to the Hebrews*. On the diverse symbolism of the dove, see Str-B's commentary on Matt 3:16 (1:123–25).

26. Luke has anticipated this scene at the synagogue in Nazareth (Matt 13:53–58; Mark 6:1–6), as can be inferred from Luke 4:14–16. He has certainly claimed to explain the sense of the baptism in the Jordan uniting both scenes as much as possible (the genealogy presents Jesus as the new Adam), connecting them with three mentions of the Spirit (4:1a; 4:1b; 4:14) and referring expressly to his consecration by the Spirit in 4:21. See Dupont, *Études*, 404–9.

27. Baer, *Heilige Geist*, 69, 136 (as quoted in sec. 2.1).

scene at the Jordan and the scene at Pentecost, which indicates the leading of the Spirit to commence Jesus' and the disciples' evangelization.[28] The difference between the Lukan baptismal text and that of Mark and Matthew should be noted, especially the use of the double article in reference to the Holy Spirit. I have already indicated that this expression, even though it is not strictly speaking Pentecostal, is characteristic of Luke, who has certainly desired to emphasize the parallel between Jordan and Pentecost (see secs 1.3 and 8.5).

Christ receives during his life that which I have called *second comings of the Spirit*: "Jesus, full of the Holy Spirit, returned from the Jordan and was led by the Spirit in the wilderness" (Luke 4:1a, 1b, 14).[29] On another occasion, Jesus "rejoiced in the Holy Spirit and said, 'I thank you, Father, Lord of heaven and earth . . .'" (Luke 10:21). This text illustrates the emphatic use of the double article and the themes of joyous exultation (ἠγαλλιάσατο) and ecstatic prayer (like the joy of the community in Acts) and praise for the greatness of God.[30] These second fillings of the Holy Spirit do not presuppose in Christ a progression in Spirit but rather a manifestation of fresh dimensions. Luke 2:40, "The child grew and became strong, filled with wisdom; and the favor of God was upon him," is parallel to the infancy story of John in Luke 1:80, "The child grew and became strong in the spirit." However, with respect to Christ, Luke avoids saying that he grew in the Spirit.[31] In his exaltation, Christ received from the Father "the promise of the Spirit," that is to say, the completeness of the Promise that is the Spirit,[32] and he poured it out on the disciples (2:33). This reception of the Spirit is presented as most solemn. It deals with the Holy Spirit of the Promise. Jesus had already received at the Jordan the Spirit that consecrated him for his prophetic

---

28. La Potterie, "L'onction du Christ." See also George, "Prédication inaugurale de Jésus."

29. Schweizer ("πνεῦμα," 404–6) observes that Luke deviates from the other Synoptics in that he does not present Jesus as a pneumatic but rather as the possessor of the Spirit. In Luke 4:1b the Lukan concept of the Spirit's manner of acting appears (see sec. 4.1), which will be the same for the disciples in the first part of Acts, without their being able to say that they are the possessors of the Spirit but rather possessors of their actions done under the influence of the Spirit. That Jesus is the possessor of the Spirit may be deduced more clearly at the moment of his exaltation (Acts 2:33).

30. See Cerfaux, "Sources scripturaires de Matt. 11:25–30."

31. Schweizer, "πνεῦμα," 404–5.

32. See sec. 3.3.

mission, but that does not refer to the fulfillment of the Promise but to his preparation.

That which I have called *second comings of the Spirit* (4:1a, 1b, 14; 10:21) are no more than renewed manifestations. In his exaltation, Jesus receives the Spirit in a different way, a way related to the Spirit as eschatological gift. Interpreting 2:33 as merely the reception of the ability to transmit the Spirit would do violence to the text by minimalizing the Promise. It is true that Peter identifies the Spirit received by Jesus with the Spirit poured out upon the apostles: "Being therefore exalted at the right hand of God, and having received from the Father the promise of the Holy Spirit, he has poured out this that you both see and hear." However, only a systematic prejudice could deny that the Pentecostal Spirit is primarily an eschatological Spirit and that his manifestations are the inbreaking of a selfless, celestial exultation. Only secondarily, and only for the apostles, will the Pentecostal Spirit be an impulse for testimony-evangelization.[33]

Jesus is established as Messiah in his exaltation, and because of this he receives the fullness of the Promise with the gift of the Holy Spirit in his true eschatological dimension. In pouring it out on the disciples, they are made to participate—as much as is possible—in the anticipation of the eschatological gift, making them participants, in a certain way, of the Promise. This anticipated possession is the guarantee of having entered into the true people of God, into the kingdom of God, and into the way of salvation. It is, therefore, Jesus Messiah who gives salvation. The Spirit, also given by the Messiah as an anticipation of the fullness, is the guarantee of the salvation known fully by Christ. The people of

---

33. ". . . that which you have seen and heard" refers evidently to glossolalia, even though it does not exclude Peter's discourse. In the understanding of the first redactor, Pentecost is eminently an eschatological event. In Luke's understanding, it cannot be reduced to a force for testimony (1:8) because this is the exclusive mission of the apostles and certain specially designated persons. Pentecost, on the other hand, is a universal gift. See Section 8.5. [Haya-Prats realizes that the gift of the Holy Spirit is poured out upon the 120 disciples, which includes the twelve apostles whom he rightly views as the initial bearers of the Christian message of testimony-evangelization. Then, the testimony of the Spirit expands in "concentric waves," Luke showing historical episodes wherein momentum is gained for evangelization via other characters like Stephen and Paul. To be clear, Haya-Prats is not restricting to apostles the fervor and spiritual impulse provided by the gift of the Holy Spirit as received by disciple-believers in the scenes portrayed by Luke. (This clarification is based on private communication with the author.) —Ed.]

God are still under way, prolonging the journey, until "the coming of the Lord's great and glorious day" (2:20). On that day, true salvation will be realized: "Then everyone who calls on the name of the Lord shall be saved" (2:21). The possession of the Holy Spirit is simply an anticipation of the eschatological fullness of salvation.[34]

8.3 The Spirit and the Church—Hierarchical and Charismatic Guidance

According to three explicit passages in the book of Acts, during Old Testament times the Holy Spirit united the people of Yahweh in the messianic hope through the inspiration of the prophets. The Holy Spirit had been given to Jesus at the Jordan as a consecration for his messianic work and, in his exaltation, as a fulfillment of the Promise. Jesus poured out the Spirit on his disciples as a foretaste of the fullness of the Promise. From this moment, the Spirit attests to the possession of the messianic people, breathing on them boldness and wisdom both for ordinary evangelization and in critical situations before tribunals. Everything that has been revealed up to this point justifies abundantly the interpretation of the work of the Spirit in prophetic guidance for the people of God. We recall here, however, certain texts in order to reintegrate them into this perspective and to define in some detail the prophetic sense of this guidance of the People of God. First, in a general manner, we will examine the texts that show the direction of the Spirit through the leadership hierarchy or through any believer in a charismatic moment, and then we will study in greater detail the process of disengagement from the Mosaic law.[35]

---

34. [Historically, Haya-Prats writes at a time of the continuing emergence of the International Catholic Charismatic Renewal (with the Belgian Cardinal L. J. Suenens' *Une nouvelle Pentecôte?* following on the heels of his thesis). He shows no tendency of advancing an agenda against this movement or its predecessor, as did some Protestant scholars of a fixed pseudo-epochalistic mindset during that time. In his demeanor Haya-Prats is similar to other Catholic scholars like his supervisor, La Potterie, and to Congar, Laurentin, Mühlen, and Sullivan, for example, who all contributed to the Renewal. Therefore, his concluding remark at the end of sec. 8.2 should not be interpreted as being offered in a polemical or condescending light, rather his entire thesis is advanced in a contemplative spirit, similar to that of the distinguished Catholic commentator Pesch in his "Gabe des Heiligen Geistes." —Ed.]

35. See esp. Congar, "Saint-Esprit"; and Bonnard, "L'Esprit Saint et l'Eglise."

Hierarchical Guidance

The first text that can be integrated into this group is Acts 1:2. Whether the expression "through the Holy Spirit" refers to the election of the apostles or to instruction concerning the last days, it assumes an intervention of the Spirit in the formation of the first hierarchical leadership group.[36] However, the Lukan origin for these first verses is improbable, and therefore, their value is rather limited,[37] but neither can it be said that they are foreign to Luke's way of thinking, since they are in line with the charismatic wisdom of Stephen and his companions.[38] In the same line of special contact between the Holy Spirit and the leadership hierarchy, the giving of the Spirit to the Samaritans is verified by the laying on of hands by Peter and John and not by the baptism administered by Philip. In the laying of Ananias' hands on Paul, the exact moment of the giving of the Spirit seems unclear, which on the other hand had to be recognized by Paul. Perhaps this reflects a reticence by the author, who wishes to reserve for the apostles the giving of the Spirit through the laying on of hands. The extension of this power to Paul in the case of the Ephesian disciples should not be wondered at, taking place as it does at a later time and, particularly, in an heir to the apostolic activity.[39] In the episode of Ananias and Sapphira (5:1–11), it is possible that a lie to the

---

36. Haenchen and Wikenhauser see the phrase as modifying the election of the apostles, whereas Conzelmann, Zerwick (*Analysis Philologica*), and Dibelius (*Aufsätze*, 81–82), though exhibiting indecisiveness, are rather inclined to see it modifying the instructions of the last days.

37. The theory that Luke wrote a single work that had been divided into two parts in order to be incorporated into the canon is well known. The division would have imposed certain reworkings at the end of the first part and at the beginning of the second. A summary of the topic may be seen in Trocmé, *Livre des Actes*, 31–34. Trocmé cites Sahlin (*Messias und Gottesvolk*, 11–18) as the initiator of this suggestion. Menoud ("Remarques sur les textes de l'Ascension," "Pendent quarante jours, Actes 1, 3") believes that Luke attributes great importance to the forty days for establishing the apostles' authority. See also Larrañaga, *Ascensión del Señor*, who defends the Lukan authenticity of Acts 1:1–14 (see 1:211–313 on literary criticism and 1:108–53, 221–75 on the forty days). The introduction form corresponds to that used five times in *The Anabasis* by Jenofonte, twice in *The Antiquities of the Jews* by Flavius Josephus, and six times in *The History of Herodian*. Luke reiterates what is in the previous book and for this reason does not provide a summary of the book at the beginning. The interruption of μέν without the corresponding δέ is typical of Luke, and he uses it thirteen times in Acts.

38. See secs. 5.3 and 7.1. Regarding the use of διά in reference to the Holy Spirit see sec. 4.2.

39. Of these passages, regarding the purpose of baptism, see sec. 6.4.

hierarchy was automatically considered to be deceiving the Holy Spirit. It would appear, however, more probable that the lie to the Holy Spirit has a more general character of provoking (5:9) the Spirit, obstructing by means of a false spirit the paradigm of extraordinary generosity that the Spirit stirs up in the development of God's people. The episode remains rather obscure, and in any case is marginal to the overall concept of the book.[40]

The expression of the called Jerusalem Council that "it has seemed good to the Holy Spirit and to us" (15:28) does not suppose an automatic identification between the Spirit and the hierarchy in such a way that the leadership's decisions are attributed to the Spirit. Rather, it addresses the contrary case, as we will see later in the discussion of the abolition of the law. The hierarchy resisted admitting that the Gentiles were free from the Mosaic law, and a manifest intervention of the Spirit was necessary in order for the hierarchy to fear provoking God should they oppose the testimony of the Spirit. It is not that the decisions of the hierarchical leadership are considered to be decisions of the Spirit; on the contrary, it is that the charismatic manifestation of the Spirit forces the hierarchy to change its decision.[41]

The text of 20:28, "Keep watch over yourselves and over all the flock, of which the Holy Spirit has made you overseers, to shepherd the church of God," attributes to the Spirit a certain degree of influence in the establishment of these members of the hierarchy. We do not know if this refers to a charismatic designation, such as the election of Barnabas and Paul in 13:2, or if it refers to the ratification by means of the Spirit of the designation made by Paul himself.[42] Whatever the sense, this text aligns

---

40. See sec. 7.3(a) on the episode of Ananias and Sapphira.

41. See in sec. 5.5(c) indications of the designs of God, and also secs. 8.3–5.

42. See sec. 4.1 on overpowering inbreakings. Schweizer ("πνεῦμα," 408–9) admits the possibility that the latter idea, that every decision of the hierarchical leadership is automatically a decision of the Spirit, has been mixed in these texts; however, he does not believe this interpretation of Acts to be probable: "Hard to assess is Acts 5:3, 9.... [O]ne can hardly think that the disciples as such are supposed to be in possession of the Spirit. The idea seems to be that of 13:9.... One might ask whether there is not to be seen in 15:28 (and perhaps 20:28) the view of a later period acc. to which the direction of a church court is *eo ipso* that of the Holy Spirit.... 20:28 is also to be read in the light of 13:1–3, though it should be noted that Luke presupposes the work of the Spirit in all instances and not just in unusual circumstances. This carries with it the possibility of a later misunderstanding which links the Spirit automatically to a correctly discharged ecclesiastical vocation..." See also Claereboets, "In quo vos S. Sanctus."

itself among the texts that attribute to the Spirit rather detailed direction of the Pauline itineraries: 16:6–7; 19:21; 20:22–23; 21:4, 11. This series of texts, even though they deal with a certain inflation of the Spirit's intervention, follow the same line of prophetic direction of the people of God in situations that appear important in Paul's story. These texts do not refer to a determination that is made hierarchically by Paul in the Spirit but, on the contrary, to a series of charismatic interventions by the Spirit that, by means of the prophets or by other obstacles, alter the determinations that Paul has already made. On the other hand, 19:21 could refer to a determination made by Paul, in the Spirit, that he would not be intimidated by the contrary counsel of the inspired prophets (21:4).

Charismatic Guidance

The direction that the Spirit impresses on the communities is not confirmed through the church hierarchy as such. The church hierarchy directs the people according to that which man has comprehended of the plans of God, but God's plans are frequently unforeseeable and it is left for God continually to reveal them. The Christian lives continually in a present of renewed attention to and dependence upon the plans of God. This continual surprise from God is a sign of his personality and of his unfathomable mystery to humans. Regarding the direction of the people, the manifestation of these frequent changes of direction in God's plans belongs to the Spirit. Although the Pentecostal manifestation signifies the leaving behind of this waywardness, for Christ showed the disciples the way to follow, they still needed the power of the Spirit. Throughout the book of Acts we find a gradually building series of circumstances that oblige us to break the established molds, including those imposed for seemingly theological reasons. These molds are eager to be smashed, not for new theological reasons, but because of urgent circumstances. Such circumstances are presented as manifestations of the Spirit or are confirmed by them.[43]

---

43. The apostles appear to have understood the universalism of Jesus as a coming of all nations in Judaism. It was the persecutions and the outpouring of the Spirit on the Hellenists that led (according to Acts) to the breaking of these molds under the Spirit's seal of approval. The traditional practices, and even the Jewish law, were a real impediment for drawing the Gentiles, as was apparent in Peter's reluctance to enter the house of Cornelius. The unforeseeable decisions of the Spirit also obliged Paul to change the intended course of his itineraries. We could perhaps add that they also

The election of the seven may have had as its basis the anecdote of the service of the widows, but reveals at its core the need to supplement the primary hierarchy of the twelve and to adapt it to the pastoral needs of the Hellenists. Those who are chosen are men full of the Holy Spirit and wisdom. Stephen appears to become immediately involved in disputes that will lead to his death and the dispersion of the Hellenist Christians. The assumption seems obvious that these disputes formed part of the discontent that initiated the election of the seven and that the fullness of Spirit and wisdom of Stephen are a basis for this new structure in the community.[44] The persecution disperses the Hellenists and carries the gospel to Samaria (Acts 8) and Antioch (11:19–20), occasioning thereby the evangelization of the Gentiles. The event verifies the charge/promise of Christ to give testimony in Samaria and to the ends of the earth (1:8); however, this has not come spontaneously from the hierarchy, who rather feels suspicious and thus send Peter and John on an inspection. It cannot be said that these initiatives proceed from the Spirit, other than by means of a distant connection with 1:8, which promised the power of the Holy Spirit for this geographic expansion of testimony but which Acts wishes to limit to the apostles. Nevertheless, the author expressly presents a confirmation of the Spirit in the laying on of hands on the Samaritans and in the approval of the Antiochians through Barnabas, "a good man, full of the Holy Spirit and of faith" (11:24).

Paul's calling coming directly from Christ was a fact that Acts could not change; however, it attributes to the Spirit the initiation of his missionary travels and the direction of his itinerations: "While they were worshipping the Lord and fasting, the Holy Spirit said, 'Set apart for me Barnabas and Saul for the work to which I have called them. Then . . . they laid their hands on them and sent them off. So, being sent out by the Holy Spirit . . .'" (13:2–4). The laying on of hands does nothing more than confirm, hierarchically, the charismatic decision imposed by the Spirit.

The most significant case is that of the transcending of the Mosaic law, and more especially, the admission of the Gentiles without their remaining under the law.

---

compelled Luke (or the traditions that he gathers) to expand his concept of testimony and of apostleship.

44. See sec. 7.1.

8.4 The Spirit and the Church—Separation from the Law

The author of Acts wishes to justify the multiplying of communities being formed by the Gentiles without their being previously submitted to circumcision and the law. Paul has justified his revolutionary paradigm with theological reasons and Old Testament symbols. Luke continues in his historical plan, organizing his narratives by means of a simple device—admission of the Samaritans and the pious Ethiopian, leading to the decisive case of the baptism of the first Gentile, attributed to Peter. From this moment, it spreads to the Gentiles in Antioch from where Paul departs for his evangelistic missions. We have already taken note of the fact that this historical progression was confirmed or at times even promoted by the Spirit. Luke, therefore, attributes to the work of the Spirit the step toward a Christianity that is separate from the law. In this separation from the law, we encounter two important moments: Stephen's discourse and the baptism of Cornelius, both of which are related to the Spirit. However, these two moments are integrated in a very distinct way into the structure of the book. What is more, some authors have seen in Pentecost a replacing of the law with the action of the Spirit. It seems improbable, though, that the story, at least in its integration into the collection of the book, has this intention.[45]

The Spirit of Stephen

The episode of Stephen is inlaid into the general plan of the book as a digression from the election of the seven. The spirit of Stephen, which is much more vigorous than that of Philip, has momentarily seized at-

---

45. The interpretation of Pentecost as a proclamation of the new law in which the Spirit takes the place of the Torah has been defended by Knox, *Acts*, in the chapter dedicated to the theology of Acts. Dupont (*Études*, 99–100) appears rather skeptical and refutes Knox's interpretation with those of Cerfaux, "Symbolisme"; Adler, *Erste Christliche Pfingsfest*; Lyonnet, "Glossolalia Pentecostes." On the other hand, Dupont himself in his article "Première Pentecôte chrétienne" amply develops the parallelism between Pentecost and the giving of the law. See also Lécuyer, "Pentecôte et loi nouvelle." In spite of the rather problematic echoes that can be shown, it is evident that Luke has not seen in this event a principle of the abolition of the law (see Haenchen, *Acts*, 172–75 = *Apostelgeschichte*, 135–39). [O'Toole, "Acts 2:30 and the Davidic Covenant," also mounts a strong argument against an intentional or implied Lukan connection to the giving of the law. —Ed.] In the case of a supposed similarity with the traditions concerning the giving of the law at Sinai, it is more about the emphasis in Pentecost to the event that consolidated the new people of God, just as occurred at Sinai.

tention. Even so, this spirit is more radical than Luke claims. For this reason, he includes it with admiration but without showing agreement with this radicalism.[46] The interest of Stephen's discourse for our study of the Lukan conception of the Spirit is, therefore, secondary. The point of connection is in the fact that Luke presents the discourse of Stephen as a demonstration of the fullness of the Spirit and wisdom that makes him irrefutable in his disputes. Nevertheless, it is improbable that he has claimed a binding guarantee of the Spirit in every affirmation of this discourse. What the Spirit compels is the overall openness of Stephen before his inveterate countrymen and the Sanhedrin.

We cannot claim here to study in a few lines the complex spirit of Stephen, but we should note that his opposition to the temple cult and to traditional practices prepares the ground for the decision of Peter endorsed at the Jerusalem Council. Stephen is accused, just as Jesus was, of "speaking blasphemous words against Moses and against God" (6:11) and "against this holy place and the law; for we have heard him say that this Jesus of Nazareth will destroy this place and will change the customs that Moses handed on to us" (6:13-14). Luke has used here the saying of Christ about the destruction of the temple that he omitted from his Gospel. He has added the theme of the changing of the law and the traditions as a consequence of the action of Christ, a totally new theme with respect to the Gospel. From Stephen's discourse, we see that the accusation with regard to the temple is accurate: "Yet the Most High does not dwell in houses made by human hands; as the prophet says, 'Heaven is my throne, and the earth is my footstool. What kind of house will you build for me, says the Lord, or what is the place of my rest? Did not my hand make all these things?'" (7:48-50).

His attitude with respect to the law would require a much more detailed study. His great esteem for Moses is evident — more as a prophet than as a leader — who he presents implicitly as an image of Christ. With

---

46. Regarding the story of Stephen, see sec. 7.1; see also the bibliography in sec. 7.1, n. 23. Bihler (*Stephanusgeschichte*, 134-67) dedicates a chapter to the theme of the temple in the NT and deduces that Stephen's attitude is a characteristic trait of Luke. Simon (*St. Stephen*) considers the Hellenistic theme to predate Luke. See esp. the interesting article by Cullmann, "L'opposition contre le temple"; the author observes that the opposition to the temple belongs to an entire Christian group, distinct from the Synoptics and Paul, that corresponds to a group prior to Jesus and that gives a name to esoteric Judaism. The Johannine writings and the letter to the Hebrews belong to this group, which, in Acts, is called Hellenists.

respect to the law, perhaps two aspects should be distinguished: (a) "the living oracles" that Moses received to "transmit to us" (7:38); "Our ancestors were unwilling to obey him; instead, they pushed him aside, and in their hearts they turned back to Egypt" (7:39), just as the actual representative of the people were doing; "[Y]ou are forever opposing the Holy Spirit, just as your ancestors used to do. . . . You are the ones that received the law as ordained by angels, and yet you have not kept it" (7:51–53); and (b) "the traditional uses" mentioned in the accusation.

Some commentators have presented Stephen as the first missionary to the Gentiles and the most radical of all. The more probable interpretation of Simon Peter is that he sees a liberal attitude within Judaism that first and foremost rejects the temple but which remains faithful to Moses and to the law.[47] Stephen's radical tone remains relatively unique in Acts,[48] as well as in the rest of the New Testament and the Christian tradition.[49] Although Luke does not claim to draw from such radical principles their logical conclusions, the reader nevertheless remains

---

47. Barnard, "Saint Stephen."

48. However, we encounter some expressions with the same tone. In the discourse at the Areopagus, Paul returns to the idea of the temple: "The God who made the world and everything in it, he who is Lord of heaven and earth, does not live in shrines made by human hands, nor is he served by human hands, as though he needed anything, since he himself gives to all mortals life and breath and all things" (17:24–25). Regarding the law, we find other deprecating expressions, such as that of Paul in Antioch, ". . . through this man forgiveness of sins is proclaimed to you; by this Jesus everyone who believes is set free from all those sins from which you could not be freed by the law of Moses" (13:38–39), and the hard expression attributed to Peter at the Jerusalem Council: "Now therefore why are you putting God to the test by placing on the neck of the disciples a yoke that neither our ancestors nor we have been able to bear?" (15:10). These texts reflect a way of thinking that is in evident tension with the life of the primitive community that met in the temple for prayer and enjoyed the respect of all people (2:46–47). Luke is evidently aligned with the universalist tendency but does not carry their principles to their more radical consequences. His conciliatory character appreciates the piety of those who live under the law but is not able to comprehend a law of such minutia. Haenchen (*Acts*, 446 = *Apostelgeschichte*, 387) comments that Luke, unlike Paul, does not see in the law a self-sufficiency that removes God but rather an unobservable multiplicity of precepts. Concerning the two aspects of Luke's attitude, see Baltzer, "Meaning of the Temple."

49. Indications can be found, however, of a similar way of thinking, even though perhaps with different nuances. See John 4:21–24 and the unique sacrifice spoken of in the epistle to the Hebrews. Christ showed his esteem for the temple with both words and actions; however, he foresaw its destruction and a worship both in Spirit and in truth. The material would require a detailed and highly nuanced study. See Cullmann, "L'opposition."

somewhat inadequately prepared for the decree that will liberate the Gentile Christians from the imposition of the Mosaic law.

The Admission of Cornelius

This episode forms the second great block in Acts. The careful preparation and the triple relating of the episode serve to engrave in the mind of the reader the grand argument that, according to Luke, led the Jerusalem Council to decide on the liberation of the Gentile Christians with respect to the law (15:8; 14, 28). The commentators find two centers of interest in this story: the problem of Jewish and Gentile Christians eating together and the problem of the admission of the Gentiles into the church.[50] It is probable that Luke took advantage of the Petrine anecdote on the purity of foods and applied it to the purification of all persons by faith. Peter's vision would have served as an introduction for the more important anecdote of the baptism of Cornelius that he wished to put forward in the Jerusalem Council. In spite of certain diverse tendencies that denote their comparative derivation, it cannot be denied that both anecdotes fit together well. In this section, we focus on the first aspect of this question, the transcendence of the law with regard to the question of food purity, without claiming a problematic reconstruction of the primitive source. Naturally, this theme is completed, as Luke intends, with the complete exemption from the law that is granted to the Gentile Christians.

The first aspect is characterized by the vision of Peter of the pure and impure animals. The voice from heaven saying, "[W]hat God has made clean, you must not call profane" (10:15 = 11:9), is expressed through a neutral pronoun, probably with a supposed ambiguity, which Peter then was unable to interpret to mean more than the animals but which he will later understand to refer also to persons. Peter remains perplexed over the meaning of the vision. In that moment, Cornelius' emissaries arrive and the Spirit expressly orders him to accompany them,

---

50. See especially the state of the question that Dupont presents in "Problèmes du Acts" (*Études*, 75–81). Van Unnik sees in this fact an expansion of the concept of the synagogue (according to Dupont's summary). This would not refer, therefore, to an entrance into the church but to a new possibility of being acceptable to God. Haenchen in his commentary also presents a summary of the critique and takes time for an interesting analysis of the entire episode. See also Dibelius, "Bekehrung des Kornelius," collected in *Aufsätze*, as is his article "Apostelkonzil." ["The Conversion of Cornelius" and "The Apostolic Council" are now in K. C. Hanson's edition of *Aufsätze*, entitled *The Book of Acts*. —Ed.]

removing all indecision (10:19 = 11:12). Peter distills the consequence of the vision and justifies his entrance into a Gentile house, applying to human beings the voice that he had heard in the vision regarding animals: "You yourselves know that it is unlawful for a Jew to associate with or to visit a Gentile; but God has shown me that I should not call anyone profane or unclean" (10:28).[51]

Still another new expression of Peter's repeats the universalist sense of the episode, but this time the formulation is more Greek. It does not depart from the point of view of legal purity but rather from the more general principle of acceptance by God, going beyond the traditional Jewish pride of God's preference for them: "I truly understand that God shows no partiality, but in every nation anyone who fears him and does what is right is acceptable to him" (10:34–35).[52] Luke anticipates here the conclusion of James in the Jerusalem Council that God chooses his people also from among the nations. The action of the Spirit in this episode comes to a climax in his manifestation upon Cornelius that would serve as divine testimony of this purification of the Gentiles. A discussion of this aspect—a more specific examination of this coming of the Holy Spirit—follows in the next section. Among these same texts, we encounter the intervention of the Spirit in the interpretation of Peter's vision (10:19, 28; 11:12) and in his explanation that it had been the same Spirit who had sent the messengers: "the Spirit said to him . . . go with them without hesitation; for I have sent them" (10:19-20). Evidently, Cornelius himself had sent them (10:5-8, 17), but the Spirit is the director both in Peter's scene and in that of Cornelius. If in this latter one an appearance by an angel is mentioned, it is probably in order to avoid a manifestation of the Spirit to Cornelius prior to the formal coming before Peter and his companions or, at least, in order to distinguish the messenger who spoke to a Gentile from the one who spoke to Peter.

51. Concerning the exclusion of the Gentiles in spite of softenings of practice in the interest of peace, see Str-B, Exkursus 15, "Stellung der alten Synagoge zur nichtjüdischen Welt," 4:353–64, 374–83; Bonsirven, *Judaisme palestinien*, 99–110. There is no shortage of teachers that have developed the universalist prophecies of the OT, but these were inevitably conceived of as an influx of Gentiles into the Jewish people by means of circumcision and accepting the law.

52. Haenchen (*Acts*, 359 = *Apostelgeschichte*, 304) on 10:34 comments, "For some Jews the phrase 'A preference of Israel would be a προσωπολημψία [an inappropriate partiality] which on God's part would be a blaspheme—Luke in no way heeds this [Für einen Juden wäre der Satz: 'Eine Bevorzugung Israel wäre προσωπολημψία Gottes' eine Lasterung—Lukas merkt das gar nicht]."

Trying to identify whether the Spirit that spoke to Peter is the Pentecostal Holy Spirit that will descend upon Cornelius is more difficult. Both 10:19 and 11:22 say simply τὸ πνεῦμα. This form can only be justified as an anaphoric of the article if the expression *Holy Spirit* had already occurred in the story, but in our case it can only allude to the voice from heaven which had spoken previously.[53] It appears more likely that the expression τὸ πνεῦμα is carefully distinguished from the expression τὸ πνεῦμα τὸ ἅγιον that will be repeated without difficulty in the descent of the Spirit upon Cornelius (10:44–45, 47; 11:15; 15:8). The comparison that Dupont suggests between this anecdote and the baptism of the eunuch implies that both stories speak of a spirit in the popular Jewish sense.[54] This probably denotes a message somewhat superior to an angel, whose message Peter simply attributes to God (10:28). Nor is the message that he contributes in harmony with that which we know about the interventions of the Holy Spirit in Acts.

In this first part, Luke has accumulated reasons that justify the exemption from the law, reasons that, in the cases of Stephen and Peter, prove too much or, at the very least, more than Luke claims and many more reasons than Peter could have thought of in that period. But it is not with reasons that Luke argues for the break from the law, but with the great manifestation of the Holy Spirit. These anecdotes, in which the Holy Spirit indirectly intervenes, are nothing more than the preparation for the decisive event, the great manifestation of the Holy Spirit as testimony to the purification of the Gentiles by faith, without the need for circumcision. Because of the importance of this theme for the work, we will study it in the following section, which is dedicated to the Spirit in the structure of Luke's work.

From this view of the texts, we may conclude that the only charisma that is reserved for the leadership hierarchy would be testimony (1:8), and that owing to the peculiar conception of the first part of Acts, which it later betrays in the case of Paul and Stephen (22:15; 26:16; and 22:20). The charisma of evangelization does not seem to be so restricted, for the seven deacons had distinguished themselves previously as "full of the Holy Spirit and wisdom" (6:3). Evidently, the apostles and the remainder of the members that are eventually incorporated into the

---

53. On the use of the article see sec. 1.2.
54. See sec. 2.2; Dupont, *Études*, 78.

leadership hierarchy enjoy the charisms and are elected precisely for being distinguished by such charisms. What we cannot say is that, in Acts, hierarchical leadership appears as a charism or that the hierarchy is in automatic possession of a certain charism, unless it be the power of testimony. This situation is perfectly coherent with a conception that sees the intervention of the Spirit as a prophetic intervention for extraordinary moments, not as the continual and constant guidance that is experienced by the visible leaders of the community.

Acts frequently emphasizes the hierarchical organization of the community. For the admission of the Gentiles, the approval of the Holy Spirit will not be enough, but rather Luke takes pains to lift up the importance of the Jerusalem Council. However, the sign for this change of attitude is the inbreaking of the Spirit in a charismatic form as a testimony to the transcendent designs of God. The hierarchical leadership reflects on this testimony and, in examining the Scripture, discovers a sense that coincides with the new situation and that, up to that time, had been hidden. On this charismatic and theological basis, the hierarchy made its decision, to which Luke ascribes great importance, even though it requires a degree of compromise, as it does for those in the Jerusalem Council.

The Spirit directs the church with intermittent charismatic interventions according to the importance of the situations. The hierarchy also possesses the charisms of the Spirit, but the great decisions come from without in order to highlight the unforeseeable liberty of the divine decisions. These manifestations of the Spirit, when recognized by the kingdom, become an official norm that appears as a joint decision from the guidance of both the Spirit and the hierarchy: "For it seemed good to the Holy Spirit and to us to impose on you no further burden than these essentials" (15:28).

8.5 The Spirit in the Structure of Luke's Work

This chapter reunites diverse texts that display the direct action of the Spirit upon the people of God in the Old Testament, upon Christ himself, and upon the community formed by him. The presentation of the actual structure of Luke's work, from what we have of the original, demonstrates that these texts correspond to other such interventions of the Holy Spirit in the preparation, formation, and expansion of the messianic people.[55]

The Gospel

Luke has received the structure of the Gospel already formed. As preparation for the presentation of the Messiah, he has added the infancy narrative saturated with manifestations of the Spirit. The tradition had already introduced the theophany at the Jordan as the solemn consecration of Christ for his messianic work. Luke emphasizes this fact by means of the anticipation of Jesus' discourse at the synagogue in Nazareth. The presence of the Spirit upon Jesus is a consecration for his evangelistic mission. Luke has presented a discernible manifestation of the Spirit, the significance of which is explained in a discourse by means of the interpretation of a prophecy. It is the same outline that he will follow in the other two great manifestations of the Spirit. References to the Spirit in the Gospel are scarce and marginal. Barrett tries to explain this silence as being part of the messianic secret that Jesus imposes during his public life.[56] In this, Luke adapts himself to his source, introducing slight reworkings in addition to those to which I have already alluded. The most important addition would be the Pentecostal Promise, which is practically a preview of the book of Acts.

Acts

In the book of Acts, Luke feels more independent and able to construct a work that is his own. We can say that the entire structure of Acts rests on two great blocks, the Pentecostal complex and the Cornelius-Jerusalem Council complex. Luke starts from Pentecost, which he probably affirms in a universal Judaism (proselytes from the Diaspora), prepared to

---

55. I utilize the general features of the synthesis that Dupont presents in his article "Le salut des gentils," which is at the same time both detailed and constructive. This article provides an important orientation for the comprehension of Acts. With respect to the diverse opinions on the purpose of the author of Acts, see the introduction to Dupont's article, and Grässer's bibliographic presentation of Conzelmann's works in "Apostelgeschichte in der Forschung," 110–13; Trocmé, *Livre des Actes*, 113–18; Ehrhardt, "Construction and Purpose." See also Guthrie, "Recent Literature," esp. 40–41; Wikenhauser, *Apostelgeschichte und Geschichtswert*, 6–36; Menoud, "Plan des Actes"; O'Neill, *Theology of Acts*, 54–70, 66–177; Reyero, "Está terminada la obra?"; Schmitt, "Église de Jérusalem."

56. Barrett, *Holy Spirit*, 140–62.

admit into the community every Gentile who first accepts the law and circumcision. This is an event, perhaps a story, that Luke finds already established. The author claims the admission of the Gentiles in the community to be enough, and enough just as they are—uncircumcised and without the need to accept the law. The official declaration will come at the Jerusalem Council: "God . . . looked favorably on the Gentiles, to take from among them a people for his name" (15:14). The argument for this decision is the case of Cornelius, in which the Spirit has been shown to be testimony of God in their favor. This testimony is confirmed by the results of Barnabas and Paul's evangelization (15:12).

From Pentecost and the life of the Jerusalem community until Cornelius and the Jerusalem Council, Luke has carefully increased the degree of openness to the Gentiles. Philip evangelized Samaria and the Ethiopian eunuch.[57] The conversion of Paul prepared the instrument for the great mission to the Gentiles. It is especially noteworthy that only after having dealt with the case of Cornelius does Luke tell us that those dispersed by the persecution of Stephen had arrived as far as Antioch and had also preached to the Greeks (11:19–20). Once the mission to the Gentiles is inaugurated by Peter, Luke narrates the mission of those dispersed by persecution and that of Paul, which would serve to confirm the case of Cornelius at the council in Jerusalem.

---

57. Grundmann ("Apostel zwischen," 125) believes that the minister of Queen Candice could not be a proselyte because the law (Deut 23:2) prohibited the admission of eunuchs into the Lord's assembly. Pieper ("Wer war der Erstling der Heiden?") agrees; so too Wikenhauser, *Apostelgeschichte und Geschichtswert*, 54. J. Schneider ("εὐνοῦχος," 765–68) believes that it only deals with a σεβόμενος τὸν θεόν; however, he remains in doubt because of the eunuch's role in Isaiah's prophecy which is not easily attainable by non-Jews. Haenchen appears to understand him to be a proselyte. Cadbury ("Hellenists," 66 n. 2) believes that Luke presents him as a proselyte without being concerned about the historic problem. On the other hand, the interpretation of Deut 23:2 depends on the scope that is given to the concept of the assembly of the Lord, which is not always agreed upon. Sahlin (*Messias und Gottesvolk*) believes that it refers to a Jew by birth, in spite of the title Ethiopian, which he attributes to a reworking by Luke of the base text, and Wanroy ("Eunuchus Aethiops") agrees. The term *eunuch* may also designate a minister or person in the king's confidence. It does not appear that we are dealing here with an application of Isa 56:3–5 regarding the admission of eunuchs. This reference could explain the intention of the Christian redactor to show the arrival of the messianic age, but such an innovative historic event could only with some difficultly be supported by this one prophecy. Regarding the importance of this episode, see Unnik, "Befehl an Philippus." When the episode is viewed in the context of the collected work, it appears clear that the author has situated it so that it can serve as a preparatory step leading to the official reception of a pagan by means of Peter.

Pentecost

In the book of Acts, the story of Pentecost occupies the key position held by Jesus' baptism in the Gospel. All of the evangelistic work of the apostles, like all of Jesus' ministry, takes place under the motivating action of the Spirit. But also in Acts, as in the Gospel, Luke avoids attributing healings and direct salvific activity to the Spirit. Adler has affirmed pointedly the importance of the Pentecostal story: "With good reason the Pentecost account was retained in its assigned place in the structure of Acts. This described, of course, the wonderful victory run of the gospel, that the spatial and national-religious limits of Judaism are broken through and the heathen world itself is conquered. The triumphal march of the world-kingdom cannot be understood apart from the Pentecost event.... Therefore, Acts had to—after the introductory and connecting chapters—open with the Pentecost account."[58]

Also, Lohse has clearly expressed:

> The Pentecost story is therefore solidly anchored within the setting of the production of the Lucan story and can only be understood in the context of Lucan theology.... The Pentecost event is used by Luke as a great portal at the beginning of the church's story, through which the reader steps in order to find an entrance into the world church. This is why it is so important for Luke that the promises of the conferring of the Spirit himself be fulfilled directly in Jerusalem, the holy city. Then from here outward the world mission begins.[59]

The Pentecostal story provokes great difficulties both in its historical interpretation and in the meaning of its descriptive lines. It is

---

58. "Mit Recht behauptet die Pfingsterzählung den ihr zugewiesenen Platz im Aufbau der Apg. Diese schildert ja den wunderbaren Siegeslauf des Ev., das die räumlichen und religiösnationalen Schranken des Judentums durchbricht und sich die Heiden Welt erobert. Der Siegeszug der Weltkirche lässt sich nicht begreifen ohne das Pfingstereignis.... Die Apostelgeschichte musste darum—nach dem einleitenden und überleitenden Kapitel—eröffnet werden mit der Pfingsterzählung" (Adler, *Erste christliche Pfingstfest*, 146).

59. "Die Pfingstgeschichte ist also im Rahmen des lukanischen geschichtswerkes festverankert und kann nur im Zusammenhang der lukanischen Theologie verstanden werden.... Das Pfingsteereignis steht nach Lukas als ein grosses Portal am Anfang der Kirchengeschicht, durch das der Leser schreiten und Eingang in die Weltkirche finden soll. Darum ist es für Lukas so wichtig, dass die Verheissungen der Geistersverleihung sich gerade in Jerusalem, der heiligen Stadt, erfüllten, Denn von hier aus nimmt die Weltmission ihren Anfang" (Lohse, "Bedeutung des Pfingstberichtes," 434).

probable that it deals with a charismatic experience of the apostles, to which Luke has given exceptional importance.⁶⁰ That which is of interest to us in this work is to understand its coherent relationship with the book as a whole.⁶¹ We have already dealt amply with the missionary sense of Pentecost (sec. 5.2), with its value as immediate testimony of the Spirit (5.4–5.5), and with its eschatological aspect (3.1, 3.3, and 8.1). I will now attempt to present the Pentecostal event, as Luke conceives it, as the solemn foundation (and growing awareness) of the new messianic people: "Die Geburtsstunde der Kirche" (The Hour of the Church's Birth).⁶²

60. Given the impossibility of providing here a bibliography on Pentecost, I refer to Dupont, *Études*, esp. 81–83 and 85–57; Mattill, *Classified Bibliography*, 338–52. In a certain sense, it can be said that the bibliography on the meaning of Pentecost in Acts can hardly be distinguished from the bibliography on the Holy Spirit in Acts.

However, I recognize here the works that have served me more directly in the elaboration of the theme in this present section: Adler, *Erste christliche Pfingstfest*; Larrañaga, *Ascensión del Señor*; Benoit, "L'Ascension"; Lohse, "πεντηκοστή"; idem, "Bedeutung des Pfingsberichtes"; Rétif, "Mystère de la Pentecôte"; Kretschmar, "Himmelfahrt und Pfingsten"; Gelin, "L'Announce de la Pentecôte"; Menoud, "Remarques"; idem, "Pentecôte lucanienne et l'histoire"; idem, "Pendant, Actes 1, 3"; Sleeper, "Pentecost and Resurrection"; Charlier, *L'Évangile de l'enfance de l'Églis. AsSeign* dedicated issue 51 (1963) to Pentecost, with articles by Jean-Nesmy, "Permanence de la Pentecôte"; R. Le Déaut, "Pentecôte et tradition juive"; Dupont, "Première Pentecôte chrétienne." Issue 52 (1965) of *AsSeign* has P. Buis' article "Don de l'Esprit Saint." Also the periodical *Bibel und Kirche* dedicated issue 21/2 (1966) to the Holy Spirit, with articles by Svéda, "Ich giesse meinen Geist auf alles Fleisch"; Voss, "Durch die Rechte Gottes; Pesch, "Gabe des Heiligen Geistes." On Pentecost as the birth of the church see n. 62 below. On the missionary impulse, glossolalia, testimony, and the eschatological gift, see the respective sections.

61. If it can be demonstrated with sufficient probability that the author of the story has thought of the spread of the law at Sinai, one would have to interpret this gifting of the Spirit as the beginning of a new people and not precisely as the substitution of the written law by an internal law, since there remains no vestige in the remainder of the book of the latter.

62. The interpretation of Pentecost as the birth of the church is a principle that has been accepted for a time. See Adler's chapter "Bedeutung des Pfingstereignis" in his *Das erste christliche Pfingstfest*: "The meaning of the Pentecost event: 'One will, therefore, not consider Pentecost day as the foundation day, but more to the point as the birthday of the Church. The descent of the Holy Spirit marked the hour of the Church's Birth' [Man wird darum den Pfingsttag nicht als den Gründungstag, sondern treffender als den Geburtstag der Kirche ansehen; die Herabkunft des Hl. Geistes war die Geburtsstunde der Kirche]" (140). The imprecise expression of what he calls "Gründungstag" (founding day) is cited by Adler in Belser, *Apostelgeschichte*, 37; and in Schaefer and Meinertz, *Einleitung in das Neue Testament*, 380. A more precise concept of "Gerburtstag" (birthday) appears in Camerlynck, *Commentarius in Actus Apostolorum*, 119; Holzmeister, "Quid Sacra Scriptura."

The interpretation of Pentecost must be sought in Peter's immediate discourse and more concretely in the citation of Joel (Acts 2:17–21). Peter interprets the Pentecostal manifestation as the sign of the fulfillment of the messianic age in which God has poured out his Spirit on all people. Jesus is the Messiah and in his exaltation he has received the content of the Promise, here designated by its most complete aspect, the possession of the Spirit (2:33). Pentecost signifies, therefore, the divine guarantee of the foundation of the true people of God. Even more, it appears to form part of the foundational gift as one of its most important characteristics. Another source for interpreting the sense that Luke gives to the Pentecostal gift is the promise of Christ on the day of ascension. In this passage, two aspects are extracted. The first more general one interprets the Pentecostal gift as the Promise of the Father that is also called baptism in the Spirit (1:4–8). The second interprets the coming of the Spirit as a power for testimony (1:8). This second aspect is that which has prevailed in the exegesis, probably because it deals with a concrete affirmation that is more intelligible than "the Promise" or "the baptism in the Spirit," and because testimony is a highly emphasized theme in Acts; the success of this text is noticeably supported by Luke's use of his favorite type of geographical program in the work, i.e., "in Jerusalem, in all Judea and Samaria, and to the ends of the earth." I believe, however,

---

[Perhaps it might be observed that the theological propensity to tag the first Jerusalem Pentecost as the birth of the church has abated somewhat and is not an exegetical issue among others (like, for example, Kremer, *Pfingstbericht und Pfingstgeschehen*), given that Acts 20:28 might be understood by Luke in the narrative context of his double work to include those who entered salvation during the earthly ministry of Jesus. The Acts commentary tradition in which scholars like Belser (*Apostelgeschichte*, 1905) and von Baer (*Heilige Geist*, 1926) are located is foregrounded by a long history of assumptions about an "apostolic age" and another "age" after that. The tendency in this Acts scholarship was to encapsulate or constrain some Christian experience in one "age" and to allow some Christian experience to exist in another "age," maximizing apostles as uniquely associated with the miraculous and minimizing the narrative role of the Spirit for disciple-believers. Salvation through the ministry of the earthly Jesus and apostles escapes the arbitrary truncation of an "apostolic age," whereas Spirit-reception through the ministry of apostles and others does not. This tendency is demonstrated mainly by scholarship following Reformed tradition, as illustrated, for example, by Schwegler, *Nachapostolische Zeitalter*; Lechler, *Apostolische und nachapostolische Zeitalter*; Weizsäcker, *Apostolische Zeitalter der christlichen Kirche*. To the contrary, in the Catholic tradition this Reformed tendency was not as dominant, and Haya-Prats also realizes, as did Jacquier (*Actes* [1926], xlvii), that while in John 20:22 the Holy Spirit is received by apostles, in the book of Acts the gift of the Holy Spirit is received by disciples. —Ed.]

that the interpretation of Pentecost as an impulse to testimony is merely one concrete application of the gift of the Holy Spirit. Testimony is the exclusive mission of the apostles—according to the idea found in the first part of Acts—while the Pentecostal gift is essentially directed to the entire new messianic people, as is evident from the citation of Joel (Acts 2:17–21), from the promise of Peter (2:38), from the emphasized identification between the gift received by Cornelius and the Pentecostal gift (as we will see in the following), and from the assumption that each new group receives the gift of the Spirit (the Samaritans and Ephesians).

The presentation of the Spirit as a power for testimony is revealed through its concrete application. Jesus has spontaneously made the more general interpretation as a Promise of the Father and as a baptism in Spirit. When the disciples interpret the Promise as restoration of the kingdom in a material sense, Jesus dissuades them from interpreting God's designs, assuring them only of the divine assistance that is of immediate interest to them: "It is not for you to know the times or periods that the Father has set by his own authority. But you will receive power when the Holy Spirit has come upon you and you will be my witnesses" (1:7–8).

Intermediate Narratives

Diverse references and episodes are joined to this Pentecostal story, on some occasions as variants of the theme and on others as steps that prepare for the second great fulfillment of the manifestation of the Spirit—the Gentile Pentecost. The variants and similarities of the Pentecostal story probably formed the redactional block that Luke encountered. However, other narratives existed from diverse origins that Luke places at intervals in order to prepare for the Cornelius episode. Pentecostal variants would be as follows: the boldness of Peter before the Sanhedrin (4:8); the new coming of the Spirit, probably upon the same disciples (4:31); the reference to the double testimony of the Spirit (5:32); and the two transitional refrains concerning the growth of the community (9:31; 13:52).[63] On the other hand, the episode of Ananias and Sapphira (5:3, 9) and the election of the deacons and the death of Stephen (6:3, 5, 10; 7:51, 55) has been included as episodes illustrative of the action of the

---

63. [Brodie (*Proto-Luke*) suggests that Acts 9:31—12:25 and 13:1—15:35 were originally redactional blocks that Luke inherited illustrating the two major breakthroughs of Peter and Paul with respect to the Gentiles. —Ed.]

Spirit. The baptisms of the Samaritans and of the eunuch (ch. 8) prepare the way for the formal admission of the first Gentile. The baptism of Paul introduces the agent for great expansion among the Gentiles.

Cornelius and the Jerusalem Council

The second great block that supports the narrative of the book of Acts is the episode of Cornelius, which leads to the council at Jerusalem. It is the second pillar upon which Luke places the security (ἀσφάλειαν) of his Gentile brothers, upon "the events that have been fulfilled among us" (Luke 1:1–4).[64] Although objectively this situation should have less importance than Pentecost, Luke develops it more, precisely because he wants to present it as an historic argument for his confirmation thesis of the privilege already obtained by the Gentile Christians. (Because of the richness of this passage, I have already made frequent use of it in sec. 3.1 on the gift of the Holy Spirit, in sec. 5.4 on the immediate testimony of the Spirit, in sec. 6.3 on faith, and in sec. 6.4a on the baptism of the Holy Spirit. In this section, I merely highlight the fundamental position that it occupies in Luke's work.)

The Cornelius complex consists of a preparation with visions for Peter and Cornelius (examined in sec. 8.3) and of the manifestation of the Holy Spirit, referred to in the following three stories: the direct narration by the author (10:44–48), the review by Peter before the community at Jerusalem (11:15–18), and the reference that he also makes as an argument before the Jerusalem Council (15:7–11). In the same council, James reaches the theological conclusion (15:13–20), and the resulting decree translates it into practice in the name of the Holy Spirit and of the leaders of the community (15:28).

These three texts (10:44–48; 11:15–18; 15:6–29) exhibit an underlying parallelism of diverse expressions as they mutually explain or complement one another. I can only indicate here the essential elements that meld the three stories, passing briefly over the nuances required by the person who is talking, whether Peter, his companions, or the Jewish-Christian community. (I also attempt to illustrate this underlying parallelism graphically in the appendix.) These texts have two dimensions, one latitudinally oriented toward a comparison with the gift of the Spirit

---

64. See Trocmé, *Livre des Actes*, 38–75, esp. 47. [See too Alexander, *Acts in Its Ancient Literary Context*, 194. —Ed.]

received by the disciples at Pentecost, and the other longitudinally oriented toward a progressive interpretation of the event.

The comparison with the Pentecostal gift is obsessive and appears either explicitly or implicitly in almost every verse. It is illustrated at 10:45, καὶ ἐπὶ τὰ ἔθνη,[65] *even upon the Gentiles*, and the use of the verb ἐκκέχυται (see 2:17, ἐκχέω); 10:46 presents the motive that allows Peter's companions to infer the equality of the Pentecostal gift, "for they heard them speaking in tongues [see 2:4] and extolling God" (μεγαλυνόντων . . . θεόν; see 2:11, τὰ μεγαλεῖα τοῦ θεοῦ). 10:47 continues, ". . . these people who have received the Holy Spirit just as we." The same comparison is found in 11:15, "the Holy Spirit fell upon them just as it had upon us at the beginning." 11:16 presents the motive for Peter's interpretation that relates the event to the baptism in the Spirit promised by Jesus (see 1:5).[66] 11:17 says, "If then God gave them the same gift that he gave us, having believed on the Lord Jesus."[67] The Jerusalem community, upon hearing Peter's justification, exclaim: "Then God has given even to the Gentiles [ἄρα καὶ τοῖς ἔθνεσιν] . . . ." (11:18). In the Jerusalem Council, Peter states expressly in 15:8-9, ". . . giving them the Holy Spirit, just as he did to us; and in cleansing their hearts by faith . . ."[68] And bringing out the consequences, he insists in 15:11, "[W]e believe that we will be saved through the grace of the Lord Jesus, just as they will." The comparison reaches its defining point in the moment that the term ἔθνη can be integrated with the term λαός (15:14).[69]

---

65. In this phrase (as in 11:18), attention is called to the rapidity with which the case of Cornelius is generalized: "even the Gentiles." Evidently, this demonstrates Luke's intention to transform an anecdote into a typical case. Dibelius ("Apostelkonzil," in *Aufsätze*, 85) has underscored the tendency of this story to make general conclusions. Also, the expression ἀφ' ἡμερῶν ἀρχαίων (15:7) presents the event as belonging to the "situations-type" of the beginning. Note that in 15:7 the term ἀρχή is applied to the episode of Cornelius, while in 11:15 the same term designates the day of Pentecost in contrast to the episode of Cornelius. With respect to the καί in the phrase καὶ ἐπὶ τὰ ἔθνη (10:45), the sense here is exaggerated. Zorell (*Lexicon*, "καί," 2:2) in certain cases attributes a value of self-inclusion and cites Luke 10:17. In the similar text of Acts 10:47, καί reinforces the comparative sense (*Lexicon*, "καί," 2:1a). [At 10:47 then, ὡς καὶ ἡμεῖς; is understood in the following way: "just as we?" or "just as we do?" —Ed.]

66. On the application of baptism in the Holy Spirit to Cornelius, see sec. 3.1; on the baptism in the Spirit, see sec. 6.4.

67. See sec. 6.3.

68. Ibid.

69. For Luke, λαός always designates the people of Israel. Precisely for this reason, it is significant that in 15:14 and in 18:10 it is applied to the pagan converts, with full

228   PART TWO: THE EFFECTS OF THE HOLY SPIRIT

This progressive explanation begins with the manifestation of the Holy Spirit in glossolalia. The interpretation for Peter's companions is simply the gift of the Holy Spirit, and for Peter, in the second telling, it is the baptism in the Spirit, and before the Jerusalem Council it is the testimony that God has purified the Gentiles by means of faith. From each interpretation, there follows in the respective telling of the stories a practical consequence. In the first story, it is Peter who draws the conclusion that they cannot withhold baptism (κωλῦσαι) from those who have received the gift of the Spirit just as they had. In the second telling, he draws the same conclusion once again (κωλῦσαι τὸν θεόν). Then the Jewish Christians in Jerusalem progress somewhat in their formulation: "God has given even to the Gentiles the repentance that leads to life" (11:18). The conclusion reached in the third telling of the story brings to light the idea implicit in Cornelius' baptism, i.e., the hindering of God (10:47; 11:17). Now it is expressed in terms of tempting God (15:10). The denial of baptism would equate to placing on the Gentiles the numbing yoke of the law, since it is by the grace of God that both Jewish Christians and Gentile Christians alike are saved (15:11). And God has given testimony by means of the Spirit that he has purified them already by faith.[70] The entire meaning of the passage is summarized in the words of James, to which we have had to look for support many times throughout the study, because they truly constitute the book's center of gravity: "Simeon has related how God first looked favorably on the Gentiles, to take from among them a people for his name" (15:14).[71] It remains only to write the legal decree that translates the Council's ruling into practice: "For it

---

consciousness that God has admitted them into his new people. Luke employs this term with its everyday sense of a multitude, but always in reference to the Israelites. When Jesus leaves the confines of Israel, Luke employs this term a single time and with it probably designates a Jewish group in that territory (see Dahl, "People"). Τὰ ἔθνη, generally in the plural, commonly designates Gentiles in the Septuagint, in the NT, and especially in Acts (Bertram and Schmidt, "ἔθνος").

70. Note the parallelism between the gift of the Holy Spirit and the baptism in the Holy Spirit, and, on the other hand, the parallelism between baptism in water and salvation.

71. James searches the Scriptures for the confirmation of the principle that they are going to accept in this meeting. The citation of Amos 9:11–12 is taken from the Septuagint, since its sense in the Hebrew would not correspond to the circumstances alluded to in his application. It is an indication of the Greek origin of this justification discourse. See Dupont, "λαός ἐξ ἐθνῶν" (in the revision of this article in *Études*, he accepts the suggestions of Dahl ["People"]); and Winter, "Miszellen zur Apostelgeschichte."

seemed good to the Holy Spirit and to us to impose on you no further burden than these essentials" (15:28).[72]

The testimony of the Holy Spirit has been the decisive event (according to Luke) that has determined the exemption from the law for all of the Gentile Christians, changing in this way the direction that the hierarchy planned the avenues of evangelization. The Spirit appears in this way as the driver of the messianic people, by charismatic means, in decisive circumstances. "The idea of allowing the Gentiles to enter the Church without any obligation to the law comes neither from Paul, nor from Peter, but from God!"[73] From this moment, the plan of Acts reaches its literary culmination. The evangelization of the Gentiles fills the scene. Perhaps the Pauline stories were completed by a later hand. But the end of the book corresponds perfectly to the geographic plan of 1:8 with the arrival of Paul in Rome, where "He lived ... proclaiming the kingdom of God and teaching about the Lord Jesus Christ with all boldness and without hindrance" (28:31).

Synthesis of the Spirit's Action

Luke's plan can be constructed around these three great interventions of the Spirit: first at the Jordan, second at Pentecost, and third at the house of Cornelius. Taking advantage of a Greek term that has already lost its numeric meaning, these interventions could be called the *Pentecost* of Christ, the *Pentecost* of the Jewish disciples, and the *Pentecost* of the Gentile disciples. In the first, the Spirit consecrates (ἔχρισεν) Jesus for his messianic ministry. In the second, the Spirit is sent by Christ upon the community as an anticipation and a guarantee of the fullness of the Promise. In the third—perhaps theoretically unnecessary in our eyes, but essential for Luke's thesis—the Spirit testifies to the sanctification of the Gentiles by faith in Jesus, without the need to keep the Mosaic law. The three neurological centers of Luke's work attribute to the intervention of the Spirit the beginning of the messianic work, its application to the community, and its extension to the Gentiles, that is to say, the

---

72. I have addressed this text in secs. 5.5 and 8.3. Concerning the problems created by the Jerusalem decree, see Dupont's review, *Études*, 72–75, and concerning the problems of the historicity of the apostolic council, see 56–72.

73. "Die Idee, die Heiden ohne gesetzliche Verpflichtung in die Kirche einzugliedern, stammt nicht vom Paulus, und nicht von Petrus, sonder von Gott!" (Dibelius, "Bekehrung des Kornelius," *Aufsätze*, 107).

extraordinary intervention of God in the decisive moments of the formation of the people of salvation. This intervention, however, neither realizes nor confers salvation. The Spirit compels, testifies, confirms, and breathes in decisive interventions, but this does not come to constitute the essence of salvation, which is reserved in Acts for the action of God or of Jesus. The work of the Spirit is to keep the people in contact with God, a work already initiated through the prophetic inspiration of the Old Testament, continued through Jesus and the church, and which, for this reason, is a work I have called the *prophetic direction of the people of God*.

Von Baer sums up the work of the Spirit as power that places the saving plan of God onto the historic scene: "The salvation plan of God for the redemption of sinful humanity is the theme of the writings of Luke. The concept through which our author leads us is not the internal moral redemption of men, but rather the establishment of God's lordship over this world."[74]

8.6 Conclusions

The intension of this chapter is to make clear a latent meaning of the diverse interventions of the Holy Spirit narrated by Luke. The common and more profound object of these interventions would be the formation and direction of the messianic salvation people. It is not that the Spirit confers the salvation. His work, like that of the prophets, is the announcing of salvation, the transmission of the unforeseeable designs of God in new, critical situations, and the intermittent stimulation of

---

74. "Der Heilsplan Gottes zur Erlösung der sündigen Menschheit, das ist das Thema des Lukaswerkes. Aber nicht die innere sittliche Erlösung des Menschen, sonder die Aufrichtung der Gottesherrschaft über diese Welt ist der Gedanke, den unser Verfasser durchführt. Die Kraft, die in allen Heilsepochen diesen göttlichen Plan verwirklicht, ist der Heilige Geist." Von Baer (*Heilige Geist*, 108–9) reviews the first part and observes generally that "This is a salvation plan, that he is involved in, and a Spirit, through which it takes effect [Es ist ein Heilsplan, der sich verwirklich, un ein Geist, der ihn auswirkt]" (110). However, translating the entire conception of Acts, it could be said that Jesus is the protagonist of the salvation plan established in the designs of God, but it is the Spirit who establishes the plan in history. This has to do with a category that is somewhat distinct from the mere sending of the Spirit by Christ. More than just sending, he had to speak of the outpouring (perhaps in reflecting upon the disciples) of the Spirit that the Father sent. It is not that Jesus continues acting in the church through the Spirit. We have already seen (in sec. 2.3) that Jesus continues achieving salvation through the power of his name. The actions of Jesus and of the Spirit are complementary.

perseverance in God's people. The Holy Spirit has prepared the messianic work, maintaining the hope of the people through prophetic inspiration (Acts 1:16; 4:25; 28:25). The immediate preparation for the coming of the Messiah is characterized by a prophetic overflow that for some time had disappeared from Israel (Luke 1:15, 41, 67; 2:25–27). Jesus himself receives the assistance of the Holy Spirit for his evangelistic work (Luke 1:35; 3:22; 4:1, 14, 18; Acts 10:38). In these texts the prophetic consecration of Jesus is addressed. In his exaltation, he receives the Holy Spirit of the Promise (2:33). This text refers to the Spirit as a gift of the eschatological fulfillment, already presented in its joyous aspect in the Jubilee hymn (Luke 10:21).

The beginning of the messianic people can be identified with the moment that Jesus receives the Spirit of the Promise and pours it out among his disciples on the day of Pentecost (2:33), with those that remain being inaugurated into the last days (2:17). The manifestation of the Spirit in glossolalia and exultant doxology constitutes the solemn guarantee of the formation of the new messianic people. Also, the new groups that adhere to the people of salvation receive a solemn testimony (5:32) of their incorporation through glossolalia (10:45; 19:6) and prophetic gifts. The gift of the Spirit poured out at Pentecost is not merely a solemn testimony. For the disciples, it is also an impulse for testimony-evangelization that continues the prophetic work of Jesus. Pentecost means a new beginning for the disciples, similar to the consecration of Jesus at the Jordan. Jesus had promised them the Spirit as an extraordinary help before tribunals (Luke 12:12), which is fulfilled especially in the presentation of the disciples before the Sanhedrin (Acts 4:8; 7:55). In a more general way, they had been promised the power of the Holy Spirit to testify "to the ends of the earth" (Acts 1:8 must refer to evangelization as well as testimony). The testimony-evangelization begins with the Pentecostal discourse of Peter and is renewed with the manifestation of the Spirit (4:31). The wisdom of the seven elected ones (ch. 6) has the same evangelistic purpose as does the boldness. Joy (13:52) and comfort (9:31) are at the time foretastes of the fullness of the promise and testimony that stimulates the growth of the people of God.

The Holy Spirit directs the progress of God's people, at times by means of the hierarchical leadership. Acts 1:2, if it is authentic, would have to be interpreted in this sense, even though it may deal with the Spirit that is in Jesus, since it is improbable that the author spoke of an action of the Spirit upon the disciples prior to Pentecost. The leadership hierarchy has the mission of assuring continuity with the work of Jesus, with Jerusalem, and with the apostles. Their typical ritual is the laying on of hands, which is frequently accompanied by a manifestation of the Spirit as a charismatic confirmation of this union and continuity. Some interpret the episodes of Ananias and Sapphira and the establishment of the Ephesian bishops as a permanent assistance by the Spirit in the decision making of the hierarchy. It is much more probable, though, that they refer to the Spirit that drives this extraordinary behavior by the people of God, or that he has designated the new representatives by means of a prophetic oracle, such as in the case of the designation of Barnabas and Paul for their first mission. The case of the Jerusalem Council shows that the joint decision of the Holy Spirit and the hierarchy has been reached by a laborious accommodation of this decision to the testimony of the Spirit manifested charismatically against all expectations. The Spirit manifests so that such a situation can be grafted into the life of the church, but this does not mean that the Gentiles should adapt themselves to the existing demands made by the hierarchical leadership but rather that the hierarchy should change its norms in order to assimilate the Gentiles.

The guidance of the people of God is realized through the charismatic manifestations. The Pentecostal manifestation unexpectedly presents faith in Jesus as a requirement for membership in the true people of God. The seven Hellenists incorporated into the hierarchy had already been characterized by their charismatic gifts. It may be said that the principal events develop in an unforeseeable way by means of the manifestation of the Holy Spirit. It is not that the Spirit contradicts the decisions of the hierarchy or dispenses with them. The Spirit reveals the designs of God that cannot be foreseen by the hierarchy; this verifies the fact in light of the Scriptures and adds to the guarantee of its approval. The baptism in the Spirit of Cornelius does not dispense with the baptism in the name of Jesus, but rather it requires its concession. The mission to the Gentiles is not fully justified until the decision of the Jerusalem Council. The proclamation of salvation has received three fundamental impulses that Luke has attributed to the Spirit, which I have called the Pentecost of Christ at the Jordan, the Pentecost of the Jewish disciples, and the Pentecost of the Gentile Christians represented by Cornelius.

The function of zealous watchfulness by the people of God in order to bring forth the message of salvation, and more intermittently the decisions made in critical moments, is what I have wanted to express under the title of "The Prophetic Direction of the People of God." It deals, therefore, with prophecy in the fullest sense. This aspect lies behind all of the Spirit's interventions in the historic dynamism of the community.

There also exist vestiges of a joyous presence of the Spirit, an eschatological anticipation that contributes only indirectly to the dynamism of the growth of God's people. This aspect is also included in the prophetic gift in its dimension of exultant doxology. The meaning of *baptism in the Holy Spirit* includes the dynamic assistance of the Spirit but probably designates more directly the anticipated joy of the eschatological fulfillment. This dynamism is secondary in the promise of the day of ascension and is only found indirectly in the case of Cornelius and of the majority of believers. This joyous aspect could not be considered as direction but rather as anticipation of the repose of God's people. Even though this is the foundation for fundamental texts, it is much less developed in Acts. The people of God are still expanding, and the work of the Spirit is not so much to cause a foretaste of the enjoyment of salvation as it is to send them on their way according to the salvific plan of God in history.

9

Conclusions

9.1 General Synthesis

ACTS OFFERS A CHARACTERISTIC concept of the Spirit. This begins to be manifested in the frequency and even more in the constancy with which it employs the term *Holy Spirit*, succeeding, definitively, in fixing this term as a proper name for a homogeneous series of interventions by God. The concept is not totally original. It is presented as the heir to the Old Testament concept of the Spirit of God, and it receives its radical novelty from the three sayings of Jesus on the Holy Spirit (sec. 1.1). I suggested as a mere hypothesis that the author of the third Gospel took a Pentecostal story in the christological-messianic sense as a foundation for the second part of his work. This story focused, preferentially, on the joyous, eschatological aspect of the gift of the Spirit and on its value as a guarantee of the messianic age. Luke, by incorporating this story into his work, shifted the accent onto the dynamic, temporal aspect of the expansion of the church, although without dispensing totally with the joyous, eschatological aspect. The originality of Luke is in relating the charismatic experiences of his communities to the sayings of Jesus and to the story that explained the post-Easter exultation as the messianic gift announced by the prophet Joel (secs. 1.3 and 4.3). The charismatic experiences of the Gentile Christians remain thus interpreted as a guarantee of the Spirit with respect to their incorporation into the people of God. They deal, therefore, in true continuity with the people of the Promise and with the original nucleus of the church established by Jesus himself.

In spite of certain divergent nuances of very debatable origin, the concept of the Spirit in the entire first part of Acts is fairly homogeneous. However, the second part, which encompasses almost the entire Pauline cycle, appears to revert back to the Old Testament topics on the Spirit. The overflowing enthusiasm and the richness of content of the first part is replaced with mere attributions of certain facts to the Spirit, introduced as a *deus ex machina* in the narrative. The contrast is especially significant in the Spirit's mode of action. In the first part, we find men who act under the influence of the Spirit, while in the second part the Spirit bursts in on the level of events, either directly or through prophetic oracles (secs. 4.1–3). I refer generally to the concept of the Spirit from the first part, although always having the second part and the data from the Gospel of Luke in mind.

The Holy Spirit is a gift of the Promise. It refers to a permanent gift or, more precisely, with a permanent offering that is perpetually verified when a situation requires the extraordinary assistance of the Spirit. The idea of an internal permanence is foreign to Luke. Nevertheless, it deals with a divine principle that will influence believers without smothering their own decisions and that will cause them to feel renewed while they complete their charge to testify unto the ends of the earth. This constant influence through the human spirit (immaterial and without any internal or external coercion) can be considered as the internal permanence of the Spirit, but Luke appears to have conceived of it as a permanent offering of new comings of the Spirit (secs. 3.1–2).

The gift of the Spirit is first and foremost an eschatological gift. This is its sense in the prophecy of Joel and in the Pentecostal story. His outpouring is a sign that the last days have begun, but these have split into an earthly period (the life of Jesus and of the church) and in a celestial state (inaugurated for Jesus in his exaltation and postponed for the church until the Parousia). These last days in his earthly arena constitute the age of salvation offered and initiated by way of the entrance of the new people of God, joined by the Messiah, until the coming of the Great Day of the Lord. The possession of the Spirit is not an arbitrary sign of salvation but is a natural sign because it promises fulfillment. Jesus received the Spirit in his exaltation and poured him out among the believers. The manifestations of this eschatological anticipation are glossolalia or prophecy as exultant doxology and an extraordinary degree of joyous exultation (secs 3.3 and 8.1).

The gift of the Spirit also has a dynamic, temporal dimension. In the historic situation, the Spirit impels testimony-evangelization and, in cases of necessity, testimony before tribunals and earthly powers. This impulse of the Spirit is manifested first and foremost in wisdom, boldness, and extraordinary faith (secs. 5.1–3). Luke has left us samples of both aspects of the gift of the Spirit. The kerygmatic, historical aspect appears in the anointing of Jesus at the Jordan (sec. 8.2), in the saying about assistance before tribunals (sec. 5.3), and in the interpretation of Pentecost as a special impulse for testimony-evangelization destined solely for the apostles (Acts 1:8; 1:21–22; 10:41; 13:31–32; see secs. 5.1–2).

The eschatological aspect appears in the exaltation of the Messiah (2:33), and in a certain manner it appeared already anticipated in the Jubilee hymn (Luke 10:21; sec. 8.2). With respect to all believers, the eschatological aspect appears in the most essential interpretation of Pentecost as a universal gifting of the Spirit and as baptism in the Holy Spirit (Acts 1:5; secs. 6.4 and 8.6). The joyous, eschatological effects of the Spirit are repeated in the annexation of new Christian groups, according to the words of Peter (2:38; 5:32) and the narratives of the Samaritans, of Cornelius, and of the Ephesians (sec. 6.4). Even though the eschatological aspect is more essential to Pentecost and continues throughout the first part of Acts, *Luke has emphasized the kerygmatic aspect more*, which predominates his work. It is probable that it is Luke who has added the interpretation of Pentecost as a special impulse for testimony-evangelization in the apostles. He has also taken advantage of the gift of rejoicing in the Spirit as a confirmation of having been incorporated into the people of God (5:32 and 15:8). This aspect, which I have called immediate testimony of the Spirit, acquires a great deal of importance in Acts. His manifestations are a testimony to the designs of God, but they must be interpreted by the community in the light of Scripture (secs. 5.4–5).

This change of emphasis results from the purpose of the work, i.e., confirming the Gentile believers in their incorporation into the people of salvation. The principal proofs of Luke would be, on the one hand, the tangible *experience of the Spirit* both in the first Gentile convert and in each new group in the community, and on the other hand, the unstoppable *expansion of the gospel* that shows the dynamic impulse of the Spirit promised by Jesus and which is transmitted with official continuity from the apostles in Jerusalem to the missionaries in the Gentile communities (unto the ends of the earth) (secs. 5.5 and 8.5).

The sanctifying aspect of the Spirit, which was initiated in the Old Testament, developed at Qumran, and is characteristic of Paul (secs. 6.1–2 and 7.4), is for all practical purposes absent in Acts. It is not that there is a total lack of relation between the Spirit and the Christian proceedings of the community. This relation can be found implicitly in the election of the seven (sec. 7.1), in the summaries of the community life (sec. 7.2), and in occurrences of resistance to the Holy Spirit (sec. 7.3). Nevertheless, this implicit relation does not present the Holy Spirit as the sanctifier of the believer, but as an impulse to display the Christian life in extraordinary works. I have called this an extraordinary activation of the Christian life. That which is lacking is the directly sanctifying aspect. The Holy Spirit is given to those who are already believers, and we do not encounter any case in which the gifting of the Spirit precedes faith. Moreover, it appears probable that faith is presupposed as a condition for the gifting of the Spirit. The Holy Spirit is granted, therefore, to those who have already been sanctified by faith. If the faith of Stephen and Barnabas is attributed to the Spirit, it is because this refers to extraordinary manifestations (sec. 6.3). The gifting of the Spirit, according to Acts, is independent of the ritual of baptism and even of the ritual of the laying on of hands, even though it is frequently manifested as a testimony in these rituals of being added to the community in continuity with the work of Jesus (sec. 6.4).

Only with difficulty is Luke able to ignore the attribution of certain directly sanctifying aspects to the Spirit; nevertheless, he has dispensed with this interpretation of the Spirit. It is probable that his attitude is due primarily to his historic concept that, even interpreting the events theologically, does not claim to explain how salvation operates. Acts claims to confirm the faith that shows God's salvific plan, but it makes no theological explanation as to how this salvation is realized in each individual believer. Furthermore, the Lukan conception could be due to a tendency toward the clarity and precision that reserves for Jesus the realization of salvation and, for the Spirit, the putting in place of God's salvific plan in its diverse historical phases (sec. 7.4). The Holy Spirit is not identified in Acts with the gift of salvation or of sanctification. In his dynamic, historical aspect, the Spirit prepares, propels, and directs the salvation plan carried out by Jesus and received by means of faith in him, by the invocation of his name, and by baptism. Likewise, healings—although anticipatory symbols of salvation—are attributed to faith in the name of Jesus, not to the Spirit.

The certainty with which Luke has attributed a series of divine interventions to the Holy Spirit, and the care with which he has avoided attributing other interventions of a distinct character to him, imply that Luke conceived of the Holy Spirit as a divine principle of activity, well characterized in himself, and different both from the direct action of God and from other indirect actions through Christ, the angels, or a supernatural force. It is not that Luke thought of a divine third person, but his attribution to the Spirit of a determined series of divine interventions surpasses a mere literary personification. The importance that Luke confers to the Holy Spirit, as a principle characterized in itself, leaves an impression of three principles in the effecting of salvation: (1) God grants salvation by sending Jesus and calling to faith; (2) Jesus confers it by means of the power in his name, especially in baptism; and (3) the Spirit performs in history the salvific plan of God and completes it as an eschatological fulfillment, to a certain degree, anticipated (sec. 4.4).

It is possible to construct the historic action of the Holy Spirit as a prophetic guidance of the people of God. Since the Old Testament, he has directed the people by means of the prophets up until the messianic salvation. Also, the prophetic work of Jesus proceeds from the consecration of the Holy Spirit. In the period of the church, the Spirit directs the new people of God in the same way, whether by means of charisms possessed by the leadership hierarchy (both common and special charisms for testimony-evangelization) or through charismatic individuals, but, above all, with his manifestations giving testimony to the new ways of God (secs. 8.1–3).

The diverse aspects of the prophetic gift reflect the magnitude of the action that the Spirit brings about by himself or through the distribution of gifts, with respect to the people of God. In the first place, there are the predictions that indicate decisions of God in circumstances of relative importance, the kerygmatic announcement that calls to mind the themes of faith in God, the transmission of divine messages in decisive circumstances of the people, and the vigilance in the carrying out of God's plans before the people and their leaders. We discover in the prophetic gift an aspect of exuberant joy in the knowledge and praise of

God that corresponds also to the gift of the Spirit, even though only as an historic anticipation of his eschatological aspect (sec. 8.1).

This synthesis is an attempt to comprehend the basis for the Lukan concept of the Spirit according to the explicit and implicit facts in his work. Based on the image that Luke himself gives of the diverse episodes, the Lukan concept of the Spirit synthesizes around three great events that provide the structure for his work: (1) the Pentecost of Jesus at the Jordan, (2) the Pentecost of the church in Jerusalem, and (3) the Pentecost of the Gentile Christians represented by Cornelius. The three great events of Luke's work refer to the three periods of the gospel leading up to its arrival to the Gentiles. They implicitly signal the intervention of the Spirit that breaks through the stagnant attitude of the people of God in order to initiate decisive new periods. The prophetic consecration at the Jordan introduces the new Moses who will reorganize the people of God. The Jerusalem Pentecost marks the birth of the church as the new people of God, heir to the Promise. The Pentecost of Cornelius—of essential importance for the Gentile Christian author—determines the turn of the church toward the Gentiles with the recognition of the superfluity of the law (sec. 8.4).

Luke attributes to the Holy Spirit extraordinary interventions of God in decisive moments in the history of his people in order to effect his salvific plan.

9.2 The Contemporary Message of the Lukan Concept

During this entire study we have made an effort to interpret the Lukan concept of the Spirit and his effects, staying within the book and its milieu. As much as possible, it was an inside look, with Lukan eyes. I wish to add a few brief reflections on the Lukan concept made from without, from the perspective of our contemporary situation.

Diverse Concepts of the Spirit of God

We have found in Acts a specific evolutionary stage of the concept of the Spirit of God. Within the book itself are found vestiges of less evolved stages. It may be said that the conception of the first part has integrated them in a rather homogeneous manner and that the second part has retained this similarity, although perhaps without its freshness and profundity. This evolution does not follow a monolineal progression in the writings of the New Testament. Acts has developed the prophetic line, fundamental in the Old Testament, the only one preserved by Jesus according to the testimony of the Synoptics. John and, most of all, Paul have continued the line of the sanctifying Spirit that produces a new supernatural life. These diverse concepts of the Spirit are certainly not conflicting. What is more, it may be said that they are complementary, provided that this complementariness is not understood as an addition of facts in order to form a unique logical scheme. They are complementary because they interpret diverse aspects of the action of God that cannot be adequately expressed in a single human formulation. We are heirs of these concepts and we need to integrate them. However, this synthesis must be realized at the level of the concepts themselves as complete organic collections, and we must avoid the temptation to retain a single concept, adding or accommodating other facts that lose their true sense when disconnected from their own organic unity.

The biblical authors have left us certain signs that they do not wish to combine the two concepts. Luke has, with difficulty, ignored the attribution of sanctifying effects to the Spirit and, thus, has not added them to his concept. More difficult still is that John has failed to recognize the Pentecostal gifting and has disregarded it, unless it be the case that he has reinterpreted it in the gifting of the Spirit on the day of Christ's resurrection (20:22).[1] In a less significant detail, Luke positively avoided attributing to the Spirit the exorcisms and healings that Matthew attributes to him, in order to reserve them directly for God, for the δύναμις, or for the salvific power of the name of Jesus. Adding this fact to the Lukan concept would betray its intention, even though it was not a point of great importance. Claiming to combine these facts and to attribute to the Spirit the final component of the activity that each biblical author has attributed to him would be contrary to the very purpose of such attributes. These attributes have served to characterize and make the divine persons recognizable to us. If we combine the diverse attributions of each biblical author, we run the risk of confusing the activity of the persons and losing in this way the traits that characterize them for us, returning to a single undifferentiated representation.

Interpreting Pentecost as a gifting of the sanctifying Spirit is not an error because the Holy Spirit really is a sanctifier, but it would practically

---

1. [See here Porsch, "Pneuma-Gabe und die Sendung der Jünger durch den Auferstandenen." —Ed.]

obliterate Luke's picture in order to paint a Pauline scene over it. It loses the Pentecost concept and only makes use of the basic structure of its scenes. Luke's concept, however, characterizes the action of the Holy Spirit in a more peculiar way than does the Pauline concept, in that it distinguishes more clearly the action of the Spirit and that of the risen Christ. We should, then, maintain the diverse biblical conceptions as inspired but necessarily inadequate expressions of the mystery. They mutually complement one another but cannot be based on a single logical concept.

The concept deals, therefore, with attributions, with interpretations of variable events in relation to a knowable cause but one that is unidentifiable through the senses. After the resurrection of Jesus, the disciples were filled with enthusiasm, joy, and boldness; they performed wondrous works and obtained innumerable conversions. They knew that it all came from God, and they interpreted it in the light of Scripture and of the words of Jesus, attributing it to God, to the name of Jesus, or to the Holy Spirit. These interpretations are inspired and are, therefore, authentic. But they are, at the same time, human and therefore limited, incapable of exhausting the infinite mystery that they express.

The Pauline conception of the Spirit is perhaps more profound, more mystic, and attributes to the Spirit an activity that is more essential in the Christian life. It has, however, the problem of leaving the distinction between the action of the Spirit and the action of the risen Christ upon Christians very imprecise. In practice, Paul has so closely identified these actions so as to essentially obscure the action of the Holy Spirit. It is this conception which has prevailed in our theology. Of the Lukan theology, only certain "summary" elements have remained, but they are not integrated. No one can dispense with Pentecost, but it has been interpreted in terms of a sanctifying Spirit, of the sacramental gift of baptism, or of some imprecise effects of the sacrament of confirmation. The Lukan concept distinguishes more clearly between the salvific action of Jesus and the action of the Holy Spirit. It is true that the action of the Spirit has two aspects, one *eschatological* as an anticipation of the fulfillment of salvation and the other *dynamic* as a guide for the people of God. The eschatological aspect is distinguished from the action of Jesus, as the effect is distinguished from its cause. The eschatalogical aspect, which is closer to the Pauline concept, has left more of an imprint on our theology than has the historic aspect, even though it is frequently confined to the somewhat hermeneutical domains of mystic theology.

The dynamic, historic action of the Spirit has remained almost exclusively associated with assisting the leadership hierarchy in their succession and in their teaching function. Missiologists have already begun to react against the forgetting of the pneumatic foundation of mission theology. The decree "Ad Gentes" from Vatican II on the missionary activity of the church has redressed this absence, as can be noted in the mission encyclics, in the plan of Vatican I, and even in first sketches prepared for Vatican II itself.

The desire to "summarize" and "draw together" the diverse concepts of the biblical authors in order to obtain a single logical schema necessarily entails the omission of data less concordant with the desired "harmony," or they appear already to be contained in a clearer and more practical form in other formulations. In order to avoid this impoverishing of theology and of the Christian life, it is necessary to return to the conception of each one of the biblical authors in his own richness.

The Spirit in the Events of the Salvific Plan

Luke has imposed his theology on the historical development of the salvific plan of God. Probably this conception is not original, but it evidently predominates his work. The Lukan categories are historical and dynamic. Participation in salvation is conceived of as incorporation into the people of salvation. For this reason, the author goes to some lengths to show the continuity of the people of salvation in the unfolding of time. Luke makes manifest the continuity of the salvific work attributing to the Spirit its development through the diverse historical periods and through tangible manifestations that guarantee its authenticity. To this continuity, by means of the Spirit, is connected the natural unity of the people in the Old Testament and the unity among the hierarchy in the new people of God.

The Holy Spirit inspires the Old Testament prophets (as well as those in the infancy narratives of Jesus and the Baptist) to announce the Messiah and the fulfillment of the Promise. The Spirit is given to Jesus at the Jordan for his prophetic mission and in his exaltation as an eschatological gift of the Promise. The same Spirit is sent by Jesus upon the community that he has brought together, as they are gathered in Jerusalem. The eschatological gift of the Spirit extends to all believers, while the prophetic gift refers to the apostles who are called to testimony-evangelization. The apostles feel insufficient to the task when faced with the development of the communities and delegate seven elected "men full of the Holy Spirit and of wisdom," who are then scattered, because of the persecution, throughout Samaria, Phoenicia, Cyprus, and Antioch. The unity of these new communities with the first community in Jerusalem is assured by means of the sending of Peter and John to Samaria and the manifestation of the Spirit in the moment of the laying on of hands. The sending of Barnabas, "a man full of the Holy Spirit," to Antioch has the same purpose as the intervention of Ananias in Paul's baptism.

The period of the evangelization of the Gentiles (and their admission as they are, without the need for circumcision) is initiated and confirmed by the Holy Spirit. But it is attributed (not without forcing certain facts) to Peter and confirmed by the community at Jerusalem and later on by a council, which made the decision in the name of the Holy Spirit and of the church.

The impulse and the guarantee of the Spirit in the historical continuation of the work of salvation is not a fact that can be proven with the senses; it is a theological interpretation by Luke. We recall that no other New Testament author alluded to Pentecost and that Paul never referred to the case of Cornelius or to the decree of the Jerusalem Council to justify the evangelization of the Gentiles. We are dealing, probably in both cases, with a theological interpretation by Luke of a historical occurrence whose importance and significance stands out by itself.

In Luke, the Heilsgeschichte (salvation history) is founded upon a theological vision of events within a Gottesgeschichte (God history). The most original portion of his concept is the discovery of the action of the Holy Spirit in a number of relatively ordinary events that fulfill the evolution of the salvific plan in the new historical periods. In order to arrive at this discovery of the Spirit in the historical development of God's people, Luke attributes special importance to the charisms, but these religious experiences are integrated into a more comprehensive approach for perceiving the Spirit.

Discerning the Testimony of the Spirit

Luke has developed, as pillars of his structure, three experiences of the Spirit: (1) that of the Jordan, (2) that of Pentecost, and (3) that of Cornelius. The intervention of the Spirit, according to Acts, is always verifiable and serves both as an impulse and as an immediate testimony of the Spirit. Paul, on the other hand, distrusts the use of the charisms, even though he was conscious of the value of those gifts of the Spirit that he himself had experienced. His argument is more directly supported in an interpretation of the Scripture. In Acts, the possibility of deception also appears in these experiences of the Spirit. However, the objections appear to come from those who are ill disposed toward Pentecost, like those who hearing of it attribute the phenomenon to intoxication. Neither do those who sow discord in Antioch appear to be well disposed, "to whom no mission" had been entrusted. The case of the prophets that correctly predict Paul's imprisonment is less clear, as they try to dissuade him from making the journey.

Peter's discourse on Pentecost confronts directly the difficulty of applying the present situation to the prophecy of Joel. This appeal to the prophets in order to interpret the experiences of the Spirit is frequent in Luke. He refers to Isa 61:1 to explain the manifestation of the Spirit at the Jordan. In the case of Cornelius, he places in Peter's mouth a reference to the promise of the baptism of the Spirit, dispensing with its temporal specificity. In the approval of James, he likewise interprets the event in the light of various prophecies. It should be noted, however, that these prophecies are generally taken from the Septuagint and that they are accommodated to the new situation.

The two aspects of mystic experience of the Spirit and harmony with the Scripture are sufficient for Peter to initiate, against all of his reservations, the admission of the Gentiles. Nevertheless, Luke knows that this argument does not silence all doubts, and he develops a further confirmation by means of the approval of the community. We have already noted that the continuity of the salvific plan is based, in addition to the impulse and the confirmation of the Spirit, on hierarchical transmission. The culminating point of Acts is not reached with the coming of the Spirit upon Cornelius but with the recognition of the church as a whole (15:12, 22), whether it be in the principles spoken of by James (15:14) or in the practice established by means of the decree (15:28).

Thus, we encounter in Acts three elements that mutually complete one another in order to discern the testimony of the Spirit regarding new historical fulfillments of God's salvific plan. None of these three elements would be sufficient by itself for recognizing with certainty the testimony of the Spirit. Mystic experience can be confused with a mere human exultation. The interpretation of the Scripture is not literal but, rather, accommodated and can, therefore, be arbitrary. It has nothing to do with planning a new attitude starting from the words of the Scripture, but rather with penetrating the intimate sense of the Scriptures by starting from situations initiated by the Spirit. It has been observed in certain spiritual movements that their forgetting of the church runs parallel to a devaluation of the tangible element of the incarnation. The Spirit cannot be separated from the church, just as it cannot be separated from Jesus. But neither is ecclesial unanimity sufficient by itself. This refers to a consistent guarantee, frequently resulting from a laborious adaptation to the charismatic testimony of the Spirit (Hellenists, the dispersion from Jerusalem, Cornelius). The hierarchical leadership appears to have inherited a governing charisma, manifesting in knowledge about the plans of God, while the Spirit reserves for himself the provoking of prophetic situations that manifest that which is unforeseeable in these plans.

Each one of these three components—experience of the Spirit, interpretation of the Spirit, and ecclesial approval—need to be balanced by the other two. The combination appears to constitute a balanced approach for discerning the testimony of the Spirit in the new historical fulfillments of the plan of God. This evidently does not have to do with an infallible formula. Neither does it follow that we can claim that Luke was conscious of it, nor that it reflected *precisely* the historical process of the expansion of the church. It is probable that neither the Pentecost of Jerusalem, nor that of Cornelius, nor the Jerusalem decree is an event so individually distinct and important that it decided the development of the community in the direction of the Gentiles. More probably, it deals with a historical synthesis of real events (charismatic gifts, Pauline approvals) occurring in the first years of the development of the church. It is important, however, to see the relevance of these three elements Luke utilizes in his interpretation of the historical development of the church in order to retain our own sensitivity to new manifestations of the plans of God.

Present Development of the Salvific Plan

God continues fulfilling his salvific plan in history. He continues producing events, foreseen or unexpected, that open new perspectives for the people of God. Evidently, the events take place as a result of tangible causes, without the senses being able to read a divine origin in them.

Nevertheless, instructed by the Lukan concept of the Spirit, such occurrences have been brought about by the Spirit and have a meaning in the history of salvation. In order to discern the testimony of the Spirit in our present period of the salvific plan, we can apply the same criterion of balance that we have deduced from the book of Acts. For example, the fulfillment of the Second Vatican Council was very much an unforeseen event and with unsuspected consequences. It has been a mystic experience lived in simplicity, both in its convocation and in many of its communications and dialogues.

I do not claim that the Council had been alluded to expressly in any text of Scripture, but neither was the substitution of Judas foreseen in any Psalm. Still, a commentary on the current experiences of the church—on the desire for unity, for justice, and for peace—that will be expressed in the midrashic style of biblical allusions may help us deepen the theological sense of our historic age and discover new applications for the biblical texts. In Luke's work, we were able to find in the infant and Pentecost narratives two perfect examples of inspired Christian midrash. The ecclesial approval of the great experience of the Spirit in Vatican II has again taken on the solemnity of an ecumenical Council, together with the unanimous joy of all believers.

Evidently, this balanced formula is not easily applied to a problem that is still in the process of evolving or to an experience that is still not accepted. In reality, Luke himself referred to events that were already accepted in the life of the church. However, this criterion of balance is able to direct the tensions between the diverse Christian impulses—mystic experience, interpretation of the Scripture, ecclesial action—toward a profile of equilibrium.

The Spirit and the Sanctification of the Christian

Our investigation started with a search for a certain influence of the Spirit on the religious-moral behavior of the Christian. From the first moment, it was clear that this theme remained marginal in the concerns of Acts. A more detailed analysis made it possible to verify a certain influence of the Spirit upon the behavior of believers. But the findings did not support a sanctifying effect of such influence but rather the unstoppable advance of the people propelled by the Holy Spirit and already enjoying a foretaste of the Promise. For a moral theology, it offered, therefore, a series of marginal (and in part questionable) facts concerning the influence of the Spirit on Christian behavior. This section brings together these influences in a synthesis, described as an extraordinary activation of the Christian life.

The unbiased study of the Lukan conception of the Spirit has shown us another interesting dimension in a theological understanding of Christian ethos. Acts does not claim to be a digression but rather a theological interpretation of the history of God's people. Without claiming to offer moralistic advice, the author can do no less than interpret the behavior of Christians in relation to the historic plan of salvation. The first consequence in order to direct Christian behavior could be the emphasizing of the importance of this ecclesial dimension of his way of acting. The action of the Christian may not simply be considered in relation to sanctification but rather to a fulfillment of the kingdom of God. This importance is made concrete in the responsibility for the positive and negative effects of the Christian's attitude with regard to the fulfillment of the salvific plan of God.

An attitude of resisting the Holy Spirit can be offered not only among those that reject the testimony of the ones whom he sends (prophets, apostles, Stephen), but also among the Christians that falsify through deception the extraordinary generosity that the Spirit creates in the community. What is more, the hierarchy itself can resist the Holy Spirit when, sticking to the letter of the law, it becomes numb to the unforeseeable designs of God, designs certified by the charismatic manifestations of the Spirit. In the positive aspect, the theological vision of Luke teaches us to discern the action of the Spirit in every notable event in the development of the church. The wisdom of its pastors, the boldness to proclaim God's word without compromise, and the mystic exaltation and the exuberant joy that expand the people of God are signs of the active presence of the Spirit in the events of the historical periods.

Luke recognizes human participation in this historical development. He knows of resistances to the Spirit, but he also knows of personal cooperation, for it is not the Spirit that speaks in the disciples, but rather they in the Spirit. He knows that man is able to prepare for the messages of God by means of good works, alms, and above all prayer: "how much more will the heavenly Father give the Holy Spirit to those who ask him!" (Luke 11:13). The charisms are frequently a point of union between the action of the Spirit in history and the cooperation of believers. Luke gives great importance to these charismatic experiences.

He appears to assume certain charisms for the election to a hierarchical office. Also, he appears to assume that certain charismatic experiences are normal among believers in the community, even though a greater or lesser period of time may pass without these experiences, even after faith and baptism are received.

The charisms today are not the exclusive possession of a certain privileged soul. The charisms for today, like those from that time, must be discovered and verified with a theological vision of history. From the human perspective, the charisms appeared as intoxication or as weakness through contamination from impure persons or foods. The charisms always appear embedded in human cooperation, but sufficient indications to recognize their origin remain for a believer sensitive to the Spirit's action.

In conclusion, we may say that the Lukan conception of the Spirit awakens the responsibility of believers in order to discover the action of God in each phase of history, in order not to oppose him and to be able to collaborate in his salvific plan. In order to reach this theological interpretation of events, it is necessary to become sensitive to the experience of the Spirit, to the intimate sense of Scripture, and to the ecclesial dialogue.

Appendix

I PROPOSE, FURTHERMORE, A synthesis of the three stories of the coming of the Holy Spirit upon Cornelius, in which we can appreciate how the movement of each individual story and that of the entire Cornelius-Jerusalem Council block moves toward the admission of the Gentiles as the people of God. The intervention of the Spirit is the testimony that they have already been purified by faith and that, therefore, to hinder them from being baptized, placing on them the condition of the yoke of the law, would be to tempt God. The following figure presents a graphic analysis of the parallels of Luke's three retellings of the Cornelius episode. I offer here a brief explanation of the legend used: underlined italics indicate the action of the Spirit; dashed underlines indicate the equality of the gift received by Cornelius and the Pentecostal gift, which is the perceivable event by which the testimony of the Spirit is recognized; solid underlines indicate the opposition of the community to the admission of the Gentiles without the need to be circumcised; italics indicate the central idea of the story of purification of the Gentiles by faith and, therefore, their incorporation, even without circumcision, into the people of God. As can be seen, I have not altered the order of the verses or the Greek words. I have only omitted secondary details. The conclusions from this analysis have been collected in secs. 6.3 and 8.5.

The Pentecost of Cornelius: An Analysis of the Parallels

Acts 10: 44–48	Acts 11: 15–18	Acts 15: 7–11, 14
44 ἔτι λαλοῦντος While still speaking	**15** ἐν...τῷ...λαλεῖν in ... the ... to speak	**7** ...ἀφ' ἡμερῶν ἀρχαίων... ... from days early...
ἐπέπεσεν τ. πν. τ. ἅγ. ... fell the Holy Spirit...	*ἐπέπεσεν τ. πν. τ. ἅγ.*... fell the Holy Spirit...	ἀκοῦσαι τ. ἔθνη τ. λόγον ... to hear the Gentiles the word...
45 κ. ἐξέστησαν...ὅτι And were amazed...because	ὥσπερ καὶ ἐφ' ἡμᾶς as also on us	καὶ *πιστεῦσαι*. and to believe.
καὶ ἐπὶ τὰ ἔθνη also on the Gentiles	ἐν ἀρχῇ. in (the) beginning.	**8** καὶ ὁ ... θεὸς *ἐμαρτύρησεν*... And ... God witnessed...
ἡ δωρεὰ τ. ἁγ. πνεύματος the gift of the Holy Spirit	**16** ἐμνήσθην δὲ ... And I remember...	*δοὺς τ. πν. τ. ἅγ.* giving the Holy Spirit
ἐκκέχυται has been poured out	ὑμεῖς...βαπ. ...πν. ἁγίῳ. you will be baptized in the Holy Spirit.	καθὼς καὶ ἡμῖν as also to us
46 ἤκουον γὰρ ... for they heard...	**17** εἰ οὖν τ. ἴσην *δωρεὰν* If therefore the same gift	**9** κ. οὐθὲν διέκρινεν And nothing distinguished
λαλ. γλώσ. κ. τὸν μεγ. θ.... speaking in tongues and magnifying God	ἔδωκεν αὐτοῖς ὁ θεὸς gave them God	μεταξὺ ἡμῶν τε κ. αὐτῶν between us and them
47 μήτι...ὕδωρ...κωλῦσαί τις (Not)...the water (to) forbid anyone	ὡς καὶ ἡμῖν as also to us	τῇ πίστει καθαρίσας... by faith cleansing...
τοῦ μὴ βαπτισθ.... not to be baptized....	*πιστεύσασιν* ... having believed...	**10** ...τί πειράζετε ... why test you
οἵτινες *τ. πν. τ. ἅγ. ἔλαβον* who the Holy Spirit received	τίς ἤμην...κωλῦσαι who was (I)...to hinder	τὸν θεόν, God
ὡς καὶ ἡμεῖς ; as also we?	τὸν θεόν ; God?	ἐπιθεῖναι ζυγὸν...; to put a yoke ... ?
48 προσέταξεν δὲ And he commanded	**18** ἀκούσαντες...ἡσύχασαν... hearing ... they kept silence...	**11** ἀλλὰ διὰ τῆς χάριτος... but through the grace ...
αὐτοὺς...*βαπτισθῆναι*. them ... to be baptized.	ἄρα κ. τοῖς ἔθνεσιν then also to the Gentiles	σωθῆναι to be saved
	ὁ θεὸς God	καθ' ὃν τρόπον in the same way as
	τ. μετάνοιαν εἰς ζωὴν repentance to life	κἀκεῖνοι. those also.
	ἔδωκεν gave	**14** ...ὁ θεὸς ἐπεσκέψατο... ... God visited ...
		ἐξ ἐθνῶν λαόν... out of the Gentiles a people...

LEGEND

Underlined Italics indicate the action of the Spirit bearing witness.

Dashed Underlines indicate the equality between the gift received by Cornelius and the Pentecostal gift.

Solid Underlines indicate the community's opposition to admitting the Gentiles without circumcision.

Italics indicate the central idea of Gentile purification by faith and admittance into God's people, even without circumcision.

Bibliography

Works following an asterisk have been employed within the editorial process or are included because of their relevance to the interpretive methodology of Haya-Prats.

Abbott, Edwin. *From Letter to Spirit*. London: Black, 1903.
Adler, Nickolas. *Das erste christliche Pfingstfest: Sinn und Bedeutung des Pfingstberichtes Apostelgeschichte 2, 1–13*. Münster: Aschendorff, 1938.
———. *Taufe und Handauflegung: eine exegetisch-theologische Untersuchung von Apg 8, 14–17*. Münster: Aschendorff, 1951.
*Alexander, Loveday C. A. *Acts in Its Ancient Literary Context: A Classicist Looks at the Acts of the Apostles*. T. & T. Clark Biblical Studies. London: T. & T. Clark, 2005.
Alonso-Díaz, J. "El bautismo de fuego anunciado por el Bautista y su relación con la profecía de Malaquías." *MCom* 38 (1962) 121–33.
———. "Hasta qué punto los elementos del rito bautismal cristiano y su profundización teológica en el Nuevo Testamento dependen de Jesús." *EstBib* 24 (1965) 321–47.
Antón, A. "El Espíritu Santo y la Iglesia." En busca de una fórmula para el misterio de la Iglesia. *Greg* 47 (1966) 101–13.
Arnal, J. *La notion de l'Esprit*. Paris: Fischbacher, 1907.
Arnaldich, L. *Los Estudios bíblicos en España 1900–1955*. Madrid, 1957. [On Acts see pp. 177–79.]
Asensio, Felix. "El Espíritu de Dios en los apócrifos judíos precristianos." *EstBib* 6 (1947) 5–33.
Assemblées du Seigneur. Nn. 51 and 52. Bruges, 1963, 1965. Correspondence to Sunday and to the week of Pentecost.
Asting, Ragnar Kristian. *Die Verkündigung des Wortes im Urchristentum. Dargestellt an den Begriffen "Wort Gottes," "Evangelium" und "Zeugnis."* Stuttgart: Kohlhammer, 1939.
Baciocchi, J. de. "Comment reconnaître la personalité du Saint-Esprit?" *NRTh* 77 (1955) 1025–49.
Baer, Heinrich von. *Der Heilige Geist in den Lukasschriften*. BWANT 3/3. Stuttgart: Kohlhammer, 1926.
Bailey, John Amedee. *The Tradition Common to the Gospels of Luke and John*. NovTSup 7. Leiden: Brill, 1963.
Baltzer, K. "The Meaning of the Temple in the Lucan Writings." *HTR* 58 (1965) 263–77.
Bardy, Ephrem. *Le Saint-Esprit en nous et dans l'Église d'après le Nouveau Testament*. Albi: Orphelins-Apprentis, 1950.
Bargon, L. "Le Signe du feu." *Spiritus* 2/7 (1961) 117–22.

Barnard, L. W. "Saint Stephen and Early Alexandrian Christianity." *NTS* 7 (1960–61) 31–45.

*Barrett, C. K. *The Acts of the Apostles, I*. ICC. Edinburgh: T. & T. Clark, 1994.

———. *The Holy Spirit and the Gospel Tradition*. London: SPCK, 1947.

———. "'The Holy Spirit and Gospel Tradition:' Important Hypothesis Reconsidered." *ExpTim* 67 (1955) 142–45.

———. *Luke the Historian in Recent Study*. London: Epworth, 1961.

Bartsch, H. W. "Zum Problem der Pausieverzögerung bei den Sinoptikern." *EvT* 19 (1959) 116–31.

Batdorf, Irvin W. "The Spirit of God in the Synoptic Gospels: An Historical Comparison and a Re-Appraisal." ThD thesis, Princeton Theological Seminary, 1950.

*Bauckham, Richard, editor. *The Book of Acts in Its Palestinian Setting*. The Book of Acts in Its First Century Setting 4. Grand Rapids: Eerdmans, 1995.

Bauer, Johannes Baptist. *Bibeltheologisches Worterbuch*. Graz: Styria, 1962.

Bauernfeind, Otto. *Die Apostelgeschichte*. THKNT 5. Leipzig: Deichert, 1939.

———. "Vom historischen zum lukanischen Paulus." *EvT* 13 (1953) 347–53.

———. "Zur Frage nach der Entscheidung zwishen Paulus und Lukas." *ZST* 23 (1954) 59–88.

*Baumert, Norbert. *Charisma, Taufe, Geisttaufe, I: Entflechtung einersemantischen Verwirrung; II, Normativität und persönliche Berufung*. Würzburg: Echter, 2001.

Baumgärtel, F. W. Bieder, and E. Sjöberg. "Spirit in Judaism." In "πνεῦμα, κτλ." *TDNT* 6:367–89.

Bayer, Hermann Wolfgang. *Die Apostelgeschichte*. NTD 5. Göttingen: Vandenhoeck & Ruprecht, 1951.

Beasley-Murray, G. R. *Baptism in the New Testament*. London: Macmillan, 1962.

———. "The Holy Spirit, Baptism, and the Body of Christ." *RevExp* 63/2 (1966) 177–85.

Behm, Johannes. "γλῶσσα." In *TDNT* 1:719–26.

Belser, J. E. *Die Apostelgeschichte*. Kurzgefasster wissenschaftlicher Kommentar zu den Heiligen Schriften des Neuen Testamentes 3/1. Vienna: Mayer, 1905.

Benoit, Pierre. "L'Ascension." *RB* 56 (1949) 161–203.

———. "Qumran et Nouveau Testament." *NTS* 7 (1960–61) 276–96.

———. "Remarques sur les 'summaries' des Actes 2:42 à 45." In *Aux sources de la tradition chrétienne: mélanges offerts à Maurice Goguel à l'occasion de son 70me anniversaire*, edited by Maurice Goguel and Pierre Benoit, 1–10. Bibliothèque théologique. Neuchatel: Delachaux & Niestlé, 1950.

Bertram, Georg. "θαῦμα, κτλ." In *TDNT* 3:36–42.

Bertram, Georg, and K. L. Schmidt. "ἔθνος, κτλ." In *TDNT* 2:364–72.

Best, E. "Spirit Baptism." *NovT* 4 (1960–61) 236–43.

Bieder, Werner. *Die Apostelgeschichte in der Historie*. Theologische Studien 61. Zürich, 1960.

———. *Die Verheissung der Taufe im Neuen Testament*. Zürich: EVZ, 1966.

Bietenhard, Hans. "ὄνομα, κτλ." In *TDNT* 5:242–83.

Bihler, Johannes. "Der Stephanusbericht." *BZ* 3 (1959) 252–70.

———. *Die Stephanusgeschichte im Zusammenhang der Apostelgeschichte*. Munich: Hüber, 1963.

*Blass, F., A. Debrunner, and R. W. Funk. *A Greek Grammar of the New Testament and Other Early Christian Literature*. Chicago: University of Chicago Press, 1961.

Blass, Friedrich, Albert Debrunner, and David Tabachovitz. *Grammatik des neutestamentlichen Griechisch*. Göttingen: Vandenhoeck & Ruprecht, 1965.

Boeckh, J. "Die Entwicklung der altkirchlichen Pentecoste." Diss., University of Heidelberg, 1959.
Boer, Harry R. *Pentecost and Missions*. Grand Rapids: Eerdmans, 1961.
Boismard, M. E. "La Révélation de l'Esprit-Saint." *RThom* 55 (1955) 5–21.
Boismard, M. E., et al., editors. *L'évangile de Jean: études et problèmes*. RechBib 3. Paris: Desclée de Brouwer, 1958.
Bonnard, Pierre. "L'Esprit-Saint et l'Église selon le Nouveau Testament." *RHPR* 37 (1957) 81–90.
Bonsirven, Joseph. *Le judaïsme palestinien au temps de Jésus-Christ*. Paris: Beauchesne, 1934. Enlish translation: *Palestinian Judaism in the Time of Jesus Christ*. Translated by William Wolf. New York: Holt, Rinehart and Winston, 1964.
———. *Le règne de Dieu*. Éditions Montaigne. Paris: Aubier, 1957.
———. *Théologie du Nouveau Testament*. Théologie 22. Paris: Aubier, 1951.
Borgen, Peder. "Eschatology and Heilsgeschichte in Luke-Acts." PhD diss., Drew University, 1956.
Boudou, Adrien. *Actes des apôtres*. VS 7. Paris: Beauchesne, 1933.
Bouman, H. "The Baptism of Christ with Special Reference to the Gift of the Spirit." *CTM* 28 (1957) 1–14.
Bourke, J. "Le jour de Jahvé en Joël." *RB* 66 (1959) 3–31; 191–212.
Bover y Oliver, José María, and Francisco Cantera Burgos. *Sagrada Biblia: versión crítica sobre los textos hebreo y griego*. Biblioteca de autores cristianos. Madrid: Editorial Católica, 1951.
Bovon, F. *De vocatione gentium: Histoire de l'interpretation d'Act 10:1–11:18 dans les six premeires siècles*. Beiträge zur Geschichte der biblischen Exegese 8. Tubingen: Mohr/Siebeck, 1967.
Braumann, G. "Das Mittel der Zeit: Erwägungen zur Theologie des Lukasevangelium." *ZNW* 54 (1963) 116–45.
Braun, Herbert. "Qumran und das Neue Testament: Acta." *TRu* 29 (1963) 147–76.
Brauns, M. "Le témoignage des mystiques et des saints." *LumVit* 8/1 (1953) 51–60.
Bribomont, J. "L'Esprit sanctificateur dans la spiritualité de Pères grecs." In *Dictionnaire de spiritualité: ascétique et mystique, doctrine et histoire*, edited by Marcel Viller, Charles Baumgartner, and André Rayez, 1257. Paris: Beauchesne, 1932.
*Brodie, Thomas L. *Proto-Luke: The First Edition of Luke-Acts*. Limerick: Dominican Biblical Centre, 2002.
Brown, E. K. "An Interpretation of the Holy Spirit in the Acts." ThM thesis, Union Theological Seminary, 1952.
Brox, Norbert. *Zeuge and Märtyrer: Untersuchungen zur frühchristlichen Zeugnis-Terminologie*. Studien zum Alten und Neuen Testament 5. Munich: Kösel, 1961.
Bruce, F. F. *The Acts of the Apostles: The Greek Text*. London: Tyndale, 1951.
Büchsel, Friedrich. "δίδωμι, κτλ." In *TDNT* 2:166–73.
———. *Der Geist Gottes im Neuen Testament*. Gütersloh: Bertelsmann, 1926.
Buis, P. "Le don de l'Esprit Saint et la prophétie de Joel." *AsSeign* 52 (1965) 16–28.
———. "Joël annonce l'effusion de l'Esprit." *Spiritus* 2 (1961) 145–52.
Bultmann, Rudolf. "ἀγαλλίασις, κτλ." In *TDNT* 1:19–21.
———. "πίστις." In *TDNT* 6:203–28.
———. *Theologie des Neuen Testaments*. Tübingen: Mohr/Siebeck, 1948.
Butler, Basil Christopher. "Spirit and Institution in the New Testament." *SE* 3 (1964) 138–65.

Cadbury, Henry Joel. "Acts and Eschatology." In *The Background of the New Testament and Its Eschatology: In Honour of C. H. Dodd*, edited by W. D. Davies, and David Daube, 300–321. Cambridge: Cambridge University Press, 1956.

———. *The Book of Acts in History*. New York: Harper, 1955.

———. "Four Features of Lucan Style." In *Studies in Luke-Acts: Essays Presented in Honor of Paul Schubert*, edited by Leander E. Keck, Paul Schubert, and J. Louis Martyn, 87–102. Nashville: Abingdon, 1966.

———. "The Hellenists." In *Beginnings* 5:59–74.

———. *The Making of Luke-Acts*. London: SPCK, 1927.

———. *The Style and Literary Method of Luke*. HTS 6. Cambridge: Cambridge University Press, 1920.

———. "The Summaries in Acts." In *Beginnings* 5:392–402.

Caemmerer, R. "The Educational Use of Scripture in the Doctrine of the Holy Spirit." *CTM* 28 (1957) 211–19.

Caldwell, E. C. "The Holy Spirit in the Book of Acts." *Union Seminary Review* 31 (1919) 21–27.

*Calvin, John. *Commentariorum Joannis Calvini in Acta Apostolorum, I*. Geneva: Ex officinal Ioannis Crispini, 1552.

Camerlynck, A. *Commentarius in Actus Apostolorum*. Rome: Desclee, Lefebure et Sacii, 1910.

Campbell, J. Y. "Κοινωνία and Its Cognates in the New Testament." *JBL* 51 (1932) 352–80.

Campenhausen, Hans von. "Tradition und Geist im Urchristentum." *Studium Generale* 4 (1951) 351–57.

Campenhausen, Hans von, and Kurt Galling, editors. *Die Religion in Geschicte und Gegenwart: Handwörterbuch für Theologie und Religionswissenschaft*. Tübingen: Mohr/Siebeck, 1957.

*Cantalamessa, Raniero. *The Mystery of Pentecost*. Translated by Glen S. Davis. Collegeville, MN: Liturgical, 2001.

Carr, Arthur. "The Fellowship of Acts 2:42 and Cognate Words." *Exp* 8/5 (1913) 458–64.

Casey, R. P. "Μάρτυς." In *Beginnings* 5:30–37.

Causse, R. "Le mythe de la nouvelle Jérusalem du Deutero-Isaïe à la 3e sibylle." *RHPR* 18 (1938) 377–414.

———. "Le pèlerinage à Jérusalem et la première Pentecôte." *RHPR* 20 (1940) 120–41.

Cerfaux, Lucien. *Les Actes des Apôtres et le Christianisme primitive*. In *Recueil Lucien Cerfaux: études d'exégèse et d'histoire religieuse, réunies á l'occasion de son soixante-dixième anniversaire*, 63–315. Gembloux: Duculot, 1954.

———. *La communauté apostolique*. Paris: Cerf, 1956.

———. "La composition de la première partie du Livre des Actes." In *Recueil Lucien Cerfaux*, 2:63–91. BETL 6, 7. Gembloux: Duculot, 1954. First published in *ETL* 13 (1936) 667–91.

———. "Première communauté chrétienne a Jérusalem." In *Recueil Lucien Cerfaux*, 2:125–56. BETL 6, 7. Gembloux: Duculot, 1954.

———. *Recueil Lucien Cerfaux: Études D'Exégèse Et D'Histoire Religieuse De Monseigneur Cerfaux*. 3 vols. BETL 6, 7, 18. Gembloux: Duculot, 1954–1962.

———. "Les sources scripturaires de Matt. 11:25–30." In *Recueil Lucien Cerfaux*, 3:139–59. BETL 18. Gembloux: Duculot, 1962. First published in *ETL* 30 (1954) 740–46; 31 (1955) 331–42.

———. "Le symbolisme attaché au miracle des langues." *ETL* 13 (1936) 256–59.
———. "Témoins du Christ d'après le Livre des Actes." *Ang* 20 (1943) 166–83.
Ceuppens, P. F. *De Sanctissima Trinitate*. Rome: Marietti, 1949.
*Charette, Blaine. "'Tongues of Fire': Judgment as a Function of Glossolalia in Luke's Thought." *JPT* 13 (2005) 173–86.
Charlier, Jean-Pierre. *L'Évangile de l'enfance de l'Église: Commentaire de Actes 1–2*. Brussels: La Pensée catholique, 1966.
Chenu, Marie-Dominique. "L'Expérience des Spirituels du XIIIe siècle." In *L'Évangile dans le temps*, 75–97. Cogitatio fidei 11. Paris: Cerf, 1964.
Cheshire, C. L. "The Doctrine of the Holy Spirit in Acts." ThM thesis, Union Theological Seminary, 1953.
Chevallier, Max-Alain. *L'Esprit et le Messie dans le Bas-Judaïsme et le Nouveau Testament*. Paris: Universitaires de France, 1958.
*Cho, Y. *Spirit and Kingdom in the Writings of Luke and Paul: An Attempt to Reconcile These Concepts*. Paternoster Biblical Monographs. Milton Keynes, UK: Paternoster, 2005.
Claereboets, C. "In quo vos S. Sanctus posuit episcopos regere Ecclesiam Dei." *Bib* 24 (1943) 370–87.
Comblin, Joseph. *Le Témoignage et l'Esprit*. Paris: Universitaires de France, 1964.
*Congar, Yves M.-J. "Actualité renouvelée du Saint-Esprit," *LumVit* 27 (1972) 543–60.
———. "L'Esprit-Saint dans l'Église." *LumVie* 10 (1953) 75–94.
*———. "The Holy Spirit in the 'Economy': Revelation and Experience of the Spirit." In *I Believe in the Holy Spirit*, translated by David Smith, 3–62. 3 vols. in 1. New York: Crossroad, 2005.
*———. "La pneumatology et théologie catholique." *RSPT* 51 (1972) 250–58.
*———. "The Positive Contribution of the 'Charismatic Renewal' to the Church." In *I Believe in the Holy Spirit*, translated by David Smith, 149–60. 3 vols. in 1. New York: Crossroad, 2005.
———. "Le Saint-Esprit et le corps apostolique réalisateurs de l'oeuvre du Christ." *RSPT* 36 (1952) 613–25; 37 (1953) 24–48.
Conzelmann, Hans. *Die Apostelgeschichte*. HNT 7. Tübingen: Mohr/Siebeck, 1963.
———. "Gegenwart und Zukunft in der synoptischen Tradition." *ZTK* 54 (1957) 277–96.
———. "Geschichte, Geschichtsbild, und Geschichtsdarstellung bei Lukas." *TLZ* 85 (1960) 241–50.
———. "Heidenchristentum." In *RGG* 3 (1959) 128–41.
———. *Die Mitte der Zeit: Studien zur Theologie des Lukas*. BHT 17. 5th ed. Tübingen: Mohr/Siebeck, 1964.
———. *Theology of St. Luke*. Translated by Geoffrey Buswell. New York: Harper & Row, 1961.
———. "Zur Lukasanalyse." *ZTK* 49 (1952) 16–33.
Coppens, Joseph. "Le don de l'Esprit d'après les textes de Qumrân et le quatrième évangile." In *L'Evangile de Jean: études et problemes*, 209–23. RechBib 3. Edited by M. E. Boismard et al. Paris: Desclée de Brouwer, 1958.
———. *L'Imposition des mains et les rites connexes dans le Nouveau Testament et dans l'Eglise Ancienne: étude de théologie positive*. Paris: Gabalda, 1925.
Coppens, Joseph, A. L. Descamps, and Edouard Massaux, editors. *Sacra pagina: miscillanea biblica*. 2 vols. BETL 12–13. Gembloux: Duculot, 1959.

Cramer, J. A., editor. *Catenae graecorum Patrum in Novum Testamentum*. Studies in Scripture, Acta Apostolorum, 3. Oxford: Oxford University Press, 1844.

Crehan, J. H. "The Purpose of Luke in Acts." *SE* 2 (1964) 354–68.

Crump, F. J. "*Pneuma* in the Gospels." PhD diss., Catholic University of America, 1954.

Cullmann, Oscar. *Heil als Geschichte: Heilsgeschichtliche Existenz im Neuen Testament*. Tübingen: Mohr/Siebeck, 1965.

———. "L'opposition contre le temple de Jérusalem: motif commun de la théologie johannique et du monde ambiant." *NTS* 5 (1958–59) 157–73.

———. "Parusieverzögerung und Urchristentum, der gegenwärtige Stand der Diskusion." *TLZ* 83 (1958) 1–12.

Dahl, Nils Alstrup. "A People for His Name." *NTS* 4 (1957) 319–27.

———. *Das Volk Gottes: eine Untersuchung zum Kirchenbewusstsein des Urchristentums*. 2nd ed. Darmstadt: Wissenschaftliche Buchgesellschaft, 1963.

D'Ales, A. "Nota a Acts 5:3." *RHR* 24 (1934) 199f.

Dander, F. "L'Esprit Saint." *LumVit* 8/1 (1953) 7–17.

Daniélou, Jean. "Le Christ prophète." *VSpir* 78 (1948) 154–70.

———. "Esprit-Saint et histoire du Salut." *VSpir* 83 (1950) 127–40.

*Danker, Frederick. *The Concise Greek-English Lexicon of the New Testament*. Chicago: University of Chicago Press, 2009.

Davies, G. "Pentecost and Glossolalia." *JTS* 3 (1952) 228–31.

Davies, G. H. "The Holy Spirit in the OT." *RevExp* 63/2 (1966) 129–34.

Davies, J. G. *The Spirit, the Church and the Sacraments*. London: Faith, 1954.

Davies, O. W. *Mélanges bibliques rédigés en l'honneur de André Robert*. Travaux de l'Institut Catholique de Paris 4. Paris: Bloud & Gay, 1956.

Davies, W. D., and D. Daube, editors. *The Background of the New Testament and Its Eschatology: In Honour of Charles Harold Dodd*. Cambridge: Cambridge University Press, 1956.

Denio, F. B. "The Scriptural Teaching Respecting the Holy Spirit." *JBL* 15 (1896) 135–50.

Díaz, J. M. "Características literarias de S. Lucas." *Cathedra* 6 (1952) 39–48.

Dibelius, Martin. *Aufsätze zur Apostelgeschichte*. Edited by Heinrich Greeven. FRLANT 60. Göttingen: Vandenhoeck & Ruprecht, 1961.

*———. *The Book of Acts: Form, Style, and Theology*. Edited by K. C. Hanson, translated by Mary Ling and Paul Schubert. Fortress Classics in Biblical Studies. Minneapolis: Fortress, 2004.

———. *Die Reden der Apostelgeschichte und die antike Geschichtsschreibung*. Heidelberg: Winter, 1949.

Dieli, L. "Marc Sources des Actes?" *RB* 29 (1920) 555–69; 30 (1921) 86–96.

Díez Macho, A. "El Logos y el Espíritu Santo." *Atlántida* 1 (1963) 381–96.

Dodd, H. *The Apostolic Preaching and Its Developments: Three Lectures with an Appendix on Eschatology and History*. London: Hodder & Stoughton, 1956.

———. *The Parables of the Kingdom*. London: Nisbet, 1948.

———. *La prédication apostolique et ses développements*. Paris: Universitaires de France, 1964.

Dumont, R. "La koinonia en los primeros cinco capítulos de los Hechos." *RevistB* 24 (1962) 22–32.

Dupont, Jacques. "La communauté des biens aux premièrs jours de l'Église. In *Études sur les Actes des apôtres*, 503–19. LD 45. Paris: Cerf, 1967.

———. "La conversion dans les Actes des Apôtres." *LumVie* 47 (1960) 47–70.

*———. "Dieu l'a oint d'Esprit Saint (Ac 10, 34–38)." In *Nouvelles Études sur les Actes des Apôtres*, 319–28. LD 118. Paris: Cerf, 1984.
———. *Études sur les Actes des Apôtres*. LD 45. Paris: Cerf, 1967.
———. "Hechos de los Apóstoles." In *Enciclopedia Bíblica*, III, 1149–61. Barcelona: Garriaga, 1964.
———. "λαός ἐξ ἐθνῶν." *NTS* 3 (1956) 47–50.
*———. "La nouvelle Pentecôte (Ac 2, 1–11). Fête de la Pentecôte." In *Nouvelles Études sur les Actes des Apôtres*, 191–98. LD 118. Paris: Cerf, 1984.
———. "La première Pentecôte chrétienne." *AsSeign* 51 (1963) 39–62.
———. "Repentir et Conversion d'après les Actes des Apôtres." *ScEccl* 12 (1960) 1371–73.
———. "Le salut des gentils et la signification théologique du livre des Actes." In *Études sur les Actes des apôtres*, 393–419. LD 45. Paris: Cerf, 1967. First published in *NTS* 6 (1959) 132–55.
———. *Les sources du livre des Actes: État de la question*. Paris: Desclee de Brouwer, 1960.
———. "L'Utilisation apologetique de l'Ancien Testament dans les discours des Actes." *ETL* 29 (1953) 289–327.
Edsman, Carl-Martin. *Le baptême de feu*. Uppsala: Almqvist & Wiksells, 1940.
Ehrhardt, Arnold. "The Construction and Purpose of the Acts of the Apostles." *ST* 12 (1958) 45–79.
*Eisen, Ute E. *Die Poetik der Apostelgeschichte: Eine narratologische Studie*. NTOA/SUNT 58. Göttingen: Vandenhoeck & Ruprecht, 2006.
*Elbert, Paul. "Contextual Analysis and Interpretation with Sensitivity to the Spirit as Interactive Person." *JBPR* 1 (2009) 1–14.
*———. "An Observation on Luke's Composition and Narrative Style of Questions." *CBQ* 66 (2004) 98–109.
*———. "Paul of the Miletus Speech and 1 Thessalonians: Critique and Considerations." *ZNW* 95 (2004) 258–68.
*———. "Possible Literary Links Between Luke-Acts and Pauline Letters Regarding Spirit-Language." In *The Intertextuality of the Epistles: Explorations of Theory and Practice*, edited by T. L. Brodie, D. R. MacDonald, and S. E. Porter, 226–54. NTM 16. Sheffield: Sheffield-Phoenix, 2006.
Elfers, H. "Gehört die Salbung mit Chrisma im ältesten abendländischen Initiationsritus zur Taufe oder zur Firmung?" *TGl* 34 (1942) 334–41.
Ellis, E. Earle. "Present and Future Eschatology in Luke." *NTS* 12 (1965–66) 27–41.
*———. "Prophecy in the New Testament Church—and Today." In *Prophetic Vocation in the New Testament and Today*, edited by J. Panagopoulos, 46–57. NovTSup 45. Leiden: Brill, 1977.
*———. "The Role of the Christian Prophet in Acts." In *Prophecy and Hermeneutic in Early Christianity*, 129–44. WUNT 18. Tübingen: Mohr/Siebeck, 1978.
Enciso, J. "Manifestaciones naturales y sobrenaturales del Espíritu de Dios en el Antiguo Testamento." *EstBib* 5 (1946) 351–80.
Fascher, F. "Zur Taufe des Paulus." *TLZ* 80 (1955) 643–48.
Fenton, John. "The Order of the Miracles Performed by Peter and Paul in Acts." *ExpTim* 77 (1965) 381–83.
Feuillet, A. "Marie et la nouvelle creation." *VSpir* 81 (1949) 472–73.
———. "Le messianisme du livre d'Isaïe." *RSR* 36 (1949) 182–228.
———. "Le symbolisme de la colombe dans les récits évangéliques du baptême." *RSR* 46 (1958) 524–44.

Filson, Floyd V. "Life Issues in Acts." *BR* 9 (1964) 26–37.
Fitzmyer, Joseph A. *The Acts of the Apostles*. AB 31. New York: Doubleday, 1998.
*———. *The Gospel according to Luke*. 2 vols. AB 28, 28A. Garden City, NY: Doubleday, 1981–85.
*———. "Jewish Christianity in Acts in Light of the Qumran Scrolls." In *Studies in Luke-Acts: Essays Presented in Honor of Paul Schubert*, edited by Leander E. Keck, Paul Schubert, and J. Louis Martyn, 233–57. Nashville: Abingdon, 1966.
*———. "The Virginal Conception of Jesus in the New Testament." *TS* 34 (1973) 541–75.
Flender, Helmut. *Heil und Geschichte in der Theologie des Lukas*. BEvT 41. Munich: Kaiser, 1965.
*Forbes, Christopher. *Prophecy and Inspired Speech in Early Christianity and Its Hellenistic Environment*. WUNT 2/75. Tübingen: Mohr/Siebeck, 1995.
Förster, W. "Stephanus und die Urgemeinde." In *Dienst unter dem Wort: eine Festgabe für Professor D. Dr. Helmuth Schreiner zum 60*, edited by Karl Janssen and Walter Künneth. Gutersloh: Bertelsmann, 1953.
———. "Der Heilige Geist im Spätjudentum." *NTS* 8 (1961) 117–34.
Friedrich, Gerhard. "κηρύσσειν, κτλ." In *TDNT* 3:683–718.
Gächter, Paul. "Die Sieben." *ZKT* 74 (1952) 129–66.
———. "Zum Pneumabegriff des Hl. Paulus." *ZKT* 53 (1929) 345–408.
Galot, J. "Vous serez mes témoins." *Spiritus* 2/7 (1961) 153–62.
Gamba, G. G. "La preoccupazione universalista del Vangelo di S. Luca." Diss., Pontifical Gregorian University, 1962. Summary reprinted in *VD* 40 (1962) 131–35.
García del Moral, A. "Sentido trinitario de la expresión Espíritu de Yavé de Is 11:2 in 1 Petr 4:14." *EstBib* 20 (1961) 169–206.
———. "Un posible aspecto de la tesis y unidad del libro de los Hechos." *EstBíb* 23 (1964) 41–92.
Gelin, A. "L'annonce de la Pentecôte." *BVC* 27 (1959) 15–19.
*George, Augustin. "L'Esprit Saint dans l'oeuvre de Luc." *RB* 85 (1978) 500–542.
*———. *Études sur l'oeuvre de Luc*. SB. Paris: Gabalda, 1978.
———. "Note sur quelques traits lucaniens de l'expresion 'Par le doigt de Dieu.'" *ScEccl* 18 (1966) 461–66.
———. "La prédication inaugurale de Jésus dans la synagogue de Nazareth." *BVC* 59 (1964) 17–29.
Gettys, J. M. "The Book of Acts." *Studia Biblica* 5 (1951) 216–30.
Gewiess, Josef. *Die urapostolische Heilsverkündigung nach der Apostelgeschichte*. Breslau: Müller & Seiffert, 1939.
Ghidelli, C. "Metodo esegetico e contenuto teologico nel discorso di S. Pietro a Pentecoste." Diss., Pontifical Gregorian University, 1962.
———. "Studi sugli Atti degli Apostoli." *SchuolC* 91 (1963) 96–108; 93 (1965) 222–28, 371–89, and 390–98.
———. "Le citazioni dell' Antico Testamento nel cap. 2 degli Atti." *ETL* 29 (1953) 289–327. Reprinted in *AtSettBibl* 18 (1964) 285–305.
*Giblet, Jean. "Baptism in the Spirit in the Acts of the Apostles." *OC* 10 (1974) 162–71.
———. "Les promeses de l'Esprit et la mission des Apôtres dans les Évangiles." *Irenikon* 30 (1957) 5–43.
*Gill, David W. J., and Conrad H. Gempf, editors. *The Book of Acts in Its First Century Setting*. Vol. 2: *Greco-Roman Setting*. Carlisle, Cumbria: Paternoster, 1994.

Gillespie, J. T. "The Work of the Holy Spirit as Shown in the Book of Acts." PhD diss., Southern Baptist Theological Seminary, 1930.
Gils, F. "L'Esprit Saint chez Saint Jean." *Spiritus* 2/7 (1961) 189–200.
———. "L'évangile du Saint Esprit." *Spiritus* 2/7 (1961) 163–79.
Glombitza, O. "Der Schluss der Petrusrede, Acta 2, 36–40." *ZNW* 52 (1961) 115–18.
Goguel, Maurice. *La notion johannique de l'esprit et ses antécédénts historiques étude de théologie biblique.* Paris: Fischbacher, 1902.
———. "Pneumatisme et eschatologie dans le christianisme primitif." *RHR* 132 (1946) 124–69; 133 (1947) 103–61.
Goguel, Maurice, and Pierre Benoit. *Aux sources de la tradition chrétienne: mélanges offerts à Maurice Goguel à l'occasion de son 70me anniversaire.* Bibliothèque théologique. Neuchatel: Delachaux & Niestlé, 1950.
Goitia, J. de. "Espíritu." In *Enciclopedia Bíblica*, III, 184–87. Barcelona: Garriaga, 1964.
———. "La noción dinámica del pneuma en los libros sagrados." *EstBib* 15 (1956) 147–85, 341–80; 16 (1957) 115–59.
Gomá Civit, I. *El Espíritu Santo y sus "charismas" en la teología del Nuevo Testamento.* Barcelona, 1954.
———. *Ubi Spiritus Dei, illic Ecclesia et omnis gratia.* Barcelona, 1954.
González Nuñez, A. *Profetas, sacerdotes y reyes en el antiguo Israel.* Madrid, 1962.
Goulder, M. D. *Type and History in Acts.* London: SPCK, 1964.
Grangette, G. "Esprit-Saint et communauté chrétienne." *LumVie* 10 (1953) 95–108.
Grässer, Erich. "Die Apostelgeschichte in der Forschung der Gegenwart." *TRu* 26 (1960) 93–167.
———. *Das Problem der Parousieverzögerung in den synoptischen Evangelien und in der Apostelgeschichte.* BZNW 22. 2nd ed. Berlin: Töpelmann, 1960.
Graystone, G. "Catholic Bibliography of Acts." *Scr* 6 (1953) 58–59.
Grundmann, Walter. "Die Apostel zwischen Jerusalem und Antioquia." *ZNW* 39 (1940) 110–37.
———. "δύναμις." In *TDNT* 2:284–317.
———. "Das hellenistische Christentum innerhalb der Jerusalemer Urgemeinde." *ZNW* 38 (1939) 45–73.
———. "Der Pfingstbericht der Apostelgeschichte in seinem theologischen Sinn." *SE* 2 (1964) 584–94.
Grundmann, Walter, Gerhard von Rad, and Gerhard Kittel. "ἄγγελος, κτλ." In *TDNT* 1:74–87.
Guillet, J. "Baptême et Esprit." *LumVie* 26 (1956) 85–104.
———. "Dans l'Écriture." In *Dictionnaire de spiritualité*, edited by Marcel Viller, Charles Baumgartner, and André Rayezvol, IV/2:1246. Paris: Beauchesne, 1932.
———. "La révélation progressive du Saint-Esprit dans l'Écriture." *LumVit* 8/1 (1953) 18–32.
———. *Thèmes bibliques: Le soufle de Jahweh.* Théologie 18. Paris: Aubien, 1951.
Gunkel, Hermann. *Die Wirkungen des heiligen Geistes nach der populären Anschauung der apostolischen Zeit und nach der Lehre des Apostels Paulus.* 3rd ed. Göttingen: Vandenhoeck & Ruprecht, 1909.
*———. *The Influence of the Holy Spirit: The Popular View of the Apostolic Age and the Teaching of the Apostle Paul.* Translated by Roy A. Harrisville and Philip A. Quanbeck II. Philadelphia: Fortress, 1979.
Günther, Ernst. *Martys die Geschichte eines Wortes.* Gütersloh: Bertelsmann, 1941.

———. "Zeuge und Martyrer." *ZNW* 47 (1956) 145–61.
Guthrie, Donald. "Recent Literature on the Acts of the Apostles." *VE* 2 (1963) 33–49.
Haenchen, Ernst. "Apostelgeschichte." In *RGG* 1 (1957) 501–07.
———. *Die Apostelgeschichte*. KEK 3. Göttingen: Vandenhoeck & Ruprecht, 1965.
*———. *The Acts of the Apostles: A Commentary*. Translated from the 14th German ed. by Bernard Noble and Gerald Shinn. Philadelphia: Westminster, 1971.
———. Review of Hans Conzelmann's *Die Mitte der Zeit*. *ZKG* 66 (1954–55) 157–60.
———. "Tradition und Komposition in der Apostelgeschichte." *ZTK* 52 (1955) 205–25.
Hamaide, J., and P. Gilbert. "Résonances pastorales du plan des Actes." *Église Vivante* 9 (1957) 95–113, 368–83.
Hammans, Herbert. *Die neueren katholischen Erklärungen der Dogmenentwicklung*. Beiträge zur neueren Geschichte der katholischen Theologie 7. Essen: Ludgerus, 1965.
Harnack, Adolf von. *Beiträge zur Einleitung in das Neue Testament*. 7 vols. Leipzig: Hinrichs, 1906–16.
Hastings, James, John A. Selbie, and Louis H. Gray, editors. *Encyclopaedia of Religion and Ethics*. 13 vols. New York: Scribner, 1955.
Hauck, F. "κοινός, κτλ." In *TDNT* 3:789–809.
*Haya-Prats, Gonzalo. *L'Esprit Force de l'Église: Sa nature et son activité d'après les Actes des Apôtres*. Translated by José J. Romero and Hubert Faes. LD 81. Paris: Cerf, 1975.
*Hays, Richard B. "Reading the Bible with Eyes of Faith: The Practice of Theological Exegesis." *JTI* 1/1 (2007) 5–21.
*Hemer, Colin. *The Book of Acts in the Setting of Hellenistic History*. Edited by Conrad H. Gempf. WUNT 49. Tübingen: Mohr/Siebeck, 1989.
Hermann, I. and O. Semmelroth. "Heiliger Geist." In *Handbuch theologischer Grundbegriffe*, edited by Heinrich Fries, 642–52. Munich: Kösel, 1962.
*Hill, David. "Prophets and Prophecy in the Acts of the Apostles." In *New Testament Prophecy*, 94–109. London: Marshall, Morgan & Scott, 1979.
Holtzmann, Heinrich Julius. *Die Apostelgeschichte*. HKNT 1/2. Tübingen: Mohr/Siebeck, 1901.
Holzmeister, U. "Quid Sacra Scriptura doceat de mysterio festi Pentecostes." *VD* 7 (1927) 161–64.
Hunken, J. W. "British Work on the Acts." In *Beginnings* 2:396–433.
*Hur, Ju. *A Dynamic Reading of the Holy Spirit in Luke-Acts*. JSNTSup 211. London: T. & T. Clark, 2004.
Iglesias, S. Muñoz. "Los profetas del Nuevo Testamento comparados con los del Antiguo Testamento." *EstBib* 6 (1947) 307–44.
Imschoot, Paul van. "L'Action de l'Esprit de Jahvé dans l'Ancien Testament." *RSPT* 23 (1934) 553–87.
———. "Baptême d'eau et baptême d'Esprit Saint." *ETL* 13 (1963) 653–66.
———. "L'Esprit de Jahvé et l'Alliance nouvelle dans l'Ancien Testament." *RB* 47 (1938) 23–49.
———. "L'Esprit de Jahvé, Principe de vie morale dans l'Ancien Testament." *ETL* 16 (1939) 457–67.
———. "L'Esprit de Jahvé source de vie dans l'Ancien Testament." *RB* 44 (1935) 481–501.
———. "Geist Gottes." In *Bibellexikon*, edited by Herbert Haag and Adrian van den Boren, 531–40. Einsiedeln: Benziger, 1951.

Isaac, Jean. *La revelation progressive des personnes divines*. Lumiere de la foi. Paris: Cerf, 1960.
Jacquier, Eugène. *Les Actes des Apôtres*. Ebib. Paris: Lecoffre, 1926.
Jaeger, H. "Parrhesia et fiducia, Étude spirituelle des mots." *StPatr* 1 (1957) 221-39.
Jean-Nesmy, C. "Permanence de la Pentecôte." *AsSeign* 51 (1963) 72-87.
Jeremias, Joachim. "Untersuchungen zum Quellenproblem der Apostelgeschichte." *ZNW* 36 (1937) 205-21.
*Jervell, Jacob. *Die Apostelgeschichte*. KEKNT 3/17. Göttingen: Vandenhoeck & Ruprecht, 1998.
———. "Das gespaltene Israel und die Heidenvölker: Zur Motivierung der Heidenmission in der Apostelgeschichte." *ST* 19 (1965) 58-96.
*Johns, Cheryl Bridges. "Of Like Passion: A Pentecostal Appreciation of Benedict XVI." In *The Pontificate of Benedict XVI: Its Premises and Promises*, edited by William G. Rush, 97-113. Grand Rapids.: Eerdmans, 2009.
Johnson, S. E. "The Dead Sea Manual of Discipline and the Jerusalem Church in Acts." *ZAW* 66 (1954) 106-20.
Johnston, L. "The Spirit of God." *Scr* 8 (1956) 65-74.
Joüon, P. "Divers sens de παρρησία dans le Nouveau Testament." *RSR* 30 (1940) 239-42.
Journet, Ch. "La Mission visible de l'Esprit-Saint." *RThom* 65 (1965) 357-97.
Käsemann, Ernst. "Die Anfänge christlicher Theologie." *ZTK* 57 (1960) 167-85.
———. "Geist und geistgaben im Neuen Testament." In *RGG*, 1272-79.
———. "Die Johannesjünger in Ephesus" *ZTK* 49 (1952) 144-54.
Keck, Leander E., Paul Schubert, and J. Louis Martyn, editors. *Studies in Luke-Acts: Essays Presented in Honor of Paul Schubert*. Nashville: Abingdon, 1966.
*Keener, Craig S. *The Spirit in the Gospels and Acts: Divine Purity and Power*. Peabody, MA: Hendrickson, 1997.
Kerrigan, A. "The 'sensus plenus' of Joel 3:1-5 in Acts 2:14-36." In *Sacra pagina: miscillanea biblica*, edited by Joseph Coppens, A. L. Descamps, and Edouard Massaux, 2:295-313. BETL 13. Gembloux: Duculot, 1959.
*Kilgallen, John J. "The Speech of Stephen, Acts 7:2-53." *ExpTim* 115/9 (2004) 293-97.
Kilpatrick, G. D. "The Spirit, God, and Jesus in Acts." *JTS* 15 (1964) 63.
*Kim, Hee-Seong. *Die Geisttaufe des Messias: Eine kompositionsgeschichtliche Untersuchung zu einem Leitmotiv des lukanischen Doppelwerks. Ein Beitrag zur Theologie und Intention des Lukas*. SklPhil 81. Frankfurt: Lang, 1993.
*Kim, Young Hwan. "A Narrative Preaching of the Holy Spirit in Luke-Acts." PhD diss., University of Wales, Lampeter, 2008.
Kittel, Gerhard. "Die Wirkungen der christlichen Wassertaufe." *TSK* 87 (1914) 25-53.
Kittel, Gerhard, and Gerhard Friedrich, editors. *Theologisches Wörterbuch zum Neuen Testament*. 10 vols. Stuttgart: Kohlhammer, 1933ff.
Klausner, Joseph. *From Jesus to Paul*. Translated by William F. Stinespring. London: Allen & Unwin, 1946.
*Klein, Hans. *Das Lukasevangelium*. KEK 1/3. 10th ed. Göttingen: Vandenhoeck & Ruprecht, 2006.
Kleinknecht, Hermann. "πνεῦμα in the Greek World." In *TDNT* 6:334-59.
Knox, John. "Acts and the Pauline Letter Corpus." In *Studies in Luke-Acts: Essays Presented in Honor of Paul Schubert*, edited by Leander E. Keck, Paul Schubert, and J. Louis Martyn, 279-87. Nashville: Abingdon, 1966.
Knox, Wilfred L. *The Acts of the Apostles*. Cambridge: Cambridge University Press, 1948.

Koch, Róbert. "Geist." In *Bibeltheologisches Worterbuch*, edited by Johannes Baptist Bauer, 422-53. Graz: Styria, 1962.

―――. *Geist und Messias. Beitrag zur biblischen Theologie des Alten Testaments.* Vienna: Herder, 1950.

―――. "La Théologie de l'Esprit de Jahvé dans le livre d'Isaïe." In *Sacra pagina: miscillanea biblica*, edited by Joseph Coppens, A. L. Descamps, and Edouard Massaux, 1:419-33. BETL 12. Gembloux: Duculot, 1959.

*Kremer, J. *Pfingstbericht und Pfingstgeschehen: Eine exegetische Untersuchung zu Apg 2, 1-13.* SBS 63/64. Stuttgart: KBW, 1973.

Kretschmar, G. "Himmelfahrt und Pfingsten (Apg 2, 1-13)." *ZKG* 66 (1954) 209-53.

Kümmel, Werner Georg. "Das Urchristentum." *TRu* 14 (1942) 81-95, 155-73; 17 (1948) 3-50, 103-42; 18 (1950) 1-53; 22 (1954) 138-70, 191-211.

*Kurz, William S. "From the Servant Isaiah to Jesus and the Apostles in Luke-Acts to Christians Today: Spirit-Filled Witness to the Ends of the Earth." In *Between Experience and Interpretation: Engaging the Writings of the New Testament* (Festschrift for Luke Timothy Johnson), edited by Mary F. Foskett and O. Wesley Allen Jr., 175-94. Nashville: Abingdon, 2008.

Kürzinger, Josef. *Die Apostelgeschichte.* Geistliche Schriftlesung 5. Düsseldorf: Patmos, 1966.

La Potterie, Ignace de. "L'onction du chrétien par la foi." *Bib* 40 (1959) 12-69.

―――. "L'onction du Christ." *NRTh* 80 (1958) 225-52.

―――. "La notion de témoignage dans Saint Jean." *SP* 2 (1959) 193-208.

―――. "Le Paraclet." *AsSeign* 47 (1963) 37-55.

*―――. "Le sens spiritual de l'Écriture." *Greg* 78 (1997) 627-45.

*―――. *La vérité dans Saint Jean.* AnBib 74, 75. Rome: Biblical Institute Press, 1977.

―――. *La vie selon l'Esprit. Condition du chrétien.* Paris: Cerf, 1965.

*La Potterie, Ignace de, and Stanislas Lyonnet. *The Christian Lives by the Spirit.* Translated by John Morriss. Staten Island, NY: Alba House, 1971.

Ladd, George Eldon. *Jesus and the Kingdom: The Eschatology of Biblical Realism.* New York: Harper & Row, 1964.

Lagrange, Marie-Joseph. *Commentaire à l'Évangile de Luc.* Ebib. Paris: Gabalda, 1921.

Lake, Kirsopp. "Baptism." In *Encyclopaedia of Religion and Ethics*, edited by James Hastings, John A. Selbie, and Louis H. Gray, 2:379-90. New York: Scribner's, 1955.

―――. "The Communism of Acts 2 and 4-6 and the Appointment of the Seven." In *Beginnings* 5:140-51.

―――. "The Conversion of Paul and the Events Immediately Following It." In *Beginnings* 5:188-95.

―――. "The Holy Spirit." In *Beginnings* 5:96-111.

―――. "Paul's Controversies." In *Beginnings* 5:212-23.

*Lambrecht, Jan. "In Memoriam: R. P. Ignace de la Potterie, S. J." *Bib* 84 (2003) 592-93.

Lampe, G. W. H. "Holy Spirit." In *The Interpreter's Dictionary of the Bible*, 2:626-39. Nashville: Abingdon, 1962.

―――. "The Holy Spirit in the Writings of St. Luke." In *Studies in the Gospel: Essays in Memory of R. H. Lightfoot*, edited by D. E. Nineham, 159-200. Oxford: Blackwell, 1955.

―――. "Miracles in the Acts of the Apostles." In *Miracles: Cambridge Studies in Their Philosophy and History*, edited by C. F. D. Moule, 163-78. London: Mowbray, 1966.

―――. *The Seal of the Spirit.* London: SPCK, 1967.

Larrañaga, Victoriano. *La ascensión del Señor en el Nuevo Testamento*. 2 vols. Madrid: Instituto Francisco Suárez, 1943.

*Laurentin, René. *Catholic Pentecostalism*. Translated by Matthew O'Connell. Garden City, NY: Doubleday, 1977.

———. *Structure et théologie de Luc 1–11*. Paris: Gabalda, 1957.

Le Déaut, R. "Pentecôte et tradition juive." *Spiritus* 2/7 (1961) 127–44. Reprinted in *AsSeign* 51 (1963) 22–38.

Leal, Juan. *Hechos de los Apóstoles*. La Sagrada Escritura, NT 2. Madrid: La Editorial Católica, 1962.

———. *La Sagrada Escritura: Nuevo Testamento. Texto y comentario por profesores de la Compañía de Jesús*. Biblioteca de autores cristainos. Madrid: La Editorial Católica, 1962.

*Lechler, Gotthard V. *Das apostolische und nachapostoliche Zeitalter*. Stuttgart: Besser, 1857.

Lécuyer, Joseph. "Pentecôte et loi nouvelle." *VSpri* 25 (1953) 471–90.

Leenhardt, Franz J., et al. *Le Saint-Esprit*. Geneve: Labor et Fides, 1963.

Leisegang, Hans. *Pneuma Hagion; der Ursprung des Geistbegriffs der synoptischen Evangelien aus der griechischen Mystik*. Leipzig: Hinrichs, 1922.

Lemonnyer, A. "L'Esprit Saint Paraclet." *RSPT* 16 (1927) 293–307.

Léon-Dufour, X. "Redaktionsgeschichte." *RSR* 46 (1958) 239–50.

Lescure, J. "Le Saint Esprit dans la Bible." *Spiritus* 2/7 (1961) 208–14.

Lieb, F. "Der Heilige Geist als Geist Jesu Christi." *EvT* 23 (1963) 281–98.

Lofthouse, W. F. "The Holy Spirit in the Acts and the Fourth Gospel." *ExpTim* 52 (1940) 334–36.

Lohfink, G. "Eine altestestamentliche Darstellungsform für Gotteserscheinungen in den Damaskuserichten." *BZ* 9 (1965) 246–57.

Lohmeyer, Ernst. *Das Vater-unser*. ATANT 23. Göttingen: Vandenhoeck & Ruprecht, 1952.

Lohse, Edvard. "Die Bedeutung des Pfingsberichtes im Rahmen des lukanischen Geschichts-werkes." *EvT* 13 (1953) 422–36.

———. "Lukas als Theologe der Heilsgeschichte." *EvT* 14 (1954) 256–75.

———. "πεντηκοστή." In *TDNT* 6:44–53.

Loisy, Alfred. *Les Actes des Apôtres*. Paris: Nourry, 1920.

Lonke, J. "Liber Actuum apte vocatur Spiritus Sancti Evangelium." *Collationes Brugenses* 42 (1946) 46–52.

López-Gay, Jesús María. *El Espíritu Santo y la missión*. Bérriz, Spain: Editorial Angeles de las Misiones, 1967.

Luck, U. "Kerygma, Tradition, und geschichte Jesu bei Lukas." *ZTK* 57 (1960) 51–66.

Lyonnet, S. "De glossolalia Pentecostes eiusque significatione." *VD* 24 (1944) 65–73.

———. "La κοινωνία de l'Église primitive et la Sainte Eucharistie." *XXXV Congr. Euc. Int.* (Barcelona, 1953) 511–15.

———. "Le récit de l'Annonciation." *AmClergé* 66 (1956) 33–46.

Lys, Daniel. *Rûach: le souffle dans l'Ancien Testament: enquête anthropologique à travers l'histoire théologique d'Israël*. Études d'histoire et de philosophie religieuses 56. Paris: Universitaires de France, 1962.

*Mainville, Odette. *L'Esprit dans l'oeuvre de Luc*. HP 45. Montreal: Fides, 1991.

Mansueto, F. "Actus Apostolorum = Evangelium Spiritus Sancti." *RCB* 1 (1956–57) 169–80.

Margoliouth, D. S. "Baptizing with Fire." *Exp* 8/13 (1917) 446–53.

*Marguerat, Daniel. *The First Christian Historian: Writing the "Acts of the Apostles."* Translated by Ken McKinney, Gregory J. Laughery, and Richard Bauckham. SNTSMS 121. Cambridge: Cambridge University Press, 2002.

Martimort, A. G. "La Confirmation." In *Communion solennelle et profession de foi*, 159–201. Lex orandi 14. Paris: Cerf, 1952.

*Martin, Francis. "Le baptême dans l'Esprit; tradition du Nouveau Testament et vie de l'Eglise." *NRTh* 106 (1984) 23–58.

*———. *Baptism in the Spirit: A Scriptural Foundation*. Steubenville, OH: Franciscan University Press, 1986.

Martin, R. A. "Syntactical Evidence of Aramaic Sources in Acts I–IV." *NTS* 11 (1964) 38–59.

Mattill, A. J. *A Classified Bibliography of Literature on the Acts of the Apostles*. NT Tools and Studies 7. Leiden: Brill, 1966.

———. "Luke as Historian in Criticism Since 1840." PhD diss., Vanderbilt University, 1959.

McClendon, J. W. "Some Reflections on the Future of Trinitarianism." *RevExp* 63/2 (1966) 149–56.

McNamara, K. "The Holy Spirit in the Church." *ITQ* 32 (1965) 281–94.

Meinertz, Max. *Einleitung in das Neue Testament*. Paderborn: Schoningh, 1933.

Menasce, P. de. "L'experience de l'Esprit dans la mystique chrétienne." In "Der Geist," *ErJb* 13 (1946) 355–84. [*Der Geist* (ed. O. Fröbe-Kapteyn; *ErJb* 13; Zürich: Rhein, 1946) is a book from an Eranos Conference. Four more of its eleven studies are cited in this bibliography below by Rahner, Schmidt, Schmitt, and Wili. —Ed.]

Menchini, Camillo M. "Il discorso di S. Stefano protomartire nella letteratura e predicazione cristiana primitiva." PhD diss., Pontificio Istituto Angelicum, 1951.

Menoud, Philippe Henri. "Les additions au groupe des douze apôtres: d'après le livre des Actes." *RHPR* 37 (1957) 71–80.

———. "Jésus et ses témoins: Remarques sur l'oeuvre de Luc." *EgT* 23 (1960) 7–20.

———. "La mort d'Ananias et de Saphira." In *Aux sources de la tradition chrétienne; mélanges offerts à M. Maurice Goguel à l'occasion de son soixante-dixième anniversaire*, edited by P. H. Menoud et al., 146–54. Neuchâtel: Delachaux & Niestlé, 1950.

———. "Pendent quarante jours, Actes 1, 3." In *Neotestamentica et Patristica: eine Freundesgabe an Herrn Prof. Dr. Oscar Cullmann zu seinem 60*, edited by Willem C. van Unnik, 148–56. NovTSup 6. Leiden: Brill, 1962.

———. "La Pentecôte lucanienne et l'histoire." *RHPR* 42 (1962) 141–47.

———. "Le plan des Actes des Apôtres." *NTS* 1 (1954) 44–51.

———. "Remarques sur les textes de l'Ascension dans Luc–Actes." In *Neutestamentliche Studien für Rudolf Bultmann zu seinem 70*, edited by Walther Eltester, 148–56. BZNW 21. Berlin: Töpelmann, 1954.

———. *La vie de l'Église naissante*. Neuchâtel: Delachaux & Niestlé, 1952.

———. "The Western Text and the Theology of Acts." *Studiorum NT Societas, Bulletin II* (1951) 19–32.

*Menzies, Robert P. *The Development of Early Christian Pneumatology with Special Reference to Luke-Acts*. JSNTSup 54. Sheffield: JSOT, 1991.

Merk, A. "Der neunentdeckte Kommentar des Heiligen Ephraen zur Apostelgeschichte." *ZKT* 48 (1924) 37–58, 226–60.

Michaelis, Wilhelm. "ὁράω, κτλ." In *TDNT* 5:315–82.

———. *Reich Gottes und Geist Gottes nach dem Neuen Testament*. Basel: Reinhardt, 1931.

———. *Täufer, Jesus, Urgemeinde: Die Predigt vom Reiche Gottes vor und nach Pfingsten.* NTF 2. Gütersloh: Bertelsmann, 1928.
Michiels, R. "La conception lucanienne de la conversion." *ETL* 41 (1965) 42–78.
Michl, J. "Der Geist als Garant des rechten Glaubens." In *Vom Wort des Lebens: Festschrift für Max Meinertz zur Vollendung des 70*, edited by Nikolaus Adler, 142–55. NTAbh 1. Münster: Aschendorff, 1951.
———. "Der Geist des Herrn ruth auf mir." *BK* 21/2 (1966) 42–45.
Minear, Paul S. "Luke's Use of the Birth Stories." In *Studies in Luke-Acts: Essays Presented in Honor of Paul Schubert*, edited by Leander E. Keck, Paul Schubert, and J. Louis Martyn, 111–32. Nashville: Abingdon, 1966.
Mollat, D. "Jugement dans le Nouveau Testament." In *DBSup* 4:1344–94.
*Montague, George T. *The Holy Spirit: Growth of a Biblical Tradition.* New York: Paulist, 1976. Reprint, Eugene, OR: Wipf & Stock, 2006.
Moral, A. García del. "Sentido trinitario de la expresión Espíritu de Javé de Isa 11:2 en 1 Pet 4:14." *EstBib* 20 (1961) 169–206.
Morgenthaler, Robert. *Die lukanische Geschichtsschreibung als Zeugnis: Gestalt und Gehalt der Kunst des Lukas.* 2 vols. ATANT 14–15. Zürich: Zwingli, 1948.
*Mühlen, Heribert. "Der Beginn einer neuen Epoche der Geschichte des Glaubens." *TGl* 64 (1974) 28–45.
———. *Der heilige Geist als Person: Beitrag zur Frage nach der dem heiligen Geiste eigentümlichen Funktion in der Trinität, bei der Inkarnation und im Gnadenbund.* Münsterische Beiträge zur Theologie 26. Münster: Aschendorff, 1963.
*———. "The Person of the Holy Spirit." In *The Holy Spirit and Power*, edited by Kilian McDonnell, 11–33. Garden City, NY: Doubleday, 1975. First published as "Die epochale Notwendigkeit eines penumatologischen Ansatzes der Gotteslehre." *Wort und Wahrheit* 18 (1973) 275–87.
*———. "The Renewal of the Church." In *A Charismatic Theology: Initiation in the Spirit*, translated by Edward Quinn and Thomas Linton, 347–60. London: Burns & Oates; New York: Paulist, 1978.
———. *Una Mystica Persona. Die Kirche als das Mysterium der heilsgeschichtlichen Identität des Heiligen Geistes in Christus und den Christen: Eine Person in vielen Personen.* 2nd ed. Paderborn: Schöningh, 1967.
Mullins, E. Y. "Holy Spirit." In *The International Standard Bible Encyclopedia*, edited by James Orr, 1414–16. Chicago: Howard-Severance, 1915.
Mussner, F. "In den letzten Tagen (Apg 2, 17a)." *BZ* 5 (1961) 263–65.
Neher, André. *L'essence du prophétisme.* Paris: Universitaires de France, 1955.
Nestle, Eberhard. "Acts 15:28 (ἔδωξε τῷ)." *ExpTim* 10 (1898f.) 143f.
New, Silva. "The Name, Baptism and the Laying on of Hands." In *Beginnings* 5:121–40.
Nineham, D. E., editor. *Studies in the Gospels: Essays in Memory of R. H. Lightfoot.* Oxford: Blackwell, 1955.
Noack, Bent. *Das Gottesreich bei Lukas, eine studie zu Luk. 17, 20–24.* SymBU 10. Uppsala: Gleerup, 1948.
Norda, Johannes. *Die Interpretation von Apostelgeschichte 20, 28 im Tridentinum.* Rome: Pontifical Gregorian University, 1942.
Nösgen, K. F. *Der Heilige Geist: sein Wesen und die Art seines Wirkens.* Berlin: Trowitzsch & Sohn, 1905.
Nötscher, Friedrich. "Geist und Geister in den Texten von Qumran." In *Mélanges bibliques rédigés en l'honneur de André Robert*, edited by O. W. Davies, 305–15. Travaux de l'Institut Catholique de Paris 4. Paris: Bloud & Gay, 1957.

Oates, W. E. "The Holy Spirit and the Overseer of the Flock." *RevExp* 63/2 (1966) 187–97.
*O'Connor, Edward D. *The Pentecostal Movement in the Catholic Church*. Notre Dame, IN: Ave Maria, 1973.
Oepke, A. "βάπτω, κτλ." In *TDNT* 1:527–46.
Oliver, H. H. "The Lucan Birth Stories and the Purpose of Luke-Acts." *NTS* 10 (1963) 202–26.
O'Neill, J. C. "Commentaries on the Acts of the Apostles." *Theology* 61 (1958) 140–43.
———. *The Theology of Acts in Its Historical Setting*. London: SPCK, 1961.
*O'Toole, Robert F. "Acts 2:30 and the Davidic Covenant of Pentecost." *JBL* 102 (1983) 245–58.
Oulton, J. E. L. "The Holy Spirit, Baptism, and Laying on of Hands in Acts." *ExpTim* 66 (1954) 236–40.
Paissac, H. "Le don de l'Esprit au chrétien." *LumVie* 10 (1953) 29–50.
*Panagopoulos, Johannes. "Die urchristliche Prophetie: Ihr Charakter und ihre Funktion." In *Prophetic Vocation in the New Testament and Today*, edited by J. Panagopoulos, 1–32. NovTSup 45. Leiden: Brill, 1977.
Patterson, J. W. "A Comparative Study of the Holy Spirit in the Gospels." Diss., Southwestern Baptist Seminary, 1955.
*Pervo, Richard I. *Acts*. Hermeneia. Minneapolis: Fortress, 2009.
Pesch, Rudolf. "Die Gabe des Heiligen Geistes (Apg 2, 38)." *BK* 21 (1966) 52–53.
*———. *Apostelgeschichte, I*. EKK 5/1. 3rd ed. Düsseldorf: Benziger, 2005.
Pieper, K. "Wer war der Erstling der Heiden?" *NZM* 5 (1915) 119–32.
Poelman, R. "L'action de l'Esprit Saint dans l'histoire du salut." *LumVit* 8/1 (1953) 33–50.
*Porsch, Felix. "Die Pneuma-Gabe und die Sendung der Jünger durch den Auferstandenen (Joh 20, 21–23)." In *Pneuma und Wort: Ein exegetischer Beitrag zur Pneumatologie des Johannesevangeliums*, 340–78. Frankfurter Theologische Studien 16. Frankfurt: Knecht, 1974.
Prenter, Regin. *Le Saint-Esprit et le renouveau de l'Église*. Cahiers théologiques de l'actualité protestante 23–24. Neuchâtel: Delachaux & Niestlé, 1949.
Preuschen, Erwin. *Die Apostelgeschichte*. HNT 4/1. Tübingen: Mohr/Siebeck, 1912.
Procksch, Otto. "ἅγιος, κτλ." In *TDNT* 1:88–115.
Pulver, Max. *Das Erlebnis des Pneuma bei Philon*. Zürich: Rhein, 1946.
Rahner, H. "Erdgeist und Himmelgeist in der patristische Theologie." In "Der Geist," *ErJb*. 13 (1946) 237–76.
Ramos, J. "Significación del fenómeno del Pentecostés Apostólico." *EstBíb* 3 (1944) 469–94.
Rasco, E. "Conzelmann y la Historia salutis." *Greg* 46 (1965) 286–391.
Rehkopf, Friedrich. *Die lukanische Sonderquelle: ihr Umfang und Sprachgebrauch*. WUNT 5. Tübingen: Mohr/Siebeck, 1959.
Reicke, Bo. *Glaube und Leben der Urgemeinde: Bemerkungen zu Apg 1–7*. ATANT 32. Zürich: Zwingli, 1957.
———. "Zum Begriffe Martys." *Nuntius* 7 (1952) 52.
*Reiling, Jannes. "Prophecy, the Spirit and the Church." In *Prophetic Vocation in the New Testament and Today*, edited by J. Panagopoulos, 58–76. NovTSup 45. Leiden: Brill, 1977.
Renié, J. *Actes des Apôtres*. Paris: Letouzey et Ané, 1949.
Rétif, A. "Le mystère de la Pentecôte." *VSpir* 84 (1951) 451–65.
———. "Témoignage et predication missionaire dans les Actes des Apôtres." *NRTh* 75 (1951) 152–65.

Reyero, S. "¿Está terminada la obra de San Lucas?" *St* 5 (1965) 273–89.
Reymond, P. "Aperçus sur l'Esprit dans l'Ancien Testament." In *Le Saint-esprit*, edited by Franz J. Leenhardt, 12–32. Genève: Labor et Fides, 1963.
Richtstätter, K. "Die Glossolalie im Lichte der Mystik." *SchuolC* 11 (1936) 321–45.
Rinaldi, G. "Stefano." BibOr 6 (1964) 153–62.
Robinson, William C. *Der Weg des Herrn: Studien zur Geschichte und Eschatologie im Lukas-Evangelium, ein Gespräch mit H. Conzelmann*. TF 36. Hamburg: Reich, 1964.
Rodd, C. R. "Spirit or Finger." *ExpTim* 72 (1961) 157–58.
Rohde, Joachim. *Die redaktionsgeschichtliche Methode: Einführung und Sichtung des Forschungsstandes*. Hamburg: Furche, 1966.
Roover, E. de. "L'éxégèse patristique de Lc 1:35 des origines à Augustin." PhD diss., Pontifical Gregorian University, 1964.
Russell, H. G. "Which Was Written First, Luke or Acts?" *HTR* 47 (1955) 167–74.
Rust, E. C. "The Holy Spirit, Nature, and Man." *RevExp* 63/2 (1966) 157–76.
Sahlin, Harald. *Der Messias und das Gottesvolk: Studien zur protolukanischen Theologie*. ASNU 12. Uppsala: Almqvist & Wiksells, 1945.
———. *Studien zum dritten Kapitel des Lukasevangeliums*. Uppsala Universitets Årsskrift 2. Uppsala: Lundequistska, 1949.
Salas, Antonio. *Discurso escatológico prelucano. Estudio de Lc. 21, 20–36*. El Escorial. Madrid: Biblioteca "La Ciudad de Dios," 1967.
Saldarini, G., and G. Biffi. "Le tre persone divine nel Nuevo Testamento." *SchuolC* 87 (1959) 241–77.
Scarpat, Giuseppe. *Parrhesia: storia del termine e delle sue traduzioni in latino*. Brescia: Paideia, 1964.
Schaefer, Aloys, and Max Meinertz. *Einleitung in das Neue Testament*. Paderborn: Schoningh, 1913.
Scharbert, J. "Verheissung." In *Handbuch theologische Grundbegriffe*, edited by H. Fries, 2:752–59. Munich: Kösel, 1963.
Schlatter, Adolf von. *Die Geschichte der ersten Christenheit*. BFCT 11. Gütersloh: Bertelsmann, 1926.
Schmid, Norbert. "Kliene ringförmige Komposition in den Evangelien und in der Apostelgeschichte." PhD diss., University of Tübingen, 1961.
Schmidt, H. W. "Der Heilige Geist und das Problem der Geschichte." *ZST* 24 (1955) 194–206.
Schmidt, Karl Ludwig. "βασιλεία (τοῦ θεοῦ) in Hellenistic Judaism." In *TDNT* 1:574–93.
———. "Das *Pneuma Hagion* als Person und als Charisma." In "Der Geist," *ErJb*. 13 (1946) 187–235.
Schmitt, J. "L'Église de Jérusalem ou la restauration d'Israel d'après les cinq premiers chapitres des Actes." *RHR* 27 (1953) 209–18.
Schmitt, P. "Geist und Seele." In "Der Geist," *ErJb*. 13 (1946) 133–85.
Schnackenburg, Rudolf. *Gottes Herrschaft und Reich: Eine biblisch-theologische Studie*. Freiburg: Herder, 1959.
———. *Das Heilsgeschehen bei der Taufe nach dem Apostel Paulus: eine Studie zur paulinischen Theologie*. Munich: Zink, 1950.
———. *Die Sittliche Botschaft des Neuen Testamentes*. Handbuch der Moraltheologie 6. Munich: Hüber, 1962.
———. "Typen der Metanoia-Predigt nach Apostelgeschichte." *MTZ* 1/4 (1950) 1–13.

*Schneider, Gerhard. *Die Apostelgeschichte*. Vols. 1, 2. HTKNT 5/1, 2. Freiburg: Herder, 1980, 1982.

*———. "Pfingsten und der heilige Geist." In *Die Apostelgeschichte* 1:256–79.

*———. "Philippus und die Samaria-Mission: 8, 4–25." In *Die Apostelgeschichte* 1:481–95.

*———. "Stephanus, die Hellenisten und Samaria." In *Les Actes des Apôtres: Traditions, redaction, théologie*, edited by J. Kremer, 215–40. BETL 48. Leuven: Leuven University Press, 1979.

Schneider, Johannes. "εὐνοῦχος." In *TDNT* 2:765–68.

Schniewind, Julius, and Gerhard Friedrich. "ἐπαγγέλλω, κτλ." In *TDNT* 2:576–86.

Schumacher, R. *Der Diakon Stephanus*. NTAbh 3/4. Münster: Aschendorf, 1910.

Schürmann, H. "Aufbau, Eigenart, und Geschichtswert der Vorgeschichte von Lukas 1–2." *BK* 21/4 (1966) 106–11.

*———. *Das Lukasevangelium, I*. HTKNT 3/1. Leipzig: St. Benno, 1970.

*Schwegler, Albert. *Das nachapostolische Zeitalter in den Hauptmomenten seiner Entwicklung*. Tübingen: Fues, 1846.

Schweizer, Eduard. "Die Bekehrung des Apollos." *EvT* 15 (1955) 247–54.

———. "Gegenwart des Geistes und eschatologische Hoffnung bei Zarathustra, spät jüdischen Gruppen, Gnostikern und den Zeugnis des Neuen Testament." In *The Background of the New Testament and Eschatology: In Honour of C. H. Dodd*, edited by W. D. Davies and David Daube, 482–508. Cambridge: Cambridge University Press, 1956.

———. *Geist und Gemeinde im Neuen Testament und Heute*. Theologische Existenz Heute 32. Munich: Kaiser, 1952.

———. "Der Heiligen Geist im Neuen Testament." *Die Zeichen der Zeit* 8/11 (1954) 401–09.

———. "πνεῦμα, κτλ." In *TDNT* 6:389–455.

———. "The Spirit of Power. The Uniformity and Diversity of the Concept of the Holy Spirit in the New Testament." *Int* 6 (1952) 259–78.

———. "Zu den Reden der Apostelgeschichte." *TZ* 13 (1957) 1–11.

Scott, C. A. "The Fellowship or κοινωνία." *ExpTim* 35 (1923–24) 567.

———. "What Happened at Pentecost?" In *The Spirit: The Relation of God and Man, Considered from the Standpoint of Recent Philosophy and Science*, edited by Burnett Hillman Streeter et al., 117–58. New York: Macmillan, 1919.

Scott, Ernest Findlay. *The Spirit in the New Testament*. London: Hodder and Stoughton, 1923.

Seesemann, Heinrich. *Der Begriff κοινωνία im Neuen Testament*. Giessen: Töpelmann, 1933.

Semain. P. "L'Esprit et le royaume de Dieu d'après Saint Luc." *RevDiocTour* 2 (1947) 481–92.

*Shelton, James B. "'Filled with the Holy Spirit' and 'Full of the Holy Spirit.'" In *Faces of Renewal: Studies in Honor of Stanley M. Horton*, edited by Paul Elbert, 81–107. 1988. Reprint, Eugene, OR: Wipf and Stock, 2007.

*———. *Mighty in Word and Deed: The Role of the Holy Spirit in Luke-Acts*. 1991. Reprint, Eugene, OR: Wipf and Stock, 2000.

*Shepherd, William H. *The Narrative Function of the Holy Spirit as a Character in Luke-Acts*. SBLDS 147. Atlanta: Scholars, 1994.

Shoemaker, William R. "The Use of *Ruah* in the Old Testament and of πνεῦμα in the New Testament: A Lexicographical Study." *JBL* 23 (1904) 13–67.

Simbolo, Il. 15: "Credo nello Spirito Santo." 16: "La Santissima Trinità." 17: ". . . parlò per mezzo dei Profeti." Exhibition in Assisi, 1958–60.

Simon, Marcel. *St. Stephen and the Hellenists in the Primitive Church.* London: Longmans and Green, 1958.

Simpson, J. G. S., and G. W. H. Lampe. "Holy Spirit." In *Dictionary of the Bible*, edited by James Hastings, H. H. Rowley, and Frederick C. Grant, 392–93. Edinburgh: T. & T. Clark, 1963.

Sjöberg, Erik. "πνεῦμα." In *TDNT* 6:375–89.

Sleeper, C. T. "Pentecost and Resurrection." *JBL* 84 (1965) 389–99.

Smidt, Udo. *Die Apostelgeschichte.* Kassel: Oncken, 1959.

Smith, R. H. "The Eschatology of Acts and Contemporary Exegesis." *CTM* 29 (1958) 641–63.

———. "History and Eschatology in Luke-Acts." *CTM* 29 (1958) 881–901.

Smulders, P. ". . . et latins." In *Dictionnaire de spiritualité*, edited by Marcel Viller, Charles Baumgartner, and André Rayez, 4/2:1272. Paris: Beauchesne, 1932.

Snape, H. C. "The Composition of the Lukan Writings: A Re-assessment." *HTR* 53 (1960) 27–46.

*Soards, Marion L. *The Speeches in Acts: Their Content, Context, and Concerns.* Louisville, KY: Westminster/John Knox, 1994.

Solignac, A. "Le Saint-Esprit et la présence du Christ auprès des ses fidèles." *NRTh* 77 (1955) 478–490.

Spicq, Ceslaus. "The Holy Spirit in the New Testament." *RevExp* 63/2 (1966) 135–47.

———. "Le Saint-Esprit, vie et force de l'Église primitive." *LumVie* 10 (1953) 9–28.

Stählin, Gustav. *Die Apostelgeschichte.* NTD 5. Göttingen: Vandenhoeck & Ruprecht, 1962.

*———. "Τὸ πνεῦμα Ἰησοῦ (Apostelgeschichte 16:7)." In *Christ and Spirit in the New Testament: Studies in Honour of Charles Francis Digby Moule*, edited by Barnabus Lindars and Stephen Smalley, 229–52. Cambridge: Cambridge University Press, 1973.

Steinmann, Alphons August. *Die Apostelgeschichte.* HSNT 3. Bonn: Hanstein, 1921.

Stempvoort, P. A. van. "The Interpretation of the Ascension in Luke and Acts." *NTS* 5 (1958) 30–42.

Strack, Hermann L., and Paul Billerbeck. *Kommentar zum Neuen Testament aus Talmud und Midrasch.* 6 vols. Munich: Beck, 1922–61.

Strathmann, H. "μάρτυς, κτλ." In *TDNT* 4:474–514.

Strecker, Georg. *Der Weg der Gerechtigkeit: Untersuchung zur Theologie des Matthäus.* Gottingen: Vandenhoeck & Ruprecht, 1962.

*Stronstad, Roger. "On Being Baptized in the Holy Spirit: A Lukan Emphasis." In *Trajectories in the Book of Acts: Essays in Honor of John Wesley Wyckoff*, edited by Paul Alexander, Jordan Daniel May, and Robert G. Reid, 160–93. Eugene, OR: Wipf and Stock, 2010.

*———. *The Charismatic Theology of St. Luke.* Peabody, MA: Hendrickson, 1984.

*———. *The Prophethood of All Believers: A Study in Luke's Charismatic Theology.* JPTSup 16. Sheffield: Sheffield Academic, 1999.

*Suenens, Cardinal Léon Joseph. *A New Pentecost?* Translated by Francis Martin. New York: Seabury, 1975. First published as *Une nouvelle Pentecôte?* Paris: Desclée de Bouwer, 1974.

*Sullivan, Francis A. "'Baptism in the Holy Spirit': A Catholic Interpretation of the Pentecostal Experience." *Greg* 55 (1974) 54–61.

*Sullivan, Francis A., Wolfgang Wörner, and Norbert Baumert, *Die charismatische Erneuerung: die biblische und theologische Grundlagen*. Graz: Styria, 1986.

Svéda, S. "Ich giesse meinen Geist auf alles Fleisch." *BK* 21/2 (1966) 37–41.

Swete, H. B. *The Holy Spirit in the New Testament*. London: Macmillan, 1909.

*Talbert, Charles H. "Conversion in the Acts of the Apostles: Ancient Auditors' Perceptions." In *Literary Studies in Luke-Acts: Essays in Honor of Joseph B. Tyson*, edited by Richard P. Thompson and Thomas E. Phillips, 141–53. Macon, GA: Mercer University Press, 1998.

Tannehill, Robert C. "A Study in the Theology of Luke-Acts." *AThR* 43 (1961) 195–203.

Tatum, W. B. "The Epoch of Israel: Luke 1–2 and the Theological Plan of Luke-Acts." *NTS* 13 (1966) 184–95.

Theissen, A. "Bibliography of Acts." *Scr* 2 (1947) 53–57.

Thornton, Lionel Spencer. *The Common Life in the Body of Christ*. Westminster: Dacre, 1944.

*Tibbs, C. *Religious Experience of the Pneuma*. WUNT 2/230. Tübingen: Mohr/Siebeck, 2007.

Tillich, Paul. *Die Gegenwärtigkeit des Göttlichen Geistes: Predigt*. Stuttgart: Evangelisches Verlagswerk, 1962.

Tosetti, Wilhelm. *Der Heilige Geist als göttliche Person in den Evangelien: eine biblisch-dogmatische Untersuchung*. Düsseldorf: Schwann, 1918.

Trocmé, Étienne. *Le Livre des Actes et L'histoire*. Paris: Universitaires de France, 1957.

Trump, S. "L'Esprit Saint âme de l'Église." In *Dictionnaire de spiritualité*, edited by Marcel Viller, Charles Baumgartner, and André Rayez, 4/2:1296. Paris: Beauchesne, 1932.

Turrado, Lorenzo. "El Bautismo 'in Spiritu Sancto et igni.'" *EstEcl* 34 (1960) 807–17.

———. *Hechos de los Apóstoles y Epístolas paulinas*. Biblia comentada 6. Madrid: Biblioteca de Autores Cristianos, 1965.

Unnik, Willem Cornelis van. "Der Befehl an Philippus." *ZNW* 47 (1956) 181–91.

———. "The 'Book of Acts' the Confirmation of the Gospel." *NT* 4 (1960) 26–59.

*———. "Luke's Second Book and the Rules of Hellenistic Historiography." In *Les Actes des Apôtres: Traditions, redaction, théologie*, edited by J. Kremer, 37–60. BETL 48. Leuven: Leuven University Press, 1979.

Vandenbroucke, F. "L'action du Saint-Esprit dans les âmes." In *Dictionnaire de spiritualité*, edited by Marcel Viller, Charles Baumgartner, and André Rayez, 4/2:1302. Paris: Beauchesne, 1932.

———. "Dans la liturgie." In *Dictionnaire de spiritualité*, edited by Marcel Viller, Charles Baumgartner, and André Rayez, 4/2:1283. Paris: Beauchesne, 1932.

Vatican Council. *Dogmatic Constitution on the Church: Lumen Gentium, Solemnly Promulgated by His Holiness, Pope Paul VI on November 21, 1964*. Boston: St. Paul Editions, 1965.

Vatican Council and Ronan Hoffman. *Decree on the Missionary Activity of the Church: December 7, 1965*. Vatican II documents. Washington, DC: National Catholic Welfare Conference, 1965.

Vielhauer, Phillipe. "Zum Paulinismus der Apostelgeschichte." *EvT* 10 (1950–51) 1–15.

Viller, Marcel, Charles Baumgartner, and André Rayez. *Dictionnaire de spiritualité: ascétique et mystique, doctrine et histoire*. Paris: Beauchesne, 1932.

Vitti, A. "L'ultimo decennio di critica sugli Atti degli Apostoli." *Bib* 12 (1931) 233–42.

*Vondey, Wolfgang. *Heribert Mühlen: His Theology and Praxis, a New Profile of the Church*. Lanham, MD: University Press of America, 2004.

Voss, G. "Die Christusverkündigung der Kindheitsgeschichte im Rahmen des Lukasevangelium." *BK* 21/4 (1966) 112–18.
———. "Durch die Rechte Gottes erhöht hat er den Geist ausgegossen. *BK* 21/2 (1966) 45–47.
Vosté, J. M. "The Acts of the Holy Ghost." *HPR* 43 (1947–48) 5–11.
Wanroy, M. van. "Eunuchus Aethiops a diacono Philippo converses." *VD* 20 (1940) 285–93.
*Wasserberg, Günter. *Aus Israels Mitte—Heil für die Welt: Eine narrative-exegetische Studie zur Theologie des Lukas*. BZNW 92. Berlin: de Gruyter, 1998.
*Weinel, Heinrich. *Die Wirkungen des Geistes und der Geister im nachapostolischen Zeitalter bis auf Irenäus*. Tübingen: Mohr/Siebeck, 1899.
Weiss, Johannes. *Die Schriften des Neuen Testaments: neu übersetzt und für die Gegenwart erklärt*. Vol. 1: *Die drei älteren Evangelien. Die Apostelgeschichte*. Gottingen: Vandenhoeck & Ruprecht, 1906.
*Weizsäcker, Carl. *Das apostolische Zeitalter der christlichen Kirche*. Freiburg: Mohr/Siebeck, 1892.
*Welker, M. *Gottes Geist: Theologie des Heiligen Geistes*. Neukirchen-Vluyn: Neukirchner, 2002.
Wendt, Hans Hinrich, *Die Apostlegeschichte*. KEK 3. Gottingen: Vandenhoeck & Ruprecht, 1913.
White, H. V. "The Holy Spirit in Life and Doctrine." *EcuR* 6 (1953) 199–202.
Wikenhauser, Alfred. *Die Apostelgeschichte*. RNT 5. Regensburg: Pustet, 1961.
———. *Die Apostelgeschichte und ihr Geschichtswert*. NTAbh 8/3–5. Münster: Aschendorff, 1921.
Wilckens, Urlich. "Kerygma und Evangelium bei Lukas (zum Act 10:34–43)." *ZNW* 49 (1958) 233–37.
———. *Die Missionsreden der Apostelgeschichte: Form- und traditionsgeschichtliche Untersuchungen*. WMANT 5. Neukirchen: Neukirchener, 1961.
———. "σοφία." In *TDNT* 7:465–76, 496–528.
Wilcox, Max. "The Old Testament in Acts 1–15." *ABR* 5 (1956) 3–41.
———. *The Semitisms of Acts*. Oxford: Clarendon, 1965.
Wili, W. "Die Geschichte des Geistes in der Antike." In "Der Geist," *ErJb*. 13 (1946) 49–93.
Wilkens, W. "Wassertaufe und Geistesempfang bei Lukas." *TZ* 23 (1967) 26–47.
Willaert, A. "Der Heilige Geist eschatologische Gave in Christus." *Coll* 3 (1957) 145–60.
Windisch, H. "Das Urchristentum." *TRu* 5 (1933) 186–200, 239–58, 289–301, 319–44.
Winter, P. "Miszellen zur Apostelgeschicte: 15:14 und die Lukanische Kompositionstechnik." *EvT* 17 (1957) 398–406.
Wood, W. S. "Fellowship." *Exp* 8/21 (1921) 31–40.
*Woods, Edward J. *The "Finger of God" and Pneumatology in Luke-Acts*. JSNTSup 205. Sheffield, UK: Sheffield Academic, 2001.
Yates, John Edmund. "Luke's Pneumatology and Luke 11:20." *SE* 2 (1964) 295–99.
———. *The Spirit and the Kingdom*. London: SPCK, 1963.
Ysebaert, Joseph. *Greek Baptismal Terminology: Its Origins and Early Development*. Græcitas Christianorum primæva 1. Nijmegen: Dekker & Van de Vegt, 1962.
Zbik, F. "O Espírito Santo Descerá sôbre Ti . . . (Lc 1:35)." *RCB* 1 (1956) 237–47.
Zerwick, Maximilian. *Analysis Philologica Novi Testamenti Graeci*. Scripta Pontificii instituti biblici 107. 2nd ed. Rome: Pontifical Biblical Institute, 1960.
*———. *Biblical Greek: Illustrated by Examples*. Translated by Joseph Smith. Rome: Pontifical Biblical Institute, 1963.

———. *Graecitas Biblica: exemplis illustratur*. Rome: Pontifical Biblical Institute, 1960.
Zimmermann, H. "Die Sammelberichte der Apostelgeschichte." *BZ* 5 (1961) 71–82.
Zorell, Franz. *Lexicon Graecum Novi Testamenti*. Cursus Scripturae Sacrae 7. 3rd ed. Paris: Lethielleux, 1961.

Index of Names

Abbott, E., 205
Adler, N., 54, 63, 152, 213, 222, 223
Alexander, L. C. A., 54, 226
Alonso-Diaz, J., 146, 147
Arnal, J., 3
Asensio, F., 7
Asting, R. K., 103

Baer, H. von, x, xviii, xix, xx, 12, 32, 35, 41, 42, 43, 44, 64, 97, 104, 125, 132, 146, 147, 148, 151, 170, 178, 183, 189, 205, 224, 230
Baltzer, K., 215
Bardy, E., 146
Barnard, L. W., 164, 215
Barrett, C. K., 115, 195, 203, 220
Bartsch, H. W., 63
Bauckham, R., 73
Bauer, J. B., 80
Bauernfeind, O., 140
Baumert, N., x
Baumgärtel, F., 7
Beasley-Murray, G. R., 152
Behm, J., 115
Belser, J. E., 223, 224
Benoit, P., 7, 167, 168, 223
Bertram, G., 123, 228
Best, E., 146, 147
Bieder, W., 7, 146
Bietenhard, H., 45
Bihler, J., 164, 214
Boer, H. R., 103

Boismard, M. E., 194
Bonnard, P., 194, 208
Bonsirven, J., 40, 62, 217
Borgen, P., 63
Bourke, J., 63
Bover y Oliver, J. M., 79, 117
Braun, H., 7
Brodie, T. L., 225
Brox, N., 97, 98, 109
Büchsel, F., 49, 152
Buis, P., 223
Burgos, F. C., 79, 117
Bultmann, R., 63, 152, 161, 163, 169

Cadbury, H. J., 3, 63, 80, 164, 167, 168, 221
Calvin, John, xix, 115
Camerlynck, A., 223
Campbell, J. Y., 170
Cantalamessa, R., xi, 71,
Carr, A., 170
Casey, R. P., 97
Causse, R., 194
Cerfaux, L., 97, 100, 115, 117, 165, 167, 168, 170, 206, 213
Ceuppens, P. F., 88
Charette, B., 147
Charlier, J.-P., 223
Chenu, M.-D., 194
Chevallier, M.-A., 147, 194, 202, 203, 204, 205
Cho, Y., 62

273

Index of Names

Claereboets, C., 210
Comblin, J., 97, 100
Congar, Y. M.-J., x, 98, 167, 194, 208
Conzelmann, H., 27, 41, 42, 62, 63, 64, 66, 67, 68, 69, 70, 109, 126, 140, 146, 194, 197, 209, 220
Coppens, J., 7, 90, 139, 150, 152
Cullmann, O., 63, 67, 164, 214, 215

Dahl, N. A., 194, 228
D'Ales, A., 178
Daniélou, J., 200
Danker, F. W., 55, 110, 119, 123, 161
Davies, G., 115
Davies, J. G., 146
Dibelius, M., xix, 10, 73, 74, 167, 209, 216, 227, 229
Dodd, C. H., 62, 63, 131
Dupont, J., xix, 6, 10, 73, 93, 115, 126, 134, 137, 169, 170, 194, 205, 213, 216, 218, 220, 223, 228, 229

Edsman, C.-M., 147
Ehrhardt, A., 220
Eisen, U. E., 140
Elbert, P., 4, 10, 89, 143
Elfers, H., 152
Ellis, E. E., 63, 200
Enciso, J., 5

Fascher, E., 149
Feuillet, A., 203, 205
Fitzmyer, J. A., 7, 66, 189, 204
Flender, H., 64, 194
Förster, W., 7, 164
Forbes, C., 7
Friedrich, G., 60, 105

Gächter, P., 3, 7, 11, 162
Garcia del Moral, A., 93
Gelin, A., 223
Gempf, C. H., 73
George, A., 32, 33, 45, 134, 206
Gewiess, J., 193-94
Ghidelli, C., 6
Giblet, J., x

Gill, D. W. J., 73
Glombitza, O., 152
Goguel, M., 3
Goitia, J. de, 5, 93, 202
Grangette, G., 194
Grässer, E., xvii, 63, 73, 220
Grundmann, W., 31, 37, 40, 164, 165, 221
Guillet, J., 3
Gunkel, H., 7, 66, 121, 133, 144-45
Günther, E., 97
Guthrie, D., xvii, 73, 220

Haenchen, E., xix, 6, 10, 42, 49, 57, 64, 67, 73, 74, 75, 78, 80, 82, 107, 109, 115, 117, 130, 131, 140, 146, 152, 161, 164, 167, 169, 178, 179, 209, 213, 215, 216, 217, 221
Harnack, A. von, 168
Hauck, F., 169
Hays, R. B., ix
Hemer, C., 10, 73,
Hill, D., 200
Holtzmann, H. J., 49
Holzmeister, U., 223
Hur, J., x

Iglesias, S. M., 199
Imschoot, P. van, 5, 87, 147

Jacquier, E., 57, 58, 93, 115, 118, 140, 143, 152, 179, 224
Jaeger, H., 110
Jean-Nesmy, C., 223
Jeremias, J., 165, 167, 168
Jervell, J., 74, 89
Johns, C. B., xi
Joüon, P., 110

Käsemann, E., 151
Keener, C. S., 106
Kerrigan, A., 63
Kilgallen, J. J., 159
Kilpatrick, G. D., 10, 44
Kim, H.-S., x, 148, 151
Kim, Y. H., x

Kittel, G., 152, 186
Klausner, J., 164
Klein, H., 62
Kleinknecht, H., 3, 12
Knox, J., 10
Knox, W., 74, 93, 213
Koch, R., 5, 78, 87, 202
Kremer, J., 224
Kretschmar, G., 223
Kurz, W. S., xi, 167

La Potterie, I. de, ix, x, xii, xix, xx, 6, 97, 121, 143, 152, 202, 205, 206, 208
Ladd, G. E., 62
Lagrange, M.-J., 183
Lake, K., 42, 80, 152, 167
Lambrecht, ix
Lampe, G. W. H., xviii, 86, 87, 146, 194, 200
Larrañaga, V., 209
Laurentin, R., 115, 172, 202, 203, 204, 208
Le Déaut, R., 223
Leal, J., 44, 152
Lechler, G., 224
Lécuyer, J., 213
Leisegang, H., 12
Lemonnyer, A., 118
León-Dufour, X., 64
Lohfink, G., 42
Lohmeyer, E., 138, 151
Lohse, E., xix, 71, 115, 131, 177, 222
Loisy, A., 63, 152
Lopez-Gay, J. M., 103
Luther, Martin, xix
Lyonnet, S., 97, 115, 121, 170, 204, 213

Mainville, O., 80, 86, 106
Margoliouth, D. S., 147
Marguerat, D., 73
Martin, F., x, xi
Mattill, A. J., xviii, 223
McDonnell, K., x
Meinertz, M., 223
Menchini, C. M., 164

Menoud, P. H., xix, 97, 98, 100, 169, 170, 178, 180, 209, 220, 223
Menzies, R. P., x, 7, 106
Michaelis, W., 43, 62, 63,
Michiels, R., 134
Michl, J., 97
Minear, P. S., 202
Mollat, D., 63
Moral, A. G. del, 93
Morgenthaler, R., 158
Mühlen, H., x, 208
Mussner, F., 67

Neher, A., 199
New, S., 135, 146
Noack, B., 62
Nötscher, F., 7

O'Connor, E. D., 167
Oepke, A., 152
Oliver, H. H., 64
O'Neill, J. C., 220
O'Toole, R. F., 115, 213
Oulton, J. E. L., 150, 163

Paissac, H., 194
Panagopoulos, J., 200
Pervo, R. I., 43
Pesch, R., 113, 169, 208, 223
Pieper, K., 221
Pious XII, xv
Poelmann, R., 194
Porsch, F., 240
Preuschen, E., 140
Procksch, O., 4, 9, 13

Rasco, E., 64
Reicke, B., 103, 178
Reiling, J., 200
Renié, J., 88, 117, 119
Rétif, A., 97, 100, 103-4, 116, 223
Reyero, S., 220
Richtstätter, K., 115
Rinaldi, G., 164
Robinson, W. C., 63
Rodd, C. R., 33

Rohde, J., 64
Roover, E. de, 202

Sahlin, H., 165, 179, 194, 202, 205, 209, 221
Salas, A., 63
Scarpat, G., 110
Schaefer, A., 223
Scharbert, J., 60
Schlatter, A. von, 71
Schmidt, K. L., 62, 228
Schmitt, J., 179, 194, 220
Schnackenburg, R., 62, 132
Schneider, G., 49, 66, 140, 165
Schneider, J., 221
Schniewind, J., 60
Schumacher, R., 164
Schürmann, H., 118, 202
Schwegler, A., 224
Schweitzer, A., 63
Schweizer, E., xviii, 3, 31, 33, 34, 63, 67, 75, 104, 120, 131, 132, 134, 139, 149, 153, 169, 200, 206, 210
Scott, C. A., 170
Seesemann, H., 170
Semain, P., 62
Shelton, J. B., x, 11, 50
Shepherd, W. H., 151
Shoemaker, W. R., 3
Simon, M., 164, 214
Sjöberg, E., 7, 195
Sleeper, C. T., 223
Smith, R. H., 63
Soards, M. L., 159
Spicq, C., 194
Stählin, G., 45
Steinmann, A. A., 44
Strathmann, H., 97, 113
Str-B, 7, 195, 205, 217
Strecker, G., 64
Stronstad, R., x, xi, 103, 200
Suenens, Cardinal, x, 208
Sullivan, F. A., 146, 208
Svéda, S., 223

Talbert, C. H., 134
Tatum, W. B., 202
Thorton, L. S., 169, 171, 172, 188
Tibbs, C., 167
Trocmé, É., xix, 10, 97, 114, 164, 165, 167, 178, 179, 209, 220, 226
Turrado, L., 147

Unnik, W. C. van, xx, 216, 221

Vielhauer, P., 10
Vondey, W., x
Voss, G., 202, 223

Wanroy, M. van, 221
Wasserberg, G., 65, 143
Weinel, H., 66
Weiss, J., 49
Weizäcker, C., 224
Welker, M., 89
Wendt, H. H., 140
Wikenhauser, A., 10, 75, 79, 115, 132, 133, 146, 152, 167, 209, 220, 221
Wilckens, U., 62, 161
Wilkens, W., 146, 153
Williams, C. B., 143
Winter, P., 194, 228
Wood, W. S., 170
Woods, E. J., 33
Wörner, W., x

Yates, J. E., 33
Ysebaert, J., 152, 153

Zerwick, M., 15, 27, 31, 51, 57, 78, 80, 81, 82, 123, 140, 209
Zimmermann, H., 167, 168
Zorell, F., 55, 123, 161, 227

Index of Ancient Literature

Old Testament

Genesis

1:1	203

Exodus

8:15	32
17:1–7	181
28:3	4, 5
31:3	4, 5
35:31	4, 6
40:34	203
40:35	203

Leviticus

10:1–5	179

Numbers

5:14	4, 5
11	124
11:16	53
11:17	15, 20, 59
11:25	15, 53, 59
11:29	5, 53, 202
14:22	181
27:14	181
27:18	59

Deuteronomy

6:16	181
9:22	181
18:15–19	197, 200
18:15	199
23:2	221
23:23	179
33:8	181
34:9	4, 6, 59, 90

Joshua

7	179
7:1–26	181

1 Samuel

16:14	59
18:10	4

1 Kings

18:10	5

2 Kings (4 Kingdoms)

19:7	5

Nehemiah

9:20	4, 20, 90

Job

33:4	90

Psalms

2:12	147
15:9	169
44:8	6
51:10–12	139, 191

Index of Ancient Literature

Psalms (continued)

51:11	4, 20
78:18	181
78:41	181
78:56	181
95:9	181
106:4	181
125:2	157
142:10	4, 20, 90
142:12	4

Proverbs

15:4	5, 157

Song of Songs

2:14	205
5:2	205
5:12	205
6:8	205

Isaiah

4:2–6	203
4:4	90, 138, 147, 191
11:2	90
11:4	147
11:12	4, 138
32:15–16	138, 191
32:15	5
42:1	5, 204
49:2	203
56:3–5	221
59:21	20
61:1	4, 33, 138, 204, 205, 244
63:10–14	179, 181
63:10–11	4, 20
63:10	89
63:14	6
66:2	35

Jeremiah

31:31–34	11

Ezekiel

2:2	5
3:24	5
11:5	5
11:19	4, 5, 90, 138, 191
36:24	11
36:25–28	191
36:26–28	138
36:26	4, 90
36:27	5
37:6	5
37:14	5

Daniel

5:12	4
6:4	4

Joel

2:27–28	15
2:28–32	5, 11, 43, 48, 50, 52, 66, 67, 77, 86, 197
2:28	6, 52
2:32	46

Amos

9:11–12	228

Haggai

2:5	59

Zechariah

12:10	90

Malachi

3:15	181

Apocrypha

Judith

8:12	181

1 Maccabees

9:27	195

Sirach

18:23	181
39:6	4, 5, 90
48:12	6, 157

Index of Ancient Literature

Wisdom of Solomon

1:2	181
1:5	4, 90, 138, 191
1:7	59
7:7	4, 5, 90
7:14	49
9:17	4, 19, 138, 191
12:1	4
16:25	49
48:12	4

New Testament

Matthew

1:8	173
1:10	173
1:13	173
1:18	10, 204
1:20	10
3:11	xi, 9, 10, 79, 147
3:16	9, 10, 20, 90, 153, 173, 204, 205
3:21	173
4:1	10, 76
6:7	81
7:11	10, 173
9:28	173
9:34	81
10:17	8
10:18	109
10:20	8, 9, 10, 76, 90, 155
11:25	10, 174
12:28	9, 10, 32, 80
12:31	183
12:32	7, 10, 20
12:35	162
13:53–58	205
13:54	161
14:20	157
15:37	157
17:2	173
17:20	144
18:15–17	178
19:17	162
22:40	80
22:43	10
24:14	109
25:21	162
26:61	8
28:19	19, 147

Mark

1:7–8	xi, 10
1:8	9, 79, 147
1:10	9, 10, 20, 153, 173, 204
1:12	10, 39, 76
3:9	9
3:29–30	183
3:29	7, 10, 19
4:28	157
5:2	81
5:25	81
6:1–6	205
6:2	161
6:11	109
8:19	157
9:2	173
10:18	162
10:19	112
12:36	9, 10, 80
13:4	65
13:5	65, 112
13:9	8, 65
13:10	65
13:11	8, 9, 10, 19, 65, 76, 109, 112, 155
14:58	8
16:16	147

Luke

1–2	14, 28, 84, 124, 195
1:1–4	226
1:14	163, 169
1:15	5, 13, 54, 195, 200, 231
1:17	81, 200
1:25	204
1:28	163
1:35	10, 13, 18, 30, 31, 35, 54, 86, 202, 203, 204, 231
1:41–42	174
1:41	5, 13, 54, 195, 231

Luke (*continued*)

1:42	174
1:44	169
1:47	169
1:49	36
1:67	5, 13, 54, 174, 195, 231
1:80	82, 206
2:10	163
2:25–35	174
2:25–27	195, 231
2:25	13, 18, 118, 158, 160
2:26	13, 18, 20
2:27	13, 81
2:40	161, 206
2:52	158, 160, 161
3:16	xi, 9, 10, 79, 147, 148
3:21	153, 173
3:22	9, 10, 20, 86, 197, 200, 204, 231
4:1	10, 13, 39, 77, 79, 81, 205, 206, 207, 231
4:14	13, 31, 37, 77, 80, 81, 205, 206, 207, 231
4:14–16	205
4:18–19	33
4:18	5, 6, 54, 77, 86, 138, 197, 200, 205, 231
4:21	205
4:36	31, 35
5:12	157
5:16	173
5:17	31, 33, 58
5:32	58
6:12	173
6:19	31
6:23	163
6:24	118
6:28	173
6:45	162
7:33–34	58
7:36–50	125, 189
8:46	31, 33, 58
9:1	31, 32, 33, 35
9:18	173
9:27	65
9:49	46
10:2	173
10:9	58, 65
10:11	65
10:13	31
10:17	46, 227
10:19	31, 32, 35
10:20	163
10:21	10, 20, 68, 80, 82, 169, 174, 206, 207, 231, 236
10:38	86
11:1	173
11:2	62, 173
11:9–10	173
11:13	10, 173, 188, 189, 247
11:20	10, 64, 92
11:48	103
12:4–12	183
12:10	8, 10, 19, 183
12:12	8, 10, 19, 34, 76, 112, 155, 159, 187, 231
12:36	10
13:1–5	180
13:17	163
14:31	36
15:5	163
15:7	163
15:10	163
16:16	64, 200
17:3	178
17:6	144
17:20–21	65
17:20	61
18:1	173
18:10–11	173
18:19	162
18:27	36
19:6	163
19:15	58
19:17	162
19:37	31
19:46	173
20:42	10
21:5	8, 158
21:7	61
21:13	103, 109

Index of Ancient Literature   281

21:15	8, 10, 76, 108, 112, 155, 159		66, 69, 76, 84, 91, 97, 99, 103, 105, 106, 108, 111, 127, 128, 197, 207, 212, 218, 224, 231, 236
21:27	31		
21:36	173		
22:19	109	1:11	27
22:32	173	1:14–15	172
22:40	173	1:14	168, 175
22:44–46	173	1:16	10, 14, 78, 84, 88, 182, 195, 231
22:54–71	8		
22:69	31	1:19	73
23:50	158, 160, 162	1:21–22	100, 236
24	50	1:22	99, 101
24:19	36	1:24	101, 171
24:41	163	1:25	42
24:48	50, 103	2–5	127
24:49	5, 30, 31, 54, 61, 91, 189	2:4	5, 13, 17, 28, 54, 57, 76, 82, 84, 171, 172, 174
24:52	163		
24:53	175	2:6	123
		2:7	123
John		2:11	172, 174, 198, 227
1:4	157, 158	2:12	123
1:27	xi	2:13	115, 172
1:32	173	2:14–39	106
1:33	xi, 9, 10, 11, 79, 147	2:14	106
4:10	49	2:17–21	43, 66, 224, 225
4:21–24	215	2:17–18	6, 57
7:39	182, 196	2:17	54, 59, 67, 76, 84, 106, 227, 231
14:26	12, 121		
16:13–15	121	2:18	54, 76, 84
20:22–23	124	2:19	34
20:22	xx, 12, 224, 240	2:20	208
		2:21–36	46
Acts		2:21	208
1:1–14	209	2:22	31, 34, 120
1:2	15, 44, 78, 84, 209, 231	2:24–47	131
1:3	62	2:24	36
1:4–8	224	2:26	169
1:4	48, 53, 60, 61, 148, 189	2:28–29	67
1:5	8, 9, 10, 15, 50, 51, 53, 61, 79, 84, 146, 147, 148, 197, 227, 236	2:29	110, 111
		2:32	99
		2:33	13, 14, 18, 19, 20, 36, 48, 52, 54, 59, 61, 66, 70, 76, 86, 92, 106, 120, 122, 202, 206, 207, 224, 231, 236
1:6	61		
1:7–8	189, 225		
1:7	35		
1:8	xi, 5, 18, 19, 30, 31, 36, 37, 50, 53, 54, 59, 61, 62, 65,	2:38–39	48, 159

Acts (continued)

2:38	13, 16, 18, 19, 48, 50, 51, 52, 54, 57, 61, 76, 115, 116, 120, 125, 137, 143, 146, 151, 152, 153, 186, 225, 236
2:39	135
2:40	34, 65
2:41–47	172, 175
2:41	146, 147
2:42–47	168
2:42	170, 171, 172, 173, 175, 188
2:43	175
2:46–47	172, 215
2:46	169, 188
2:47	135, 175, 189
3:6	46
3:12–26	65
3:12	31, 33, 91
3:14	158, 160
3:15	99, 106
3:16	46
3:18	78
3:21	78
3:22–23	197, 199
3:22	147
3:26	137
4:1–3	147
4:1	81, 157
4:2	106
4:3	103
4:4	168
4:7	31, 33, 45, 46, 91
4:8	5, 8, 14, 34, 54, 59, 76, 82, 84, 91, 109, 114, 116, 225, 231
4:10	46, 120
4:12	46, 47, 58
4:13	76, 110, 111, 112, 123
4:16	123
4:17	106
4:19–20	106
4:20	36, 76
4:21	120
4:24	173
4:25	10, 14, 15, 55, 78, 84, 87, 88, 182, 195, 231
4:27	6
4:28	35
4:29–31	46, 111
4:29	110
4:30	34, 36
4:31–35	175
4:31	5, 13, 15, 19, 34, 37, 54, 59, 76, 82, 84, 91, 98, 106, 107, 110, 111, 116, 123, 126, 173, 225, 231
4:32–35	168, 176
4:32	71, 168, 170
4:33	34, 91, 99, 106, 111, 175, 189
4:36–37	170
4:36	118
5:1–11	178
5:3	8, 14, 39, 87, 225
5:4	87, 170
5:5	168
5:8	178
5:9	8, 14, 29, 39, 181, 210, 225
5:11–16	168, 175
5:11–12	175
5:11	175, 209
5:12	36, 157, 172
5:13	120, 168, 175
5:15–16	175
5:19	40
5:20	106
5:24	123
5:29	37
5:31	36, 137
5:32	5, 16, 50, 54, 59, 75, 77, 84, 89, 98, 99, 114, 116, 125, 140, 186, 225, 231, 236
5:41	162, 163
5:42	106, 168
6:1–7	187
6:1	117, 164
6:3	14, 57, 76, 82, 83, 84, 91, 99, 112, 116, 156, 157, 158, 161, 218, 225

6:5	14, 35, 57, 76, 82, 84, 91, 109, 117, 119, 143, 145, 156, 157, 158, 159, 161, 225	8:14–25	16
		8:14–20	116
		8:15–19	17
		8:15–17	115
6:6	164, 173	8:15	16, 54, 76, 143, 173
6:7	117, 168	8:16	5, 54, 58, 143, 145, 146
6:8	34, 35, 91, 144, 157, 161	8:17	16, 18, 54, 57, 76, 84
6:9	165	8:18	5, 16, 17, 54, 57, 75, 123
6:10	8, 18, 37, 57, 76, 82, 83, 91, 107, 108, 109, 112, 126, 144, 158, 159, 161, 187, 225	8:19	16, 18, 35, 54, 57, 76, 84
		8:20–24	178
		8:20	48, 49, 84, 87
		8:22	137, 173
6:11	214	8:24	173
6:13–14	8, 214	8:27	58
6:13	99	8:29	18, 38, 55, 73, 84, 88
6:15	40, 109	8:31	37
6:24	118	8:38	145, 146
7:10	158	8:39–40	107
7:17	61, 64, 117	8:39	18, 29, 39, 71, 149, 163
7:22	36	9:1–18	42
7:25	36	9:1–9	42
7:30	40	9:10	42, 43
7:31	43	9:11	173
7:35	40	9:17	5, 14, 54, 76, 82, 107, 116, 149
7:37	199		
7:38	40, 215	9:18	146, 149
7:39	147, 215	9:21	58
7:48–50	214	9:27	111
7:50	36	9:28	111
7:51–53	215	9:29	164, 165
7:51–52	195	9:31—12:25	225
7:51	8, 20, 182, 225	9:31	18, 19, 57, 59, 70, 117, 145, 162, 163, 168, 225, 231
7:53	40		
7:55–56	109		
7:55	14, 42, 43, 57, 58, 76, 82, 84, 112, 126, 156, 158, 225, 231	9:34	46
		9:36	135, 157, 158, 160
		9:40	173
8	105, 107, 150, 212	10–11	127
8:1	165	10:2	135, 158, 160, 173
8:3	165	10:3	123
8:4–5	165	10:4	135, 173, 175
8:8	150, 163	10:5–8	217
8:10	31, 91	10:9	173
8:12–17	144	10:13	39
8:12	62	10:15	216
8:13	31	10:17	123, 217

Acts (*continued*)

10:19–20	217
10:19	18, 29, 39, 55, 73, 84, 88, 217, 218
10:20	39
10:22	39, 99, 135, 158, 160
10:28	217, 218
10:30–31	173, 175
10:34–35	135, 217
10:34	217
10:35	158, 160
10:37–38	205
10:37	146
10:38	6, 30, 31, 35, 54, 77, 82, 91, 158, 160, 200, 202, 205, 231
10:39	99
10:41	42, 99, 100, 101, 236
10:42	100, 105, 128
10:43	99, 137
10:44–48	49, 141, 226, 250
10:44–47	19
10:44–45	218
10:44	5, 14, 17, 28, 54, 84
10:45–46	50, 174
10:45	18, 28, 48, 49, 50, 54, 58, 76, 123, 227, 231
10:46	115, 198, 227
10:47	14, 28, 50, 51, 54, 76, 218, 227, 228
10:48	146
11:5	173
11:7	39
11:9	216
11:12	18, 39, 55, 73, 84, 216
11:15–18	49, 141, 226, 250
11:15	5, 14, 17, 28, 50, 54, 84, 197, 218, 227
11:16	8, 9, 10, 15, 28, 51, 77, 79, 146, 147, 227
11:17	5, 36, 49, 50, 51, 54, 76, 140, 145, 172, 186, 227, 228
11:18	137, 227, 228
11:19–20	165, 212, 221
11:19	165
11:20	144, 164
11:21	36, 168
11:22	218
11:23–24	118, 144, 162
11:23	162, 163
11:24	57, 76, 82, 91, 117, 144, 145, 156, 157, 158, 159, 161, 163, 187, 212
11:26	57
11:27	196
11:28	15, 18, 75, 78, 79, 80, 85, 126, 196
11:30	36
12:5	173
12:7–11	40
12:14	163
12:15–16	40
12:15	40
12:23	40
12:24	117, 168
13:1—15:35	225
13:1	196
13:2–5	108
13:2–4	19, 88, 212
13:2	14, 17, 28, 55, 73, 84, 87, 126, 210
13:3	173
13:4	14, 17, 18, 19, 28, 73, 85, 87, 126
13:6–12	57
13:9–10	75
13:9	5, 14, 28, 34, 54, 76, 82, 117
13:10–11	178
13:10	157
13:11	34, 36, 117
13:15	118
13:22	99
13:23	61
13:24	146
13:31–32	100, 101, 236
13:32	61
13:38–39	215
13:38	37
13:39	137
13:46	111

Index of Ancient Literature   285

13:48–49	168	16:16	173
13:48	135, 163	16:18	32, 46
13:52	54, 57, 59, 70, 76, 82, 117, 145, 159, 162, 163, 168, 225, 231	16:19–40	122
		16:25	173
		16:31	138
14:3	36, 111	16:33	145, 146
14:9	161	17:24–25	215
14:22	173	18:2	58
15	140	18:5	75, 100, 107
15:3	163	18:8	145, 146, 168
15:6–29	226	18:9–10	42
15:7–14	49	18:9	43, 44
15:7–11	141, 226, 250	18:10	227
15:7–9	141, 142, 143	18:11	57
15:7	142, 227	18:24–28	149
15:8–9	120, 227	18:24	36
15:8	5, 14, 28, 50, 51, 54, 59, 76, 89, 98, 114, 127, 142, 216, 218, 236	18:25	44, 82, 111, 146
		18:26	111
		19:1–7	16, 151, 186
15:9	120, 138, 142, 186	19:1–2	143
15:10	181, 215, 228	19:2–6	115
15:11	142, 227, 228	19:2–3	92, 146
15:12	34, 111, 127, 221, 244	19:2	16, 18, 54, 76, 116, 132, 143
15:13–20	226		
15:14	127, 142, 181, 216, 221, 227, 228, 244, 250	19:3–5	146
		19:3	151
15:15	77	19:4	146
15:18f	145	19:5–6	151
15:20	63	19:5	146
15:22	244	19:6	14, 16, 17, 54, 115, 120, 231
15:26	121		
15:28	14, 20, 55, 87, 88, 127, 210, 216, 219, 226, 229, 244	19:7	116, 174
		19:8	111
		19:10	168
15:31	118, 163	19:11	31, 36
15:36	196	19:13–20	57
15:37–40	118	19:13	46
16:5	168	19:20	37, 168
16:6–7	44, 74, 88, 108, 211	19:21	15, 18, 44, 75, 80, 85, 211
16:6	18, 19, 43, 80, 85, 126	19:28	157, 158
16:7	43, 45, 55, 84, 126	19:32	123
16:9–10	43	20:16	36
16:9	74	20:21	100, 107
16:13	173	20:22–23	88, 211
16:14	135, 137	20:22	18, 44, 58, 74, 80, 82, 83, 85, 108, 126
16:15	145, 146		

Acts (continued)

20:23	14, 18, 44, 57, 75, 79, 80, 84, 126
20:24	100, 107, 108
20:28	14, 55, 80, 84, 87, 88, 210, 224
20:32	36
20:35	55
20:36	173
21:4	18, 44, 78, 79, 80, 85, 126, 196, 211
21:5	173
21:9	196
21:11	14, 18, 39, 44, 57, 75, 79, 80, 84, 88, 196, 211
21:12	126
21:22	58
21:24	15, 75
21:31	123
22:5–16	42
22:6–11	42
22:12	99
22:15	107, 109, 218
22:16	137, 146
22:17–18	42, 43
22:17	44, 173
22:18	103, 107
22:20	218
23:8–9	40
23:9	40, 174
23:11	42, 43, 44, 100, 107, 109
25:5	36
26:1	75
26:6	61
26:9–18	42
26:10	55
26:13–18	42
26:16	107, 218
26:18	35, 138
26:19	42
26:22–23	100
26:22	107, 109
26:26	111
27:23	40, 44
28:3	62
28:8	173
28:23	100, 107
28:25	10, 14, 55, 78, 85, 88, 182, 195, 231
28:31	62, 111, 113, 128, 168, 229

Romans

1:4	11, 90
4:13–20	60
5:15	49
5:17	49
8:9	11, 81, 90, 139
8:11	19
8:14	11, 90
8:15	11, 59, 90
8:16	122, 139
9:4	60
9:8	60
9:9	60
11:8	11, 59, 90
12:12	169
15:8	60

1 Corinthians

1:9	79
1:14	151
1:24	161
2:12	59
2:14	11, 90
3:16	11, 90
5:1–5	178
6:11	11, 90, 139
6:19	19
7:40	11, 90
10:9	181
12:3	11, 90
12:13	171
12:14	115
14	11, 114, 122, 199
14:23	115
15:8	42

2 Corinthians

1:20	60
1:21	6
3:17	11, 90

5:5	59	6:4	49, 171
7:1	60	6:6	49
9:15	49	6:12	60
13:13	171	6:15	60
13:14	171	6:17	60
		9:15	60

Galatians

		10:26–31	184
3:2	59	10:36	60
3:14	59, 60	11:9	60
3:16–29	60	11:13	60
4:6	59, 122, 139	11:17	60
4:23	60	11:33	60
4:28	60	11:39	60
		12:16–17	184

Ephesians

1 Peter

1:7	11, 59	1:12	12
1:13	59, 60		
1:17	90, 161		

2 Peter

2:12	60	1:21	12
3:6	60	3:4	60
3:7	49	3:9	60
4:7	49		
4:30	11, 90		

1 John

6:2	60	2:25	60
6:18	169	5:15–17	184

Philippians

2 John

2:1	171	8	157

Colossians

Jude

1:9	161	20	12

1 Thessalonians

Revelation

4:8	59, 90	2:5	58

2 Timothy

		8:3	58
1:1	60	9:1	58
1:7	59		
4:22	90		

Hebrews

1:9	6
3:8	181
4:1	60
6:4–8	184

About the Book

THIS THESIS BY GONZALO Haya-Prats, written in the Catholic interpretive tradition under the supervision of Johannine scholar Ignace de la Potterie at the Gregorian University in Rome, reflects a faith tradition that historically remained open to the miraculous and resisted regulations on activities of the Holy Spirit in the Book of Acts. Accordingly, Haya-Prats interprets the workings of the Spirit from a perspective of narrative sensitivity. He is deliberately diligent to exercise due care so as not to obscure narrative flow and connectivity, despite any ecclesial or interpretive precedents that might be of influence to the contrary. His exegetical method is to let the original meaning be discerned and discovered according to the author's intention as closely as possible. With this sound interpretive approach Haya-Prats achieves a remarkable degree of freshness and insightful vision that all readers of Luke-Acts will welcome. Students and scholars alike should find this timely and thoughtful thesis to be a valuable and long-lasting contribution to New Testament studies.

This English edition is made more accessible by including translations of all contemporary foreign languages, and editor Paul Elbert offers occasional explanatory notes that engage current scholarship relevant to Haya-Prats's presentation.